# EUROPE: AN INTIMATE JOURNEY

Jan Morris was born in 1926 of a Welsh fath............. .......... and when she is not travelling she lives with he.. ......... ...... ... Morris in the top left-hand corner of Wales, between ... mountains and the sea. Her books include *Coronation Everest*, *Venice*, The Pax Britannica Trilogy (*Heaven's Command*, *Pax Britannica* and *Farewell the Trumpets*), and *Conundrum*. She is also the author of six books about cities and countries, two autobiographical books, several volumes of collected travel essays, and, more recently, the unclassifiable *Trieste and the Meaning of Nowhere*. *Hav*, a novel, was published in a revised and expanded edition in 2006.

Further praise for *Europe*:

'Jan Morris writes beautifully. Her unique literary manner miraculously combines in itself all the best elements of British travel writing . . . [*Europe*] will keep warming your soul for many years to come.' Vitali Vitaliev, *Observer*

'More than just a travel memoir, this book is a wonderful rediscovery of a continent that we often pass over in our quest for far-flung travel. Jan Morris conducts a close examination of the similarities and diversities that created the European character. Her knowledge of her subject makes this book educational in the best possible sense.' Tara McNicholas, *The Times*

'A coherent and revealing portrait of a continent seeking to reinvent itself after centuries of turmoil.' Michael Leapman, *Country Life*

'[Describes] the space-time continuum of the continent of Europe – not just its grand history, but the prawn-eaters of the Grand Café in the main square of Oslo; the six reasons why the former residence of Romanian royalty may not be entered (of which only the sixth is that it is closed); an old woman's gift of a sprig of rosemary in a Portugal long since rendered unreachable by the distance that is time.' Vera Rule, *Guardian*

'May all the colour, superstitions and quirks of the countries of our continent, may the very differences so delicately portrayed by Jan Morris in her writing, survive.' Michael Portillo, *Mail on Sunday*

*by the same author*

HEAVEN'S COMMAND: AN IMPERIAL PROGRESS
PAX BRITANNICA: THE CLIMAX OF AN EMPIRE
FAREWELL THE TRUMPETS: AN IMPERIAL RETREAT
CORONATION EVEREST
VENICE
CONUNDRUM
TRIESTE AND THE MEANING OF NOWHERE
A WRITER'S WORLD
HAV

# EUROPE

*An Intimate Journey*

JAN MORRIS

*faber and faber*

First published as *Fifty Years of Europe: An Album* by Viking in 1997
Published by Penguin Books in 1998
First published as *Europe: An Intimate Journey* in 2006
by Faber and Faber Limited
3 Queen Square London WC1N 3AU

Printed in England by Mackays of Chatham Ltd, Chatham, Kent

All rights reserved
© Jan Morris, 1997, 2006

The right of Jan Morris to be identified as author of this work has been asserted
in accordance with Section 77 of the Copyright, Designs and Patents Act 1988

*This book is sold subject to the condition that it shall not, by way of trade
or otherwise, be lent, resold, hired out or otherwise circulated without the publisher's
prior consent in any form of binding or cover other than that in which it is published
and without a similar condition including this condition being imposed on
the subsequent purchaser*

A CIP record for this book
is available from the British Library

ISBN 978-0-571-23312-0
ISBN 0-571-23312-0

2 4 6 8 10 9 7 5 3

*For*
ELIZABETH

*From Reykjavik to Ljubljana,*
*Cheerful Cork to weird Tirana,*
*No exotic route avails*
*To clear my homesick mind of Wales.*
*Where my Love is at,*
*And also Jenks the cat.*

★

Except for sporadic quotations all the responses in this book are my own, ranging from the adolescent to the all too mature. It is a purely personal and entirely subjective album of Europe

*Trefan Morys, 1997*

★

# CONTENTS

# AN INTRODUCTION

## 1 On the Audace Jetty

On a fine warm day in my twentieth year, in the summer of 1946, I started to write an essay about nostalgia, sitting on a bollard beside the sea on the Molo Audace in Trieste.

There are curious connotations to the name of this jetty, which protrudes into the harbour from the piazza at the formal centre of the city. It commemorates the day in 1918 when the Italian destroyer *Audace*, 1,017 tons, tied up there to disembark a company of soldiers and claim Trieste on behalf of the Kingdom of Italy – for the previous century it had been part of the Austro-Hungarian Empire. Although the place was no more than half Italian-speaking, and was debatably part of the Italian peninsula, this was in effect a last coup of the Risorgimento. The *Audace* was ecstatically welcomed with bands and rhetoric, at least by the local Italians, and the pier was at once renamed for her.

She was not, however, originally an Italian warship at all. She was laid down in Scotland in 1912 to a Japanese commission, but was transferred to the Italian Navy when Italy entered the war against Germany in 1915. After her moment of glory at Trieste she continued to serve with the Regia Marina until 1943, when the Italians surrendered to the Allies in the Second World War: she was then seized by the Germans and went to sea with the Reichsmarine. In the end she was sunk in a battle off the Dalmatian coast by her creators the British – both Britons and Germans, I have no doubt, if not Italians too by then, altogether unaware of her place in history. When I sat there that afternoon I did not know the story of the *Audace* either: but in retrospect her career seems to offer, with its mingled allusions of pride and pathos, absurdity, irony and oddity, not a bad beginning for a book about Europe.

## 2 A transient

It was nostalgia I was writing about then, though, Trieste having brought on a vicarious spasm of it. The second German war had ended, and I was in the city as a member of an occupying army, during a hiatus before our transference to British imperial duties in Palestine. This was my introduction to Europe. Anglo-Welsh though I am, I thought of myself then as firmly British, and I looked at everything around me, I fear, slightly *de haut en bas*.

As Alan Moorehead once wrote, in those days the British travelled all the world like the children of rich parents. Not for a moment did I think of myself as European. I was a privileged transient from another kind of country, an oceanic country whose frontiers extended from Tasmania to Newfoundland.

I was billeted in a tall old apartment block up on the cathedral hill, with a violent shimmering view over the bay – its blues hotly blue, its evening sunshine blinding; and having time on my hands, especially in the afternoons, I would often walk down the hill, past the Roman amphitheatre, down the ceremonial staircase built by the vanquished Fascists, over the Piazza dell' Unità d'Italia where the British and American flags flew side by side above the former Governor's Palace, to find a convenient spot for composition at the harbour's edge.

I had come to Trieste across a shattered, bewildered and despondent continent, which looked as though it could never recover. We knew only the half of it then, the full horrors of the Second World War and its aftermath having not yet been revealed, but it was quite enough to make me feel that I could never experience Europe in any state of grace or glory. The continual civil wars which had wracked the continent throughout the century – French against Germans, British against Italians, Czechs against Poles, Spaniards against Spaniards, Gentiles against Jews – had reached a devastating climax, and I saw all its nations as in a fearful dream, blurred and disjointed. Millions of homeless people swarmed here and there across its frontiers, or lay despondent in refugee camps, bureaucratically categorized as 'displaced persons'. Great cities lay in ruin. Bridges were broken, roads and railways were in chaos. In the eastern forests savage partisans were still at each other's throats. Homesick armies were dispersing in triumph or in ignominy. Conquerors from East and West flew their ensigns above the seats of old authority, and proud populations would do almost anything for a pack of cigarettes or some nylon stockings. Europe was in shock, powerless, discredited and degraded. 'When the waters recede,' wrote Thomas Mann from his exile in the United States, 'Europe will have changed beyond recognition, so that one will hardly be able to speak of going home . . .'

Although I had never been on the continent before, I had been brought up to a vision of it. My English mother had been a student in Leipzig before the First World War, and had brought home a taste for the easy charm of the Leipzigers that she consummated, I like to think, by marrying a Welshman. Her memories had coloured my childhood ideas of Europe. It was a roseate,

Old German Europe that I chiefly had in mind, and I thought of it as a romantic whole. Great writers and musicians walking the streets – lovely parks with lakes and gazebos – architecture of ancient splendour – merry student life in sunlit cafés – grand old cities of culture and history – all these, and a muddle of other Mendelssohnian notions, added up to my European ideal. It was no wonder, when I compared the actual present with the fanciful past, that nostalgia was the subject of my afternoon essay; and to make it all the more poignant it happened that the particular city I saw around me, my first European city of residence, was not shattered at all. It is true that the Western Allies, with the apostate Italians, were squabbling with Marshal Tito the Yugoslav over the future of Trieste, while in Moscow Stalin schemed to get control of it as a Mediterranean outlet for the Soviet Union. But the city had been spared the worst of war's destructions, and stood there a little forlorn perhaps, but virtually intact – one of the fortunate moiety of European cities to look almost as they did before the war began.

In its prime it had been the principal seaport of the Habsburg Empire, a free port linked by railway direct with Vienna. Its hinterland had been the whole of central Europe, and it had acquired the ample and assured physique of nineteenth-century Mitteleuropa. Around its medieval core a grand city of commerce and finance had arisen, lining the shores with quays and warehouses, stretching inland with ornate parades of banks and exchanges and agencies and shipping offices. There were coffee-shops where littérateurs and heroes of the Risorgimento had written and plotted. There was an opera house Verdi had composed operas for. There were memories of Stendhal, Svevo, Winckelmann, James Joyce. Schooners and elderly steamers still came and went from its harbour, as in old postcards, and across the bay there stood the sweet Victorian pleasure-castle of Miramare, once the home of a Habsburg archduke, by then the headquarters of an American general.

So I was able to summon an all but genuine sense of nostalgia (nostalgia comes rarely, after all, when you are nineteen years old). Trieste made me homesick for a Europe that was gone, that I had never known except in fancy, and when I looked over the city roofs to the harsh limestone Karst above, I could imagine all the famous European capitals that lay beyond, some ruined, some bemused, one triumphant: from Belgrade and Bucharest, not so far to the east, over the Alps to Vienna, and Prague, and Geneva – to Berlin still in nightmare, and an ambivalent Rome, and Paris humiliated, and Lisbon and Madrid untouched, and away to Stockholm and Oslo and Copenhagen (and over to London, too, the city victorious, except that I did not think of London as being in Europe at all . . .). In 1946 one no longer often saw the bill of lading '*Via Trieste*', which had once directed so much of the world's trade towards the heart of Europe: but it certainly applied to me.

I was sitting, there on my bollard, at one of the continent's fulcra, where Slavs, Teutons and Latins met, or turned their backs on one another, where the Balkans began and the Mediterranean reached its northernmost tide-reach up the wide fjord of the Adriatic. Trieste, however, had lost the advantages of its situation. Thirty-odd years earlier it had become a historical backwater, when the Habsburg Empire came to an end and the seaport forfeited its true *raison d'être*. No longer was this the proud gateway through which the traffic of an empire passed to and from the world outside. A hush of limbo lay over the city, especially on such a hot summer afternoon, when only an occasional schooner loitered in from Istria, and a few men fished with their lines from the quayside, now and then wandering over to see how the fellow along the quay was doing. Around the bay Miramare stood hazy on its promontory. In my memory the light was dazzling that afternoon, and the limestone ridges running away into Italy looked bleached with heat and drought.

## 3 *What became of Waring*

I never did finish my maudlin essay (though I still have a draft of it, in a dog-eared notebook under the stairs): but the sensations it tried to record were to mark me for life, and I was always to associate the city of Trieste with my conception of Europe. To this day I love its feel of mordant separateness, as though time is always passing it by. It suggests to me a watcher on the shore, looking back over the ridge to the places where history is on the go, and recognizing faintly within itself, as in echo from long before, all the grand movements of peoples, moneys, dynasties, armies, beliefs and aspirations that have formed the tumultuous continent beyond.

Now, half a century on, I have returned to Trieste to sort out my own lifetime's experience of Europe, to write this introduction in a room above the harbour, and to use the city as a point of reference for my impressions and reflections – just as I tried, so long ago, to give form there to my nostalgia. Thomas Mann was wrong, I think. If he could come back to the continent now he would know he was home after all, and my fifty years of Europe have turned out to be fifty complex years of a return to glory, if not to grace.

Decade by decade I have watched Europe recover from its wounds of war, endure and escape the traumas of Communism, regain its assurance, and try to make something altogether new of itself. Some countries have risen to fresh distinction, some have been abased, some have gone on fighting that incessant civil war, but after centuries of violent rivalry, and successive attempts to make a comity of it by fair means or foul, at the end of the twentieth century Europe really is tentatively shuffling towards some kind of unity – the only adult objective for a mature community of neighbours. I myself long ago grew out of my British imperialism, found myself in Welshness, and came to realize that I had also been a European all the time; and although I have always been a solitary traveller, an onlooker, in Trieste now I no longer feel an outsider (still less, unfortunately, a child of rich parents).

It is a great place for contemplative escape anyway, a great place for sitting on quaysides in the sunshine, thinking about history and toying with the idea of writing essays. I feed upon the city's pungent blend of the pompous, the creative, the raffish, the significant and the melancholy, and see in it always the shade of Browning's elusive Waring – 'What's become of Waring/ Since he gave us all the slip?' For Waring showed up, as you may remember, wearing a wide straw hat in the stern-sheets of a boat in the Bay of Trieste: somewhere beyond the Molo Audace, I like to suppose, out there towards Miramare, bounding beneath a lateen sail 'Into the rosy and golden half/O' the sky'.

# I

## HOLY SYMPTOMS

*

*High above the Molo Audace, at the summit of Trieste, the cathedral of San Giusto stands beside a castle on the top of a hill. It is dedicated to St Justin, but is equally devoted to the well-known Roman martyr Sergius, because at the very moment when he was decapitated for the faith in Syria, in the fourth century A D, a halberd fell out of the skies into Trieste, and has been preserved in the city ever since, besides appearing on the civic coat of arms. The view from San Giusto's campanile is magnificent – a grand panorama of sea and mountain, city, port and suburb, looking south and east to Croatia and Slovenia, north towards Austria, westward across the gulf to Venice. Such a noble prospect sets one thinking about a definition of Europe.*

*I did not think much about definitions when I first came here. I thought of Europe simply as 'abroad'. The rest of the world seemed on the whole rather less foreign, and huge swathes of it were actually British. Fifty years later, defining the continent is much less simple for me. I take it to end at the frontiers of Turkey and the old Soviet Union, but that is a matter of prejudice or convenience. It is an invented place anyway. Geographically it is no more than a peninsula protruding from the land mass of Asia, with attendant islands and archipelagos. Culturally it has always been a shifting confusion of languages, peoples and traditions. Politically it is a movable feast: of the thirty-five sovereign States in my idea of Europe, nine have been created or resurrected during my half-century. Sweden was not considered a proper European country until the seventeenth century. Greece, for all its classical pedigree, was hardly a part of Europe until it gained its independence from the Turks. Spain often feels, as Auden once said, as though it is 'tacked on to the bottom of Europe'. Within living memory people in northern Bulgaria called going to Vienna 'going to Europe', and British people to this day say they are visiting Europe when they cross the English Channel. It seems to me that down the centuries only religion has given the continent any lasting common identity.*

*Judaism has sometimes been powerful in Europe; the threat and presence of Islam has crucially affected its history; but paganism and Christianity have been the continent's universal defining factors, and the one long ago mastered the other. 'Populus et christianitas una est,' declared the Emperor Charles the Bald in the ninth century; nine centuries later the Treaty of Utrecht was still talking about a 'Republica Christiana'; Gladstone thought the Concert of Europe symbolical of Christian unity. Europe and Christendom were synonymous, and even now, if you happened to fall from outer space anywhere in Europe, somewhere in sight there would probably be a steeple, a dome, a belfry-tower or the silhouetted mass of a monastery. But God knows* the Christian temples raise their crosses to heaven in very different styles and tones of voice, and looking down at Trieste from its cathedral tower we can see for ourselves the bewildering variety of the faith. The domed neoclassical church down there, presiding over a canal full of boats, is the Roman Catholic church of Sant Antonio Taumaturgo – St Antony the Wonder-Worker. The one with the two towers is the Greek Orthodox church of San Nicolò. With a street map in our hands we may be able to place the pretty little Anglican Christ Church classically pedimented, and the Evangelical church with its tall neo-Gothic steeple, and the seventeenth-century Jesuit church of Santa Maria Maggiore, and the eleventh-century church of San Silvestro where the Waldensians worship, and the big Serbian Orthodox church with a Byzantine dome; and there is a Benedictine church down there, and a Franciscan church, and the former church of the Armenian fathers, where they now have Catholic services in German, and a Methodist chapel somewhere, and the neat little private church that the crooked millionaire Pasquale Revoltella built as a mausoleum for his mother and himself. In the autumn of 1995 I came up here to the cathedral with a television crew, in search of material. It turned out to be the festival day of St Sergius, and there on an altar was displayed the miraculous halberd, with policemen guarding it, and a mighty choir singing, and priests in golden vestments processing all around.

And that's just the Christians! There were religions in Europe long before Christ, pagan beliefs of many kinds, cults of the Greeks and Romans which have entered all our myths – and even before them, and far more compelling for me, the misty megalithic religion, which seems to have been as widespread as European Christianity would ever be, and probably longer lasting. Looking back upon my half-century of Europe, then, trying to give shape to my responses from my vantage point in space and time, I recall first a few random and decidedly mixed symptoms of its sanctity.

# 1 *The rocks*

I am an animist or pantheist myself. I believe all Nature to be God, and like Pasternak's Dr Zhivago I reverence the forces of earth and sky as my own ancestors. Years ago I found myself profoundly moved by Dafydd ap Gwilym's great Welsh poem '*Offeren y Llwyn*', 'The Woodland Mass', which imagines a forest as a place of worship, with the golden leaves as a chancel roof, and the nightingale raising the host '*a charegl nwyf a chariad*' – 'with a chalice of ecstasy and love'. So I have always been moved too when, all across Europe, I have found relics of the religions that preceded Christianity. In this continent people were exploring the mysteries of theology for several millennia before the news of Christ came out of the East, and when they were not contemplating the sacred wonders of the sun and moon, or the numen of forests, or idols of one sort or another, it seems to me that they were generally venerating rocks. In Malta and Orkney, Ireland and Corsica, from the myriad menhirs of Carnac in Brittany to the grand ensemble of the English Stonehenge, the rocks were elevated into sanctity. Sometimes they were given priestly significance too, as intermediaries with the heavens; but while the arcane powers of the heavenly bodies have unfortunately been discounted (nothing could be much less magical, it turns out, than the moon), the rocks themselves defy geological analysis to retain their enchantments still. To my mind they are the holiest things in Europe. Reverently indeed, and affectionately, I place my foot into the sacred footprints incised in stones in the west of Europe – supposed now, of course, to be the footprints of Christian saints or pilgrims, but to my mind the stamps of far older divines. I love the texture of the old stones, roughened sometimes by lichen. There are some rocks which seem to me warm to the touch, as if there is a gentle fire inside them – nothing as savage as flame, more a meditative smoulder of wood-ash. Also some, especially near my home in Wales, have a sweet and comforting smell to them, like the smell of donkeys.

# 2 *Touching things*

Surrounded still by pagan legend, many a sacred boulder has lingered into our own times as palladium or public charm, and the passion for touching things, a favourite form of modern European mumbo-jumbo, undoubtedly descends from the reverent caressing of such significant stones, by way of relics of the Cross. Nowadays most of the objects people publicly touch for luck are made of bronze or some equally wearable metal, and are visibly polished or worn down, but they are all of stony pedigree. I enjoy watching people perform the touching process (when I am not performing it myself). In some places they touch the lucky object as a matter of course, without thinking about it; in others it seems to be a genuinely spiritual experience; in others a semi-joke.

¶ The figure of the mythical Cuchulain in Dublin's General Post Office, a focus of the rebellion against English rule in 1916, has been a talisman only since then, and is less than a century old anyway, but has already been given the gloss of sanctity by much credulous fingering (regular customers touch it with a sort of intense matter-of-factness, rather as they dip their fingers into the holy water on their way into mass). 'Who is that figure?' I once asked a woman as she joined me in the queue for stamps, having made her ritual touch. 'Sure I don't know his name,' she said, 'but he's a well-known lucky feller.'

¶ Till Eulenspiegel, that archetypal rascal of German myth, is the personage to touch at Mölln in Schleswig-Holstein. He sits in bronze below the church in the old market-place of the town, a setting of such fairy-tale picturesqueness, with its gable roofs and half-timbering, that the whole thing might be an illustration from a children's pop-up book. Till has only been there since 1951, but such is his tactile allure that already two of his toes, and one of his long fingers, have been rubbed through to the brass.

¶ At Dijon in France women touch the little figure of an owl on the Rue de la Chouette as casually as they might pull on a glove – except that, since it is perched rather high on a wall, small ladies have to jump a bit to reach the bird, and children have to be lifted one after the other, their mothers never interrupting, all the same, the flow of their own conversations.

¶ On the other hand people in Brussels seem a little self-conscious as they approach the reclining figure of the local fourteenth-century hero Everard 't Serclaes, off the Grand' Place. They look around and smile rather defensively as they stroke it – even more so, I fancy, if they reach up to touch the little dog in the plaque above the champion's figure, which is almost as worn as he is.

¶ Almost all visitors touch the lucky figure of St John of Nepomuk on the Charles Bridge at Prague (he was martyred in 1393 by drowning in the river below). This is one of the supreme tourist icons of Europe, and it is entertaining to see how anxious they all are to proclaim their scepticism: 'It's only for fun,' they one and all seem to be saying as they pose for the camera; 'of course we don't take it seriously . . .' But I have seen young Czechs at twilight touching it with real reverence.

¶ Outside the Rathaus in the city of Dresden there stands a large bronze of the god Bacchus, riding what looks like an extremely drunk small donkey. One of the god's toes gleams with the wear of devotees' fingers, and I am not surprised: through all the horrors of war and miseries of Communism this merry figure, on his cheerfully inebriated ass, must have offered some symbolic reminder of happy times and irresponsibilities.

¶ Nobody sniggers, nobody looks self-conscious, nobody's mind is elsewhere when they pause to touch foreheads with the bare bronze head of Maestro Mateo, the architect of Santiago Cathedral in Spain, who kneels for ever beside its western door. Santiago de Compostela is one of the supreme pilgrim sites of Europe, and Mateo is the gatekeeper at the end of every pilgrimage – the gatekeeper of fulfilment. Who would be foolish or ungrateful enough not to bump heads with him, there at the door of his magnificent building, with the gleam of its altars waiting inside?

¶ I have noticed that in Bucharest, on the hill which leads from the Patriarchal Cathedral to the concrete modern quarters below, many people touch a particular lamppost. I don't know why. When I asked one citizen why he did it, he asked me if I would care to change some US dollars at extremely favourable rates.

## 3 *The old religion*

Many of the old stones are totems of the megalithic faith, whatever that was: the most widespread of the religions, it seems, that gives some specious cohesion to the idea of Europe before Christianity arrived – specious, because modern scholarship seems to show that it did not after all constitute any grand unitary system. There are said to be almost as many megalithic monuments still extant on the continent as there are Christian churches. Nowadays they are ever more vulnerable to archaeology and tourism, two disciplines about equally immune to reverence and numen which have done more than time itself to take the magic out of megaliths. I cheer when their arcane virtue triumphs anyway! For instance I know a rock near Reguengos, in the Alentejo country of Portugal, that has merrily survived all scholarly or bureaucratic attention. It is a very tall and flat-topped fertility symbol. Lovers who succeed in throwing a stone to the top of it can be assured of a happy romance, and the Rocha des Enamoradas is littered with successful pebbles, and frequented by scores of weekend couples who, having parked their cars across the road, throw their stones up there only half in self-mockery. At Riga in Latvia some phallic-looking stones stand on the banks of the River Daugava, in the heart of the city: I don't know if they are themselves of any ancient sanctity, but I do know (because I have watched them from my hotel window) that two or three times almost every day brides go there all in white to be photographed beside them, honouring if only unconsciously the lusty rites of their forebears.

Once I stopped for a picnic lunch off the road between Vitoria and Pamplona, in the Basque country of Spain: and as I spread out my cheese, wine and bread-hunks on the grass, I caught sight of five or six little cypress trees, planted in formal gravity upon a nearby mound. I wandered over to see why they had been planted there, expecting to find some florid Catholic shrine or memorial of the Spanish Civil War. Instead I discovered in the hollow beyond the mound an inexpressibly ancient stone cromlech. It looked rather toad-like – greyish, speckled with lichen, squat. Authority had fenced it with those cypresses as if to reduce it to a more prosaic status, like a cemetery or a commemorative slab: but the wind whistled superbly through its great ugly boulders that day, and made the line of trees seem a finicky irrelevance.

# 4  *The Paladins*

For my tastes the grandest and strangest of all the megaliths are the tall menhir-statues of Filitosa on the Mediterranean island of Corsica. They are called the Paladini, the Paladins, and they have a majesty all their own. The archaeologist Dorothy Carrington, who first made them known to a wider world, claims that they are 'perhaps the earliest portraits of individual human beings in western Europe', the predecessors of a hundred thousand equestrian marshals, marmoreal statesmen, bronze Lenins and anonymous mourning soldiers. Dr Carrington thinks they are probably about 5,000 years old. When I discovered them for myself in the 1970s not much had been done to temper their arcane authority. A track led through the fields to them, but it was

muddy and slippery and unwelcoming to tourist groups, and the fields
themselves were unkempt, with brambly bushes here and there, a few clumps
of neglected olives, and a smell of the sea. It felt essentially an ordinary,
workaday place, which ought to have had cows in it, and perhaps sometimes
did: but the five pillars stood there marvellously recondite, maybe a little
sinister. They looked aloof and scornful. Were they really human heroes?
Were they gods? Were they phallic emblems? Were they good or bad?
Nobody knew then; nobody knows now. While I was considering them a
mist came drifting off the sea, and for a moment they looked like so many
twisted and time-worn crucifixes.

## 5 Śwíatowit

I suppose you could always see in those Paladins what you wanted to see,
and they may have been idols all the time. The line is thin between a simple
megalith and a graven image, as you may see if you ever visit the archaeological
museum at Kraków in Poland. There lives Śwíatowit, the very last survivor
of the pagan gods of the Slavs. He is about a thousand years old, and none
of his comrades has ever been found. He stands in an alcove of his own in
the museum, against a photographic background of a birch-wood, and at
first sight he may seem no more than another standing stone, seven or eight
feet tall. When you get close to him, though, you find he has crossed the
line between rock and idol. His body is no simple pillar of stone after all,
but is carved all over with mystic images of animals and people: his head has
four faces, one on each side, and is crowned with a bowl-like hat. A copy
of this arcane divinity stands at the foot of the hill that leads up to the castle
and cathedral of Kraków, the stateliest place in Poland: and especially when
there is snow on the ground, and Śwíatowit stands there silhouetted grey
and enigmatic in his bowler, looking all ways at once, you may think he has
not lost his powers even now.

## 6 Cheerfulness creeps in

Enigmatic in a more cheerful way are the queer stone maze-games which
the ancients have left, here and there across the continent, to intrigue us still.
Sometimes they are large enough to walk through, sometimes just scratches

in a rock. They are traditionally associated, nearly everywhere, with the city of Troy, and are sometimes named after it. Just outside Visby, the capital of the Swedish Baltic island of Gotland, there is a famous example which has always been known to the islanders as Trojeborg – Troytown – and is as casually accepted by the people as an amusement park. It seems almost new, and to this day hosts of children entertain themselves by following its paths, their laughter echoing through the woods and up the hillside behind. I did it myself, all on my own one bright spring morning, and felt remarkably close to the prehistoric designers, who, whatever their reasons for making it, surely had fun trying it out.

In Gotland there are also many ship-graves – graves of prehistoric notables laid out in the shape of galleys. These too, though clearly sacred sites, possess none of the melancholy one rather expects of megalithic monuments. They lie dreaming on woodland glades, clambered over delicately by flowers and creepers, or bask in a self-satisfied chieftainly manner in grasslands above the sea, inspiriting all who visit them. I like to think this is because they retain some of the boisterous convivial temperament of the nobles buried in them, and the confidence of their beliefs. Prehistoric places can feel much less reassuring when they have clearly lost their holiness, when their gods and ghosts have gone. I was decidedly disturbed by my only visit (one was enough) to the cave called Idheon in Crete, on the slopes of Mount Psiloritis. This was an extremely sacred place in ancient times – Zeus was said to have been born in it – but it did not comfort me. Dusk was falling as I reached the place, but it was not the high loneliness of it or the greyness of the scene that chilled me. It was the feeling that, for all the faith and reverence expended there down the centuries, not one shred of emotion lingered. The wind had scoured it all, and the cave was just a hole in the rock.

## 7 *Old music*

Music must always have echoed around these holy places and their rituals, and in northern Europe there still exist some of the instruments played by the priests or acolytes of long ago. In Denmark they have hauled out of bogs some thirty examples of the lur, the bronze horn that sounded among the rocks at least a thousand years before the birth of Christ. They have long wiggly worm-like tubes, carefully fashioned mouthpieces and decorated flat bells, and, since they were evidently sometimes used as war-trumpets, loose metal plates that jangled to make the general effect more terrifying. At the National Museum at Copenhagen several of these things are strung on wires within a glass case, their convoluted tubes twisted this way and that, looking like so many sea-snakes or amoebas. Sometimes pairs of them are removed from the museum and played on ceremonial occasions, producing then what must be the oldest sound in Europe. Opinions seem to differ about its nature. The National Museum calls it deep and plangent, rather like the sound of a trombone. Grove's *Dictionary of Music and Musicians* (1940 edition) thought it rough and blatant. The French writer Marcel Brion called it a sombre, tragic call. A frank Danish lady told me it was horrid. But we are at liberty to imagine for ourselves what the lur sounded like in the hands of its original masters, and I prefer myself to think of its call as hoarse, breathy, gusty and intermittent, like the sound of a sea-wind through a crevice in a cliff, or the voice of a Corsican paladin.

## 8 *Two magical stones*

I visited two of the most magical of European stones on a single afternoon in London. First I took a cab and went to see the London Stone. 'To the London Stone!' I theatrically cried, and the driver understood me, although nobody really knew what the London Stone was, or ever had been. Perhaps it was something very holy once. Perhaps it was something lewd. Perhaps it was the central milestone of Roman Britain. Perhaps it was a column at the gate of the Roman governor's palace, a symbol of his authority. By medieval times the legend had arisen that its possession guaranteed mastery of the capital itself – 'Now London is mine!' cried the rebel Jack Cade when in 1450 he struck it with his sword – and it was eventually built into a wall of St Swithin's church in the City of London. This was bombed in the Second World War, and an office of the Oversea-Chinese Banking Corporation now stands upon its site, almost opposite Cannon Street railway station. In a wall of the bank a last fragment of the London Stone was carefully preserved. My taxi-driver knew exactly where to find it. I could only just see it from the street, half-hidden behind an iron grille, but inside the building the Chinese bankers displayed it with some reverence behind a sheet of glass. It looked like an ancestral totem there, or perhaps something to do with *feng-shui*.

Next I went to Westminster Abbey, and among all the cluttered paraphernalia of English historical pride, the shadowy statues, the flowery memorials to poets, statesmen and generals, the jumble of royal mementoes, the daily multitude of tourists, glowering for all to see I found the Stone of Scone, 335 pounds of rough-hewn limestone also known as the Stone of Destiny. Its prehistory was stunning. Was it not the very stone upon which Jacob rested, when he saw the angels coming? Did it not reside for a thousand years upon the Hill of Tara, mystic seat of the high kings of Ireland? Its history was extraordinary too. For several centuries it was kept at the Scottish village of Scone in Tayside, and there it became so revered a symbol of Scottishness that the kings of Scotland were crowned upon it. When the English invaded Scotland in the thirteenth century they took it away to London and built around it their own coronation throne, upon which kings and queens of England were consecrated ever after. Farcical muddles, contradictions, misunderstandings and escapades attended the Stone of Scone, and some Scots believed that it was only a copy anyway, and that the original was hidden somewhere in Scotland. When I went to Westminster to see it, whether or not it was the true talisman, it lay there beneath the seat of the throne as a broodingly charismatic emblem of historical dreams and resentments. But hardly had I made my pilgrimage that day than the British Government, inspired less by altruism than by expediency, after 700 years returned the Stone of Scone with preposterous flummery to the Scots (who prudently deposited it this time in Edinburgh Castle, the most secure of all their fortresses, and charged visitors of all persuasions £5.50 to see it).

## 9  *Chimerical aspects*

There were chimerical aspects to the old beliefs that I greatly enjoy, bridging as they do the gap between intellect and instinct. They call it crypto-zoology nowadays, but the Loch Ness Monster is distinctly holy to me. Whether it exists in the flesh or only in the mind, it is undeniably a truth of some sort, peering at us from the murky past like the goggle-eyed insect in cuckoo-spit. Some cynics say it is no more than an unconscious memory of the dinosaurs, but I do not doubt that it was once a religious conception, a figure of good or evil, born out of the rocks. All over Europe such creatures are remembered – lakes and rivers from the Baltic to the Black Sea boil, hiss and steam with their legendary thrashings. The last of the Welsh dragons spent his nights in the dragon-chamber high in the church tower of Llandeilo Graban, and beside the doorway of the great cathedral of Kraków there hangs a bundle of queer, crooked, immemorial bones to remind the faithful of the holy animals of long ago.

Most of their sanctities have been frittered away into folk-tale or tourism, and outsiders make a joke of the Loch Ness chimera, draw silly cartoons of it and call it 'Nessie'. To many Scots people living around the loch, though, it is as real as the lake itself. Long before the engines of publicity fell upon the mystery, they had been brought up in the everyday knowledge of creatures out there in the water. Their fathers and grandfathers had known of them, and never doubted their existence; in the Gaelic language they were called nothing so insulting as 'monster', but *each uisce*, 'water-horse'. I have met several sober people who assure me they have witnessed Loch Ness water-horses, who see nothing comical in the idea of them, and who talk without self-consciousness about their experiences. In 1985 the postmistress of Dores told me that she occasionally saw a creature or two playing off the point below her house. It was usually about teatime, she said.

## 10  *Looking for witches*

The idea that the megalithic cults gave rise to a benevolent European witchcraft has apparently been discredited by scholars. Religious witches and warlocks throughout Europe think otherwise: they maintain white witchcraft to be an ancient and benign matriarchal faith, inherited from most ancient times and given a bad name by macho Christian persecutors. I prefer to agree with them, because I feel a sympathy for what I read about their practices: their reverence for the old stones, their taste for harmless private ritual, their belief in a universal Mother-God all seem to make theirs one of the less unappealing of organized religions, even if it is tangled up with Aquarianism, New Ageism, Flower Peopleness, feminist dogma and neo-Tolkienism. But of course for most people a witch is a witch is a witch, and belief in witchly *maleficium* certainly survives. Not only schoolgirls, in twentieth-century Europe, stick pins in wax effigies of their enemies, and nobody denies the power of suggestion, for good or for ill. In Normandy in the 1970s bad witches were still often blamed for miscarriages, children's sicknesses or butter refusing to churn, and good witches ('blessers' they used to be called) were frequently called in to put things right. Recognizing your witch is, of course, always a problem. In sixteenth-century Europe the only sure sign was thought to be something called 'the witch's mark' – a sort of teat on a woman's body, usually near the pudenda, which showed where her devilish familiar – rat, toad, hare or cat – had sucked her blood; yet even in my time people in different parts of the continent have confidently asserted the presence of genuine, old-school witches.

A few years ago in the Sierra Nevada of Spain, for example, I was assured that witchcraft both malicious and benign was flourishing. I should look out, they said, for herbalists and magic potionists in the hill-villages. Sure enough, idling through one such hamlet I saw a notice in a window advertising an infallibly curative and rejuvenative jelly, and went inside to inquire. The room was pitch-black but for the flickering light of a television showing, at that moment, a young American male in bed with two nubile girls. Amidst the gloom, surrounded by dim glass jars of liquids and boxes of desiccated vegetables I could just make out two grimly antediluvian figures: a withered old man with a stick, sitting in an armchair, and a fierce stooped-shouldered woman at a velvet-clothed table. They stared at me in grisly silence. Real witches? I hardly liked to ask – '*Excuse me, do you happen to have a teat near your pudenda?*' – and thinking that they looked decidedly more malicious than benign, I bought a bag of figs and ran. Then again, I was intrigued to learn that a village in Corsica which really did seem to me of black vibrations was a notorious residence of the Mazzeri – powerfully scary seers and sorcerers who had the power to foresee death, could be in two places at the same time, and lived in a dream-world all their own. How chill and penetrating were the eyes, at least in retrospect, of some of the villagers I interviewed!

Near my home in Wales a woman who habitually left field gates open, allowing sheep to wander, was alleged only half in fun to be a witch, but for myself I agree with the English sage Reginald Scot, who wrote in 1584 that malevolent witchcraft was a matter for 'children, fooles and melancholike persons'. It is not witches we should fear, but witch-hunters.


## 11 '*Mere superstitions*'

'Mere superstitions,' say Christian theologians about all these remnants and echoes of old faiths, but of course they have long spilled over into the Christian consciousness too. It is belief that does the trick. Contemporary European beliefs run the gamut from trust in lucky numbers to the conviction that the bread and wine of the Eucharist really are, despite all taste and appearance, transmuted by magic mantras into the flesh and blood of Christ. At Namur in Belgium people revere a reliquary supposed to contain some of the Virgin Mary's milk! Thousands of Neapolitans are persuaded to this day that on the feast of St Januarius the solidified blood of that martyr is miraculously liquefied, although it is 150 years since the Oxford scholar William Buckland, falling on his knees before the liquefaction, licked the blood and pronounced it bat's urine. Adolf Hitler, the dominant European of his time, belived in the tomfoolery of astrologers. In the streets of Bucharest, after nearly half a century of dialectical materialism, it was common to see well-dressed, perfectly modern members of the bourgeoisie crossing themselves before braving a traffic intersection; in Zagreb market-men do the same thing, without looking up from their commerce, when the cathedral bell sounds the angelus. I myself have not walked under a ladder for years, and invariably reach out of my bedclothes to touch my wooden bedstead if a rashly complacent thought enters my mind. Like nearly everyone, too, I frequently offer a silent prayer at moments of stress or frustration – always opening archaically, I have observed, with the phrase 'Please O God', inexpungible echo of an Anglican childhood.

Charms, magic crystals, holy oils, tarot cards, vampirology, exorcisms, the prophecies of fortune-tellers, prayers for rain or victory, sacred relics, touching things – Europeans still have faith in all these nostrums. In the months before the Second World War the then-famous astrologer of the London *Daily Express* repeatedly assured his readers, having consulted the constellations, that there would be no war in Europe. When the Germans invaded Poland, precipitating the maelstrom, the headline above his column read 'HITLER DEFIES THE STARS.'

## 12 *In between*

Being a sort of permanent compromise myself, I especially enjoy the syncretics of European religion, places and rituals where old faiths impinge upon new. Gandhi used to say that all religions were right, and all were wrong. Certainly they are all related, however much they detest each other, and when its time came Christianity never did quite throw off its pagan inheritances. Of course the Christian Establishment did its best, being particularly severe about the rocks. Lighting candles at stones, declared St Martin, Bishop of Dumium, in 574, was nothing more or less than devil-worship, and the Decree of Nantes, in 658, ordered bishops to 'dig up and remove and hide in places where they cannot be found those stones which in remote and woody places are still worshipped'. In ancient churches all over Europe I have been pleased to find elfish figures, little green men or chimeras, deftly translated from one belief to another – from one sect to another too, for they have often been willy-nilly inherited through doctrinal revolutions and reforms, and it is fun to see them mischievously peeking out from rood screens and choir stalls in austere churches of Protestantism. Often you will find a rock of ancient faith nervously incorporated in a church wall, just in case, or standing outside a Gothic porch like Banquo's ghost, or converted into a cross or a Calvary. At Gamla Uppsala, where Sweden's primeval kings are buried, the little church beside the burial mounds was built on the site of Sweden's last active pagan temple – perhaps on the same foundations, perhaps even to a similar design. The imagery of the rock proved inexpungible, too. 'Upon this rock I will build my church,' said Jesus himself of Simon Peter. 'Rock of Ages, cleft for me,' sing faithful Anglican congregations to this day. 'When God made the rocks he made the fossils in them,' declared the brave fundamentalist John Keble. When Charlemagne set up his imperial capital at Aachen in the eighth century of the Christian era, his royal chapel was built with infinite subtlety of biblical allusion, following the proportions of the mystic numbers in the Book of Revelation; but although one of his own edicts, in 789, had execrated 'before God' all the holy stones, still his own throne, the supreme seat of earthly power, was made of rough marble rock.

Beside a road in central Portugal I once came across a little building which seemed to speak to me direct from the in-between days of European religion. The chapel of São Brissos was famous actually, but I had never heard of it before. Its basis was an ancient cromlech, three stones in tripod with a boulder on top, but a Christian church had been built within and around it. All was whitewashed, with a blue margin around the base, and pagan and Christian were inextricably united. On one side there was a door, and a window with white lace curtains, looking rather cosy: on another the rocks were bare and lightly touched with lichen, and looked as though they had been there since the Ice Age. They held regular Christian services in this primeval structure, so a passing bicyclist informed me, and I had to assume that the priests of the rock had been obliged to give way to the priests of the Cross. I could not help wondering, though, whether the devotions of the present congregation were not partly pagan too, and sure enough long afterwards I came across this observation about São Brissos, and other such hybrids, in an official

Portuguese publication of 1992: 'Local people are aware of the religious character of dolmens and . . . it is in the interest of those who hold power in society that these monuments be integrated into the official order of things.'

## 13 *Regression*

As it happens those who have held power in society have often been under the spell of the rocks themselves, almost into our own times. The common people of Europe frequently used the ancient megaliths as Christian shrines, as tombs, as barns, as cowsheds and even occasionally as cafés. The governing classes more often made new ones, because in the eighteenth and nineteenth centuries it became modish to commission mock-megalithic monuments, garden follies and hilltop ornaments. Some were very convincing shams. Most strangers who penetrate to the so-called Druids' Temple near Masham in Yorkshire, England, take it to be as old as Merlin. Actually it was built in the 1820s by a local squire, William Danby, to give work to local people at a time of hardship. Hidden away secretively in a pine plantation on the moors, it is a very elaborate approximation of Stonehenge – smaller, but more so. Within a circle of standing stones and capstones there are ceremonial pillars, platforms, altars and chambers, and among the trees around stand sundry dolmens and triliths. When I was there an elderly man I found intensely studying the ensemble asked me how old I thought it was. I told him about Mr Danby, and he said I had cruelly shattered his illusions, especially as it had taken him two days to find the place.

In Germany megalithic monuments were often associated with more dreadful pagan traditions, warlike gods and Wagnerian legends, and so had a particular appeal for the balefully mystic Nazis. It is said to have been Heinrich Himmler, the commander of the SS and chief scourge of the Jews, who inspired the most ambitious of all megalithic shams, the vast pagan place of ceremony at Sachsenhain, near Verden in Lower Saxony. Built in the 1930s, it was meant to commemorate 4,500 Saxon slaves slaughtered there by the Franks – a slaughter, that is, of healthy Nordic pagans by effete Christian intruders from the South. Accordingly 4,500 boulders were taken to the site and erected in a vast circular avenue, perhaps a mile and a quarter round. I suppose it is the largest neo-antiquity ever made. Sometimes the avenue opens out into platforms, sometimes it is joined by lesser paths of boulders, and it surrounds a pleasant grassy meadow, with a stream running through it, and cows grazing, and cherry blossoms in season, and a tump, whether natural or man-made, conveniently sited at the edge of it.

When I was led to Sachsenhain I was at first rather charmed by the place. It suggested to me Christ Church Meadows at Oxford, harmlessly transformed under the influence of some eccentric scholar. But as I walked around the avenue myself (birds singing, a couple of women exercising their dogs) I thought about the fanatic ceremonies the Nazis held there at solstice times, proclaiming their allegiance I suppose to the virile and ethnically impeccable Old Gods of the Germans. I fancied then their torchlight parades processing between the rocks, ritually challenged by other companies of cultists at symbolical intersections, shouting slogans, singing hymns of hatred, pausing at platforms for curses or incantations; and in the flicker of their torches I saw the glinting narrow eyes of the High Priest Himmler, behind his steel-framed glasses. Even phoney megaliths can be powerfully evocative.

14  *Inscription upon an entirely bogus mock-megalithic folly erected by George Law, Bishop of Bath and Wells, circa 1840*

> Here where once druids trod in times of yore
> And stain'd their altars with a victim's gore
> Here now the Christian ransomed from above
> Adores a God of Mercy and of love.

15  *We Druids*

Those Druids came somewhere between the megalithics and the Christians, and they are relatively familiar to us. Nobody knows what a priest of the megalithic religion looked like, but we all think we know the look of a Druid. Druids survived into historical times, and left some of their mysteries behind. In Wales the classical forms of alliterative verse, still enthusiastically practised by poets young and old, are said to be inherited from the mnemonics of the Druids, and costumed Druids preside over the Eisteddfod Genedlaethol, the itinerant national cultural festival, attended by flower-maidens of the forest. I am myself a Druid on those occasions, a member of the White Order of the Gorsedd of Bards. Our rituals and regalia are in fact of eighteenth-

and nineteenth-century origins, devised by a half-crazed genius littérateur called Iolo Morgannwg, and given substance by the painter Hubert Herkomer and the sculptor Goscombe John, who between them designed a glorious set of neo-Druidical robes and insignia – blue, green, white, gold, silver and ermine.

Before the grand occasions of the festival, we members of the Gorsedd (a body of bards which Iolo resurrected, or perhaps invented) assemble in some nearby school to Druidize ourselves in flowing robes and headdresses. There is no denying comedy to this process. The setting is generally prosaic – the usual deal tables and metal-framed windows of a country school, the playground empty outside, the air smelling slightly of chalk and india-rubber. The bards range from scholarly dissertationists to opera singers or poetical anarchists. The Mistress of the Robes is a motherly soul like a minister's wife at a chapel fête. And there we cheerfully transform ourselves, with laughter and badinage, into figures from a mythical past. The men's shoes tend to protrude awkwardly beneath their robes. The women's earrings are not invariably in keeping. Some people have trouble getting their headgear right. Never mind, off we go in a mass of whites, greens and blues, to clamber into the buses that will take us to the Eisteddfod field – through their windows we can be seen peering out, often incongruously spectacled, to wave greetings to un-Druidical friends and relatives lining the route. Outsiders often sneer at this charade, but they do not understand it. It has its funny aspects, but it represents a conviction and a comradeship as strong as any forest-oath of the original Druids. When I first assumed the dignities of the Druidic Order of the White Robe it was one of the proudest moments of my life.

## 16 *Atavism*

In the most varied European places one discovers religious atavism ('some strange recurrence,' as Walter Bagehot defined it, 'to a primitive past'). When St Bernadette saw her apparition of the Virgin at Lourdes in 1858, she called it *'une petite demoiselle'* – a fairy in the local vernacular. As late as the 1880s, in England, the Revd John Atkinson was told disconcertingly that 'the priests of the old religion were more powerful conjurors than you church priests'. Even Friedrich Nietzsche, declaring God to be dead, allowed that the divine shadow might still lurk in caves! Inside the Church of England church at Haworth in Yorkshire, where the Revd Patrick Brontë brought up his genius daughters, in the 1980s I found a branch of a tree set up as a votive. Among its twigs the local population had expressed its hopes and yearnings as fervently as any African tribeswoman propitiating evil spirits. 'Please Let Me Be Mark Aspen's Girl Friend,' said one childish scrawl on a crumpled piece of lined writing-paper, 'Please Let Me And My Sister Be Friends Again,' said another, and there were several heartfelt pleas requesting a victory for Halifax Town in their Saturday match. Tatters of rags on Polish bushes – discarded crutches in holy places of Spain or Italy – midnight processions and miraculous cures – *'Please O God make me find the car keys'* – all such feral manifestations, conducted now under the aegis of the Cross, remind me still of the rocks.

## 17 *In love with death*

A death-cult, some scholars think, was part of the megalithic religion. If so, it has certainly been inherited by modern Europeans. Mummies and corpses, blood and bones go naturally enough, I suppose, with a culture which was founded upon death by torture, and no ghoul or necrophile need feel deprived in Christian Europe. Dead people are available everywhere, together with innumerable anatomical pieces pickled in reliquaries. There are mummified nuns in Dublin, calcified monks in Naples, leathery corpses from the marsh at Schleswig, perfectly preserved 2,000-year-old people from Trundholm Bog in Denmark, a charnel-house lined with the bones of 5,000 dead bodies at Évora in Portugal and the skeleton of the philosopher Jeremy Bentham, wearing nankeen trousers and bedroom slippers, sitting in a glass case at University College, London. If you drop fifty forints into a slot in Budapest the mummified hand of St Stephen will automatically be illuminated. At the Capuchin catacombs in Palermo, Sicily, the desiccated corpses of generations of citizens are on display, guarded by friars and climaxed by the body of a child labelled 'BAMBINA – SLEEPING BEAUTY GIRL'. 'Be very careful,' one of the friars said in a flat sort of voice as I left this macabre exhibition – 'watch out for robbers.' I thought there was a queer look in his eye, rather like the stare of those Corsican villagers, and hardly had I left the sacred premises than two thugs on a motor-bike snatched my bag and left me destitute.

## 18  *The mountain*

I am sure that sages long before St Patrick frequented the mountain called Croagh Patrick, on the west coast of Ireland in County Mayo, from whose summit the saint expelled all serpents from the island. It is the epitome of a holy rock, with Druidical associations too. The Irish call it 'The Reek', and it rises bare and bold from the sea-coast, overlooking a bay littered with a hundred islands. Nowadays the crowds who make the Croagh Patrick pilgrimage on the last Sunday in July ostensibly make the climb in search of Christian solace, but when I joined them I am sure I was not alone in feeling instincts far more elemental. We could hardly claim to be aspiring to the sun or the moon – we could scarcely see the top of the mountain itself for the rain – but we were certainly in intimate contact with the rocks.

Some 20,000 of us made the climb. We would have been more, I was told, were it not for a Roscommon–Mayo football match being played that afternoon. At the bottom of the mountain tinkers and their boys sold us rough-cut sticks – 'Reek Sticks' in the vernacular – and all that day, huddled in anoraks against the drizzle, the pilgrims set off up the mass of the mountain, some alone, some in groups, some laughing and singing, some saying Hail Marys all the way. It was like moving with the crowd along a city shopping pavement. There were imps and there were elders. There were rugged old ladies. There were teams of soldiers in uniform. Some of the tinkers loped along on the edge of the crowd, and prancing urchins brandished their sticks. Many zealots climbed barefoot, with facial expressions of excruciating dedication and blood mixed with mud oozing from their toes. Halfway up was easy, but then we saw in front of us, stretching away into the mist and rain, a steep wall of rubble with no track at all. 'Jesus,' said a man beside me, 'will you look at that?' They call the scree 'Hell before Heaven', and up it we laboured gritting our teeth. Sometimes people fell over; often they stood still and silent, breathing heavily, praying for help or trying to make up their minds whether to give up or go on. Occasionally stretcher men came stumbling down with casualties, bloodied and bandaged, *pour encourager les autres*. 'When you get to the top,' said my man, 'your soul will be cleansed, and you can start sinning all over again.'

And sure enough at the top, in a small glass-fronted oratory, non-stop masses were being said, the amplified voices of the priests strangely thudding through the mist, while a crowd of pilgrims milled around the summit. Some

were buying tea and buns at ad-hoc refreshment stands. Some were queuing
to make their confessions. Some wearily made the statutory seven circuits
of the stone called St Patrick's Bed – bumping now and then into me, until
I realized I was circuiting the wrong way round. I loved the pilgrimage to
Croagh Patrick, bruised and breathless though I was. 'Your first time?'
sympathetic voices kept asking me, when at last I slumped heavily on the
ground to eat a sandwich, and I told them yes; but I didn't feel it was, any
more than I have ever felt a stranger to those warm donkey-rocks at home.

## 19  *The last pagans*

The best place of all to sense the lingering power of the old gods is Lithuania,
which was the last European country to accept Christianity – thirteen
centuries after the birth of Christ. So inescapable still are signs and echoes
of the old beliefs that I sometimes think the Lithuanians are not entirely free
of their paganism even now. Reminders of Perkūnas, the Thunder-God, are
everywhere, and sometimes images of him too: a formidable Thunder-God
figure, a true idol, stands in a square at Kaunas, the former capital of the
country, and the cathedral below the castle at Vilnius, the central national
symbol, occupies the site of a temple in his honour (there is said to be a
pagan altar somewhere among its foundations, but during a long chill tour
among the miscellaneous coffins, corpses and sacred relics stored down there
I failed to discover it). In 1996 they erected in the cathedral square a statue
of one of the supreme national heroes, Grand Duke Gediminas, the founder
of the city. This was specifically conceived both as a riposte to the style of
the Soviet Russians who had ruled the country until a few years before, and
as a declaration of national meaning. It is my favourite equestrian statue in
the world – partly because the Duke is not galloping triumphantly into the
sunset, as he would be if the Communists had made him, but simply stands
beside his horse's head in a posture of generous magnanimity; partly because
it was erected directly above an ancient holy stone of the pagans.

Not far away, off a quiet backstreet, is the small redbrick church of
St Nicolas. It is a fine little building, secluded within its surrounding walls,
and very stalwart. So it had to be. It was built by the German merchant
community of the city in the early years of the fourteenth century, well before
the conversion of the Lithuanians to Christianity. Those pious Germans, when
they assembled for Sunday service, knew that the heathen were all around

them, with their sacred rocks and trees and springs, and old Perkūnas was being worshipped with who knew what profane and horrid rites up the road below the castle.

## 20 *The Hill of Crosses*

Even the site most profoundly sacred to Lithuanian Catholics seems to me to reflect convictions older than Christ. Kryžių Kalnas, the Hill of Crosses, is another famous symbol both of religious devotion and of national pride. It is the strangest place. Since the early nineteenth century at least, and probably far, far longer, people have regarded it as holy. Over the generations they have implanted its mound with a tangled forest of crosses, of wood, of iron, of stone, tall carved crosses, crosses made of old pipes, crosses exquisitely sculpted, crosses in rows, crosses in clusters, crosses piled and stacked there in an indistinguishable jumble. Around almost every cross hundreds of lesser crosses are hung, together with tangled masses of rosaries, and between them little alleys have been trampled by the pilgrims who come here in an endless flow from every corner of Lithuania. The whole hillock looks *molten*, as if all its myriad symbols have somehow been fused together, leaving jagged protrusions everywhere. There is an overpowering sense of mystic primitivism to this place, and as a pantheist I myself honour it as much for its abstract holiness as for its Christian meaning. In the days of Soviet rule in Lithuania the Communists loathed it either way. They rightly saw it as a focus of patriotic defiance, too, and did their surly best to put an end to it. They bulldozed away some 6,000 of its crosses, and forbade the erection of any more, but of course it did them no good. Patriots and pietists crept in there at night and planted new crosses anyway, and since the collapse of Communism thousands more have gone up, spreading out across the meadows about the mound; even as I stood there one afternoon thinking about it all, on the banks of the little reedy stream which runs nearby, I heard on the quiet pastoral air a pounding from somewhere in the thicket of crosses, as yet another was hammered in. How could a measly local commissar prevail against the combined forces of Christ, patriotism and Perkūnas the Thunder-God?

## 21  *In a class by herself*

Long ago Christianity won in Europe, triumphing over diverse permutations
of paganism, displacing the whole pantheon of the Greeks and Romans,
humiliating all the Perkūnases, surviving countless heresies and schisms of
its own. '*Le roi est mort, vive le roi!*' wrote Sir James Frazer, in 1880, imagining
the angelus sounding on the wind from Rome over the Temple of the
Golden Bough at Nemi. Glass weakened the primeval power of stone, and
a new order of divine beings took over. They are with us still. I have more
than once encountered people who have seen the Virgin Mary, and once
met a lady who had come across Jesus Christ himself. They had, however,
never actually spoken to these holy persons, who had crossed their paths in
stately silence, so in 1994 I was excited to discover, during a visit to the
pilgrimage site of Fátima in Portugal, that the legendary Sister Lúcia, who
had enjoyed long conversations with the Holy Mother in 1917, was still
alive. She was in a class by herself among Christian seers of her time. Her
accounts of the miraculous encounters had made Fátima one of the great
shrines of Christendom – it was the headquarters of the Blue Armada, an
anti-atheist movement alleged to have tens of millions of members in more
than 100 countries. Also she was the keeper of the mysterious Third Secret,
something either so awful or so banal that it had never been revealed to the
world, but was known only to Popes and innermost confidants of the Vatican:
shut away, as Cardinal Ottaviani, Prefect of the Holy Office, said in 1960,
'in one of those archives which are like a very deep, dark well, to the bottom
of which papers fall and nobody is able to see them any more', and so
tantalizingly mysterious that in 1981 a former Trappist monk hijacked an
Irish airliner in an unsuccessful attempt to force its extraction. Sister Lúcia
was almost certain to be beatified after her death, and the vast basilica at
Fátima, attended by a ceremonial square twice as large as St Peter's Square
in Rome, stood ever ready for her funeral.

A priest at Fátima told me all this, and when he happened to remark in
the course of conversation that Sister Lúcia was alive and well at a convent
at Coimbra, I did not waste a moment. Sister Lúcia! A prodigious and fateful
mystery in herself, who was likely to be honoured for ever and ever, who
had lived a life of magical revelation, whose tomb awaited her within
that mighty church, whose sainthood was assured, whose Third Secret lay
immured in a bottomless archive and was hijacked for by Trappists! Within

the hour I was at the door of her Carmelite convent, where she had lived with her memories and her Secret for almost half a century.

I did not meet her, though, and perhaps it was all to the good. What would I have said to her? I was only an inquisitive pagan. The young nun who opened the convent door, revealing a cadaverous hall suggestively within, regretted that Sister Lúcia could not talk to me, even through a grille. I mumbled something about only wishing to have her blessing: but I was prevaricating, and the young nun knew it.

## 22  *Seeing things*

It was a colossal event when the Holy Mother appeared to Sister Lúcia at Fátima in 1917; Bernadette of Lourdes saw Our Lady in 1858, became a saint, and had a movie made about her; but by the later years of the twentieth century holy apparitions were all the rage among European Christians. It was a sign of the times, perhaps. The sudden prevalence of sacred visions and miracles in many parts of the continent went well with the taste for Unidentified Flying Objects and other Unsolved Mysteries of the television culture. In Italy innumerable Madonna images were seen to weep tears of water or of blood, although the Church itself recognized the authenticity of only one, and scientists dismissed them all as frauds or natural phenomena. Ireland proved to be the great place for your Moving Virgins, and sacred statues all over the island miraculously shook and swayed, sometimes attended by insubstantial visitants delivering didactic messages about divorce and clean living. I looked in one rainy afternoon at a Marian grotto among a dark grove of trees at Cappoquin in County Waterford, where an image of the Virgin had repeatedly moved, been transfigured and made pronouncements, such as 'The World Must Behave', 'Thanks for the Hymns' or 'The People Must Go to Mass More.' A solitary family sat there doggedly in the wet, in a kind of gazebo above the grotto: mother, father, adult son and daughter, they waited there as in trance, clutching rosaries and staring fixedly at the statue on its rock, willing it to shift perhaps, praying for a sacred manifestation, lips moving sometimes but bodies still as images themselves. They were like addicts at a gaming table. The rain fell all around, and dripped heavily off the roof of the gazebo.

The most baffling of these visitations was the marvel of Medjugorje, a hill-hamlet in Bosnia where a group of children, in 1981, claimed to have had a vision of the Virgin Mary. Ever afterwards they reported almost daily access to the Madonna, nobody being able to shake their evidence, and although the Catholic hierarchy disassociated itself from the affair, the hamlet became another of Europe's great pilgrimage places. Throughout the wars in Yugoslavia (which did not reach Medjugorje, considered by the faithful a miracle in itself) pilgrims came from many parts of the world in the hope of sharing the visionaries' experience or, as second best, seeing a subsidiary phenomenon, the dancing of the sun. By the time I got there the little cluster of houses in the mountains had become one of your archetypal Christian shrines, in the Fátima tradition (the Medjugorje children were given Secrets, too). A brand-new sanctuary had been built, with two square towers, and around it on the bleak and stony site had arisen all the essentials of the pilgrim destination – bazaar-like shops aglitter with holy trinkets, pizza restaurants, heaps of bed-and-breakfast places, gas stations, taxi ranks, banks. Several million people, I was assured, had gone to Medjugorje since the original visions, but on my winter day there you would never guess it. It was drizzling there, too. The sanctuary was empty. The shops were deserted. The taxis waited forlorn at their ranks. I went to the Hill of Apparitions, where the children had first seen their visions, and there up the stony track I saw my only pilgrims, clambering under a line of black umbrellas towards the sacred summit. The rain poured down, the clouds scudded overhead, and even for the most visionary the sun of Medjugorje did no dancing.

### 23 *An Irish eyewitness account of the sun dancing, quoted in* Carmina Gadelica, *by Alexander Carmichael, 1900*

The glorious bright-red sun was after rising on the crest of the great hills, and it was changing colour – green, purple, red, blood-red, white, intense white, and gold-white, like the glory of God of the elements to the children of men. It was dancing up and down in exaltation . . .

### 24 *Toenails*

Another phenomenon of my European years has been the appearance of a highly mobile Pope, riding around in a vehicle called a Popemobile which has always reminded me of the glass cage Adolf Eichmann sat in during his death-trial in Jerusalem. The Polish Pope John Paul II is a terrific traveller, a terrific showman too, and for the first time he brought the mysterious power of his office into every part of Europe – who could possibly have guessed, fifty years ago, that a Pope would ever come to *Cardiff*? I have never met a Pope, but I was acquainted with an Archbishop of Canterbury once. We shared a birthday – with Gandhi, too – and we also shared the circumstance that every five years or so the big toenails of our right feet came off. His had been damaged in a tank during the Second World War, mine by a block of ice in the Himalaya. He was the spiritual head of some 70 million Anglicans throughout the world, with 800 archbishops and bishops, but I have to say that I never found myself daunted by his eminence. It might have been a different matter if I had shared a disposable toenail with a Pope, because even in the mind of an animist the Bishop of Rome has some transcendent majesty. Canterburys come and go, and retire as it were to their maiden names, but a Pope is a Pope for ever. The Pope is the Big Time. Nearly 900 million Catholics pay allegiance to the Pope. There have been venerated relics in cathedrals, bowed to by cardinals, honoured by princes, less majestic than the toenail of a Pope.

## 25  A dead Pope

I saw a dead Pope once, and he was refulgent even in corpsehood. Pope Pius X had been Patriarch of Venice before his ascension, and when I was living in that city in 1959 he paid a posthumous revisit to his old patriarchate. We watched his passing from our balcony over the Grand Canal. Embalmed though he was by then, he moved by with infinite condescension. Gondolas full of priests came first, cushioned deep in their seats and rowed by white-robed gondoliers. Then came a series of dream-like barges, their velvet draperies trailing in the water behind. And finally in a blaze of gold came the Bucintoro, successor to the magnificent State barge of the doges of Venice, rowed by a crew of tough young sailors to the beat of a drum. Bells rang, plainchants sounded from loudspeakers across the city, and to the solemn boom, boom of the drum the cadaver of the Holy Father, flat on his back in a crystal coffin, sailed by as to the manner dead.

## 26  *A live Pope*

In life too a Pope still has an aura all his own, and to my mind the best of
all European pilgrimages remains the Easter pilgrimage to St Peter's Square
in Rome to witness His Holiness speaking to his 900 million across the
world. It may be a hackneyed spectacle, even a cliché among ceremonies,
and what the Pope says is unlikely to set hearts on fire, but the very
predictability of it is half its strength. It is as it always has been. 'Upon
this rock!' The immense good-humoured crowd, disgorged from a myriad
coaches, walking leisurely up the Via della Conciliazione, seeping out of the
back-quarters of the Vatican, contains all the requisite nuns, pasty-faced
seminarians, Poles, American tourist groups, Irish enthusiasts, backpackers,
enormously old arthritic ladies and couples from England on All-Inclusive
Easter Breaks. The Swiss Guard, though not quite so stalwart nowadays as
their reputation says they used to be, still look stylish in their sixteenth-century
liveries, with pikes over their shoulders. The soldiers who turn up on parade
march about with the true Italian military panache of tossing feathers and
high-pitched bands. There are the statutory television cameras all over the
place, and properly fussy chaplains appear now and then on the papal balcony
to mess about with the lectern, adjust the microphone and look important.

When at last His Holiness appears, attended by an obsequious cardinal or
two, and further attentive acolytes with hands clasped in the mantis position,
then it really is like seeing God himself up there, so old and distant, so
angelically attended; and when his voice comes echoing over the great piazza,
slightly delayed, it seems, like a conversation on a bad overseas telephone
connection, at once very near and far away, it might indeed be the voice of
Heaven, so unimpeachably platitudinous are its sentiments and so irreproach-
able its turn of phrase – just the sort of speech of welcome we may expect,
if we are fortunate enough one day to stand at the gates of paradise.

## 27  *Christian power*

'How many divisions has the Pope?' Stalin sneeringly but ingenuously asked.
In fact, of course, Christian power has been incalculable in European history,
and it is the presence of the Pope, far more than the President of Italy, that
makes Rome one of the great cities of the world. Many other European

cities have become internationally important specifically because of their Christian connections – the great pilgrimage destinations, like Santiago de Compostela in Spain; the great centres of dissent or heresy, like Canterbury, Avignon or Luther's Wittenberg; powerful archbishoprics like Trier or Mainz; or cities which have been the sites of crucial Christian conferences, affecting the fate of the continent. Constance – Konstanz in German – is one of these. It is a middle-sized city, situated grandly at the site where the Rhine flows out of Lake Constance, but otherwise not very remarkable. The resonance of its name depends still upon the fateful Christian Council which was held here between the years 1414 and 1418. The Council formally condemned the propositions of the heretics John Wyclif and Jan Hus, treacherously burning Hus at the stake (he had gone to Constance with a safe conduct), and it succeeded in ending the Great Schism which had divided the Catholic Church between rival Popes at Rome and Avignon. But when I wander the streets of the city I do not see in my mind's eye the empurpled ecclesiasts at their conclave in the cathedral, or the triumphant Martin V who emerged as the one and only Pope. I see instead the amazing ragbag of followers who jammed the city for four years, and have remained part of its legend ever since. Going to the Council of Constance in 1414 was like going to an Olympic Games city today. Heads of State, ambassadors, scholars and lawyers filled these old houses, together with thousands of servants, guards and courtiers, and the city was turned into an enormous trading fair and emporium. Some 100,000 people, it is said, came to Constance for the Ecumenical Council, and most of them were not greatly interested in theology, for they included every sort of trader, mountebanks and con men of all kinds, peregrinating actors, street musicians, clowns and vast numbers of prostitutes. I can see them clearly still, milling around the cathedral square while Hus was burning: and I can imagine the squabbles there would be now over the sale of television rights, or the propriety of displaying advertisements around the stake.

## 28  The uses of faith

During my fifty years Christianity in Europe has been most obviously influential when it has provided defiance in oppressive times, or plain pleasure. (Nowadays it seldom represents, as it still does in America, social pride or business advantage.) I shall never forget the magnificent outpouring of ritual

and ceremony which surrounded the Catholic Church in Poland in the days
when it stood alone against the dingy autocracy of Communism – so resolutely
that every chapel of the pilgrimage church at Czestochowa, the holiest shrine
of Polish Christendom, was bugged by the secret police. It hardly struck me
as a sacramental effulgence, though. In Warsaw on a weekday evening in
the 1950s one often saw citizens slipping into church, out of the cold and
snowy city, rather as commuters elsewhere popped into a bar before catching
the train home: entering hurriedly, crossing themselves as one might sign in
at a club, and emerging a few moments later buttoning up their coats, pulling
on their thick gloves, and hurrying away to the trolley-bus – stocked up, as
it were, with some reviving stimulant. And when on a festival day Catholicism
displayed itself in all its glory, all shine and incense, all tremendous fugues
and stately priests, then the huge shabby congregation was elevated in the
same way as an audience at some brassy musical in the capitalist West, given
just for an hour or two a spectacular escape from reality.

Was it really remorse when, in the later years of Franco's dictatorship, the
burghers of Málaga or Seville took to the streets on a saint's day carrying
their enormous images of the Virgin, led by an official on a horse with sword
drawn and medals jangling? Group by group came the penitents then, with
tall conical hoods on their heads and wands in their hands, looking eerily
from side to side, swaggering in a rather lordly manner, and behind them
vast gilded icons swayed in the lamplight, carried by ranks of bent-backed,
cowled and cassocked devotees. A hooded major-domo kept them in time
with the clang of a bell, rather like that drummer with the dead Pope, and
in a sad and dreadful rhythm they made their slow way through the streets.
Yet I used to notice that when they stopped for a rest those sweating slaves
of God often waved convivially to friends in the crowd, called for Coca-Colas
or lit cigarettes. Those were not really processions of contrition: they were
partly reflections of the forces that ruled Spain then, Church and State in
almighty tandem, but partly expressions of the national delight in effect.

In the spring of 1996 I was walking through Bratislava, the capital of the
newly created Republic of Slovakia, in search of my supper, when I became
aware of groups of merry and noisy young people all making for some
common destination. A promising wine-cellar? Some jolly café with music?
I fell in with the stream of them, feeling like a wine-and-music evening
myself, and found myself drawn into the jam-packed and festively rococo
church of the Jesuits, where the undergraduates of the university, all apparently
in the highest of spirits, were assembling for their student mass. In Ireland I

sometimes suspect that the harshest rituals of Catholicism are undertaken in a spirit of enjoyment – masochistic enjoyment, perhaps, like the wonderfully jolly ascent of Croagh Patrick. One of the most demanding of Irish pilgrimages takes the faithful to a grim island in Lough Derg, a remote and dispiriting mountain lake in Donegal, where they endure a three-day fast, a twenty-four-hour vigil, barefoot peregrinations over stony tracks and the compulsory recitations of 63 Glorias, 234 Creeds, 891 Paternosters and 1,458 Hail Marys. I was once at a wedding reception at Drogheda, away on the east coast, when I heard a woman ask a worldly young guest with a carnation buttonhole and a glass of champagne where he was going for his holidays that year. I expected Barbados or Mykonos, but no. 'I thought of giving myself,' he said, 'the three days at Lough Derg.'

## 29  A prince of the Church

Certainly the best-known Catholic martyr of my time was considered in his lifetime more an ideologue than a saint. Cardinal József Mindszenty first came into my life in 1949, when during my vacations from Oxford I was sub-editing on *The Times* in London. He was the Primate of Hungary, and a nightly stream of news passed through my hands concerning his trial for treason at the hands of the Communist Government in Budapest. After days of torture and a show trial he was sentenced to jail for life, but re-entered the news even more spectacularly when he was briefly set free during the Budapest Rising of 1956. The Communists having regained control, he took refuge in the United States Embassy in Budapest, and there he remained for fifteen years, repeatedly refusing invitations to go into exile abroad. For people of my generation Mindszenty was a household name, a living symbol of anti-Communist inflexibility – he later fell out with the Vatican itself because he thought it too soft on Stalinism.

Mindszenty died and was buried in Austria, but when the Communists finally lost power in Hungary, in 1991, his body was reburied in the basilica at Esztergom, the seat of the Hungarian primates, and there I made a pilgrimage to his tomb. What a conclusion for a prince of the Church! The huge domed basilica of Esztergom stands on a high bluff above the Danube. Far below it a broken bridge to the Slovakian shore, blown up during the Second World War, adds an extra note of tragic violence to a truly epic site, and in front of the building a vast never-completed piazza, leading upwards to a classical colonnade, makes you feel you are approaching one of Christianity's power-centres. The church is claimed to be the fifth largest on earth, and its treasury contains a fabulous hoard of gold and silver objects. Mindszenty is buried in its crypt, which is sustained by walls fifty feet thick, is guarded by two female colossi representing Resurrection and Immortality, and is pervaded by an atmosphere of immensely portentous gloom. Many of his predecessors are commemorated by tablets in the walls, and one of them is portrayed in effigy sheltered beneath the wing of a gigantic black angel: but nothing down there matches the significance of Cardinal Mindszenty's tomb, which is one of the great shrines of Hungarian Catholicism. When I was there, two decades after his death, a mass of wreaths, ribbons and memorial messages still surrounded it, together with photographs of papal visits to the sacred site. An organ played gigantically in the basilica above, and as I emerged into the sunshine I reflected wryly upon the days, long before, when I had wrestled with the problem of writing a two-column headline around a name with ten letters in it.

## 30  *True faith*

But at some places, in eastern Europe especially, one may still experience Christian belief at its most transcendental. One such site is the city gate called Aušros Vartai, the Gates of Dawn, at Vilnius. The city is largely Polish in population, and the holiest thing in it for Polish Catholics is a miracle-working icon of the Madonna which is housed in a little chapel above the gateway. Old pictures show the street below crowded with kneeling worshippers, gazing up at the chapel above, and in the late 1990s I found the strength of adoration unabated. The Gates of Dawn remained a place of daily pilgrimage, conducted so far as I could see in a spirit of purest devotion. Mass was said there every day, its music sounding in the street below (the chapel windows were opened, to allow people to see the Madonna): and when one weekday morning I found my way into the staircase which leads up to the holy place, it was crowded almost to suffocation with Christians in a state of ecstasy – some singing, some praying aloud, some trying to shuffle up the steps on their knees, all pressing joyfully towards a glimpse of the sacred picture, radiant there in black and gold among a shimmer of priestly ritual.

Another gateway alive with faith is the right-angled Stone Gate which leads into the upper town at Zagreb, in Croatia. On a Sunday especially this provides an unforgettable spectacle of Christian dedication. In the gate's shadowy interior there stands another miraculous Madonna icon, within a grille, and before it the faithful stand in silent supplication, or kneel in rows of pews half-concealed in the darkness. A small cavernous shop sells votive candles, and these the supplicants hand over to attendant nuns to light and put in place. There were two candle-nuns when I was there – unsmiling, preoccupied women. A mass of candles burned before them on a large tray, its flickering light a blaze in the gloom, and they worked incessantly with metal spatulas to make room for more. The scores of candles had coagulated into one big waxy flaming mass. The nuns separated them into clumps, as though they were working on a cake in a medieval kitchen, cutting them into slices, shifting them here and there, scooping huge lumps of molten wax out of the tray, slicing, scooping, shifting without a pause, while the faithful stood silent and immobile before the Madonna, dim figures crouched in the pews behind, and a line of believers queued with unlit candles to add to the furnace. Cut and scoop, cut and scoop, the nuns continued with their sacred duties, silhouetted against the flames (it sacrilegiously occurred to me) like a pair of imps in Hades. From outside the gate sounded a monotonous sing-song mantra, kept up by two beggar children, one on each side of the path – faltering sometimes when they ran out of breath, renewed whenever a likely votary emerged.

## 31  *Passion Flower*

Such has been the popular force of faith like this that even in my time un-Christian ideologies of Europe have sometimes requisitioned the trappings of Christianity. When I was working on a book in Spain in the 1960s an undeclared anathema applied to the name of Dolores Ibárurri Gómez, 'La Pasionaria', one of the supreme Communist heroines of the Spanish Civil War. Under the left-wing Republic of the 1930s she had been elevated to an eminence hitherto only occupied by the Virgin Mary herself. In the great political processions her icon was actually carried in place of the Madonna's, preceded by candle-bearers and drummers just as in the Easter processions of other times. Her Civil War battle-cries were quoted like holy decrees – '*No paserán!*', '*Better to die on your feet than live on your knees*' – and even her nickname referred explicitly enough to the Christian story. This flaming prophet of Marxism was created in the pattern of holiness. If history had gone a different way we might well have had miraculous statues of her, or liquefactions of her blood. During my time in Spain La Pasionaria was an exile in Moscow; but religions being what they are, whether sacred or secular, after the death of the Catholic dictator Francisco Franco she came home again, and died in 1989 as a respected member of Spain's new democratic parliament.

## 32  St Scrooge's Day

Some of the great festivals of Christianity, themselves inherited from paganism, have maintained something of their immemorial popular sanctity. Going to church on Easter Sunday, a purely Christian festival, is still a great occasion among congregations across Europe – almost obligatory, for example, among millions of organically agnostic Anglicans – but I have never noticed that it has any immediate effect on the manners or morals of the continent. On the other hand Christmas, directly descended without a doubt from pagan celebrations of the winter solstice, still works. Christmas Day is St Scrooge's Day. Perhaps because it is a children's festival, because the Christmas story is so charming and Christmas carols are such good tunes, somehow on Christmas Day all Europe is a better place. Pickpockets stay home on Christmas morning. Grumps are less grumpy then. Smiles come easier, and all across the continent one feels the peoples moving into a slower and gentler mode, as the goose, the duck or ever more commonly the tasteless turkey browns in the oven. One Christmas in Vienna I went for a stroll in a park before returning to the Sacher Hotel, where my own Christmas dinner was roasting. There was hardly a woman in the park. Everywhere the husbands of Vienna, with their children, aimlessly but expectantly loitered, expelled from under the womanly feet of the city while Gretchen and Helge got on with the job. Christmas is a time when old hierarchies are restored. 'For Heaven's sake,' I could hear the housewives of all Europe grumbling that day, 'go and get yourself a bit of fresh air, and take the children with you!'

## 33  *Christmas with the Pickwick Club*

Scandinavian Christmases are especially convincing. Santa Claus lives up there, after all (visited, on direct flights to Swedish Lapland, by countless package tourists and their children – who sometimes find it bewildering that only the day before they had seen the old gentleman in a plastic grotto at Toys 'R' Us). At Christmas a smell of spiced mulled wine, onomatopoeically called *glögg*, pervades the city markets of Scandinavia, and the stewardesses of Scandinavian Airlines put candled crowns on their heads and appear in aircraft cabins to sing squeaky hymns. Some of my own happiest Christmas memories are of the restaurant called the Operakällaren in Stockholm, where dark falls long before the festive meal is over, and through the great plush dining-room the flambeaus outside send their lurid light.

There, as evening draws on, and more and more of the Operakällaren's house aquavit is poured by merry waiters of the old school, the Christian spirit of Christmas seems to me exemplified in a way Dickens would have loved – almost as though one is dining with the Pickwick Club itself. All ages are there, and everyone gives the impression of being related to everyone else. Marvellously goes the elk-meat, swiftly pass the herrings, one great salmon succeeds another on the buffet, and very soon you find yourself on familiar terms with the Swedes at the next table, complimenting them on their fluent English, admiring little Eva's Christmas frock or little Erik's blue bow-tie, exchanging grandmotherly confidences with Mrs Andersson, toasting them all with yet more aquavit. Stockholmers are not especially religious people, and I imagine they have been eating those Baltic herrings and downing fiery liquids at least since the days of the heathen kings of Old Uppsala up the road: but still if I wanted to show visitors from outer space an exhibition of Christianity ritually in action I might well take them behind the flambeaus to try a Christmas smorgasbord at the Operakällaren. Devilish good dinner, as Mr Jingle would say – cold, but capital – pleasant people these – well behaved, too – very.

## 34  *Are Christians kinder?*

Of course spirituous conviviality is not what Christianity is about, and, Christmas or no Christmas, people from Iceland to Bulgaria generally assume that practising Christians will probably be kinder persons than the rest of us. Perhaps they are. In Bucharest, not I think the most compassionate of capitals, I once paid a visit to the little Patriarchal Cathedral. It was a festival day of some kind, and the church was full of people queuing up to kiss the sacred icons. Old women in kerchiefs, distinguished-looking gentlemen, ragamuffins, drop-outs, through the candle-lit musty space they patiently shuffled; and when they emerged from behind the iconostasis a tall thin priest was standing there to bless them and sprinkle them with holy water – stiffly, with jerky bird-like movements, right and left, one after the other. At first it seemed to me a perfunctory devotion, and I sat watching the scene out of the shadows with a cynical eye: but presently there entered the church a madwoman, all disjointed, paraplegically stumbling and falling here and there, shouting what I took to be imprecations. I thought they would eject her, or at least try to silence her, but they took no notice of her insanity, allowing her to lurch and shove and shout her way among the waiting faithful. Now and then a kindly hand reached out to pat her on the shoulder, or help her through the crowd.

Oh, often enough the spirit of kindness still finds a practical outlet in Christianity. Where better to test it than in Rome, just down the Tiber from the Vatican itself? One Christmas morning I was loitering with literary intent around Trastévere, a not yet gentrified quarter of poor people and Bohemians, when I heard the hum of voices and the clatter of crockery from inside the church of Santa Maria. Poking my nose inside, I found the enormous dark space of the church filled with row upon row of trestle tables, and at them sat several hundred poor Romans, eating a substantial Christmas dinner by courtesy of the Christian ethos. They were being served by obvious members of the Roman jet set, mostly young and very smart, often beautiful too, who bustled around with soup ladles and bowls in a furore of charitable purpose. (But at the very bottom of the church, all the same, away in the shadows at the gloomiest end of it, the Gypsies of Trastévere had been cautiously segregated.)

## 35  *Two monks*

Christianity certainly affects its practitioners in different ways, sometimes diametrically opposite ways. On a single European journey I felt the full blast of devout contrast in the presence of two young members of the monastic orders. The first was a Benedictine at the Bavarian monastery of Andechs, not far from Munich. I can see his face now. In his late twenties, I would guess, he looked like an interrogator more than a confessor, far more accusatory than forgiving. Tall, thin, pale, unsmiling, cold-eyed, pious as all hell, when I asked him the way to the monastery cemetery he did not at first reply at all, but simply turned his cod-like features upon me with raised eyebrows. When at last he gave me a curt and loveless answer I hardly had time to thank him (not that I was planning to be very fulsome about it) before he turned on his heel with a swish of his cassock, pushed his way arrogantly through the crowd of tourists, and disappeared inside the church. I hope he choked on his vespers.

The second monk was about the same age, and was an Augustinian at the hospice on the Great St Bernard Pass between Switzerland and Italy. He and I were talking in a hospice corridor when we were approached by a somewhat eccentric old man. His bristly white hair was cut very short, his beard was stubbly, he was wearing shorts and shabby boots, and slung all around him was a wide variety of rucksacks, sticks and mugs. He reminded me of a famous Sherpa who was known to the uninhibited British Everest climbers of the 1930s as 'The Foreign Sportsman'. This esoteric ancient interrupted our conversation to ask the young monk (whom he called 'Father') if he could have a room for the night. The Augustinian turned to him with the kindest of smiles, and with only a single question: 'Did you come on foot?' The dear old codger most certainly had – how else? Excusing himself from me, the monk relieved him of his more disposable equipment and conducted him down the corridor with all the care, courtesy and respect of an assistant manager at a five-star hotel – 'No need to register now,' I could imagine him saying, 'we can look after all that when you've settled in.' May all his monkly life be happy, and when he reaches the reception-desk of heaven – '*Did you come on foot?*' – may his welcome be just as professional.

## 36  *Two saints?*

Yes, Europe still produces holy persons, and some no doubt, like Sister Lúcia of Fátima, will eventually be canonized. I have met two possible candidates. I once ran into Agnes Gonxha Bojaxhiu, Mother Teresa, the Albanian heroine of the Calcutta slums, at the door of a house I was visiting. She was still travelling widely then, and I was not altogether surprised to meet her, or to feel her little cold hand in mine. She was much smaller than I had supposed, though, and reminded me irresistibly, with her chirpy voice and bright eyes, of a diminutive sex therapist of American television known as Dr Ruth, famous for her frank talk about things like masturbation. Mother Teresa offered me no counselling during our brief conversation, but she did give me a holy leaflet, and went off in high spirits, having just persuaded our common host to commit several hundred thousand dollars to a new hospice.

My other potential saint was Francis Aungier Pakenham, Knight of the Garter, seventh Earl of Longford, Baron Longford, Baron Silchester, Baron Pakenham, an Anglo-Irish aristocrat, writer and politician who made himself famous in England by publicly befriending the most squalid, degraded and unlovely of criminals. The tabloid press derided him for it. The broadsheets mocked him as a holy fool. Comedians sneered at him. Cartoonists lampooned him. He became a figure of public fun. But when from time to time I saw his lanky bespectacled figure uncoiling itself from his seat to greet me, kind smile at the ready, I always felt that I was in the presence of sanctity. It takes guts to be a martyr, to have arrows stuck all over you or be pulled apart on wheels: but it perhaps takes a truer holiness to be laughed at by louts for your convictions.

## 37  *The decline of faith?*

It is conventionally assumed that the Christian faith is now declining in Europe. Even in 1851, in that supposed stronghold of Christianity, Victorian Britain, an official census showed that only half the population of churchgoing age actually went to church. A century and a half later, almost nowhere in Europe could boast as much. Virgin birth, the meaning of the Trinity, the divinity of Christ, the infallibility of Popes – the certainties of dogma were generally open to question, and only the more elemental sub-sects prospered.

As I have travelled around Europe I have witnessed with my own eyes the diminution of traditional Christianity, just as I have seen visually enacted the population explosion of India. The priests, nuns and seminarians who used to throng the streets of Spain are no longer there, and their dark conventual buildings are often shuttered or demolished. Mendicant friars, once the familiars of our Venetian neighbourhood, are a rarity on the streets of Venice now. Big comradely congregations no longer pour out of the chapels of Wales on a Sunday morning, and visiting preachers are no longer carried off in triumph to Sunday dinner at the tables of hospitable elders – mutton, roast potatoes and mint sauce over an earnest discussion of the morning's sermon. I was in a bookshop in Dublin some years ago, browsing through the stacks, when I heard over the radio on the proprietor's desk a scandalously funny programme satirizing the Catholic hierarchy. I could hardly believe my ears, to hear such outrageous talk in a country where Roman Catholicism had for so long been omnipotent, but the bookseller seemed indifferent. 'Sometimes they're comical,' was all he said – 'it depends on the material.' More recently, walking down Cathedral Street in the same city I was saddened to find 'For Sale' signs outside McCaul's, a venerable and celebrated clerical outfitters. In its windows there was displayed its very last generation of cassocks, clerical bibs and remarkably undesirable mud-coloured shoes for nuns – since the early 1980s the collapse of demand among nuns had been 'particularly dramatic', Mr Padraig McCaul told the press next day, and I must say I was not surprised. Some authorities suggest that Sister Lúcia's Third Secret concerns nothing less than the decline of faith within the Church of Rome itself. The process is known as 'Diabolical Disorientation'.

## 38  Fire and brimstone

Yet you would hardly know the faith was in any trouble at all, from the continuing passions of its sects. In the Czech Republic in 1995 I found Protestants violently objecting to the canonization of Jan Sarkandner, a seventeenth-century Catholic priest, claiming that, far from being martyred by fanatical Moravian noblemen, as the Vatican maintained, he had himself recruited Cossacks to persecute Bohemian Calvinists. Enormously assertive fanes are still being built: the mammoth church (with attendant airport) commemorating miraculous events at Knock in Ireland; the Arctic Cathedral at Tromsø in Norway, which looks like an angular Sydney Opera House;

the monastic church at St Blasien in Germany, which was conclusively rebuilt in 1983, and has a dome smaller only than those of St Peter's in Rome and St Paul's in London. Jehovah's Witnesses knock ever-hopefully on the doors of Europe, and in many parts of the continent charismatic Christians are talking in tongues, laying on hands, falling in convulsions or literally rolling in the aisles in paroxysms of holy laughter. If you have doubts about the energy of sectarian conviction, nearly at the end of the twentieth century, come with me now to the bridge over the river at Derry in Northern Ireland (Londonderry to the English) on a July day in the 1980s, when the men and boys of the Protestant Orange Order are celebrating a famous victory over the Roman Catholics three centuries before. Never will you see a parade more aflame with righteous pride, more militant, more arrogant or more horribly fascinating. It makes those Spanish processions seem ordinary. Nowhere in the world have I seen faces as fiercely individual as the gingery and florid faces of the disciplined Orange bourgeoisie, beneath their statutory bowler hats and tam o' shanters, or more elfish than the faces of the drummer boys twirling their sticks, beating their drums, as they march and remarch across the bridge over the River Foyle.

What fire! What brimstone too! The Catholic population of Derry keeps well away, in its barricaded enclave called the Bogside up the hill, and the Protestants march back and forth all day, waving their banners, beating their drums, playing their trumpets – little boys of five or six, white-haired elders with rows of medals, prancing and strutting, grinning right and left, brandishing their swords or their walking-sticks, twirling their batons, tara tara, thump thump, while swaggering in the middle of it all comes the presiding champion of the anti-papists, a large Presbyterian clergyman with a cohort of aides, cheered all across the bridge by his adoring fellow-bigots.


### 39  From 'Remorse for Intemperate Speech', 1932, by W. B. Yeats

> Out of Ireland have we come.
> Great hatred, little room,
> Maimed us at the start.
> I carry from my mother's womb
> A fanatic heart.

## 40 *Too many bells*

At least the Christian cacophony of bells is beginning to fade. The American writer Elmer Davis, who was a Rhodes Scholar, once described Oxford as a place where too many bells were always ringing in the rain. I have always been of the same mind about bells, and as it happens Oxford bells were the worst of all for me. There the bell Great Tom at Christ Church rang 101 times every night at five past nine, honouring some antique and long-inoperative regulation – enough to drive a saint crazy; and every now and then the air of the city was split asunder with the awful rehearsals of the chain-ringers, clanging down the campanological octaves over and over again. Venice is terrible too, with the variously grating, shovelling, booming, tinkling and jangling of its church bells. The chimes of carillons, all too often sickly and funereal, inescapably ring out across many European cities – Antwerp in Belgium, for instance, where whenever you think the recital has ended, and settle down gratefully to read your book, dear God the famous carillon is sure to start again. (Its carillonneur is a civic celebrity, once pointed out to me with infinite respect as he strode across Grote Markt to his performance, and Dante Gabriel Rossetti once wrote a poem about its muscular peals – 'circling thews of sounds at sunset'.)

There are church clocks in Portugal that strike the hour twice, in case you miss it the first time. The clock in the Mint Tower at Amsterdam strikes the next hour at the half-hour too. And who has not gone to bed in some sweet hostelry of France, when the last swallow has returned to its nest, the restaurant chairs have been up-ended, and the final desultory murmur of gossip has died away from the cottages round about, to find that every fifteen minutes – *crash!* – the bell of the church of Notre-Dame-des-Insomniacs, immediately across the picturesque alley from your bedroom, is obligingly going to tell you the time all night?

## 41 *In the cathedrals*

I was amused one day to read an entry in the visitor's book of Our Lady's Cathedral at Antwerp (into which I had retreated, I dare say, to escape the carillon). 'Seeing this superb cathedral,' wrote L. R. Bultoen on 15 February 1995, 'we are very proud of being Belgian.' When the builders of Antwerp began work on their masterpiece in the fourteenth century, there was no such place as Belgium, and no Belgian nationality to be proud of, but still the Cathedral of Our Lady has long since become a national possession, and L. R. Bultoen can be forgiven for feeling some proprietorial satisfaction. Many of the continent's greatest cathedrals are only sublet, so to speak, as houses of God. Some give the impression of being thriving commercial undertakings, even if all their profits are ploughed back into the business. Some are essentially art galleries. Some double as concert halls or even theatres. And many are frank displays of national history, disguised as places of memorial, dedication or reconciliation, but really galleries of self-esteem.

Spanish cathedrals can be gloriously bombastic, with their great golden grilles, their mighty tombs of kings, queens and champions, the pipes of their organs like artillery massed for action. Pope John Paul II himself described the Wawel Cathedral at Kraków as containing 'a vast greatness which speaks to us of the history of Poland, of all our past'; forty-one monarchs are buried there, together with sundry martial heroes, making the building a mighty shrine not so much of God as of Polishness – as the Pope said, the sanctuary of the nation, which cannot be entered 'without an inner trembling, without an awe'. Generally pre-eminent in this kind, though, are the cathedrals of England, making many of their domestic visitors – at least those of a certain age – decidedly proud to be English. Few of them nowadays greet you with much sense of holy mana. They are too far gone for that – at the cathedral of Oxford I was once greeted by an effusive functionary officially called a Welcomer. God may be all-powerful still in his own quarters of these buildings, around the high altar, but everywhere else the officers of English history are paramount, and are registered only incidentally by their claims to Christian virtue. Here they march elaborately by us, wall by wall, the public-spirited local magnates, the gentlemen of illustrious but never-flaunted pedigree, the generals tried, tested and found true in foreign battlefields. Unwaveringly just judges have spent their lifetimes in Bengal, successful West Indian merchants have generously shared their good fortune with society at large, aldermen have been three times elected with public acclaim to the mayoralty. As mysterious as any holy shroud or saint-fragranced handkerchiefs are the faded cobwebby standards that rot the generations away in the ceilings of regimental chapels; as holy as any Bible are the great memorial books, their hand-lettered pages turned week by week within their oak-framed glass-cases, which list the names of the victorious English dead (for all are victorious in the end, in the wars of the English).

## 42  *Age shall not weary them*

In my time the memorials of the Second World War have, as it were, overlaid
the memorials of the First, and often enough the inscriptions of one have
been added to the epitaphs of the other. I find them all profoundly saddening,
but I have to say they do not always stir me to feelings of reconciliation.
The Germans, in the national change of heart that followed the defeat of
their Nazi cause, commemorated their war dead with some of the most
exquisite of war-cemeteries, but there is gall to my tears when I wander
around their graves. I remember a particularly lovely one not far from Athens,
its hundreds of silent gravestones unobtrusively laid out among the myrtles
and the olive trees: but even as I mourned for the poor young fellows lying
there in death, I imagined how they probably were in life, fresh out of the
Hitler Youth, swanking around Attica as a master race. They should not
have been there at all! And I was certainly not moved to Christian charity
by the tremendous memorial to the U-boat crews of the Second World War
which stands beside the Baltic outside Kiel. A huge, predatory and magnificent
figure of a sea-eagle stands above this edifice, looking anything but remorseful.
Inside, the submarine crews are listed boat by boat, and when I was there a
Dutchman near the gate told me particularly to look out for the name of
Lieutenant Commander Prien, the brilliant submariner who had penetrated
Scapa Flow to torpedo the British battleship *Royal Oak* in 1939. This was a
mistake on his part. I loved the *Royal Oak* and all she stood for, so venerable
and so stately, and when I found Prien's name on the wall I thought less
about him and the crew of U47 than about the men of the grand old
battleship, all 833 of them, deep in the cold waters of the North.

We are all children of our times – to a visitor of a later generation such a
response would not occur. I wonder, all the same, about the true meaning
of the bombed churches and sacred objects left unrestored across Europe as
reminders of war's horrors – the hulk of the Kaiser Wilhelm Memorial Church
in Berlin, the remains of the old cathedral at Coventry, the melted-down bells
of Lübeck's Marienkirche. How much do they speak of Christian forgiveness,
and how much of reproach?

## 43  *The little hero*

Who could fail to be touched, though, of whatever nationality, whatever age, whatever ideology, whatever background of faith or experience, by the sculpted Monument to the Little Insurgent, which stands beside the ramparts of the Old Town in Warsaw? It remembers the tragic heroism of the Warsaw Rising of 1944, when the Poles in a splurge of hopeless romantic courage rose in arms against the overwhelming forces of the Nazis who oppressed them. A very small boy, in a steel helmet far too big for him, holds a sub-machine-gun as if it were a toy, and bears himself ready for all comers, as so many children of Warsaw truly did at that great and awful time. It is a sentimental little image, and rightly so. There are nearly always flowers at the foot of it.

## 44  *God's system*

Anyway, if religion can give us a groping sort of definition of Europe, what makes a metaphysical unity of this continent is art, which to a pantheist like me is the ultimate revelation of the divine. In my view European religion has been the acolyte of art, rather than the other way round. Edward Gibbon said Europe was no more than 'a system of arts and laws and manners': the laws and manners came from Christianity, but the arts came from God, and the true human glory of Europe, as I have learnt to see it, lies in the fact that in every corner of this continent, for thousands of years, people have been inspired to make beautiful things, in the service of one god or another, or of no consciously recognized god at all. The rankest amateur, painting the slushiest water-colour of Swiss waterfall or Grand Canal, has contributed to the oneness of Europe ('The lake here,' wrote Cézanne of the lake of Annecy in France, 'lends itself admirably to the line-drawing exercises of young English misses'). The particular combination of mode, time and harmony which has made European music different from Asian and African music has been a defining factor of the continent; so, for centuries, was the use of perspective. Even the nature of Europe must bow before its art: as Gustav Mahler observed to the conductor Bruno Walter when they travelled through the Alps together, 'No need to look – I've already composed them.'

Art is unity is God, and the absurd rules that some European nations have devised for keeping works of visual art within national boundaries seem to me downright irreligious. Fortunately they cannot prevent the grand distribution of genius across all the frontiers of Europe. One cathedral leads you to another across this magnificent corner of the earth. In the glory of an Italian palazzo you may recognize, as in family likeness, the charm of an English country house. Shakespeare, who is undoubtedly one of God's own personae, belongs to everyone in Europe. Mozart worked in London as in Salzburg. Napoleon invited Goethe to go and live in France. Samuel Beckett was French as well as Irish. Voltaire, Rousseau, Byron, Balzac, Dostoevsky, Shelley, Liszt, Hans Christian Andersen and Tchaikovsky all, at one time or another, lived and worked beside Lake Geneva in Switzerland. Above all else (except perhaps marijuana), rock music has linked the young of modern Europe – it was a civic celebration to match the fantastic festivities of old when in the 1980s the rock-and-roll group Pink Floyd played on a raft in the Bacino di San Marco in Venice. I strolled into Notre-Dame in Paris one evening to find a glorious German choir singing Bach's St Matthew Passion before the high altar, while all around the dim-lit cathedral young French people sat on the floor, or leant against pillars, reverent and entranced; and I once listened to just the same music, performed to just the same effect, in a bare and clinical church hall in a suburb of Reykjavik.

## 45 'Sweet Rosemarie'

Loiter with me now for a moment or two, on a winter day in 1996, in an alley off Ban Jelačić Square in Zagreb, down the hill from the Stone Gate. A man bundled in a greatcoat is playing an instrument of his own invention, consisting of rows of wine and mineral-water bottles strung on a contraption rather like a washing-line, and tuned by their varying contents of liquid. He is playing with great delicacy a piece you and I both know well, but can't for the life of us place, and around him a smiling crowd has gathered, amused by the instrument, touched by the tune. In the front row of the audience a small child of two or three in a woolly blue and white jumper suit, with hat to match, is performing a shuffly sort of dance to the beat of the music.

It is a curiously affecting performance, partly because of the sweetly familiar music – what *is* that tune, damn it? – played upon so homely a device, but partly because the musician is one of a grand company of street performers who greet us nowadays all across Europe, a league of artists of varying talent but generally cheering message. They are a true concert of Europe. I remember, off the top of my head, a trombonist and a cellist playing a Marcello sonata in a park at Weimar, and a juggler of genius outside the Beaubourg in Paris, and brilliant Gypsy fiddlers, and a virtuoso flautist in the Kurfürstendamm in Berlin, and pavement portrait-painters in Prague, and rustic bagpipers in Rome, and mimes and clowns all over the place, and my son Twm with his harp and his Welsh songs in the cathedral square at Freiburg, and a young woman with an oboe in an underground train in London (where they call it 'busking' – a word which originally meant, it seems, 'cruising as a pirate').

They are no pirates to me. They are part of Europe's holy fabric, and except for the mimes and clowns I am always glad to see them. And hang on, I think I've remembered what that tune is. Isn't it one of those charming Fritz Kreisler fripperies they used to play in Palm Court cafés, with a lady violinist in a satin blouse, and the grammar-school music-master moon-lighting at the piano? *Schön Rosmarin* – isn't that it?

## 46  *Old friends*

Art makes Europe European – Joyce's Dublin, Cervantes's Spain, Camoëns' Portugal, Dickens's London, Kafka's Prague, Proust's France, Rembrandt's Holland, Bach's Germany, Sibelius's Finland, Ibsen's Norway, Mozart's Austria, Leonardo's Italy – all made common property by art's genius. You may find works by the divine Giorgione not only in his native Venice but in Amsterdam, Bassano, Bergamo, Berlin, Budapest, Dublin, Florence, Glasgow, London, Madrid, Milan, Monaco, Naples, Oxford, Padua, Paris, Rome, Rotterdam and Vienna. After a lifetime of familiarity with repro-ductions of his *Sleeping Venus*, all unexpectedly I came across its original among the war-ruins of Dresden. I was not in the least surprised. I was not even ecstatic – merely pleased to see it there. It was like coming across an old friend in the street one day, not far from home.

# 2

## THE MISHMASH

*

*Time and again history has disrupted the shaky identity that religion has given Europe, and shattered art's unity. The result is a maze of frontiers, enclaves, minorities, irredentisms, ethnic anomalies and political fragmentation, and Trieste is just the place for contemplating it. This city is hemmed in by artificial frontiers, inhabited by people of several races, complicated by the detritus of abandoned empires and by the effects of unnecessary wars. Even in my time its circumstances have repeatedly shifted. It has been a foreign-occupied port, a free territory, an Italian prefectorial capital, a last capitalist outpost on the edge of the Communist world, a watchpost for the conflict in Yugoslavia. It has been an evocative relic of the lost Austro-Hungarian Empire. Before the final collapse of European Communism bus-loads of shoppers used to come here from many countries of eastern Europe. A Balkan market near the bus station catered especially for them, beneath the flowering chestnuts of the Piazza della Libertà, and there they wandered in their thousands – Hungarians, Romanians, Bulgarians, Serbs, Croats, Bosnians, Hercegovinans – stocky, calculating people, festooned with ill-wrapped packages and occasionally pausing, so the evidence showed, to write graffiti in the Cyrillic script. They were reenacting the time when Trieste was the great entrepôt for them all, and when I once asked a man from Budapest if he had enjoyed his trip, he said it had been 'an experience of nostalgia' – nostalgia, I suppose, like my own on the jetty that day, for a state of things he had never known. During my time the Director of the Trieste Opera has been the Barone Rafaelle Douglas de Banfield-Tripcovich, composer, businessman, politician and Honorary French Consul; he is a worldly, elegant, hand-kissing sort of man, the son of a Slav countess and the most highly decorated officer in the Austro-Hungarian armed forces, and his inherited title – Baron of Trieste – was awarded to his father by the Emperor Franz Josef himself.*

*Trieste hardly has a nationality. It is like no other Italian city, and to be a Triestino is to be a special kind of Italian citizen – many Triestini would rather not be Italian anyway. In this city the lines between fact and fiction, past and present, the explicit and the enigmatic, let alone between one ethnicity and another, always seem to me uncertain. If Trieste ever felt impelled to advertise itself on road signs, like towns in France ('Sa Cathédrale, Ses Grottes, Ses Langoustines'), it would have no problems. This is a city unique and altogether original, and it could simply announce, on one very large placard, 'Sua Triestinità': its Triesteness. It is the perfect place to disappear into, and sometimes over the years, as my Britishness has refined itself into Welshness, and I have found myself distracted by the impotence of the small nations and minorities caught in the apparently unravellable tangle of the continent, I have been tempted to disappear here myself. I would take an attic flat somewhere behind the Piazza dell'Unità d'Italia, among the bookstalls and the junk shops, thence to emerge in ageing anonymity, wearing slippers and a wide straw hat, to write philosophical essays all day long in the sunshine.*

*Thus I would escape from the mishmash of Europe, for what would race, frontier or nation mean in such a condition of liberty? I would be escaping from Europe's complexities, the arbitrary sham of the lines that criss-cross the continent, the bits and pieces clinging to the edge of it, blurring its outlines, messing things up.*

# 1 *Dôle*

For me the epitome of the European frontier will always be one of those high railway stations in the lee of the Alps where the transcontinental steam expresses used to stop, in the days when most of us travelled across Europe by train. It always seemed to be the middle of the night when we reached these places. There was always snow on the ground. The train would stop with a hiss of brakes, a clanking and a sudden utter silence, broken only by spasmodic coughs from the locomotive. Blurrily through our steamed-up sleeper windows we would peer into the night, which appeared to be almost absolute. A few dim bulbs. A deserted station. No sign of a town – only a name on a lamppost, which might have been Brig or Domodossola, but in my memory seems always to have been Dôle.

Was there really such a place, I used to wonder? Where were we? We might have been altogether abandoned, remote from anywhere, until far away along the train we heard the stamping of feet and the sliding of corridor doors. '*Passeports s'il vous plaît – passeports mesdames, messieurs – tous les passeports!*' – louder and louder through the hush until our own door abruptly opened, jarring our nerves however long we had been expecting it, and there was the customs man holding his hand out, with a policeman looking over his shoulder. Sometimes they would want to inspect your luggage, snarled around by blankets in the awkward jumble of your berth, but only as a matter of form, scarcely examining it when you managed to open it at last. Then you heard them moving away up the train again – '*Passeports! Tous les passeports!*' – fainter and fainter towards the engine. The silence was resumed – the smothered silence of a snowy landscape, broken only by distant banging of doors and a few sleepy murmurs up and down your carriage, before the train slowly eased itself off again with a judder of couplings and a creaking of woodwork, and made for its tunnel under the Alps.

For years I thought of Dôle only as that funereal halt in the night, just a station, a silence and two official faces at the sleeper door. It was only recently that, travelling to Switzerland by car, I found myself in the town itself. It had been there all the time! It turned out to be forty miles from the frontier proper, and was a comfortable place of steeples and bridges and happy squares, where Pasteur was born, and where I enjoyed a delightful meal of little trout and local Sauvignon in the garden of La Petite Auberge, on the other side of town from the railway station. It shows how hallucinatory frontiers can be.

## 2  God's frontiers

The proper limits of France, declared Cardinal Richelieu in the seventeenth century, were the Alps, the Rhine and the Pyrenees. A web of artificial frontiers has been imposed upon Europe – even weather maps often end abruptly at national borders – but others were God-given. 'See how the wand'ring Danube flows,' wrote Jonathan Swift, who never set eyes on that river, 'Realms and religions parting!' Rivers and mountains, straits and lakes have separated peoples always, and some remain as political frontiers to this day – the Alps (parting France, Switzerland, Germany, Austria and Italy), the Pyrenees (parting Spain and France), the Danube (Romania, Yugoslavia, Hungary, Slovakia and Bulgaria), the Morava (Slovakia and the Czech Republic), the Great Belt (Sweden and Denmark), the English Channel (Britain and everywhere else), the Rhine (Germany, France and Switzerland).

Especially the Rhine, because you cannot travel along it without remembering the mighty confrontation here between the great rival forces of the Latins and the Teutons. The Rhine has been a frontier as potent in men's minds as on the map. 'The Watch on the Rhine', Max Schneckenburger's nineteenth-century paean to Germanness, was more than just a poem, a ballad or a slogan, but an expression of immemorial instinct – after the Prussian victory over France in 1870 Bismarck said the song had been worth three extra divisions to the German armies. The 'Marseillaise' was written as the battle-hymn of a French army specifically charged with the defence of this frontier. Even the British sang about it, in the First World War hit 'Mademoiselle from Armentières' – 'Two German officers crossed the Rhine, *Parlez-vous* . . .' At Rüdesheim on the German side the immense Franco-Prussian War memorial, its triumphant Germania presiding over an eruption of eagles, crests, sculpted generals and angels of victory, towers above both banks of the river to set an arrogant seal upon its meaning (although one of the first air raids to hit German soil in the Second World War was mounted in 1940 by the Luftwaffe itself, which mistook Freiburg im Breisgau for Colmar on the other side of the Rhine . . .).

Strasbourg, a few miles back from the river in the French province of Alsace, is a comforting place to escape from these absurd old enmities. Sometimes it has been French, sometimes German, as the tide of rivalry has swept this way and that across the Rhine – 1870 French, 1871 German, 1918

French, 1940 German, 1945 French. It has been a city of war, violence, oppression and furious patriotism. Bismarck said that Strasbourg, with the rest of Alsace, was no more than a glacis for the defence of Germany. Kaiser Wilhelm II unleashed his most Germanic architects upon it. General Joffre announced, when his armies entered Alsace in 1914, that it would now be French for ever. Hitler declared, in 1940, that it was to be considered 'part of the German Fatherland itself', banned the French language, and Germanized everyone's names. Nowadays Strasbourg looks to me about equally German and French, and people appear to speak the two languages indiscriminately, and divide their diet equably between sausage and *coq au vin*. Voltaire once wrote of Alsatians that they were 'half-German, half-French and completely Iroquois'; but today the passions are calmed – for the moment anyway. Nobody is going to scalp you as you wander Strasbourg's handsome streets, and overlooking a park in the Avenue de l'Europe, providing an optimistic conclusion to the long bitterness of the Rhine, in 1979 there was opened for business the glassy assembly house of the European Parliament, with the flags of half Europe fluttering side by side outside – enough to make those ferocious old nationalists of the Rhine, the Bismarcks and the Joffres, the Kaisers and the Adolf Hitlers, squirm in their graves.

## 3 *At the front*

For them a frontier meant more or less the same as a front line, and so it did in Roman times. The fortified frontier of the Roman Empire in Europe, the *Limes* ('path'), marked the northern boundary of certainty, beyond which anarchy reigned. It still vestigially exists, in fits and starts from Scotland to the Black Sea. At its western end stand the windswept masonries of Hadrian's Wall, undulating across the bleak landscapes of the Anglo-Scottish border from the Atlantic to the North Sea. At the other end old maps still show it, in castellated conventional signs, marching past the Danube estuary to the Black Sea (where the poor poet Ovid, exiled in AD 8 by the Emperor Augustus to the hell-hole now called Constanța, dreamt of home and happier times almost within sight of it). Between these two extremes, the desolation of the West, the melancholy of the East, here and there across the sweep of Europe there are still traces of the *Limes*, sometimes in stretches of wall, sometimes in turf-covered dykes and ditches, sometimes in the form of advanced outposts thrown across a natural barrier – at Budapest (Aquincum), for instance, where unfortunate pickets were posted to forts on the wrong side of the un-bridged Danube.

The line ran a few miles north of Bad Homburg in Germany, and in 1899 Kaiser Wilhelm II had one of its frontier forts meticulously reconstructed. He claimed to have done the work, so it says in Latin above one of its gateways, in pious memory of his parents, but there were doubtless political motives too. His own home kingdom of Prussia lay north of the line, in barbarian country, and he had barbarian yearnings himself, sponsoring neo-pagan monuments and encouraging his soldiers to fight like Huns; but he also loved to see the emergent German Empire in classical terms, sometimes Grecian, sometimes Latin, and when he and his entourage attended the official opening of his pastiche the courtiers were obliged to wear togas. Purists scoff at the reborn fortress of Saalburg, and think it grossly overdone, but when I once spent an afternoon there I thought it truly evocative. It stands on the edge of a wood, and, although it is a popular place for an afternoon's outing from Frankfurt, still manages to feel fairly remote and frontier-like. Everything is in place, carefully restored or rebuilt, down to the water-wells and the baking-ovens; I could fancy the tramp of Roman sandals and hear the commands of centurions (though I dare say I got their imperative moods wrong). Snow was on the ground when I was there, in wisps and slivers among the trees, and I even managed to feel a little homesick, imagining myself posted there for frontier duty from warmer, easier places. A mile or so away, through the woods, runs the grassy mound that is the *Limes*, the end of all order: beyond it, away in the mists of the ominous North, strangers waited.

## 4  *The gate-tower of Trier*

Not far behind the frontier, on the Mosel river, the Romans built their chief administrative capital in north-west Europe, Augusta Treverorum – Trier to the Germans, Trèves to the French. The northern gateway to this fortified city, which still stands, is the greatest surviving Roman building north of the Alps, and is a kind of paradigm of frontierness. The Porto Nigra looks out from its city walls in a posture of majestic suspicion, as though it is perpetually expecting the worst of any approaching travellers. Its twin watch-towers are semicircular, allowing sentries on three floors a field of view in all dangerous directions, and their windows are like sleepless, lidless eyes. It took me a long time to realize what these rounded towers of Trier reminded me of: they are like the rounded superstructures of old-fashioned New York tugboats. Writers have been describing the gate-towers of Trier for a thousand years and more, but I flatter myself that nobody before me has stumbled upon this simile.

## 5  A nasty legend

By medieval times mishmash had long set in. For centuries petty princes and ambitious ecclesiasts established frontiers of their own, their own *limites* with their own private Dôles. In those days 'princes and princes' mistresses', as Hitler disapprovingly recalled, 'haggled over State borders'. Many such piddling frontiers, as it happened, reached down to the banks of the Rhine, like the policies of strip-farms along the St Lawrence, and probably the most famous frontier posts in Europe are both German Rhine island-castles, where local potentates once collected their own customs dues from the passing shipping. One is the Pfalzgrafenstein – the Pfalz for short – a white hexagonal fortress near Kaub from which the officials of the Counts Palatine of the Rhine exerted their authority, and which has long provided a sort of logo for the Rhine tourist trade. The other is the little thirteenth-century castle called the Mäuseturm, the Mice Tower, which stands in a posture of ineffable authority, painted yellow, at the mouth of the Rhine gorges near Bingen. This used to collect traffic tolls for the archbishopric of Mainz, one of those diocesan sovereignties, and legend has long linked its name with the horrible death of a tenth-century incumbent. Archbishop Hatto, it used to be said, was a viciously oppressive landlord, and during a famine he ordered that some of his poor tenants should be burnt alive in a barn, accusing them of gobbling up precious corn 'like so many field-mice'. The mice of his estate, incensed as much by the calumny as by the cruelty, swore revenge and chased him so mercilessly from cathedral to palace to country house, nibbling all the way, that he determined to retreat to his customs post in the middle of the river. As the English poet Robert Southey interpreted him, ' "I'll go to my tower on the Rhine," he replied./'Tis the safest place in Germany;/The walls are high and the shores are steep,/And the stream is strong and the water deep." ' Not high, steep, strong or deep enough, though. Hundreds of thousands of mice swam across, climbed the tower and ate the archbishop

– 'They gnaw'd the flesh from every limb,/ For they were sent to do judgement on him!' It is all lies. Archbishop Hatto was, by scholarly account, a kindly priest and generous landlord, the tower had not been built in his day, and probably 'Mäuseturm' should really be 'Musterungturm' – inspection tower.

## 6  Safe haven

Another customs place of unpleasant suggestion – another haven, too – is the sea-castle of Bourdzi, which stands on a reef on the Gulf of Argolis in southern Greece, and is linked to the town of Nauplia only by a causeway. It is an extravagantly pretty, picture-postcard castle, lying there in the blue of the sea with the Argolis mountains beyond. The Venetians built a fort here in the days when they ruled these parts, and when the Turks seized Nauplia in 1540 they too erected a castle on the site. All ships were obliged to stop there to pay their dues as they entered the harbour, but the fortress acquired a more baleful function too: casting around for a place of retirement for their superannuated executioners, not highly regarded as neighbours in Greece, the Turkish governors fixed them up with quarters inside the walls of Bourdzi.

## 7  Waiting

Beloved of guidebooks are those places where a national frontier runs absurdly down the main street of a village, or divides a city. Constance, for instance, is split in this way between the German Konstanz and the Swiss Kreuzlingen. The frontier post is in the middle of a city street, making for traffic jams, and during the Second World War if an escaping prisoner from a German camp could find his way to Konstanz he had then only to cross the road to be safe in neutral Kreuzlingen. Equally memorable, to my mind, are frontier posts that seem to have sprung up in a purely theoretical way nowhere in particular. Halfway across empty wastes you find them, on little-used highways in the rain, with their officials lounging about in a hut lonely miles from the nearest café, and a vehicle arriving only every half-hour or so. Then I like to imagine the diplomatic negotiators of long ago, in wigs perhaps, crouched over a mahogany table like pious Jews over the Torah, with their silver protractors and unrolled parchment maps, marking the hypothetical line across marsh or mountain, wheat-plain or tundra, which would satisfy the dignities of their respective masters – honoured so wanly now, on drizzly afternoons a couple of centuries later, by those poor bored functionaries, feet up beside their television sets waiting for the next car.

## 8  *Frontiers in the imagination*

Some frontiers are only in the imagination. Prince Metternich used to say the frontier of Asia was at the Landstrasse, the street which ran away towards Hungary from Vienna's city walls, and it is possible to feel the same even today, if you ever drive out from the city into the back-country of Hungary or Slovakia, where people speak in unknown tongues. They say that Konrad Adenauer, the first Chancellor of West Germany after the Second World War, cherished similar feelings about the *Land* of Prussia. He was a Rhinelander, and whenever his train crossed the Elbe, on its way eastward to Berlin, he too would groan, '*Hier beginnt Asien*,' and pull the blinds down. The English, in their jingo days, meant the same when they said that wogs began at Calais.

## 9  *Special trains*

In an aesthetic sense the definitive frontier is surely the Brenner Pass, in the Alps, which separates not only Austria from Italy, but the German world from the Latin world. The Romans knew it well, there has been a carriage road through it since the eighteenth century, a railway since 1867, a motorway since the 1970s. The way to the Brenner from the south sweeps magnificently through a spectacular mountain setting, ornamented in a painterly way with castles and churches and trim ancient villages – all deep blues, vivid greens and the white of the high snows. The frontier stands at about 5,000 feet, and in the course of a few hours you can speed from the dusty heat of the Po valley to the celestial cool of the Alps, from the Mediterranean to Mitteleuropa. In 1940 Adolf Hitler and Benito Mussolini held a fateful meeting at the Brenner, each going there in his special train, and I cannot cross the pass myself without seeing the two dictators primping themselves for the meeting as they approached each other from north and south along the tracks. In those days the Führer was still respectful of the Duce, as his senior in the hierarchy of dictators, but who can doubt that Mussolini too wanted to be seen at his best? Imagine the last-minute cleaning and polishing of their respective trains! Imagine the engines so competitively burnished, the crews in their newly pressed uniforms, the flags flying, the gilded fasces and the gleaming black swastikas! As they steam through the mountains, doubtless Duce and Führer both, summoning their valets, stand before their mirrors to prepare themselves, swaying a little with the movement of their carriages, occasionally stumbling with a lurch, the one combing his small black moustache, the other adjusting his Sam Browne belt to fit his pouter-pigeon chest: a last flick of the valet's clothes-brush, a last practice of the pose, and when the two trains reach the frontier (the Führer's was late, in fact) out into the snowy sunshine step the two autocrats, all smiles, salutes and speculative inspections, like a pair of ruthless beauties meeting at a charity ball.

## 10  *Beuno's frontier*

At another extreme of significance, the border between Wales and England is mostly unmarked, and visitors often do not know which country they are in. This was not always so. In the days when the pagan Saxons were kept out of Wales by the Celtic Christians of the place, the Welsh language provided a metaphysical frontier of its own. The seventh-century Celtic divine Beuno was walking once upon the banks of the River Severn, meditating no doubt upon the Celticity of Christ, when he heard from across the stream the sound of brutal syllables. Merciful Heaven, they were the sound of the English language! and instantly St Beuno knew that the heathen were at the frontiers of Wales. I think of him when I drive through the border village of Llanymynech, in the same Severn valley, because this is indeed one of those guidebook places where a political line runs clean through a community, bisecting in this case the long bar of the White Swan, and actually dividing graves in the village churchyard, so that some parishioners lie there with their heads in England, their feet in Wales. The language in Llanymynech nowadays is an only moderately Welshified sort of English, and St Beuno might not be very happy there: for even metaphysical frontiers are not inviolate, though they certainly last longer than most.

## 11 *Gun-frontiers*

For three centuries, for example, the empire of the Habsburgs was bounded by an intangible demarcation called the Military Frontier, a 750-mile autonomous zone, mostly along the Danube, which did not depend upon fortifications. It was deliberately peopled with wild and warlike folk of many races, who owed their loyalty only to the Emperor himself, and for generations successfully held off the predatory Turks. Its southern anchor was the fortress of Senj, on the Dalmatian coast, which acted as base for a terrifying but officially encouraged clan of pirates called the Uskoks, and it re-entered history in the 1990s when, as Vojna Krajina, it had also become a frontier between Catholic and Orthodox Christians, and a cockpit of the Yugoslav wars.

Europe is creased, though, with the remains of more orthodox military barricades, and they have nearly all been failures. Did the *Limes* keep the barbarians out? Often on the frontiers of France, in the Ardennes mountains, in the Jura, away in the Alps facing Italy, even on the French island of Corsica, I have come across remnants of the Maginot Line, the chain of fortresses, tunnels, blockhouses and military roads, built in the 1930s, by which the French fondly hoped to keep themselves permanently secure. It was named for its creator, André Maginot the Minister of War, included the highest motor-road in Europe (over the Col du Galibier, above Besançon at 10,636 feet), and was said in my youth to be the biggest man-made work since the Great Wall of China. Often there is little more than a tumbled pillbox to be seen now, half-hidden by brambles; but sometimes I discover deep in woodland, or below the crest of a ridge, a brown steel dome like a helmet, with blank gun-slits in it, and casements all around. The fortifications look beautifully made to me, craftsmen's work, with finely sculpted shapes, textured concrete walling, steel doors that exquisitely fit their frames. They speak to me paradoxically not only of heroic memories, and of humiliations too (the Germans simply circumvented them when they overran the frontier in 1940), but also of things subtle and graceful in France. There seems nothing brutal to them, and in fact the Maginot Line was the last in a great heritage of a particularly French art: the art of fortification, which had reached a climax with the glorious fortresses and castellations of Marshal de Vauban in the seventeenth century. Only one of the Line's hundreds of forts ever fell to the Germans, and none at all to the invading Italians at the other end of it, but it made no difference anyway, and Maginot's name has become synonymous with defensive complacency. 'From the Great Wall of China to the Maginot Line,' declared the gung-ho American general George Patton, 'nothing anywhere has ever been successfully defended.'

## 12  Frontier styles

My family and I lived for a time near the Swiss frontier in France, in the mountains of Haute-Savoie east of Geneva. If we wanted to go seriously shopping we had to cross out of one country into the other, and this was like a demonstration of national characteristics. On the French side the gendarmes were jolly, careless, and often had wine on their breaths. On the Swiss side the police were cool, diligent, courteous and unsmiling. My car in those days was an elderly Rolls-Royce, grand, decorative and sufficiently previously-owned to raise an indulgent smile in a Marxist, and it incited mixed responses in those officials. The French were delightedly amused by it, and sometimes asked permission to sit at the wheel or try the squashy grey leather seats behind. The reaction of the Swiss was different. To them a Rolls-Royce was an image of wealth – there were more Rollses in Geneva than in any other city of the continent – and a quaint middle-aged example like mine, not old enough to be a valuable antique, certainly not new enough to be a status symbol, confused their responses. They habitually greeted us with a mixture of respect and condescension, covering all contingencies.

While we were living there, in 1956, war broke out in the Middle East, and the British were involved with the French and the Israelis in fighting against the Egyptians. I was commissioned by the *Manchester Guardian* to go out and report the war, so I piled into the old Rolls and drove down to Geneva to catch a flight to Tel Aviv. How cock-a-hoop the Swiss were when they discovered where I was off to – their centuries of neutrality were paying off once more! Gently commiserating were the French, who did not laugh at the car at all now, but grasped my shoulder and wished me luck.

## 13  A haunted frontier

One of the saddest European frontiers, for much of my half-century, has been the line dividing the six counties of British Northern Ireland, the fief of those bowler-hatted gentry and wild drummer-boys of page 48, from the independent Republic of Ireland. Guerrilla war plagued the region – the unofficial Catholic Irish Republican Army on one side, the British and diverse Protestant paramilitary groups on the other – but in some parts the border was altogether unguarded, and there was nothing but a road sign to warn you that you had reached the end of one State and the start of another. Often this occurred in remote rural lanes. The silence was complete among those backwaters of Derry or Armagh, the damp green of the fields seemed stealthily absorbent, as if all manner of secret things were concealed beneath the turf, and I used to creep over the line with a chill running down my spine. Who was watching me, through high-powered binoculars out of sight? What bad men were lurking in those ditches?

Every Irishman knew the unmanned frontier places, and they were conduits for a shadowy traffic of drugs, arms and miscellaneous contraband. I once asked a woman in Clones, County Monaghan, why some crossings were marked on my map with flags. 'That's the places,' she said, 'you're not allowed to smuggle things through.' The ones with the flags were eerie in a different way. Often it was only when you were well over the border into Northern Ireland that you found your road suddenly masked by a blank mass of concrete and sandbags, rather like a spirit wall keeping devils out of a Chinese courtyard. A traffic-light summoned you on, and behind the barrier stood a couple of young soldiers, helmeted in camouflage suits, the one pointing an automatic weapon directly at you, the other shouting the number of your car to an unseen colleague – a moment or two of distinct discomfort, until after a few perfunctory questions, and a brief search of the car with the gun more or less at your head, those young toughs of the frontier gestured you through the barricade.

It was a haunted frontier then. Some of its spectres you could never see, priming their bombs in farmhouse armouries, or under cover drinking stout in pubs. Others you could: through the gun-slits of high ugly blockhouses, built of drab brown concrete and surrounded by rolls of barbed wire, often you could make out silent figures staring at you, over their gun-barrels no doubt. In the desolate border village of Crossmaglen in Armagh, where crude hand-scrawled posters gave notice that somebody or other was a Traitor to Ireland, and one of those awful fortresses loomed over the village and all its life, I stood in the deserted square to copy an inscription, in Irish and in English, in honour of local republican patriots. 'Glory to you all,' it said, 'praised and humble heroes, who have willingly suffered for your unselfish and passionate love of Irish freedom.' I stood there for a moment thinking about the pity of it all: and when I turned to go, from a slit in the blockhouse a hand sadly waved me goodbye.

## 14 *Modern times*

In the worst times of the troubles Belfast itself, the Northern Ireland capital, was like a frontier city, rigidly divided between its Protestant and its Catholic communities, and patrolled constantly by British soldiers. In the very centre of the city I once saw a patrol of five or six infantrymen moving cautiously and watchfully through the streets in the prescribed mode – guns cocked, helmeted heads constantly turning right and left, lead man well in front, rearguard walking backwards with his finger on the trigger. As they passed an office of the National Westminster Bank, one of them peeled away while the others paused and crouched there covering his back, ready for instant fire. He put his card in the bank's automatic cash dispenser, he tucked his money away in a pocket of his camouflage suit, and they proceeded grimly on their prowl.

## 15 *Another kind of frontier*

Wedged between drab tenement blocks off Złota Street in Warsaw stands a fragment of another kind of frontier. It is only a few yards long, about twenty feet high, but it has a dreadful significance, for it is the last remaining piece of the Warsaw ghetto wall. During the Nazi occupation of Warsaw in the 1940s this construction enclosed a huge area of the city, imprisoning several hundred thousand Jews who were later shipped away in cattle-trucks to be murdered in neighbouring death-camps. I had some difficulty finding it, on a winter morning when the streets were deep in snow and a steady sleet fell upon the city, but when at last I found my way through the slushy gates, yards and alleyways, and saw its ugly brown mass towering there before me, I knew at once what it was. In my imagination at least it was unmistakably a frontier between life and death.

## 16 *The Curtain*

But the most notorious European frontier of my time has been the Iron Curtain, the ideological barrier which, at the command of Soviet Russia, fell in 1945 from Lübeck Bay on the Baltic to Trieste. It bisected Europe, split Germany into two States, and formed the western borders of East Germany, Czechoslovakia and Hungary, as of Communism itself. It was given its name by Winston Churchill, and the Cold War between Communism and capitalism made it hideously suspicious and unwelcoming. Like the Roman *Limes*, it separated not just States, or peoples, or territories, or histories, but ideas: on the one side of it (the Roman side, in Western eyes) were free enterprise, liberty, accountability: on the other side (the barbarian side, or baboonery, as Churchill would have said) were tyranny, collectivism and deceit. The Iron Curtain was hundreds of miles of barbed wire, watch-tower and minefield, with an awful sameness to it. Travelling from west to east through it was like entering a drab and disturbing dream, peopled by all the ogres of totalitarianism, a half-lit world of shabby resentments, where anything could be done to you, I used to feel, without anybody ever hearing of it, and your every step was dogged by watchful eyes and mechanisms. Some of this was doubtless paranoiac fancy, but much of it was all too true, and wherever you were travelling behind the Iron Curtain it was only wise to assume that your room was bugged, that your friendliest informant worked for the secret police, and that your curriculum vitae was on a file somewhere.

The Curtain cast a chill far across Europe, and incited every kind of skulduggery, from State espionage to old-school whisky smuggling. I never visited a Communist capital, in the worst years of the Cold War, without feeling myself to be a character in a novel or a movie – with some reason, for newspaper correspondents in those times and places were generally assumed to be agents on the side. When the first spy books of John le Carré appeared, heralding a new genre of fiction and cinema, we all saw ourselves somewhere in their pages or sequences. On a journey to Budapest once I was asked by a friend to take a package of books to a diplomat serving in one of the embassies there. I did not ask what the books were, and asked no questions either when it was suggested that I hand them over at a rendezvous in the middle of the Chain Bridge, linking Buda and Pest across the Danube, lately rebuilt after its destruction by the German Army. It was just like a film. Promptly at the appointed time I started out across the walkway of the bridge, and presently I became aware of a particular figure approaching me among the pedestrians from the other end. I saw both of us as it were through a long-focus lens, shimmering a little, the distance distorted as we neared each other. We met. We exchanged compliments. We shook hands. I handed over the package, and to dark portentous music – all drums and cellos – I returned to the Buda shore as the credit titles rolled.

## 17 *Into the new world*

One of the most theatrical manifestations of the Iron Curtain occurred if you drove northwards out of eastern Austria towards the then Czech city of Bratislava. There the wire and watchposts of the Communist frontier were backed immediately by one of Europe's most spectacular housing developments. Right and left beyond the frontier, masking the horizon as far as one could see, extended the vast new town called Petržalka – a communal forest of high-rise tenements, a tundra of concrete, treeless, chimney-less, spire-less, all new, all right angles, one block in merciless enfilade behind another. It was a declaration of a brave new world, where nothing was frivolous. More than 100,000 people had been resettled in this living-machine: between the blocks you might just make out the old towers of Bratislava over the Danube, and the burnt-out fifteenth-century castle on its hill.

## 18 *Enjoy yourself*

Even going into Yugoslavia, in the Communist Tito's day, could be a disheartening experience. I often did this out of Trieste. In the days when the Iron Curtain still stood, but Communist Yugoslavia had opted out of the Soviet system, people from all the Yugoslav republics came to Trieste at weekends to shop, sell things or engage in under-the-counter transactions. On Sunday nights they went home again, loaded with cookers, televisions, videos, toys and clothes, until their stuffy buses were jam-packed with boxes and packages, and there were bundles under the seats, and clothes in plastic bags hanging from the roofs, and the faces of the shoppers looked out from their windows like refugees on the move. Rogues and opportunists of every kind came too, dealing in gold and jeans and other gilt-edged commodities of the day, so that when the time came for them to go home again the

Yugoslav frontier officials were less than relaxed. It took many hours, on a Sunday night, to get into Yugoslavia. I can see now the hundreds of cars lurching and overheating in the gathering dark, the ad-hoc hamburger bars beside the road, the occasional bully-truck forcing its way through by sheer weight and horsepower, those pale weary faces at the windows of buses, and at last the dim-lit frontier post, and a joyless official with a red star on his cap. A slow flicking through the pages of our passports, a silent gesture of release, and away with us into the dark Communist half of the continent. 'Cheer up,' I said to the frontier official once. 'Enjoy yourself,' the man lugubriously replied.

## 19 *Warmth in a frigid world*

Behind the Iron Curtain, however, within what President Reagan called 'The Evil Empire', frontier posts between the various subject States could be islands of unexpected cheerfulness. I suppose there was always a faint hope that things might be brighter in the next of the People's Republics. I remember with pleasure taking notes in a café at a lesser border post among the woodlands between Czechoslovakia and Poland, both of them then in the depths of Stalinist oppression. How it revivified me, after a few weeks among the metropolitan apparatchiks! Excited students tumbled out of buses beneath the dark trees, cluttered with sleeping-bags and backpacks; businessmen in wide black hats like villains in old thrillers sat about doing murky things with banknotes; big Polish truck-drivers in leather jackets drank flagons of beer, sometimes joined by policemen with what we used to call burp guns on their shoulders; and more or less camping out on the edge of the forest, all around the border post, was a shifting audience from the local village, fine plump mothers, adorable little girls with pigtails, just watching the show. 'Change money?' dubious loiterers occasionally asked me – always a leitmotif of travel in eastern Europe; and although in those days I preferred not to take the risk, having had a nasty scare in Warsaw once, still the black-market inquiry gave me, like the show and bustle of the frontier itself, a warm sense of collusion in a generally frigid world.

## 20  *On the edge*

Within a loop of the Curtain stood the easternmost place in West Germany,
in the days of the Cold War. It was a small fishing-village called Schnackenburg, in Lower Saxony, built in a bend of the River Elbe which there formed
the frontier between the two Germanies. This really seemed like the edge
of civilization. It was a delightful little place, all by itself on the river's bank.
It had a fishing-harbour, and a small market-place shaded by chestnuts, and
a couple of streets of pleasant wood-and-brick houses. All around was green
farmland, and the village was protected from river floods by a high levee, in
the Mississippi manner. Up there, if you looked behind you to the west,
you would see the village sheltered snugly behind its grassy embankment, a
family-looking place where everyone knew everyone else, and the men met
genially in the evening at the inn, or gregariously tended their nets and
outboard motors in the harbour, and the small boys messed about at the
water's edge, and the women gossiped over their washing-lines – a little
epitome of old-fashioned riverine Germany. If you looked to the east,
though, over the wide river, you seemed to be looking at nowhere. Over
there the scrubby lowlands, speckled with the odd thicket of willow, looked
dank, desolate and possibly land-mined. It was as though nobody went there
any more, as though some grim catastrophe had drained the life from the
countryside. There were many places in eastern Germany then which had
not seen a foreign face, Russians apart, since the 1930s. The two banks of
the Elbe were like different worlds, and now and then a grey patrol boat of
the Communist DDR – the Deutsche Demokratische Republik – cruised
watchfully upstream, maintaining the distinction.

## 21  *The Wall*

The apex, the epitome and the most public shame of the Iron Curtain was
the Berlin Wall, which for twenty-eight years separated the western half of
the old German capital from the eastern, and stopped the people moving
from one part to the other. Each half was an ideological surrogate: the one
of Washington, the other of Moscow. The civic effect was bizarre, and made
nonsense of a great city. All the old centres of power were in the East, while
West Berlin was in effect a city of suburbs. It was as though London were

to be divided by a frontier running north to south through Hyde Park Corner. Whitehall, Buckingham Palace, the City of London would be in one part, while the other would have as its epicentres Knightsbridge and Sloane Square. All the pomp would be on one side, most of the fizz on the other. Sidling squalidly through the city, scrawled with graffiti on the capitalist side, hideously blank on the Communist, the Berlin Wall put a seal upon this idiocy, and might have been deliberately designed to discredit what it stood for. I always used to think that if Communism had evolved a sense of humour the ideology might have succeeded, but it remained profoundly laughless from start to finish, and the Berlin Wall was its proper artistic memorial: not only overbearing, and dogmatic, and ugly, and unkind, but impregnated in its every foot with a complete absence of merriment. It accurately emblemized, for all the world to note, the contrast between the Communist and capitalist ways of life.

I well remember crossing into East Berlin for the first time in the 1950s, before the Wall went up, and seeing before me as in some fearful fantasy, more UFA than Hollywood, the vast and colourless space of the still uncompleted Stalinallee (later to be renamed Karl-Marx-Allee). It seems in my memory to have been all dark, without street lights at all, certainly without trees, only the awful hulks of new rectilinear buildings, one after the other down the enormous highway, all treeless, all lifeless, all loveless, all humourless, all phantasmagorical. No less vividly do I recall coming the other way, out of Russia through the DDR into the West. Then, as I remember it, having passed through the morose inquiries of the East German checkpoint and the hardly more engaging inspection of the American, I seemed to come up against a wall of light, a hallucination precisely the opposite of the one on the other side – everything dazzling, colourful, effulgent, inviting. I did what many travellers did in those days, when they came to Berlin out of the Soviet Union: I took a taxi straight to the Hilton Hotel and asked if they would mind keeping my tin of Caspian caviare in the kitchen freezer. Such were the contrasts the Berlin Wall was so perversely determined to emphasize.

## 22  *Making up for things*

The Communist system looked ghastly to the outsider, and was hideously cruel to many of its citizens, but it had its compensations. When it collapsed, plenty of its elderly subjects would miss it, and go on voting for its electoral candidates. Jobs were generally secure, in the lands of the informers and the political police, pensions were paid, there was little public crime, behave yourself and you were generally left alone. Even among the dissidents there was the tingle of excitement that went with danger, and I had a lot of fun with people behind the Iron Curtain, even in the most frightening years of Stalinist oppression. As the Bulgarian novelist Ivan Vasov declared, during the nineteenth-century Turkish occupation of his own country, oppression can make people happy – deprived of political liberty, they make up for it in life, love and music.

## 23  *Celebrations*

Anyway, the Iron Curtain was lifted in the end, and the dreadful Wall came down. In 1990 I peered through one of the first holes in it, and saw on the other side two soldiers listlessly kicking a steel helmet around a dusty yard, as in a morality play. The whole world shared the excitement when the deprived East Germans came swarming in their thousands through the abandoned check-posts in their wretched little Trabant cars, popping and smoking and breaking down among the svelte modern motors of the West. I found this spectacle infinitely pathetic, especially when one saw a sweating paterfamilias from East Berlin, helped by his embarrassed children, desperately pushing his stalled car out of the traffic – his wife looking cross in the front seat, BMWs swarming all around. Still, it was delightful to be able, in those early months, to swan at will across that once implacable border, and I recall with pleasure a Sunday morning beside the Müggelsee, in a corner of East Berlin that would have been depressing indeed a few weeks before, and was overlooked still by grim black factories of the Workers' Paradise. Walking through the woods there that day I heard a strain of German music – ho-ho, thump-thump music – and presently found at a waterside hotel several thousand East Germans celebrating their emancipation – laughing, singing, dancing, beer-drinking, one band playing the old oom-pah-pah, the other exploring the less raucous fringes of rock. All was comradely and sentimental, the very spirit of *Gemütlichkeit*.

## 24 *Pollution*

The next day I had a meeting with two Berlin officials, one from each side of the abandoned barricade. The man from the west was dressed in the coolest Western style, and gave me an elegantly embossed visiting-card with translations in English and Japanese. The man from the east wore an ill-cut dark suit without a tie, and offered me only a piece of pasteboard with his name typed upon it, and a crookedly stamped logo on the back. It was to be many a year before the effects of the Iron Curtain were dispersed. You were no longer threatened by secret policemen when you passed the shadow of the Curtain, but you felt yourself oppressed still by a sense of hangover – a frayed, bloodshot, badly cut, grubby feeling. Some of it really was grubbiness. Many of the old frontier towns of the Communist world were horribly run-down, their buildings peeling and unpainted, their streets potholed, their clothes dowdy, their wattages low as ever, and everywhere that depressing lack of colour. On their outskirts, factories like mills from the Industrial Revolution still belched their soot, while the cars and trucks on the roads pumped black exhaust smoke into an atmosphere that was already opaque. Monotonous estates of high-rise tenements loomed over historic cities. A squalid mafia proliferated. It was pollution of every kind, and I used to feel that the very minds of those places had been made soiled and sordid, after so many years of degradation. If you crossed from Austria into Czechoslovakia at the start of the 1990s the immigration people were civil enough at the frontier, and no armed guards brandished their Kalashnikovs ominously around your car, but when you drove away an unexpected kind of functionary still let you know that you had crossed the old Iron Curtain. In twos and threes along the road the prostitutes stood in welcome, some bunched together in bus shelters, some thumbing trucks, most of them just hanging around kicking their stiletto heels – they called the road to Prague in those days 'the longest brothel in the world'. But at least the women smiled. That was something.

## 25  *From a speech by Václav Havel, President of Czechoslovakia,*
### *1 January 1990*

We live in a contaminated moral environment. We fell morally ill because we became used to saying something different from what we thought. We learnt not to believe in anything, to ignore each other, to care only about ourselves . . . The [Communist] regime reduced gifted and autonomous people, skilfully working in their own country, to nuts and bolts of some monstrously huge, noisy and stinking machine . . .

## 26  *Old hotels*

It was surprising how quickly, nevertheless, I began to find hotels of the former Communist Europe downright nostalgic. Some, of course, were very soon internationalized, and became much like hotels anywhere in the West – the Bristol in Warsaw, for whose management, back in the 1950s, I had banged out a simple brochure on my portable typewriter, presently became a member of the Leading Hotels of the World association. But I rather missed the old hotels, the Party hotels, the bugged and commissared hotels. I still come across one occasionally, in some less than completely reconstructed People's Republic, and when I check in there back it all comes, at least in memory! Here is the stony-faced receptionist demanding your passport. Here is the sly porter wanting to change your money. Ahead of you down the brown corridor with its wrinkled carpet and forty-watt bulbs, as you are conducted to your room, strides the statutory burly figure with his coat slung over his shoulders and a mock-leather briefcase in his hand. On tables all around are distributed the ill-printed hotel brochures, not unlike the one I wrote for the Poles, with their pages decoratively pleated, like napkins. Armies of fraternal delegates have walked these passages before you. KGB squads have skulked about up here. And when you reach your room at last, dim and stuffy at the back of the building, why! it is the very room you had all those years before, in the days when you could still see the big red star shining from the House of the Party over the rooftops. 'Sixty blogods to the dollar,' the porter urges once more – 'you won't do better than that': and 'OK,' you say this time.

## 27 *By the way*

By the way, I recently went back to Schnackenburg, and found that by the fishing-harbour they had created a little Museum of the Border Zone, to commemorate the bad old days. It was closed when I was there, but a peer through its window gave me a nasty turn. In the gloom of the half-shuttered room there were life-size dummies of Communist frontier guards, as they used to be. One rode a motor-bike, and had an automatic weapon strapped across his chest. One was evidently a general and was being driven by his orderly in a sort of Russian jeep. There were flags around, and rusted notices saying 'HALTE!', and seen so indistinctly through the window those grim mannequins looked truly sinister. A bare wooden table stood in the middle of the room, as though for interrogations; and outside, on the slipway, high and dry on props stood that grey DDR patrol boat.

In his book *Apples in the Snow* (1990), Geoffrey Moorhouse has a brilliantly prophetic passage, almost surreal, about the toppling of all the hundreds and thousands of public statues of Lenin in the USSR creating such a mighty surplus of bronze that the whole world's metal markets would be knocked askew. During the Communist hegemony in eastern Europe there were almost as many public statues of Stalin, and these too were one and all eliminated in a couple of years. The very last of them survived into the middle 1990s in Tirana, the capital of Albania, where it stood prominently on a plinth beside the main avenue of the city, second in importance only to the mighty bronze of Enver Hoxha, the local dictator, in the great square up the road. Stalin's effigy was removed when the regime fell, but in 1996 it still existed, in a shed on the city outskirts. I went and saw it there. It looked in good order, the old tyrant standing in the approved posture of commanding benevolence, but I saw no future for it.

## 28 *The end of the frontier?*

Frontiers in Europe are losing much of their meaning now, and with luck they may fade away altogether. In some ways I shall be sorry to see them go. The frontier has been an essential part of the European ethos, after all, throughout my fifty years – when I first travelled from England to Italy as a civilian, I had to get a transit visa to cross France. But before long, I suppose, the queues of trucks lining up at Europe's frontier posts will be no more than a folk-memory, like my steam engines coughing at Dôle, and already most customs officers, in most parts of Europe, wave the motorist through without a glance. Ernest Bevin, the British Labour Foreign Secretary, once said that the ambition of his foreign policy was to enable a Briton to go down to Waterloo station and take a train to Paris without needing a passport. I suppose it is only natural that by the 1990s the surliest frontier in western Europe was his own, the frontier of an island kingdom which had maintained its pride and its sovereignty for nearly a thousand years by reason of its insularity. It was a disagreeable experience, all the same, to observe the merciless faces of Her Majesty's customs officers, interrogating some unfortunate black traveller with a baby on her arm, or rummaging through the backpack of a student vacationer, beneath the unforgiving lights of the green channel.

## 29  Bits and bobs

Wandering one day in the 1960s through the French department of Roussillon I suddenly and quite unexpectedly found myself confronted by a frontier post with a Spanish flag above it, and an announcement that I was entering Llivia, in the Spanish province of Gerona. It was hardly more than a small and shabby village, connected by a dead straight, specially constructed and officially neutral road with the nearest Spanish city, Puigcerdá. The place was unmistakably Spanish, in architecture, language and spirit, and turned out to be a kind of historical quibble. The region had been divided between France and Spain in 1659, and this countryside with all its villages was assigned to the French: a canny Spanish argument maintained that Llivia was not a village but a town, and so for ever after its people were connected with their fatherland only by that geometrical umbilical, from which even in my day it was forbidden to stray.

Even in a Europe without frontiers, such bits, bobs and anomalies of history will always survive. For the moment they are almost inescapable. There is a Slovakian enclave on the Hungarian side of the Danube. At the southern end of Spain the British flag flies over a colony largely inhabited by people of Italian, Spanish, Maltese and North African descent. An infinitesimal strip of Bosnia-Hercegovina runs through Croatia to the Adriatic. A curious pocket of Germany exists at Büsingen, on the Swiss side of the Rhine, where the currency is Swiss but the postage stamps are German – a delightful mixture of old river town and spanking modernity, where nationality seems to have lost much of its meaning.

Luxembourg (population 407,000) has been an independent Grand Duchy only since 1867, but when you drive into its spiky capital you certainly know you are entering a sovereign State: as one of the richest cities of Europe and a centre of Europeanism, it is an exhibition of nineteenth-century grandeur and twentieth-century excitement. Before you can become a citizen of San Marino (population 24,000) you have to have lived for fifty years (which Heaven forbid) in that minuscule, steep and touristy mountain republic in the middle of Italy, which has maintained a sort of independence since the fourth century AD. The chief executive of the State of the Vatican City (population 1,000) is the Pope: it has its own railway, heliport, newspaper, university, diplomatic service and radio station, broadcasting in thirty-four languages. Half the world scarcely realized that Monaco (population 30,000) was an independent State at all until the marriage of the actress Grace Kelly to Prince Rainier in 1956: in fact it has been ruled by the same princely dynasty since the thirteenth century, within just the same territorial bounds (except those extended by profitable landfill), and finding it there today, as you drop out of the French Maritime Alps into the arid glitter of its skyscrapers, yachts, hotels and jet-set villas, is one of Europe's most curious moments of historical paradox. The first time I drove to the Republic of Andorra (population 62,000), up the twisting highway through the Pyrenees from France, the compass in my car went berserk. Its needle swung hilariously this way and that, affected I suppose by deposits in the stark mountains all around. This was apposite, because the little State seems to exist outside natural laws. Its titular heads of State, the Co-Princes of Andorra, are the President of France and the Bishop of Urgel, a small diocesan city in northern Spain, and for 700 years it has maintained its improbable but generally imperturbable independence, living in recent years by the profits of tourism and obliging tax arrangements, but officially denied recognition by the Government of Japan. No wonder my compass floundered.

## 30 Fürstlichkeit

Then there is the mountain Principality of Liechtenstein, which lies between
Switzerland and Austria. Liechtenstein (population 31,000) is like a drift on
the map, so unobtrusive that on the motorway through Switzerland from
Bad Ragaz to Lake Constance you can easily pass it by without noticing –
especially since, as Switzerland handles its external affairs anyway, the only
frontier or customs posts are on the Austrian side. It is, however, a sovereign
State of a most particular kind. It is the epitome of *Fürstlichkeit* – princeliness.
From the jumbled centre of its only city, Vaduz, a lively cacophony of
restaurants, banks, tourist shops and car parks, you may see high on a rocky
outcrop above, as in legend or allegory, the castle of its ruling prince – as I
write, Hans Adam II. His dynasty has provided sovereign rulers of this place
since 1719, and there is no ignoring it. Princes and princesses abound, not
only Prince Hans Adam himself and his wife Princess Marie, but their
children and daughter-in-law the Princes and Princesses Alois, Maximilian,
Constantin, Tatjana and Sophie: without even counting uncles, aunts and
cousins that I know not of, this amounts to one Royal Highness for every
4,500 inhabitants, and constitutes a royal presence of almost Saudi profligacy.
Princely portraits are everywhere, princely crowns and princely crests, pictures
of princely weddings, princely banners, princely epithets and princely honorifics. The stamps, of course, have princes on them. The currency would too,
if there were a currency – Swiss francs are used in Liechtenstein. Even the
wine comes from princely vineyards, by way of princely-employed retailers,
and is likely to have a princely title on its label, and an embossed crown, and
a crest with eagles and an orb.

I spent a few days in Liechtenstein in 1996, and thought that on the face
of it nowhere could be much happier. There is no poverty, and when one
Sunday I went up into the mountains for an alfresco lunch, beside the little
lake at Steg, the crowds of jolly well-behaved people up there, messing about
in boats, cooking barbecue meals, striding away up mountain paths, drinking
steins of beer at café tables, seemed to me most enviable. It turned out,
though, that all was not entirely content in Liechtenstein that week. Almost
for the first time in history, among the legislators in the modest Parliament
building, almost directly below the castle, there had been stirrings of anti-
*Fürstlichkeit*. As a republican myself I was not, of course, surprised. Despite
what the publicity brochures said ('the prince and the people rule together'),

Liechtenstein was an all-but-absolute monarchy. The allegory of the castle on the hill was perfectly true. All those crests, titles and flags were not mere ornament. Liechtenstein's economy depended partly on a thriving industrial sector, and partly upon one of the world's most successful banking and financial structures, and in the entire national enterprise Prince Hans Adam II was by far the largest shareholder. What the Prince said went!

Since then I have watched the papers for news of more general dissent in Liechtenstein: but when I remember that sunny lunch-time by the lake, the cars streaming up from Vaduz (in Liechtenstein there is one for every two persons, young and old), I don't seriously expect to find any.

## 31 *On the Rock*

I suppose the most surprising of these anomalies, during my half-century, was that of Gibraltar, still a British Crown Colony when the rest of the British Empire had all but disappeared. By the 1990s it was propagating an image of itself as a sunny if not ritzy tax haven for the very rich, but when I was working in Spain thirty years before I used to think it a gloomy relic indeed, standing there vastly humped across Algeciras Bay, or looming darkly over Andalusian landscapes. To generations of Britons, and to many foreigners too, it had long been instinct with imperial romance – one of the great fortresses by which the island people had sustained their maritime supremacy around the world. William Makepeace Thackeray (1811–63) likened it to a great blunderbuss, seized by the British 'and kept ever since tremendously loaded and cleaned and ready for use'. Richard Chevenix Trench (1807–86) said 'it made the very heart within one dance'. 'At this door,' wrote Wilfrid Scawen Blunt (1840–1922), who hated almost everything about the British Empire, 'England stands sentry. God! to hear the shrill sweet treble of her fifes upon the breeze, and at the summon of the rock gun's roar to see her redcoats marching from the hill!' Even Joyce's Molly Bloom had proud memories of Gibraltar, for it was there that she was kissed by Lieutenant (or so she fondly thought) Mulvey, Royal Navy, beneath the Moorish wall.

Nobody has been more susceptible to the imperial aesthetic than I have been, but still Gibraltar always struck me as a sorry disappointment. It might look heroic from the deck of a passing ship, standing there so terrifically with Union Jacks all over the place, but on the ground it was just a shabby barracks-town, with dingy shops and nasty little pubs where the soldiers drank, and vast bare slabs of granite rising everywhere. Even the Rock Hotel, a flowered oasis in the midst of all this drab stoniness, could let the imperial aficionado down. I once overheard two very old-school American matrons commenting upon the grumpy hotel porter who had just dumped their bags unceremoniously on the lobby floor. 'What an unpleasant man!' said one. 'What can you expect?' responded her Sister of the American Revolution. 'He is *British*, my dear, and *male.*'

## 32  *Looking for Wends*

There are innumerable ethnic muddles and anachronisms, too, which are generally noticed only when they flare into violence – Serbs in Croatia, Albanians in Yugoslavia, Croats in Bosnia, Germans in Romania and the Czech Republic, Kashubians in Poland, Finns in Sweden, Greeks and Albanians in southern Italy, Austrians in the north, Russians and Tartars in the Baltic countries, communities of many origins scattered still along the eastern marches of the continent. The district called the Vojvodina in Yugoslavia is home to Hungarians, Romanians, Macedonians, Serbs, Slovaks, Greeks, Bulgarians, Gypsies and according to some authorities at least a dozen lesser ethnicities: in 1991, well before the break-up of the old Yugoslavia, less than 7 per cent of its people thought of themselves as 'Yugoslavs' (which only means 'South Slavs' anyway).

In Germany, near the Czech and Polish borders, there are some 50,000 Slav people called Sorbs, who speak Sorbian and have a literature of their own. Somebody told me that others, calling themselves Wends, still talked their language and pursued their customs in the very heart of the country. The Wends had once been a powerful group of tribes, so irredeemably heathen that in the twelfth century the Roman Catholic Church authorized a crusade against them: this culminated in the destruction of a gigantic figure of their god Światowit, whom we met on page 17: the image stood at the tip of the off-shore island of Rügen, and the soldiers of Christ toppled it ceremoniously into the sea.

I was intrigued to think that a pocket of this people might have survived deep in western Germany, so in 1995 I went to the corner of Lower Saxony still called Wendland to see if I could find them. It is a sweet triangle of farmland well outside the usual tourist route, and on the map it was certainly littered with some encouragingly Tolkienian place names – Satemin,

Mammoisel, Gohlefanz. I was not really surprised to learn that the Wendish language was last heard here some time in the 1800s, and it soon became clear to me that under the Nazis, who categorized Slavs as subhuman, many citizens had preferred to forget their Wendishness: but I was delighted to discover that the old pagans, long since assimilated into German Christianity, had left behind them a series of villages peculiar to themselves. They are roughly circular assemblies of brick timber-framed houses, grouped around village greens, generally with a church just outside the circle. They suggested to me extremely sophisticated, advanced and comfortable Zulu kraals. No straggly suburbs spoil the elegance of the Wendish *Runddorf*, which may be no more than five or six houses anyway: it stands there in that green landscape wonderfully serene, with holy texts inscribed on its housefronts, and the names of long-dead burghers.

Very few of the inhabitants claim Wendish origin, which I had rather expected to find trendily fashionable, but the misty identity of the Wends is not entirely dispersed. When I was there the German authorities were proposing to dump nuclear waste in a disused salt-mine in the country. The people were up in arms against it, a Free Wendland Republic had been declared, and the Wendish slogans that greeted me everywhere, the unfamiliar flags that fluttered, must have amused the shades of those vanished indigenes (though the waste went into the salt-mine anyway).

## 33 Finding the Karaim

I did better with the Karaim (or Karaites), one of the smallest and most interesting racial and religious minorities in all Europe. They are Jews of a very particular kind, who originated in Baghdad, or perhaps Persia, and broke from the main body of Judaism in the eighth century, maintaining that nothing but the Bible itself was holy, that the Talmud was impious and rabbinical religion false. Sober and ascetic, with a rich literature, they held themselves austerely aloof from Christians and Muslims alike. Many Karaim found their way to the Crimea, and there at the end of the eighteenth century they were befriended by the Empress Catherine II of Russia, who transferred some of them to her territories in Lithuania on the Baltic. I had read that they had provided guards for the Grand Dukes of Lithuania at their castle of Trakai, set among a sequence of lakes near the centre of the country, so in 1996 I went there to find them.

Trakai is a spectacular place. The fifteenth-century Gothic castle, heavily reconstructed, stands on an island at the head of a peninsula, attended by a small town largely made of wood – streets of elegantly shabby planked houses interspersed with beech trees along the water's edge. There were plenty of signs of Karaim occupation. Many of those houses, I was assured, had been put up by the Karaim. A street was named for them, and so was an island near the castle, presumably where the Duke's bodyguard had been quartered. But when I followed my map to the Karaim Museum, a little square building like a village hall, I found it all abandoned; and the Knessa along the road, the Karaim equivalent of a synagogue, was in the hands of decidedly Gentile workmen. 'Karaim?' I asked the doorkeepers at the castle, but they firmly shook their heads. Were the Karaim all dead, then? Had the damned Nazis murdered them?

No, it turned out. Among anti-Semites they had never been regarded as *entirely* Jewish – rather odd, as the Karaim believed themselves to be more truly Jewish than anyone else. The tsarist Russians had given them full citizenship. The Nazis decreed that they were not biological Jews but only converts from other races, and though in the event this did not prevent their general massacre in the Crimea, it apparently saved them in Lithuania. Where were they, then? Where were the Karaim? I asked everyone I met in the streets of Trakai, and eventually I found them, in the persons of two extremely jolly, very healthy-looking, wonderfully extrovert middle-aged women, living in two of those old wooden houses.

They were not at all what I expected – not in the least sober, ascetic or aloof. About 150 of their people, they told me, still lived in Trakai, in the very same streets to which they had migrated from the Black Sea two centuries before, and they led me to a shop where I could get a true Karaim delicacy, a kind of pie called a *kibini*. However horrible it might prove to be, I jumped at the chance to taste it. Could anything be more romantic, I thought, than to sit beside the lake, looking across to the castle, eating a pie which had come to this corner of Europe by way of Baghdad, the Crimea, the patronage of the Empress of Russia and the employment of the Grand Dukes of Lithuania? The Karaim ladies laughed at my enthusiasm, but the *kibini* turned out to be delicious – though not very different, actually, from a Cornish pasty.

## 34  *Serbian high spirits*

Most minorities tend in their exile to become more than naturally themselves. However at Szentendre in Hungary there is a small community of Serbs, perhaps a couple of hundred of them, who have created down the generations a town which seems to me the utter antithesis of everything we think of as Serbian nowadays – everything, that is, warlike, obdurate, dour. Szentendre stands beside the Danube a few miles north of Budapest, and the Serbs settled here in the late seventeenth century as refugees from the Turks who still occupied the Balkans. They brought their own patriarch with them, to be the head of a Serbian Orthodox Church in exile, and they made the little riverside village a showplace of their religion and enterprise. Two centuries later it became a favourite artists' hangout, and it is now the first place foreign tourists visit when they want an excursion out of the capital. It is an exquisite little town running down a hillside to the river, where the ferries put in from Budapest, brightly coloured, with cobbled alleys full of art galleries and souvenir shops, fine old houses of the Serbian merchants, half a dozen onion-domed Serbian churches and a lovely baroque square, in the centre of the town, where they stage plays on summer evenings. I discovered this light-hearted place at a time when the Serbian homeland was plunged in misery, threadbare in the aftermath of a civil war and presided over by a disagreeable neo-Marxist bully. Heaven knows the Serbs of Szentendre have known troubles enough, during their three centuries in Hungary, but still how lucky, I thought as I pottered around those beguiling touristy streets in the sunshine, pausing to look at a water-colour here, an embroidered blouse there – what a stroke of luck it was that those fugitives of long ago chose such a happy destination to escape the furies of the Turk!

## 35  *Islands*

Now consider the islands of Europe. Just think of them, for ever distracting the diplomats and confusing the cartographers! There are thousands upon thousands of islands in Europe. Two of them are outside my window in Wales: one of them the traditional burial-place of 20,000 Celtic saints, the other inhabited only by sheep. There are said to be 80,897 islands off the coast of Finland alone, and another 20,000 at least in the Swedish archipelago.

There are Greek islands in the lee of Turkey. There are British islands twenty
miles off France. The Norwegian islands of Spitzbergen are inhabited mainly
by Russian coal-miners. Cyprus is ruled half by the Greeks, half by the Turks.
The Scottish island of Barra is a Catholic enclave in a sea of Protestantism.
The very last place the British Empire annexed was the island rock of St Kilda,
in the Atlantic; one of the first it voluntarily abandoned was Heligoland in
the North Sea (swapped with the Germans for Zanzibar). The island of
Monte Cristo, of the eponymous Count, is an uninhabited nature reserve.
On the sweet nuns' island of Fraueninsel, in the German lake Chiemsee, is
buried General Alfred Jodl, executed for war crimes after the Second World
War. And especially curious among so many curiosities are the Åland islands,
in the Gulf of Finland. There is the true essence of islandness! When I saw
them from an aircraft flying in from Helsinki they seemed to lie so thick and
green upon the surface of the sea that it looked as though a whole continent
had been fissured by some appalling calamity and was drifting about in bits
down there.

I knew something of the Åland islands already, because although only
25,000 people live there, the islands are famous for their shipowners – the
last of the ocean-going merchant sailing-ships were owned by an Åland
company, and many of the great ferries which ply the Baltic now are
Åland-registered. What makes the islands special, though, is their peculiarly
satisfactory constitution. Most of the islanders are Swedish by descent, speaking Swedish, and in the redistribution of Europe after the First World War
they mostly wanted to join Sweden and live their lives in the Swedish
language. Finland, however, was the *de-facto* sovereign of the island, and the
matter went to the League of Nations for arbitration. A favourite Åland
picture shows a dozen whiskered and cravatted statesmen, sitting in a room
with Lake Geneva and the Alps showing theatrically through the windows,
decreeing the future of the Ålanders. They did well. They ruled, in 1921,
that while the Finns should retain their sovereignty, the Ålanders should
keep their language, and the islands should form a demilitarized autonomous
province within the State of Finland. So they have remained. The big modern
building in the middle of Mariehamn, their capital, is not as you might expect
a municipal leisure centre, but the Åland Parliament. The civic museum
is full of national symbols, relics and trophies, including a huge metal
representation of the island constitution, as proud as the American Declaration
of Independence in its shrine at Washington, and a very large version of
those bigwigs in Geneva (who were presided over by a Japanese). The

Ålanders have their own flag and postage stamps. They are excused all military service. They own all those ships. They are terribly patriotic, as well they might be, and when I once came across an Åland schooner about to sail home from the Swedish island of Gotland, its crew urged me to come with them rather as though they were beckoning me away to the Autonomous Province of the Hesperides.

## 36 And talking of Gotland . . .

Talking of Gotland, come with me now to one of the medieval churches that are scattered through that big Swedish island of the Baltic and are its special glory. The church rises above the flatlands like a mailed knight, burly and muscular, and close beside it stands a fortified tower, garrisoned by rooks. Around the building a glorious meadow extends, in a flourish of cornflowers, daisies, buttercups, dandelions and cow-parsley, all among the fresh grass as in meadows long ago. The parson's trim manse may be nearby, together with a cottage or two and a church hall, but there is no sign of any village. The church is its own settlement, and in neat order around it lie the generations of its congregations – row upon row of Bergströms and Ericssons and Angströms. The church towers above them implacably, and often rooks fly restlessly about it, in a raucous symbolical way.

Open the tall wooden door, though (Gotland churches are seldom locked), and instantly we feel ourselves in some benevolent old homestead. There is a smell of old books. The box pews are brightly if simply painted, and there may be ancient frescos on the whitewashed walls – saints, angels, Christ in glory, the Last Judgement, a humiliated dragon perhaps. A sailing-ship model hangs from a rafter; beside the reading-desk of the high wooden pulpit stands an hourglass, to keep clerical verbosity in check. The altarpiece is painted in muted medieval colours. There are ancient gilded memorials to local families. A chair for the verger is draped with a comforting sheepskin. At the chancel arch there stands a magnificent wooden crucifix, ten or twelve feet high, exquisitely carved, nobly painted, and attended on each side by heart-rendingly poignant figures of mourning.

What d'you say, now? Stirred and touched as we are by our visit – oh, and wait a moment, we must put a few kronor in the collection box by the door – shall we find a roadside café and have a saffron pancake? Saffron pancakes are another Gotland speciality.

## 37  *Smouldering still*

I first set eyes upon the Greek island of Crete from the deck of a passing
troopship soon after the Second World War, and it seemed to me then to
be positively smouldering with the furies of battle. Thirty years passed before
I set foot on the place, thirty years in which tourism had penetrated every
last cove of the Grecian seas, and ancient lifestyles had been whittled away
from Tenedos to Ithaca: but, by God, I found it a furious kind of island still.
The mass of it looked hacked all about with ravines, twisted this way and
that, and the deep shadows scored in its mountain flanks made everything
seem more tremendous. I thought it *brutally* built. What could be more
violent than the mighty gorge of Samaria, a chasm of Dantean suggestion
flapped about by strident birds and frequented by the great goat which the
Cretans magnificently called 'The Wild One'? I admired Crete most of all
when the clouds that hung so often about its mountain summits spread over
the island as a whole, swirling among the defiles with their mists and
rainstorms. Sometimes then, when the driven cloud was tinged with sunshine
from below, the place looked all afire: the winds rushed up the valleys like
jets, and when it thundered the crack of it sounded among the highlands as
though caves were there and then being split in the mountain face. I
have been back to Crete several times since then, always expecting to be
disillusioned, and finding it more littered with tourism every time I go: but
I have never quite got over my first reactions, and it seems to me to be
smouldering still.

## 38  *A dance and a gate*

One evening, not so long ago, I came across a dance in a Cretan courtyard.
The lights were very bright there. The deafeningly amplified music was a
quavery sort of oriental theme. A high gate closed the yard, but along the
wall of the road above, from windows and shadowy terraces all around, a
crowd of villagers watched. Beneath the lights inside, a long circling line of
Cretans – men and women – danced a strange dance. I was bewitched.
Gracefully, jauntily, thoughtfully, swankily, the dancers tripped their complex
steps, and the music blared through the pergola. Round and round they
went, to and fro, and sometimes the man at the head of the line, detaching

himself momentarily from the rest, threw himself into a spasm, leaping, kicking his feet together, twirling about in an ecstasy of conceit and accomplishment, before the convulsion left him and he subsided into the music's rhythm. I was reminded sometimes of a revivalist meeting and sometimes of a fairy ring, and when I tore myself away the half-tone music of the loudspeakers tracked me into the night.

The timber gate of my yard at home in Wales is a ramshackle old monster of a gate, patched here and there, nailed all over with bits of wood and iron, sagging on its hinges rather, kept together by a heavy wooden latch which doesn't quite fit. The cat Jenks can squirm underneath it. I keep it only because it reminds me of gates in Crete, the storms and bad things they exclude, the mysteries they keep in.

## 39 *The café with two doors*

It was in 1974 that the island of Cyprus was forcibly divided into two republics by a Turkish invasion – the Greek Cypriot Republic of Cyprus in the south, the generally unrecognized Turkish Republic of Northern Cyprus in the north. Long before that, though, the island was horribly split between the two peoples, and for most of my years in journalism it provided what used to be called in the trade a running story. The British were still half-heartedly governing the island in those days, and when the news did not concern Greeks and Turks massacring each other it concerned Greeks in revolution against the British (they wanted union with Greece itself then – it was only later that they decided upon a republic of their own). All was skirmish and threat, armoured cars and ambushes. Terrorists lurked in mountain caves. Steel-helmeted soldiers patrolled city streets. I was standing in the doorway of my hotel in Nicosia one morning, waiting to go and interview the Governor, Field Marshal Sir John Harding, in his palace along the road, when a boy came by on a bicycle and threw a sheet of paper at my feet. It was signed by the Greek guerrilla leader who called himself Dighenis, and it said that the guerrillas had captured 'a Briton named CREMER, who is a high-ranking officer of British military intelligence', and that if the dictator HARDING did not cancel the death sentences imposed on the freedom-loving patriots ZAKKOS, MICHAEL AND PATATSOS before twelve noon the next day, CREMER would be executed. 'There will be no further warning.'

I gave the paper to the dictator HARDING when I met him later that morning, but I am ashamed to say I can't remember what happened either to the high-ranking intelligence officer or to the freedom-loving patriots. It was the summer of 1956, and to tell the truth the British were getting rather tired of the whole business. At that time the walled city of Nicosia was bisected by a barbed-wire barrier, separating the Greeks from the Turks: but at one place along it there stood a small corner café with two doors, one opening into the Greek quarter, the other into the Turkish, and through its grubby dining-room there moved a casual succession of housewives and businessmen, moving from one implacably hostile territory to the other. They seemed to see nothing strange in the arrangement. They came and they went, clasping their shopping-bags and order-books, in at one door, out the other, with only a nod of the head to the proprietor, or a pause to rearrange their bundles. It was as though the barbed-wire barrier were no more than a political pretence, nothing to do with real people.

I deceived myself that summer that this was a reflection of the island's condition as a whole – that the Greeks and Turks themselves were getting sick of their enmities. I thought the island had a *constipated* feel. But the Cypriots were like the people of Northern Ireland, and did not tire of quarrel. On and on, down the years, the conflict simmered and flared. The British Government left. The Turkish Army came. The café with two doors was only an illusion, and the Greeks and the Turks went on furiously resenting one another.

## 40  Un-Homeric

Most Mediterranean islands project powerful images. They are gloriously suggestive, like Corsica, where in every dozen bottles of the local wine one is likely to be fragrant with the sweet flower-smells of the maquis. They are ominous, like Sardinia, where the international rich live in luxurious villas on the shore, cap-à-pie against kidnappers. They are tourist-blighted islands of the Aegean. They are celebrated for their residents – Napoleon (Elba), Chopin (Majorca), Tiberius (Capri), Ulysses (Ithaca?). However, there is one at least which seems to have no popular image at all: the Italian island of Ischia, in the Gulf of Naples. Most foreigners, I find, think it is in Greece – 'Well it *sounds* Greek, doesn't it?' Ischia has no high-flown connotations. It is the Mediterranean smoothed down rather, with none of the hazards and few of the excitements: rather a middle-class, middle-aged kind of island. Its shape is elegant and its countryside is pleasant, and as it happens the entire island is curatively volcanic. Healing steams and boiling waters burst out everywhere: out of springs and conduits, out of holes in the ground or sands of the beaches, spouting through pipes, filling swimming-pools. The island's white wine, far from tasting of wild blossoms, is said by connoisseurs to have a recognizably volcanic flavour, and to be very good for rheumatism.

Ischia is a Thermal Paradise, say the publicists – has been since Greek or Roman times – and there are hundreds of spas in the island, incorporated in hotels or half-hidden beneath palm trees and bougainvillaeas in hillside terraces. Thousands of pilgrims go there in the cause of good health, and give the island its manner of complacently bourgeois respectability, so curious to encounter in those blue salacious seas. An almost palpable satisfaction hangs over Ischia, and makes me feel that the very substances of the place are reasonably happy to be there. I was loitering one evening along a beach where sulphurous steam actually comes up through the sand, at the very edge of the sea, and childishly fancied to myself the sensations of one of the gentle waves which came rippling ashore with the evening tide. In it comes, I thought, fresh and inexperienced from the Tyrrhenian Sea, hoping for Capri perhaps, or the far Ligurians, and in a trice it finds itself running away into a hole in the volcanic Ischian sand. *Mamma mia*, it's hot down there! A stunned moment or two among the volcanic ardours, and that little Tyrrhenian ripple is hot enough to boil an egg in. It does not complain, though, I like to suppose. It may not have found itself any Homeric strand or romantically stormy foreshore, but it must be snug enough down there, in the bowels of the Thermal Paradise.

## 41 *A chance meeting?*

On a bus in Capri I chanced to meet, I can't remember how, a man who introduced himself as Boris Alperovici, the third husband of Gracie Fields. She was a famous star of the past, a Dame of the British Empire, formerly a household name in her native England but somewhat diminished in the public eye by having gone off to America at the start of the Second World War. By then she was living in elderly retirement in her villa on the island. Boris took me along to visit her, and she received me graciously, and told me anecdotes of her theatrical life, and had coffee served to me by her seaside swimming-pool. It was just as though the old lady were some great Hollywood actress at the height of her career, and she evidently enjoyed it all as much as I did. Afterwards Boris gave me a lift back to my hotel: and when I got home to Britain I was surprised to meet other people, too, who had chanced to encounter Signor Alperovici on the Capri bus, they couldn't quite remember how, and had sat gratefully drinking coffee at the feet of Our Gracie.

## 42  *Presidency of the mavericks?*

All islands are unique, of course, but some are uniquer than others, and one of the uniquest is undoubtedly Malta, variously described by its visitors down the centuries as the Head, the Heart, the Navel and the Arsehole of the Mediterranean. Almost within sight of Sicily yet further south than Tunis, less than 125 square miles in area but crowned with a capital worthy of a Great Power, Malta is a true loner, and has a marvellous history of sieges, grandees, Admirals of the Fleet and knights of chivalry. Half a century ago it was still a British colony, the main base of the British Mediterranean Fleet, and I thought it at once touchingly and painfully British. The mostly Italianate proletariat of Valletta seemed to me almost indistinguishable from the British tabloid public, talking blurred varieties of regional English and keenly concerned with football pools, while the Maltese aristocrats I came across were ornamentally Anglophile, despite their long exclusion from the Union Club. The food was overwhelmingly cabbage and Brown Windsor: warships lay magnificently in the harbour.

By the late 1980s, the Empire having long collapsed, things were very different. By then everything Maltese appeared to be in flux – economics, the law, manners, values, Malta's place in the world at large. Who would ever have guessed that the arrival of Beaujolais Nouveau would be advertised in Sliema – like greeting a Pope in Cardiff? Or that *Der Spiegel* would be on sale at the Valletta news-stands? Cappuccino was fast replacing the dreadful instant coffee of the British past, and there were several indecorous Italian TV channels for every one in English. I visited a law court when I was last there. The case concerned heroin-trafficking, and, the small court being rather full, I sat in the front row, occupied otherwise only by a single man. All was remarkably informal, but I was puzzled to see no sign of the accused. When I left the court and asked a policeman where the prisoner's dock was, he told me I had been sitting in it, together with the day's villain (who got five years, I saw in *The Times of Malta* next day).

The essence of *fin-de-siècle* Malta, it seemed to me, was that fluidity. Almost everything seemed flexible, and innumerable joints and junctions, social, economic, financial, historical, articulated the nature of society. Long ago it occurred to me that a pleasant kind of nation would be provided by a confederation of all the circumpolar peoples – the Lapps and the Inuits and the nomadic Siberians: and sitting over my coffee in Malta's Republic Square one morning, beneath the statue of Queen Victoria still given magnanimous hospitality there, I wondered if there could not be a parallel alliance of Europe's misfit nations: the ones that do not conform, the raffish ones, the sinuous ones, which would compete only in their individuality. Malta might well qualify for the presidency of such a maverick alliance, adding a louche lustre to its heritage of knights and admirals.

## 43 *A paradox of the sands*

A strange sight to see is the causeway that leads to the island of Sylt. Sylt is a sandy, heathy, eroding, elongated island of the Friesian group, off the North Sea coast of Schleswig-Holstein in Germany. For centuries it was a community of fishermen and sailors, extremely simple, extremely pious, isolated, and little visited by strangers. Then in 1927 they made a railway causeway to connect the mainland with its solitary town, Westerland, and it has never looked back. You still cannot drive a car to Sylt, but you can load one on a train, and this is what makes the Hindenburg Damm such a curious spectacle. It crosses a lagoon-like stretch of sea, polders and sandbanks, half sea, half land, mysteriously opaque on a misty morning, frequented only by seals and seabirds – the waterscape of Erskine Childers's thriller *The Riddle of the Sands*. But all day long, every half hour or so, a long double-decker transporter train chugs over that desolate expanse, pouring hundreds upon hundreds upon hundreds of cars into the little island – so many cars you would think it might sink beneath the weight of them. Scores of other trains come in too, local trains from the mainland towns, inter-city trains from the heart of Germany, not to mention frequent flights to Sylt Airport, because by now this tiny place is one of the most popular of all German seaside resorts. Walkers and windsurfers flock to its magnificent beaches. Coveys of city children are chivvied into outdoor pursuits. Knockabout holiday-makers

by the million eat ice-creams in the streets of Westerland, which reminds
me very much of that favourite Australian sand-and-hamburger retreat Manly,
New South Wales. And yet only a few miles away on the same island there
basks in the sun of privilege one of the exclusive enclaves of Europe, the
holiday hamlet of Kampen.

Every reader of the German tabloids and gossip journals knows about
Kampen. Kampen is where all the celebrities go: the film and television
people, the magazine publishers, the trendier industrialists, the millionaire
authors. All the glitz is there. It is the Hamptons of Europe. Rigid planning
has meant that it remains a very pretty little place. Nearly all its houses are
thatched, each is surrounded by a statutory amount of heathy land, there are
a town pond and a lighthouse above the beach, and at first sight it all seems
modest and demure. Don't you believe it. Kampen is rolling in money, and
if you look a little harder you will see the unmistakable signs of it: expensive
boutiques, a branch of Cartier the jewellers, three or four posh hotels, a golf
club, discreet antique stores, a nightclub, a couple of discos, and a plethora
of limousines. At the end of the long weekend all those big cars roll down
to the station at Westerland, and when the transporter trains cross the
causeway you may see their owners sitting in the front seats of their cars,
high on the upper deck, smoking cigars and gossiping still on their way home
to Hamburg and the Ruhr.

## 44  *Talking rhymes in Klaksvík*

The most exhilarating moment I ever enjoyed in Europe happened on a
high windy hillside in the Faroe Islands, flying a kite. I was standing then all
at sea in the North Atlantic, halfway between Denmark and Iceland, some
200 miles north of Scotland, and all around me were the symptoms of this
situation – foam-surfed cliffs, gusting winds, screeching seabirds, the smell
of salt, the sting of spray. The lower moorlands were flecked with flowers –
blue, yellow, pink and white. A myriad birds squawked, trilled, squeaked,
piped, chuckled, gasped or throatily gurgled, and occasionally warned me
off their nesting-grounds by hurling themselves melodramatically at my head.
Far below me, beside a gully, there was a huddle of bright-painted houses,
and a small white church. Fishing-boats laboured through the winds. In the
distance along the coast I could see a few cars crawling along a precipitous
mountain road to disappear into a tunnel, but I felt entirely separate up there

in the pale northern sunshine, detached from time itself, flying my fine red kite in the ocean wind.

There's islandness for you! Like the Ålanders, the Faroese more or less govern themselves, though slightly and profitably subject to the sovereignty of Denmark. Their little capital, Tórshavn, culminates in a spit called Tinganes, no more than a couple of hundred yards long, and so narrow that you can often see the water on either side – a toy-like labyrinth of wooden buildings, mostly black. Some are roofed in turf, some in corrugated iron, and between them a narrow ancient alley wanders. On the rocks at the end of the promontory are carved some antique initials and designs, like doodles: these are homely reminders that as late as the sixteenth century the Ting, the parliament of the Faroe Islands, met alfresco on the rocks at the end of Tinganes. Now it meets indoors, but not far away, and not with much pretension, for it occupies a building rather like an English village hall. I stood on tiptoe one day to spy through the windows of this modest power-centre, and there inside were the rows of desks, for all the world like schoolroom desks, from which the parliamentarians governed the destinies of the 47,000 islanders – together with epic paintings of Faroese history hanging inspirationally on the walls, and a big handbell for the disciplinary use, I presumed, of the Prime Minister.

The badge of Faroese nationality is the island language, which is akin to Icelandic with Gaelic touches, but behind the language there survives a host of old traditions. The Faroese build their small boats recognizably in the Viking kind, with high prows and gracefully curving hulls. They roast puffins, very deliciously I have to say. They net fulmars and snare guillemots and take their children along to slaughter pilot whales on beaches. They shear their sheep with knives. Sometimes, if they are old and male, they wear woollen hats like goblin caps. I never actually saw them chain-dancing or poem-declaiming, both hoary local pastimes, but I did repeatedly bump into groups of traditionally dressed folk-persons, buckled and aproned, on their way to or from festivals of one sort or another. 'We have been telling rhymes in Klaksvík,' one practitioner told me as we sat together on the deck of a ferry, a celestial scene of mountain and fjord streaming by. 'Long rhymes?' I ventured to ask, thinking I might be fortunate to have missed them. '*Extremely* long,' he said with pride.

## 45  *We neurotics*

Then there are the minority nations – not just enclavists, or ethnic segment-
arians, or members of compulsory federations, or islanders, but peoples who,
though clamped within the frontiers of greater States, still consider themselves
complete nations in themselves, inhabiting their native territories. They have
all been mucked about by history in one way or another. Often they were
long ago deprived of their native ruling class, and so reduced to subordinate
impotence, probably sustained as nations only by their languages, their
landscapes and their ancient monuments. It is a long time since any of these
unfortunates have grabbed complete independence for themselves, and they
have not been a threat to the peace of Europe in my time, but down the
generations their resentments stir and grumble, sometimes bursting into
activism, sometimes dormant for decades. I know the sensations well, because
the very archetype of the half-suppressed nation is my own paternal people,
the Welsh, and in some ways nobody is more characteristic of their anxieties,
resentments and neuroses than I am myself.

One of the ancient Celtic peoples of Europe, the Welsh have been subject
to English rule since 1284, but although their country has been persistently
and relentlessly Anglicized, and flooded with English settlers, still it remains
a recognizably separate place. The Welsh language may be spoken by only
a fifth of the people, but it is full of pith and enterprise, expressing itself in
everything from the traditional strict metres of the most ancient Welsh poetry
to rock lyrics and avant-garde novels; and those Welsh who do not speak
the language, having been deprived of it by the forces of history, politics and
economics, are still almost to a citizen proud of being Welsh.

But if Wales has always been a nation, it has decidedly not been a State.
Politically unsure of themselves, conditioned by centuries of scorn and
subjection, the Welsh still seem to doubt their ability to run their own affairs.
Years ago I defined the Four Torments of Wales, like the curses of a Celtic
fairy tale, and the older I got the more I realized that I was myself a victim
of them all. There was the Torment of the Confused Identity – when was
a Welshman not a Welshman; were some more Welsh than others? There
was the Torment of the Torn Tongue – the anxieties of a society ripped
apart by love, contempt, longing for or rejection of its native language and
culture. There was the torment of the Two Peoples – the ambivalence of
the Anglo-Welsh relationship, bittersweet, love-hate, never altogether frank.

And behind these conscious malaises there was the more elemental *angst* which was the Torment of Dispossession – the yearning, profound and ineradicable, for a nation's own inviolable place in the world. These are neuroses, every one, but I suspect that *mutatis mutandis* they are common to patriots in all the minority nations of Europe.

## 46  *We happy few*

They are more understandable, perhaps, in Wales than elsewhere, because the 2.8 million Welsh live beneath the immediate blast of the most powerful and corrosive cultural influence on earth – Anglo-Americanism, backed by the language, preferences, talents, techniques and hard cash of several hundred million people. It is hard to keep the flame of simple patriotism alive in the face of such a mighty onslaught. 'Where are our castles?' asked the Slovak patriot Vladimir Mináč, complaining that without their own emblems of power and authority his people were seen as a peasantry without a history. In Wales we do have some castles of our own, strongholds of our long-lost native princes, but they are far outmatched in foreigners' minds by the immense fortresses erected by the English as badges of their supremacy. When in 1981 the titular Prince of Wales, heir to the throne of England, was married to almost universal sycophancy in Westminster Abbey in London, I decided as a republican, and as a Welsh separatist too, to join a demonstration of disloyalty on a mountain called Mynydd Carn in the Preseli hills of the Welsh south-west. Rather than engage in the royalist brouhaha, we were to celebrate there the anniversary of a battle fought in 1081 between Trahaearn ap Caradog, on the one side, Gruffydd ap Cynan and Rhys ap Tewdwr on the other. It may seem an obscure alternative, but it was probably the best that anyone could find.

Rain fell persistently in Wales that day, and the few of us, we happy few, crouched in the damp lee of a rocky outcrop near the summit of the mountain to exchange mildly subversive and self-congratulatory small talk, probably noted by an infiltrator or two from the police. When we felt we had made our point we hastened down to our cars again, but I admit that as I drove away I did feel a certain sense of wasted effort: that the handful of us should have been up there on the bare and drizzly mountain, observed by nobody but ourselves, while the rest of Wales had joined the entire world around the television set, oohing and aahing at its monarchical glories. But then we were celebrating a passion, they were merely watching a soap opera – soon (as it turned out) to be sadly discredited. While there have certainly been moments when I have despaired for Wales, assumed that after 800 years of fitful resistance all was lost at last, and half-resolved to run away to Trieste, so far the nation has always come back to shame me. Sometimes I feel that we are condemned for ever to live in a political limbo, fighting always, sometimes surging forward, sometimes in dispirited retreat; but often again I feel that little by little Wales is refinding itself after all, redefining itself perhaps, and that before my children die it will be fulfilled in independence: that is to say, in the liberty to be itself.

## 47  North Britons

The Scots in the mid-1990s were in some ways more, in some ways less subject to the domination of the English, and, except for the relative weakness of the Scots Gaelic language, were just as Scottish as the Welsh are Welsh. One day in 1993 I was in Huntingdon, in southern England, and was shown the house of John Major, the Prime Minister of the United Kingdom. It was the perfect picture of your pretty English bourgeois villa, surveying a landscape as flat and ordered as a suburban back lawn. Almost immediately afterwards I drove to Scotland, and looking around me then at that spectacularly different country, so distinctive of tradition, so unmistakable of style, I marvelled at the aberration of history that allowed the kind of people who lived up there to be governed, generation after generation, by the kind of people who lived in Huntingdon. Unlike Wales, Scotland stood within the United Kingdom of its own free will, theoretically an equal member, not a subject nation, and as I travelled through the country one ineffably Scottish sight and experience after another brought home to me the anomaly of it all.

There was the sculpted Callant of Hawick, an obviously delinquent youth sitting loose-limbed on his horse, like a cowboy, and brandishing in the very spirit of reckless adventurism the flag he captured from the English in 1514. There was the terrific nineteenth-century memorial to the dead of the Black Watch regiment, in the half-ruined medieval cathedral of Dunkeld: such a furious tangle of recumbent corpses and shattered equipment, carved with such tragic passion, that it seemed to me like a Scottish *Guernica*. There was the elderly man with sparse gingery hair strolling hands in pocket towards a pub on an Edinburgh corner, followed forty or fifty yards behind by his extremely aged collie dog; sometimes the man looked round with an encouraging smile, and the dog smiled gamely back, and so they progressed in perfect rapport, like figures in a Burns poem, until the pair of them disappeared into the malty shadows of the pub. And I called on Hugh McDiarmid the great poet, Marxist and nationalist, who led me into his sweet Lanarkshire cottage over the most famous of all his lyrics, inscribed upon its threshold:

> The rose of all the world is not for me,
> I want for my part
> Only the little white rose of Scotland
> That smells sharp and sweet – and breaks the heart.

How perfectly extraordinary, I thought then, that any citizen of this singular country would *not* wish it to control its own destinies! In population Scotland was about the same size as Denmark and Finland, and bigger than Ireland or Norway. In history it was proud and fascinating. In terrain it was self-contained and majestic. It contained two of the great cities of Europe, and some of the most glorious landscapes. It was a highly educated society, full of able economists, technicians, industrialists and administrators. How could it fail? 'We have lost the fire in our bellies,' somebody told me in reply, and it was true that however patriotic the average Scot was for most of the time, when it came to national destinies he felt caution to be canny. Perhaps he distrusted the devil he did not know, even if it was his own: or perhaps he was just happy enough as he was, plodding down to the corner pub with his old dog following.

## 48  South Britons

Over the water in France the Breton patriots look with envy upon the Welsh and the Scots. They are fellow Celts, and fellow Britons too, descended from tribespeople who came from Cornwall in the sixth century. Their language is akin to Welsh, and there are always Breton scholars and artists working and wandering in Wales, and vice versa. One of the leading Welsh rock groups of the 1990s has sung many of its songs in Breton. Tourists might suppose that on the whole the South Britons were lucky, like the Serbs of Szentendre, when they emigrated across the Bay of Biscay to eat magnificent seafood on splendid unspoiled beaches, but Breton nationalists do not always agree. The French Government in Paris makes few concessions to them. The Breton language is given little encouragement, and as every year passes it retreats further and further into the enclave of the aged – even they are reluctant to talk it to strangers. It is a happy triumph for any Breton-speaking singer or actress when a contract invites her to perform, whether on stage or on the television screen, not in French but in Breton.

When I first went to Breizh – Brittany – soon after the Second World War, a murky cloud hung over the reputation of the Bretons. Like the Irish, some of their patriots had assumed that the enemy of the enemy was their friend, and that collaboration with the Nazis might be the best route to self-determination. It was a tragic delusion. Some were imprisoned after the war, some were shot, some went into exile in Wales and Ireland. Even now lingering suspicions and resentments haunt the Breton cause, and give the centralists in Paris sufficient excuse to keep the clamps on Breton nationalism. Yet the Bretons remain more recognizably themselves than any of the other Celtic minorities. High-speed trains streak from Paris to Rennes (Roazhon in the Breton language), motorways link the once remote Breton coast to the French centres of power, but powerful strains of custom and heredity still distinguish the Bretons from the French. Memories of Celtic holy men are honoured, if only by the elderly, in elaborately fretted medieval churches. *Pardons*, festivals, of local saints, are celebrated enthusiastically with processions, displays of holy relics, music and dancing. Hundreds of old women in Breton towns still wear, as everyday costumes, the high white coif of their tradition, often above long braided hair.

In the region called Bro Vigouden (Bigouden in French), in the south-west, there is a well-known clan of Breton women with genetically odd-sized legs, so that on market day you may sometimes see people limping about lopsidedly, as though they have been punished by a cruel spell in a fairy tale; the coifs of this clan have even got taller in recent years, more assertive perhaps, and are now so unwieldy that women have to bend sideways almost double to get into cars – especially awkward when they also have one leg longer than the other. In rainy weather they wear supermarket shopping-bags over the top of them. I have before me some photographs of several hundred such ladies, all of them old, assembled for a reunion at Pont an Abad (Pont l'Abbé to the French) in the 1990s, and I doubt if anywhere else in Europe at the time could have offered such a spectacle: severe, tough, creased faces peering back at me from below their peculiar head-dresses – the braided hair of

maidens on septuagenarian widows – fringed shawls and embroidered lace
– the towering white forest of coifs swaying and bobbing, this way and that,
as the company limped towards its celebratory victuals.

## 49  *Wanting an old lady*

Perhaps in the end a few such quirks, and some odds and ends of folklore,
will be all that is left of Bretonism, but for the moment there remain echoes
at least of the Celtic culture, very old, holy and serene. In the 1970s my small
daughter and I looked up from the waterfront of Douarnenez to see an old
woman smiling down at us from an upstairs window. She was not wearing
that white coif, but she had a shawl around her shoulders, her face was
infinitely wrinkled, and her smile was so kind that it seemed to be coming
to us from different times altogether – before the Fall perhaps. 'I want that
lady,' my small daughter said.

## 50  *Heart in a hard city*

The most vivid of the European minority nations are the Catalans, one of
the five or six peoples long ago subjected to the supremacy of Castilian Spain.
They had an empire of their own once, and they were always a tough and
brilliant lot – history tells of few fiercer, more arrogant, more merciless and
more often victorious soldiers than the fourteenth-century mercenaries called
the Grand Company of Catalans. They are just as hard and successful
now, the great achievers among the European minorities, and their capital,
Barcelona, is the minority capital *par excellence*. Half the influences that have
moulded the continent have touched down in Barcelona at one time or
another. The Greeks and the Romans were there; Spaniards and Frenchmen
and Italians have left their mark – ideologies from Catholicism to anarchism,
tastes of the Provençals, manners of the Moors, all heated up, enriched,
spiced and garlicked by the peculiar pungent genius of the Catalans. I have
disliked the city for thirty-five years, but I cannot deny its buzz.

I spent the Christmas of 1994 in Barcelona, and patriotic buzz was everywhere. The city was in Spain, but only just of it. In the Plaça Sant Jaume
the offices of a genuine Catalan Government, with real authority, flew

the Catalan flag in a properly sovereign style. The Catalan language was ubiquitous, and people who did not speak it seemed a little embarrassed to be asked. By the standards of minority capitals Barcelona seemed to me astonishingly self-confident, conscious of its status as the metropolis of a vigorous industrial country with its own history, its own language, its own literature, its own architecture, and most decidedly its own character.

I wish I could say I relished that character, but I didn't. There was not much on the surface of things that moved me or gave me hope. I disliked the little-black-dressed and waistcoated rich, all heritage and condescension, to be seen taking tea on squashy sofas at the Ritz. I distrusted the gangs of bravoes urgently traversing the Plaça de Catalunya, or riding their motor-bikes sinisterly muffled down side-alleys. I felt no spontaneous emanations of human warmth and geniality when I wandered into the city's cafés and brasseries. I missed, in short, the consolation of kind hearts *en masse*. Of course these were subjective responses of the most simplistic kind – people who live in Barcelona swear to me they love it. All the same, it came as an unexpected relief to me that afternoon when I chanced to see an elderly lady in a red coat, flanked by an attentive young couple, walking vigorously but a little stooped towards the Rambla. She looked frail, I thought. She looked somehow too gentle for Barcelona. The passing pedestrians took no notice of her – why should they? – and it was almost like a hallucination when, as she drew nearer, I realized her to be Lady Thatcher, the former Iron Lady of Europe. Vicious opponent though I was, to an almost Catalan degree, of Thatcherism and all it represented, I was touched and even strangely comforted to see her there. She seemed to be paying particular attention to heroic statues.

## 51  *A Lapp artist*

The Lapps are more often called the Sami now, but you know who I mean – those befurred short people, in flapped hats and trousers tied with thongs, so often to be seen in pictures driving their reindeer across the tundra of Norway, Sweden and Finland. In the 1950s they were still all known as Lapps, and a sturdy group of them gave me a kind welcome when I walked into their settlement somewhere around Kiruna, in northern Sweden, where I had wandered off from the guest-house of a local iron-ore mine. They were seasonal nomads, and had settled there with their herds for the winter.

They took me to their school, and I was astonished by the beauty of the pictures one boy was painting, bold of composition, limpid of colour. I bought one, and its solemn creator, five or six years old, signed it carefully on the back for me. It showed, in a semi-abstract way, a pale, cold, extremely Lappish landscape with reindeer, and spoke to me so hauntingly of those Arctic horizons, the very lip and antithesis of Europe, that for years afterwards it hung in my house, until its paper browned and its colours faded. I put it away then, sentimentally, wondering where those reindeer were grazing now, and what had become of the little Lapp artist.

## 52  A propagandist

Nobody has ever baffled me like the Basques did when I first went to their country in 1962, under Franco's dictatorship. They seemed to me at once raw and mystic. I understood not a word of their esoteric language, the use of which was officially discouraged anyway. The very place-names of the country – Oxocelhaya, Itxassou – made me feel I had somehow strayed out of Europe altogether. At first I thought the Basques entirely materialist. In the towns every other building seemed to be a bank, and everywhere groups of businessmen discussed what I took to be contracts or stock prices in sober grey suits over plates of eel-spawn. In the country, life seemed to be almost mechanically practical, and visiting a farmhouse was rather like opening the windows in an Advent card: here to reveal the farmer oiling his scythe, there his wife stirring the soup, the daughter of the house sewing in one room, the son at his homework in another, and handily available in the middle of the building a couple of milking cows.

But I presently became aware of a more emotional streak in the Euzkadi, as the Basques call themselves. Twenty-five years before there had briefly been a Basque Republic, suppressed by General Franco when he won the Spanish Civil War, and now and then I had come across its relics: a faded patriotic poster, escaping the vigilance of the Guardia Civil, a postage stamp, a banknote pushed wryly to the back of a drawer, about as worthless as a currency could be. Over the border in France there was still a Basque Government in Exile, but within Spain Basque nationalism seemed to be permanently stifled.

Then I came to Guernica, from time immemorial the shrine of Basque liberties, where for centuries an Euzkadi parliament had sat in sovereignty.

In 1937 German bombers had destroyed the centre of it, on Franco's behalf, and since then it had obviously been deliberately run down. It was a sad sight to see. All the virtue seemed to have left the Oak of Guernica, successor to a pedigree of trees which had been sacred to the Basques since at least the fourteenth century. The remains of its shrine were dusty and forlorn. Grass grew in the cracks of the legislative benches all around. To restore the place would clearly be an act of hostility to the Spanish State, and if anyone tried, I thought, in no time at all he would be in one of the Generalissimo's jails. As I stood meditating there, a large man in a long blue greatcoat engaged me in conversation: and when I tentatively raised the subject of the Basque identity he was not in the least inhibited after all. On the contrary, he explained it all to me in a booming and grandiloquent voice that must be audible, I nervously thought, as far as Madrid itself. He would tell me what the Basques were, cried this reckless patriot, and he would tell me what they were not. I wrote his words down word verbation in my notebook, and this is what he shouted. 'We are NOT a region, NOT a group of provinces, NOT a language, NOT a folk tradition, but a NATION, EUZKADI, THE NATION OF THE BASQUES!!!'

## 53 *The grunt beyond the mystery*

When I next came to the Basque country, fifteen years later, things had greatly changed. The aged Franco had relaxed his grip, the Basque language was less severely proscribed, and a surge of Euzkadi nationalism was now inescapable. Fiery sermons were being preached. Police clashed with pro-testers at violent demonstrations. There were strikes which were hardly strikes, really, but patriotic gestures. A Basque underground army, an army of terrorists to its opponents, was fighting with bombs and machine-guns a perpetual war against Spanish authority. I was far more aware this time of yet another side of Basqueness, the grunt beyond the mystery: the brutal energy which had made this people pre-eminent in every kind of crude contest – the chasing of bulls through the streets of Pamplona – the trapping of migrating pigeons in Pyrenean passes – the awful sport called goose-game in which a live goose was hung head-down from a wire, and men tried to decapitate it with their bare hands – the thrilling energy of pelota – the innumerable Basque competitions of strength or appetite, beer-swilling, log-chopping, stone-cutting, steak-eating. So it was to be for the rest of the twentieth century, as the unappeasable Basque patriots fought on for their liberty, once again achieving autonomy of a kind but never relaxing the fury of their demands. Whenever I read of another arrest or explosion, another set of dirty tricks by the police, another terrorist ambush, I remembered that bawling propagandist at Guernica.

## 54 The unchosen

The old Ottoman Empire, before the First World War, was officially said to include seventeen and a half nationalities. The half was the nation of the Gypsies – to whom it has only in my own time become the courtesy to give a capital G – and they remain a nation that is not a nation, a nation without frontiers, without a capital, without a homeland, without myths, without heroes, without monuments, without a Book. There are Gypsies and Gypsies, of course, and in some parts of Europe the oriental Romany strain has been so diluted that it is hard to know the difference between a Gypsy and a tinker, traveller or layabout. Over much of the continent, nevertheless, the name of 'Gypsy' means much what it always meant, and incites persecutions and even pogroms to this day – the inherited reaction, since classical times at least, of the settled to the nomadic. Especially in eastern Europe the Gypsies have born the brunt of prejudice. If they could not be exterminated, as the Nazis wanted, surely they could be turned into ordinary citizens like everyone else! The Polish Communists forced them into settlement, calling the process 'The Great Halt'. The Albanian Communists herded them into tenement blocks. The Bulgarian Communists forbade all mention of them, ignored them in census, and made them change their names. Nothing seemed to work. By the 1990s there were said to be some 8 million Gypsies – the biggest and fastest-growing minority people in Europe.

Various Gypsy institutions had come into being, in attempts to give some more conventional nationhood to the race – in the elections for the Bucharest City Council in 1996 the Gypsies' National Party got 1 per cent of the vote, rather less than the Motorists' National Party; but anyway no uniform of State, no lapel badge or armband, could be more unmistakable than the all but indefinable splash of bright colour which was the mark of the Gypsy still. In every country the Gypsies were among the least-educated people: what a prodigious source of talent had gone neglected! In some parts of the continent they were universal scapegoats too, and almost everything, from

petty thieving to State corruption, was blamed on them. In Romania especially,
by then the centre of gravity of European Gypsydom, every conversation
seemed to get around to something the Gypsies had squatted in, spoiled,
infested or were likely at any moment to steal. When I once surmised that
perhaps their ill-treatment by the dictator Nicolae Ceauşescu had something
to do with their own behaviour, *pshaw!* they said – everyone knew Ceauşescu
was a Gypsy himself.

## 55  *The romantics*

I was always a sucker for the romance of this disturbing people. In 1953 I
wrote some articles about Gypsies for the London *Times,* and spent some
time searching them out. In those days continental Gypsies sometimes crossed
the English Channel in the course of their wanderings, the Romany language
was quite widely spoken in Britain, and everything about the English Gypsies
charmed me. I attended a Gypsy funeral in the marshes of Essex, where the
wooden caravan of an old lady was ritually put to the flames, like a Viking
longboat. Gravely around the pyre stood all the members of her tribe – and
tribes there really were then, sharing the old English Gypsy names, Lee,
Boswell, Hearne, Stanley, and unmistakably allied in the brown, big-nosed,
dark-eyed, solemn dignity of their faces. 'I don't believe in God,' a Hampshire
lady told me, 'but I believe in the Blessed Lord because I've seen his photo.'
Another observed, 'Whenever I make myself a cup of tea I looks up to
Heaven and I says, "Very much obliged to you."' I learnt to admire and
envy the Gypsy ways. I made a pilgrimage to the grave of Abram Wood,
the most famous of the Gypsy harpers of Wales, who was buried heroically
in 1799 high above the sea at Llangelynnin – outside the church porch. Every
Christmas I went out in the countryside around our house to share a whisky
with an old Gypsy couple who still lived literally in the hedgerows, protected
only by a crude canvas sheet among the prickles.

I loved the dazzle of the Gypsies, too. I was bowled over in the 1960s by
the theatrical allure of the Sacromonte people, in their caves at Granada in
Spain – bold, insolent, magnificent people, I thought, whose heel-stamping,
castanet-clicking, nasal-voiced dances may have been, as cynics so often told
me, devised especially for the tourist trade, but which seemed to me to come
straight from their irrepressible hearts. I loved to stumble across one of those
great splashes of muddle, life, dust and colour that was a Gypsy encampment.

There was one on the Argolis shore near Nauplia in Greece, down the road from Mycenae: the people lived beside the sea in big circular tents, like Mongols, and there was a lively coming and going of Gypsy women with their baskets from town, and youths lounged against tent-poles as they lounge in old pictures of the Levant, and there were old cars here and there, and carts, and a wide gallimaufry of panache beside the blue water of the gulf. And what of the Gypsy violinists of eastern Europe, who so miraculously ignored the drab norms of Communism? They brought to their art a marvellous mixture of cynicism, mischief, arrogance and collusion, flinging out across their café tables a sort of defiance – challenging their dazed audiences to call their bluff or dare dispute their supremacy, with much the same charm and grace that Charlie Chaplin undoubtedly inherited from his Gypsy grandmother. They were hardly trying to please. They were expressing their own liberty and superiority, like kings in disguise. Nothing was more inspiriting, in the dark days of Hungarian Communism, than to walk along to the old Gellért Hotel in Buda, a faded prodigy of art nouveau, and hear the Gypsy fiddlers soaring and diving through their melodies: and thirty years later I most gratefully slipped a few notes into the carefully sited jacket pocket of a Bulgarian virtuoso – while the music played on.

## 56  Sight-reading

In the ill-lit pedestrian tunnel that went under the Elbe at Dresden, in Germany, I once heard ahead of me strains of those same violins, from a couple of Gypsies playing Viennese waltzes. I was in a stingy mood, and determined to give them nothing. As it happened there was nobody else in the tunnel at that moment, and as I passed the musicians, still eloquently playing, I felt their eyes thoughtfully following me. I was decidedly self-conscious, knowing very well that I ought to put something in the open violin-case at their feet, and as I walked towards the daylight my resolution wavered. 'You should be ashamed of yourself,' said I to myself, so when I emerged into the open I dug a few coins out of my purse and re-entered the tunnel. Melodies from the Vienna woods were still sounding in its twilight, and the Gypsies were not in the least surprised to see me back. They had read me like a book, and were expecting me. I put my coins in their violin-case, and they both bowed courteously, without a smile. I bowed back in admiration.

## 57  *In a woodland glade*

But there is no pretending that everything about the Gypsies fits my romantic
fancies, and even my sympathies were strained when I drove one day in the
1960s, with a car full of my family, into a woodland glade in the interior of
Corfu. It was such a glade as plays are set in, banks where the wild thyme
blew, gnarled old olives like oaks in Windsor Park, and I stopped the car
with a view to having a picnic. Instantly there fell upon us a posse of savage
Gypsy women, from their tents and caravans in the woods. These were not
the patrician Lees and Boswells of my memories, graceful violinists or stately
Welsh harpers! These were scrabbling, raggedy, predatory primitives, dressed
in vivid torn cottons, holding babies as monkeys hold them, swarmed around
by children, banging on the car, clutching at the door-handles, pushing their
thin grasping hands through the open windows. To the begging demands
of the Gypsies outside were added the banshee yells of my terrified children
within: and so, hooting my horn furiously, skidding wildly through the
undergrowth, I put my foot down and got the hell out of there.

Alas, by the 1990s a more muted image of those woodland furies was the
general image of Europe's Gypsies. The endearing sales talk of the old
door-to-door clothes-peg seller or iron merchant had become, in most
people's minds, the threatening whine of the street mendicant. Technology
had deprived the Gypsies of their ancient crafts: poverty had made them turn
more and more to petty crime. By now they haunted the railway stations of
half the continent. They swarmed the streets of Bucharest. They were the
street-thieves of Prague and Sofia. They touched one's shoulder, feather-light,
as they begged in the streets of Tirana. They camped in the undeveloped
bomb-sites of Berlin. I found them once squatting in the very heart of the
European Community, among the tower blocks of the Brussels bureaucracy.
If you wanted to hear how Europeans had talked about Jews before
the Second World War, you had only to hear them talking about Gypsies
sixty years on. My own archetypal Gypsy figures of the 1990s were the
groups of children who prowled the streets of Rome, seizing upon likely
tourists to mouth their stylized litanies of hard luck, catching hold of skirts
and coat-tails, scurrying and dancing from one side to the other, scampering
off like shadows when they were thwarted in their pickpocketing. Poor little
souls, they held cardboard boxes in front of them, the better to hide their
thieving fingers.

## 58  *The chosen*

Last in this parade of the exceptions, paradoxes and anomalies that have so complicated and enlivened my vision of Europe – last to appear but, as in the old music-halls, top of the bill – must come the Jews. They entered Europe long, long ago, and they were like the comets of this continent, repeatedly streaking through its history in brilliance and in tragedy. They were its allegorical familiars, a 'headstrong, moody, murmuring race', as the English poet John Dryden said of them in the seventeenth century. Their great men and women reached the summits of Europe – socially, economically, intellectually, artistically. Their poor were among the poorest of all, and from the *shtetls* of Poland to the tenements of London's East End the image of the Jew was the image of deprivation. It was also the image of the stranger: however profoundly assimilated, however successful and admired, the Jew remained the outsider. His religion if he had one, his appearance, his temperament, the impression he gave of wider and older loyalties, the mystery that so often seemed to surround him, the envy he inspired, the Christian superstitions that branded him an enemy of the faith, the conspiratorial legends that had been built up around his people down the centuries – they all combined to make him the ultimate loner of Europe.

And I write in the past tense because in the end they all combined, too, to destroy him. The emblematic tragedy of twentieth-century Europe, changing the very nature of the continent, was the deliberate extermination of Jewry at the hands of the Nazis and their sympathizers, which has meant that during my fifty years the Jews of Europe have been mostly ghosts. Wherever I go I find them, in vanished ghettos and in concentration camps, and I hear their sad melodies from hotel balconies, and wander among city streets somehow missing their salt.

## 59  *The Jew's House*

I walked one day along the coastal path that leads to the famously picturesque Cornish village of Polperro, now one of the great tourist sites of southern England, not so long ago a remote fishing-port speaking its own Celtic language. Hardly had I entered the little town, past its picture-postcard fishing-harbour, where a large cat sat licking itself on the mud of a low tide, than I saw on the wall of an ancient building a noble proclamation: 'The Jew's House'. The words thrilled and fascinated me. Who was that Jew? How did he ever come to live in this distant corner of a western island? Did he move around that waterfront in black hat and ringlets? Were bar mitzvahs once celebrated in his cream-tea cottage? Might I have once seen through his narrow windows the seven-branched candelabrum of Israel? What became of him in the end? Was he burnt, or banished, or did his seed gradually mingle down the generations with the alien corn, until his very Jewishness was lost, and he was remembered only by those enigmatic words on the house by the harbour?

I was later assured that the words were really a corrupt translation of old Cornish – Tŷ Io, 'Thursday House' – and nothing to do with Jews at all. This did nothing to change the emotions I felt that day. For me there had been a Jew of Polperro, if not historically at least figuratively, and he can stand for me as an epitome of his people. Even in my time, when so many of the Jews had been murdered or dispersed, I could find their traces and sometimes their lingering presence in the remotest parts of the continent, where they had often arrived long before in threes and fours, a couple of families here, a solitary entrepreneur there. Into my own corner of Wales, in the peninsula called Llŷn that protrudes into the Irish Sea, the family of Pollecoffs (probably once Polyakoffs of Poland or Russia) long ago found their mysterious way, to become leading citizens of a district that could hardly have been more foreign to them: in the 1990s, though the last of the family had gone, still the name of their draper's shop – Pollecoffs of Pwllheli – resounded through the columns of our telephone directory.

## 60 *Dust in the temple*

Even in Wales, a country not generally xenophobic, the Jews have had their troubles. In Pwllheli the Pollecoffs provided mayors for the town, but at the industrial end of Wales, during the Depression of the 1930s, the handful of Jewish shopkeepers sometimes found themselves scorned and persecuted. Still, it was nothing compared to the unimaginable swell of hatred which fell upon the Jews of Germany at the same time, and upon all the Jews of continental Europe soon after. I had little idea, when I first sat upon that bollard in Trieste, about the scale of the tragedy that had befallen this people – and certainly no premonition that for the rest of my life their fate would dog my footsteps around the continent. My first immediate intimation of the Shoah, the Holocaust, came when, wandering all uninformed around Trieste, I came to the immense and magnificent synagogue of the city. It was built to a cathedral scale – Mr Bultoen of Antwerp would have been proud of it. Its structure breathed cultivated wealth and confidence, because the Jews of Trieste had long been financiers and *commerçants* of international influence. By the 1900s, when that great building went up, they controlled much of the trade passing through the chief port of the Austro-Hungarian Empire, and into their hands and networks Vienna itself entrusted its interests. Brilliant Jews from Freud to Svevo had lived and worked in the city: even Mr Bloom of *Ulysses* might be said to be half Triestino, since James Joyce created much of the character when he was living here.

However, when I crept tentatively into the synagogue that day (for I had never been in a synagogue before), I found it in a state of misery. All its sheen was gone. Its fabric was decaying, and even its holiness seemed somehow half-hearted. Dust lay everywhere. I was not altogether surprised to find it in this state – most things in Europe were in a state of neglect or abeyance anyway, waiting to be revived – but I remember still the black shock I experienced when the reason for its condition dawned upon me: that almost all the Jews of Trieste, almost every one, had been taken away and murdered.

## 61 *The void*

I suppose the shades of murdered Jewry will haunt Europe for centuries. If nothing else, the remains of the Nazi concentration camps will see to that. Some are just desolate and abandoned sites, some are museums. Some are in forlorn brown landscapes of Poland, some close to exquisitely civilized cities of Germany itself. Coachloads of visitors go to visit them, in mourning or in voyeurism, and Jews from the four corners make their pilgrimages to the places of sacrifice – for as a sacrifice I long ago taught myself to think of it, a terrible and inexplicable atonement for us all. When I was young I considered the Shoah a totally meaningless expression of evil, but I came to see it as an allegorical burnt-offering. I was once walking towards the entrance gate of Buchenwald when a big group of tourists had just arrived. They were milling this way and that, trying to get the hang of the place, some making for the bookshop, some for the film-show, talking in many languages, but through their agitated forms I saw sitting on a bench a solitary impassive figure, absolutely still and silent. He was patently a Jew. He sat there immobile, like a statue: and it was only when the crowd had dispersed, and he was left all alone there on his bench, that I saw him remove the spectacles from his eyes, to wipe the tears away.

For years after the war I used to notice, on the wrists of academics or of fellow travellers in buses, the tattoo marks of the concentration camps. They reminded me of Masons with their secret handshakes. By the 1970s I hardly ever saw those fateful brands. Most of the survivors had gone to join the murdered, and all over Europe they had left a sad void behind them. Jewishness had all but abandoned the continent – if not as absolutely as the Nazis wanted it, at least on a scale to make some of the oldest and most historic places *judenfrei*. Only a handful of Jews was left in the famous Jewish Town of Prague, where the tombs of a thousand years were tumbled together in the heart of the old ghetto, littered still with mourning-stones. At Vilnius in Lithuania, 'the Jerusalem of eastern Europe', virtually the whole Jewish community had been murdered in the extermination camp of Paneriai, only a few miles outside the city: the celebrated Great Synagogue and its library had been destroyed, together with some ninety-five smaller temples, and a Jewish quarter once famous for its culture and learning had been utterly expunged, only its street names remaining. If the city of Amsterdam somehow seemed short of pith or irony, it was because its Jews were gone. In Berlin an entire wealthy, cultivated and patriotic community, once vital to the nature of the capital, had vanished for ever. In the innumerable *shtetls* of Poland scarcely a Jew remained. One could easily travel from one end of the continent to another, through half a dozen ancient capitals, without seeing evidence of a living Jewish presence.

What must it have been like, then, to be a Jew of a certain age revisiting Europe after the Second World War and remembering all the life and variety of Jewishness that was lost? I have imagined sometimes how it would be to come home to my own country and find my people gone. Gone the little group of veterans on their bench outside the lifeboat station – dead the pubs where the Welshmen go – abandoned Siop Newydd the grocer, and Medical Hall the chemist's shop on the corner of Stryd Fawr – Twm Morys and his poetry only a memory – nobody left to sing the old songs. No longer would cheerful Dewi the Post come bustling up Trefan lane, or the old ladies sit in their gossiping rows at the health clinic. The Welsh language would be for ever silent, the chapels defaced, and all my dear friends and neighbours would be mere shadows in the streets of our *shtetl*.

## 62  *What did I expect?*

As the twentieth century approached its end, I found everywhere signs of
resurgence, among the remaining European Jews. Lucky Britain, of course,
had never lost its Jews, and only in the 1990s, as month by month the London
obituaries recorded the passing of yet another eminent Jewish citizen, did I
really realize what a prodigious influx of refugees had enriched the national
life since the 1930s. But elsewhere in Europe too, although there were still
attacks on synagogues and desecrations of Jewish graves, in general it seemed
to me that the Jews had regained their confidence. The virile example of
Israel, like it or not, had helped to expunge the old images of Jews in their
millions going passive to the slaughter: as was said even by Guy de Rothschild,
the banker, Israel had liberated 'part of our inner ego'. The immense power
of American Jewry was like money in the bank for the remaining European
Jews, and the very idea of Jewishness, for so long a slur or an accusation, had
acquired glamour and prestige. The ghetto at Venice – the original ghetto,
which I remembered as a dingy and half-abandoned semi-slum – had become
a sight of the city, its synagogues restored and active, its treasures proudly
displayed. The diamond district of Antwerp, one of the most important in
the world, hummed once more with the activity of its Jewish cutters,
polishers, sawyers and choppers – a proper Jewish quarter come to life again.
Eighty thousand Jews lived in Budapest, making it once again among the
great Jewish cities of Europe, and their towered Great Synagogue had been
magnificently restored. In Gibraltar Jews were prosperous and influential. In
Prague the tiny remnant of that Jewish Town, almost as stifled under
the Communists as it had been under the Nazis, had been miraculously
regenerated as a community, and thousands of respectful tourists passed
through its cemeteries and synagogues. In Vilnius a few thousand Jews had
returned, a solitary synagogue was active again, a National Jewish Museum
had been started, and there was a kosher restaurant – 'call in advance for
group bookings'. In Kazimierz, the old ghetto of Kraków, tourists flocked
to eat kosher luncheons in the reconstructed square, to visit the new Jewish
Cultural Centre, to follow the trail of Steven Spielberg's holocaust film
*Schindler's List*, to place their reverent stones upon the grave of the holy
Rabbi Remu'h, or to go on tours to Auschwitz. In Bratislava, where most
of the Jews were murdered or deported by the Nazis, where the Jewish
district beneath the castle had been destroyed by the Communists, and where

there was still a rumorous suggestion of anti-Semitism, there arose on the very site of the old quarter a spanking modern pension, Chez David, strictly kosher, gleamingly comfortable, and much in demand among tourists Jewish and Gentile. At Tomar in Portugal they told me that the little synagogue had recently celebrated its first Yom Kippur since 1497, when Jews had either to leave the country or convert to Christianity: families forcibly converted then were reverting to Judaism, and 'secret Jews' who had semi-clandestinely kept the faith through all those centuries were coming into the open again. Lights were hopefully shining in the synagogue at Sarajevo, when I passed by one dismal evening in 1996. In post-Franco Spain I found a cantor from North Africa giving a singing lesson next door to his synagogue high in a modern office block. In post-Fascist Turin I learnt for the first time that the shining pinnacled Mole Antonelliana, which towers above the city as its universally recognized emblem, had begun life as a spectacular project for a synagogue. Even in Germany, though pathetically few and sometimes abused by louts, the Jews presently recovered their assurance. Years ago, from my bedroom window at the Kempinski Hotel, on Kurfürstendamm in West Berlin, I used to look directly down upon the Jewish Community Centre. It incorporated the doorway of a synagogue that had stood on the site until it was burnt by the Nazis in 1938, and was then almost the only Jewish institution still active in the city. Even then I was amazed at the evident wealth and certainty of the Jews who used to arrive to enter its gates, elegantly on foot or swishily in their expensive cars. But what did I expect? Striped suits of the concentration camps? Ghetto rags?

## 63  *The frisson*

Up a dingy flight of stairs in Vienna I went to visit Dr Simon Wiesenthal, the Nazi-hunter. He seemed to me in every way a figure from the past. For one thing he was unmistakably a Jew from the pre-war Europe, a Polish Jew, a survivor of the camps. Short, balding, in his seventies, he was surrounded in his cluttered room by certificates of merit and scrolls of gratitude, for he was an award-winning Nazi-hunter. Then again, he was implacable in a way that younger European Jews I had met no longer were: they were unforgetting, of course, but did not harbour revenge. Wiesenthal undoubtedly did. He would call it retribution, and he had devoted his life to tracking down the last of the Nazi murderers and seeing that they were punished – year after year, decade after decade, while those once-swaggering SS men grew frail and forgetful, and Wiesenthal himself entered old age fired still by his tireless and merciless search for justice. If he had anything to do with it, he said, no single Nazi murderer, however old and grey, would ever be allowed to die in peace. I thought his office, up above Salztorstrasse, unforgettably baleful. The files that filled its walls were dreadful files of death and torture. Wiesenthal talked disturbingly about wicked men still alive and flourishing in Europe. Just along the road was the old Jewish quarter of Vienna, and its concomitant the Gestapo headquarters.

Many people, and not only Jews, greatly admired Dr Wiesenthal. Many more, and not only Gentiles, disliked him, and feared what he stood for. Not least the Viennese, whose communal conscience about the Jews was less than clear, very much wished he would go somewhere else. There had been an attempt on his life a few weeks before my visit, and a police guard had reluctantly been given him. That day's sentry looked up at me as I left Wiesenthal's office. He was a blond long-haired youth with a gun on his lap, lounging there on a bench with his feet on a chair, chewing something: and as he insolently stared at me, and at the old gentleman saying goodbye to me at the door, I felt an uneasy frisson.

# 3

## NATIONS, STATES AND BLOODY POWERS

*

*As I say, in Trieste, or Trst as the Slovenes prefer, or Triest as the Austrians have it, you are not quite sure what nation you are among. If a nation can be defined as an amalgam of ethnicity, language, history and landscape, or as James Joyce's Mr Bloom more succinctly thought 'the same people living in the same place', then the nationality of Trieste is far from absolute, and when the city soccer team plays elsewhere in Italy its players are sometimes sneered at as Slavs or Germans. As the Mayor exclaimed to me, one day in the 1970s, 'We are the furthest limit of Latinity, the southern extremity of Germanness' – he could have said a western protrusion of Slavness too, but that might have been politically incorrect. When I first came here Trieste's Statehood was just as debatable. The Yugoslavs had some claim to it by force majeure (they had played a powerful part in forcing the Germans and Italian Fascists out), by history (they had been fellow citizens, with the Triestini, of the lost Habsburg Empire) and by blood (outside the city centre most of Trieste's people were Slovene). The Italians could claim it because it had been in more ancient times an Italian seaport, and because they had been awarded it as spoils of victory after the First World War. History had thrown it about between sovereignties, and was still tossing it then – in 1947 it was declared a free territory under United Nations protection, almost a State itself, and only in 1954 did the city become once more part of Italy.*

*Who can really take Statehood seriously, in such a place? It is fashionable in late-twentieth-century Europe, as it struggles towards (or against) unity, to talk about Nation-States, as though nations and States were synonymous. They seldom are really. One of the very States which was squabbling about Trieste fifty years ago is a State no longer, and turns out to have been no more than a jumble of nations forcibly fused – Orthodox Serbs, Catholic Croatians, Muslim Bosnians, Kosovo Albanians, Slovenes, Montenegrins, Macedonians, all given the same passport and called Yugoslavs. Trieste attracts mavericks and outsiders because here they can feel (speciously, I fear) beyond the constraints of the Nation-State. Karl Marx once reported that the place had been built up by 'a motley crew of . . . Italians, Germans, English, French, Greeks, Armenians and Jews'. 'In Trieste, ah Trieste, ate I my liver,' wrote Joyce of his residence in the city; the phrase is really a translation of a local idiom – eating one's liver means eating one's heart out – but somehow it does seem to express the seaport's sense of esoteric enclave.*

*There are not many places in Europe that give me this feeling. The continent has generally been dominated by a few self-important States that diplomacy and history call Powers, and over the years, as I have become more and more loyal to Wales,* which is not even a State, let alone a Power, I have found myself increasingly exasperated by their childish arrogances. Powers come and go, rise and fall, but in their fortunately transient climactic days they lord it over nations and States alike, and the war memorials of Trieste tragically and nonsensically illustrate the effects. The memorials mostly date from the First World War, when the Italian Kingdom was fighting the Austro-Hungarian Empire (both undeniable Powers in those days), and their names are nationally meaningless – Borgello side by side with Brunner, Silvestro with Liebmann, Zanetti with Zottig and Blotz, so that it is hard to know which side any of them died for. As for the figure of the naval officer outside the Marine Terminal, it represents an Italian Triestino who fought for Italy, was captured by the Austrians who then ruled the place, and was accordingly shot for treason (a class of crime I myself decline to recognize).

'And so it goes on for ages and aeons,' wrote Ogden Nash, 'between these neighboring Europeans . . .' What a farce it has all been! The prejudices of nations have been bad enough, and the ambitions of States, but the bloody Powers have been the curse of Europe.

## 1 *The small Swiss coin*

I was on a troop train on my way from the English Channel to Italy. The Second World War having been won, the Swiss Government now allowed the victorious Western Powers to pass their armies through its neutral territory, and a marvel of the journey was to emerge briefly from the blighted and dingy landscapes of the warring States into a Switzerland that still looked *creamy*. Nothing could be more glamorous than the neon advertising signs, in reds and blues and yellows, that I was seeing almost for the first time in my life, and I remember how shamelessly, when the train passed through the lakeside suburbs of Lausanne, I peered through the windows of apartments to catch glimpses of the well-lit padded comforts within. When we drew into Lausanne station smiling Swiss ladies were waiting for us with cisterns of hot coffee, buns and sandwiches – miraculous sandwiches of white Swiss bread, light and crusty, like manna after several years of our brownish wartime kind.

Just as the train began to move on, while I hung out of the window absorbing these novel scenes, I caught the eye of a small well-dressed man standing indecisively on the platform. Shyly smiling, he hastened towards me. The train gathered speed. The man burst into a trot. The train went faster. The man lost his smile and ran. He held out his hand to me. I held mine out in return. The train got into its swing. The man panted anxiously. I stretched as far as I could out of my window. Our hands touched, just in time, and there passed from one to the other a small Swiss silver coin. It was not a valuable coin, but as a token it was priceless. Surely he meant it as a token? I clasped it sentimentally anyway, and waved my thanks as long as the man was still in sight – standing there motionless now, unsmiling, indistinctly raising his small white hand in response.

## 2 *State of nations*

He might have spoken French, German, Italian or Romansh, but he certainly thought of himself as Swiss – as Swiss as the coin itself, which appeared to be new-minted. The Swiss are the one people who have given dignity to the idea of the Nation-State by turning it into a State of Nations, to my mind a model for us all. They have not compromised either their Statehood or their nationhoods. Their four languages remain more or less inviolate, but in all their autonomous cantons the Swiss are the Swiss are the Swiss.

Yet they are not universally admired in the rest of Europe. In the nineteenth century the world seems to have regarded the Helvetic Confederation with almost fulsome respect. Its citizens were sturdy mountaineers and farmers, nature's gentlemen. They could teach even Victorian Britain something when it came to mighty works of engineering, and they were a nation of soldiers too, every man with his own gun above the mantelpiece. However, they preferred not to fight in either of the two world wars, and this rather altered their reputation. Neutrality enabled the Swiss not only to evade the tragedies which had befallen the rest of Europe, but even to profit from them, and by the time I came to Europe the notion of Swissness had come to seem a less noble abstraction. The English in particular now scornfully resented it. Few phrases have more exactly expressed a historical resentment than the famous remark in Carol Reed's film *The Third Man* (1949), about the creativity of the Swiss: 'They had 500 years of democracy and peace, and what did that produce? The cuckoo clock.'

The Victorians would have been astonished by this calumny, but Britons have been quoting it ever since. Nobody had yet heard it when our troop train passed through, but many of the officers on board would certainly have relished it, even as they accepted their coffee from those courteous volunteers: it perfectly expressed the sour judgement of a battle-scarred, impoverished imperial kingdom of epic suffering and performance upon a comfortable, well-heeled, chocolatey republic which hadn't done a damned thing to help save civilization as we knew it.

### 3 *Style and the Swiss*

The more elegant would doubtless have sneered at the Swiss as unstylish, too, and it is true that for years after the war the Swiss bourgeoisie seemed resolutely determined never to break out of the ordinary. (Mussolini, who despised the ordinary, had called theirs 'a sausage-making democracy'.) But actually Swissness can be truly splendid. Swiss bridges are wonderful, especially the lovely spans with which the engineer Robert Maillart gave an unprecedented beauty to concrete. Swiss chalets, though relentlessly trivialized by developers and speculative builders, and made the architectural equivalent of the cuckoo clock, can be magnificent objects – stately homes *par excellence*, built for men of stature by master craftsmen, heroic homes, as strong as they are hospitable, and sometimes inhabited by the same family for centuries. The high mountain passes of Switzerland, with their superb roads and brilliantly lit tunnels, their railway lines circling and recircling in the hearts of mountains, their crowning forts, their tremendous sense of scale, purpose and infallible calculation, are like the constructions of a super-Power, not of a petty land-locked republic. A tall-funnelled steamer of the Swiss lakes may look quaint at a distance, but when it comes into port it is an ensemble of grandeur, swanky as can be, and the very image of competence. I find something grand in the Swiss Army too, with all its half-hidden bunkers and hangars: especially at weekends when the citizen soldiery turns out in the mountains, polishing its saddles at cavalry depots among the trees, clambering up hill-tracks in pairs with radio aerials flopping, or reverberating the thunder of its artillery in impossibly inaccessible valleys. It has scarcely fired a shot in anger for 150 years, but then that is what is grand about it.

## 4  New Model Swiss

By the 1990s the Swiss were much more stylish, anyway. In some Swiss ski-resorts there is a Kinderland, and on the slopes around it New Model Children, raised to modern perfection from the start, are daily on display. Dressed as they are in apparently brand-new baby ski-suits, generally with brightly coloured helmets on their heads like infinitesimal astronauts, they seem incapable of getting wet, muddy or even untidy, and are congenitally immune to hazard. Sometimes with ski-sticks, sometimes without, often hardly big enough to be out of their carry-cots, they hurtle with terrific insouciance down the slopes and out of sight, to reappear a few moments later returning imperturbably up ski-lifts. They hardly ever fall over, and if they do they pick themselves up in a trice with a magical disentanglement of their skis. They never cry or grumble. They never hurt themselves. When the time comes for them to go home, and they are led away to their always spotless family cars, their rosy little faces express no resentment at all, but only a healthy satisfaction with their day's sport, and a proper gratitude to their parents.

Who themselves look, when they are in the mountains, preternaturally young and vigorous. High up the mountainside, when I have been taking my leisurely morning exercise, I have come across stalwart groups of great-grandparents, I swear it, sticks in their hands, smiles on their faces, striding sun-flushed and companionable towards their hearty luncheons: and once I observed far above my head, riding all alone on a chair-lift on his way to the highest ski-runs, a white-bearded ancient of such majestic splendour and vivid gear that he was like a Zeus of the snows. It is as though in some clinic of unimaginable hygiene, reachable only by funicular, these people have on the one hand had all their confusions smoothed by fatherly Jungians, while on the other hand they have been administered tremendously effective virility pills.

## 5 Old Model Swiss

I made a pilgrimage once to the field of Rütli, the lakeside meadow where, at least according to pious legend, in 1291 the Swiss highland rebels met to defy the authority of the Holy Roman Empire and bring into being a Swiss Republic. On the Sunday I walked down the track from the heights above, thousands of Swiss country patriots were making their way to and from the hallowed site, swarming through the woods and arranging picnics on the sward. I offered a cheerful good morning to everyone I met, and could not help admiring the utter lack of ingratiation, the courtesy tinged with decidedly suspended and unsmiling judgement, with which most of them responded.

This seems to me a peasant-like characteristic, and in many ways Switzerland is still a nation of bucolics. There may be New Model Swiss in the ski-resorts, but they are mostly Old Model in the rural lowlands. I am often struck by the number of twisted, stooped or withered old people I see there – people of a kind that have almost vanished from the rest of western Europe. They are one generation removed from the goitre, that talismanic ailment of mountain folk: and though the Swiss have a longer life expectancy than any other Europeans, and the remotest Alpine farm is likely to possess every last gadget of domestic convenience, still the faces of those crooked ancients, hard-hewn, bashed-about, gaunt, seem to speak of centuries of earthy hardship, isolation and suspicion. It was in Switzerland, in 1782, that the last European witch was publicly burnt.

## 6  Two pretty children

In the mountain resort of Flims, one afternoon in the early 1990s, I saw three small Swiss girls on their way home from school. They were standard graduates of Kinderland, not in the slightest goitrous or bucolic. They looked like modernistic elves, with bright-coloured rucksacks on their backs, and they were burbling brightly to each other as they climbed the hill to their homes above the town. They paused for a bit of a gossip and leg-swinging at a bench beside the road, and when they got up to go one of them, meandering off by herself, chanced to leave her sun-glasses on the bench. In a trice the other two, laughing and giggling, threw them on the ground and stamped them into pieces before my eyes, alternating kicks in the prettiest way.

## 7  The end of history?

I sometimes stay at a place called Weggis on Lake Lucerne, as Swiss a place as one can imagine, where ladies in hats stroll talkatively along promenades, where bands play in bandstands and swans and ducks are fed by plump infants in pushchairs. It is a place of sexless charm, kind but condescending, hanging on the air like lavender. It is a hive, nest or cliché of Swissness. Sometimes as I potter around the lake, however, I come across small and unobtrusive boundary markers. Four cantons surround Lake Lucerne – *Lac des Quatres Cantons* – and each to a large degree governs its own affairs: yet only those modest stones, sometimes far from roads, mark the frontiers between them. I find them very moving. Not for centuries has one of those cantons gone to war with another, or tried to impose itself upon a neighbour. The stones represent a gentle apotheosis of the nationalist idea. I would not at all mind a Europe similarly demarcated, so that only a block marked 'France', say, with a concrete cock on top, will tell travellers that they have left Germany or Italy, and must swop dictionaries for another language. Marx wrongly thought that Communism offered the complete solution to the insanities of the Nation-State: when I am in Weggis I half-cherish the hope that the end of history will be Swissness.

## 8  Or Yugoslavity?

It is sad to think that I once thought it might be Yugoslavity. Absolutely my
favourite road in all Europe used to be the coastal highway which ran down
the coast of Dalmatia from Trieste to Montenegro, because I saw it as a
proclamation of unity, and hoped that, when cohesion was finally achieved,
Yugoslavia's brutal postwar Communism would mature into libertarian
socialism. The road was fast and usually empty, and passing motorists would
cheerfully warn you, with flashing lamps and hooting horns, if there was a
speed trap around the corner. The glorious Dalmatian shoreline swept by
panoramically, all creeks and inlets and islands and ships. Every now and
then one came across a marvellous old Venetian town, with a gnarled
cathedral in the centre, winged lions of St Mark all over it and snub-nosed
Adriatic fishing-boats nestling each other in the harbour. Sometimes I made
a detour up the road to Mostar, where a lovely old Turkish bridge spanned
the Neretva river in a high and graceful span. Sometimes I stopped off for a
night or two under the golden walls of Dubrovnik, or in Split, whose
inhabitants seemed to me to be the handsomest people in all Europe. The
light, in my memory at least, was always brilliant. My BMW of the time
always went beautifully. I played Bach, Mozart and Sinatra on my cassette-
player. Once I saw Marshal Tito, the dictatorial President of the Yugoslav
federation, in a white uniform, speeding by in his limousine towards his
retreat in the Brioni islands.

   The road started in the Istrian peninsula, which had once been Austrian,
and then Italian, and was now part of the Slovene People's Republic. A little
lower down it entered the Croatian Republic. For a few miles it passed
through the Bosnian Republic. It skirted Dubrovnik, which had been for
several centuries the independent Republic of Ragusa, then ran through a
coastal strip of the Montenegrin People's Republic, until at last it stopped
short at the frontier of Albania, in those days as frowardly unwelcoming as
Tibet (the few travellers permitted to cross the border had to walk through
a tank of disinfectant). Most of these territories had once been part of the
Austro-Hungarian Empire. Some had been Roman. Some had been ruled
by the Turks. Bits of them had been, until the Second World War, Italian.
Some were chiefly Catholic, some Orthodox, some Muslim. Now, thanks
very largely to that portly white-jacketed grandee I saw in the back of his
Mercedes (who had himself started life as a corporal in the Austro-Hungarian

Army), they were all within the bounds of a single Federal State, and long
before the emergence of the European Union one could drive from one end
of Yugoslavia to the other without producing a passport or changing currency.

I used to be happy and hopeful driving down the Dalmatia highway,
supposing that all the tumultuous history of the country was reaching some
well-surfaced serenity. More recently a magazine commissioned me to drive
a new Alfa Romeo down it, picking up the car in Venice and returning it
there at the end of the journey; but it could find nobody to insure such a
venture, in the Yugoslavia of 1994.

## 9 A different country

Next time I did make a journey through what we had by then learnt to call
The Former Yugoslavia there was no such abstraction as Yugoslavity. Perhaps
there never had been. It seems extraordinary, in retrospect, that when we
foreigners used to travel so blithely through the Yugoslav federation we were
seldom aware which constituent republic we were in. I generally did not
think of the Yugoslavs who lived in the very outskirts of Trieste as anything
but Yugoslavs, or just Slavs – it seldom occurred to me to call them Slovenes.
It is true that now and then my reporter's instinct warned me that something
dangerous was brewing over there, but I never dreamt that in the 1990s the
country would collapse in a struggle horribly reminiscent not so much of
the Second World War but of those indiscriminate, almost indefinable
ethnic-religious-hereditary conflicts of the Middle Ages. Next time I went
to Dubrovnik it was scarred with shell-fire, and in the balconies of hotels
there forlornly fluttered the washing of refugees. Next time I went to Split
convoys of armoured trucks were lumbering out of the docks. The bridge
at Mostar had been blown up. The frontier with Montenegro was closed.
My next Yugoslav motor-journey was not down that happy coastline but
across the cruel mountains of Bosnia in the aftermath of the fighting, and it
aroused in me sensations not of hope but of despair or even self-reproach.

I had been in Sarajevo, and finding the airport snowed-in I took a night
ride in a mini-bus down to the sea. The snow in Bosnia-Hercegovina was
deep, the road was unpredictable, every now and then we were stopped at
roadblocks in the middle of nowhere, and the awful gorges through the
mountains loomed around us dark and dangerous. Sometimes we clattered
across a temporary iron bridge, beside a blown-up original. Sometimes,

shadowy in the night, an armoured vehicle stood guard beside a road junction. The only other traffic on the road consisted of huge tanker trucks labouring up to Sarajevo from the coast, their headlights showing far, far away on mountain curves. And, most disturbingly suggestive of all, ever and again I looked through my window to see scattered ruins passing dismally by outside – house after house gaping in the darkness, with no sign of life but for a single dim light, perhaps, on a ground floor, or a melancholy fire burning in a brazier. I dozed uncomfortably off somewhere around Konjic, and when I woke up I looked out of the window again, into the grey dawn, to see the ruins passing still.

They were not the usual ruins of war – not compact villages knocked into general shambles by blanket bombing, street fighting or concentrated artillery bombardment, like villages of France, Germany or Italy in the Second World War. They were generally strings of detached houses, well separated, each one of which had been individually and deliberately destroyed. In the same way, Sarajevo did not look in the least like those cities of Europe which were bombed into desolation in the Second World War. It was not a wasteland of burnt-out shells and skeletonic blocks. But there was hardly a building in the city centre which had not been specifically targeted, sometimes half-collapsed in a mess of beams and boulders, sometimes just pitted all over with shell fragments or snipers' bullets. All this gave me an impression of particular and personal hatred. It looked such a *spiteful* sort of destruction. Bosnia had been ravaged, it appeared, not by ignorant conscript armies clashing, but by groups of citizens expressing their true emotions. A. J. P. Taylor once wrote that the Great War had begun as the most popular of wars, but I had a feeling that the War of the Yugoslav Succession was undertaken even more genuinely from the human heart. And what did that say, I could not help wondering as those shattered houses passed me in the dark, about the human heart?

There were four other passengers in the mini-bus that night – a Swede, a Finn, a Croat and an Englishman. We were all there to make money in one way or another. Behind us a second bus-load was following through the darkness. At about two in the morning we stopped, and our driver got out and peered rather helplessly into the black emptiness behind him, up the highway banked with snowdrifts. 'What's happening?' said the Englishman in front of me. 'What have we stopped for?' The driver explained that the other bus seemed to be lost: there was no sign of its lights, and he was worried that it might have got into trouble back there. The Englishman stretched, pulled his coat more tightly around his shoulders, and settled down to sleep again. 'Who cares?' he said. But he may have been joking.

## 10  Growing old

How strange to be a Yugoslav, of whatever nation, who was born when I was born! When I was first in Sarajevo, before the Yugoslav wars, the very name of the place had a different meaning for the world. By the 1990s it stood for cruel sieges, snipers, hopeless negotiations, ethnic cleansing, poverty and public hardship. In the 1970s it had recalled only, for me as for most of the world's inhabitants, the assassination of the Archduke Franz Ferdinand, heir to the throne of Austro-Hungary, which led immediately to the First World War. I went at once then, as every visitor did, to the place where Gavrilo Princip fired the fateful shot, on 28 June 1914. He had been among the crowd at the end of a bridge, later renamed in his honour, over the Miljačka river; and there was a small museum in memory of the occasion, and some footprints incised in the pavement to show just where Princip had stood, and a plaque on a wall which every tourist liked to photograph. It was all pointed out to me with some pride: Princip was a Yugoslav patriotic hero, and there were ceremonies at his grave on the anniversary of the murder. Twenty years later, when I returned to Sarajevo, a city all bashed about and wasted, I went back to Princip's Bridge out of curiosity, to see how history had treated the site. It was a rainy dusk. The bridge was there still, over the rushing narrow river. So was the museum, though it was closed. But the paving-blocks were knocked about, cracked and puddled, and I could find no sign of the footprints. I stumbled about trying to locate the famous plaque upon the wall, but passers-by told me not to bother. It had been removed, they said. We were not in Yugoslavia any more. We were in Bosnia-Hercegovina now, and Gavrilo Princip had been a Serb.

In Zagreb I was introduced, as it happened, to a woman born there in the year before me, 1925. We inspected each other with interest, and after discussing our respective personal lives spent half an hour exchanging our experiences of history. Mine were soon told. Hers were more complicated. She had been born into a Yugoslav monarchy, in a city that was (and still is) in many ways a characteristic provincial capital of the Austro-Hungarian

Empire. She was old enough to remember the assassination of King Alexander of the Yugoslavs in 1934 (her mother cried, she said). She remembered the arrival of the German Army in 1941, and the odious Croatian Fascist State of the Second World War, with its brutal Ustashi guards, its concentration camps and its ethnic massacres. Two of her brothers, she told me, had run away to fight with the Communist partisans. She had been in the crowd in the central square that welcomed the proclamation of the Yugoslav federation in 1945. She had been present when Croatian soldiers attacked the Zagreb barracks of the Yugoslav National Army in 1991, heralding the end of it. She had lived through the miseries of the Yugoslav civil wars. Now she was looking forward eagerly to the putsch which must before long, she felt sure, rid Croatia of its present dictatorial president and make a real democracy of it.

And yet, she said, she felt no older than she had felt thirty or forty years before. 'Well,' said I conventionally, 'it's all in the mind anyway.' She eyed me thoughtfully then.

## 11  *Or Irishness?*

In the Republic of Ireland there exists a genuine and peaceable Nation-State – perhaps it is all to the good that the Protestants of the North, mostly of Scottish descent, have not been reunited with the South since the British sliced them off in the 1920s. Nowhere in western Europe has history moved faster than in Ireland – which in this century has matured from a hangdog, rebellious and poverty-stricken British possession to a confident and progressive sovereign member of the European Community. Even in my time there were wrecks of Anglo-Irish houses all over the country, never rebuilt after the old troubles, or allowed to fall into dilapidation with independence. There were innumerable semi-wrecks of Anglo-Irish people, too, surrounded by grand memories in unheated mansions, recalling the wars and high jinks of their youths in the drawing-room of the Kildare Street Club. When I first went to Ireland it was easy to meet people who remembered the Protestant Ascendancy – which meant, in effect, the British Empire – if not in full swing, at least in vibrant style. I envied them. It all sounded shamefully delightful. Who would *not* like to have been The Most Honourable the Marquess of Waterford, living with his exuberant children, his devoted family servants and his hundred horses among his wide woods at Curraghmore?

In those days, when foreigners spoke of the Irish style, as often as not it was the Anglo-Irish style they really meant. The Irish Joke, of course, never referred to the Marquess of Waterford, but Irish Dash, Irish Pluck, the Luck of the Irish, a Touch of the Irish – all these abstractions were fostered, in outsiders' minds, less by the native Celts than by the occupying Britons. It is true that the line between the two was blurred, people of impeccable Norman origins swearing to their own undying Irishness, unmistakable members of the Ascendancy turning out to be descended from native chieftains, but still Anglo-Ireland was essential to the Irish mystique.

## 12  *Too late!*

Where is it now? Even its ruins are disappearing, one by one, and the governing class of Ireland is now the courteous, cultivated, worldly, clever and sometimes corrupt progeny of its tenants. Back in the 1960s, contemplating one of the more spectacular of those Ascendancy ruins, sentimentally I remarked to a passing Irishman that it seemed a shame all the festive and colourful life of the house should have come to an end. 'Oh,' he replied, 'wouldn't you say it was too late for that kind of fandango?' I remembered his words when, decades later, I sat down to a contemporary equivalent of those old hedonisms – a first-class Irish country lunch at a famous pub near Galway City. I had never been there before, and found it gloriously high-spirited. The place was full of well-heeled and entertaining Galwegians, as Irish as could be, eating crab claws, scampi and fresh fish in the dining-room, or at wooden benches outside. Ever and again another car turned up full of eloquent anticipation. 'On a day like this,' my companion said to me, 'honest to God there's nowhere on earth I'd rather be than Moran's.' We were sitting in the open air, overlooking the water and the Volvos, and I had washed down half a dozen Galway oysters with a glass of Guinness. Finding this insufficient for my needs, I ordered the same again, and while waiting for it to arrive I took a stroll up the road to look at the view. Honest to God, there on the skyline I saw in unmistakable silhouette the very same ruin whose outdated merriments that passer-by had long before dismissed. It still looked grand up there – a big square block with the sun shining through its gutted windows – but the oysters, the Guinness and the Galway company had done their trick, and I no longer wished I could hear the music of the hunt ball, or see the young Etonians and their girls larking about in the rose-garden.

## 13 *On the move*

As the century closes, Ireland, which is the youngest country in Europe, and one of the best-educated, is still on the move. Do you recall the seditious radio programme that so astonished me in that Dublin bookshop, making fun of the Catholic Church? By the 1990s scandals among the Church hierarchy had become so common, and so highly publicized, that it was hard to remember which divine had been involved in which (there were four Catholic arch-bishops in Ireland, and thirty-one bishops). 'Let me see now,' I heard myself saying warily one morning, 'is the Bishop of Ferns the one who – well, er, you know – that woman?' 'No,' came the matter-of-fact response, 'you're thinking of the Bishop of Galway. The Bishop of Ferns is the one who's away in America for detoxification.' Of course there was a sadness to such developments, the discrediting of old certainties, the abandonment of old ways, but the Irish seemed to be taking it in their stride. Theirs was a laughing country still, and rich in quirk and variety to a degree that most countries of the West had almost forgotten. When I ventured to complain one lunch-time about a mildewed baked potato, 'Oh what a shocking misunderstanding,' cried the café pro-prietress in a truly fastidious choice of euphemism, and gave me a free pudding. Deep in the country one day I came as in a daze to a village where every house had recently been repainted in colours of blinding variety – pinks, blues, reds, dazzling yellows – while the single street was astonishingly festooned with drooping electric wires, and paved mostly with mud. It was a Civic Trust nightmare! When I went into a shop to ask the meaning of it all (there was none), merciful Heaven, disoriented as I was it seemed to me like stepping into the attic storeroom of some crazed recluse – broken boxes, splintered crates, piles of newspapers, paint-pots, random vegetables everywhere, stacks of cans tumbled in corners, shadowy high shelves jammed with packages, a potato or two rolling across the floor, and somewhere amidst the chaos a composed urbane shopkeeper, awaiting my order for all the world as though she were standing behind the confectionery counter at Fortnum & Mason's.

No doubt there were all sorts of things wrong with that republic – drugs, organized crime, violence – but still the Irish seemed to be running better than most in the general pursuit of happiness. Modernizing things without ruining them is a problem every society faces – how to make things more efficient without making them less entertaining. If any State can get away with it, Ireland's the one.

## 14  *The wind-rose*

The Portuguese were a Power in their time. They were neutral in the Second World War, but they were still imperialists long after it – their African empire collapsed only in the 1970s, and they stayed even longer in Macao, their colony on the coast of China. The spoils of empire are apparent in Portugal to this day, in the grand palaces of Lisbon and Oporto, and the vulgar country homes of recently returned colonialists. I can well remember the Portuguese in their imperial mode, when they fought with all the paraphernalia of troop carrier and camouflage suit to keep the blacks of their African possessions in subjection. I remember the tough Portuguese mercenaries who, deprived of a war by the independence of Mozambique, came over the border to fight the blacks of the old Rhodesia – sunning themselves, between skirmishes, with cigars and whisky beside the swimming-pools of Salisbury. Even in the 1990s, in Portugal itself, one sometimes came across reunions of those old veterans, jovial with regimental banners and *vinho verde*, celebrating the last of their imperial wars.

I am imaginatively seized myself by relics of the Age of Navigators, the golden age of Portugal's power, when Portuguese seamen ranged the seas in trade and conquest under the auspices of the fifteenth-century Prince Henry. The best of these souvenirs is the great wind-rose set up by Henry for the instruction of his captains at Cape St Vincent, the south-western extremity of Europe. It is a huge compass chart laid out on the ground to record the strengths and directions of prevailing winds, and it was built within the purlieus of a dramatic headland fortress. When I was there it was sadly neglected, and looked rather like a run-down rock garden, but it stirred me all the same. As I stood beside it in the evening I could see those caravel captains clustered there so long before, worrying their way through the new devices of seamanship; and, if I turned my head a little, there was the very ocean they had made their own, taking the lessons of the wind-rose with them to Brazil, to Angola, to the Cape of Good Hope, to Mozambique, to Goa, to Macao, to all those places that the Portuguese discovered for Christian Europe, and mastered for themselves.

## 15  *Peace and quiet*

But a Portuguese family arrived while I was meditating by the wind-rose, and stood staring silently at this emblem of old adventures without a sign of emotion. The Portuguese in general seem to have put Powerhood behind them, and adjusted their temperament to the times. Their frontiers have remained virtually unchanged since 1139. They got rid of their last dictator in 1970, they had their last revolution in 1974, and they are now the most tranquil of the Europeans. Peace and quiet is the thing in modern Portugal, which is why the Algarve, south of Lisbon, long ago became the favourite resort of elderly northerners of gentle tastes (though mass tourism has since whittled down the old discretion). The Portuguese can drive as maniacally as anyone else, but in most circumstances they are remarkably restrained. They are conquerors no more. Their smiles are kind but vestigial. Their waves of the hand are solemn. Their courtesy is reserved, and especially in the countryside it takes application to amuse them into riposte or badinage. From the heroic cliff-tops of Cape St Vincent, near the wind-rose, people fish with rod and line, dropping their mussel bait through the gusty winds all down the face of the precipice to the ocean far below. This eccentric technique naturally attracts foreign sightseers, but the anglers appear to think it a perfectly conventional way of fishing, as they allow their reels to release a few hundred feet more line to the tossing waves below. 'Any luck?' they say to each other, just as though they are sitting on a canal bank drinking tea from Thermos flasks and waiting for their floats to bob.

Parts of Portugal are among the poorest regions in western Europe – women still wash their clothes in rivers, mules and donkeys pull ploughs – but there is no sense of primitivism to this country. Even the animals and children are gentlemanly. In the village of Vila do Bispo once I discovered all the village dogs crowded in the market square waiting to have their compulsory inoculations, and there was not a single snarl among them. I was taken aback to find my hotel in Lisbon disturbed one day by a truly demoniac pack of infants. They screamed along hotel corridors into the small hours. They banged on strangers' doors. They were extremely ugly and seemed to have no discipline whatever. I was quite relieved to learn, when I inquired at the front desk about them, that they were not Portuguese at all, but child-members of a Russian ballet company performing in the city. 'Bring back Stalin,' said I to the concierge: but he only smiled, very Portuguesely.

## 16 *The sprig of rosemary*

I was driving along a country road in Portugal when I spied a tray of oranges for sale outside a cottage. It was blazing hot, and I stopped to buy some. Nobody attended the fruit, so I selected three oranges for myself and knocked upon the cottage door. Nobody came. There was no sign of life. I peered through the windows, I walked around the back, and in the end I opened the front door. It was very dark inside, but when my eyes accustomed themselves I saw that fast asleep on a bed in a corner of the room was a small old lady. I coughed and shuffled my feet, and without a start she awoke. Her very first reaction was to smile. Her second was to reach for her straw hat from a nearby chair and put it carefully on her head. She seemed entirely composed, entirely balanced. She accepted my few coins for the oranges, but then, hustling me kindly outside, picked me two apricots from another box and gave me those as a present. All the time she smiled, and laughed at my phrase-book Portuguese, and bustled around looking for other kindnesses to perform. She was one of the *blithest* people I have ever met, closely related I would guess to the old Breton lady that my daughter coveted on page 103. When we had said goodbye, and I had returned to the car, she came running out of the garden gate again, smiling still, clutching her hat on her head, to give me a sprig of rosemary.

## 17 *The juvenile social worker*

On my very first evening in Sweden, in the 1950s, I impertinently adopted as my paradigm of the country an antiseptic woman I saw having dinner in my hotel restaurant. She was very handsome, and very cool. She looked as though she had been to her hairdresser's half an hour before. She was eating alone, with a bottle of German white wine, but seemed not in the least lonely or bored. It took her only a moment to decide what she wanted from the menu, and her orders to the waiter were polite but brisk. Her mastication was regular, as if she were timing herself for statistical purposes. Sometimes I thought she was breathing to a conscious rhythm, too. When I engaged her in conversation she was courteous but unforthcoming, her pale blue eyes engaging mine with absolute confidence and no perceptible interest. She was all I expected of Sweden, I thought, and she could never have guessed how delighted I was when she told me her profession. 'Juvenile social worker,' she said in her impeccable English, taking an extraordinarily deliberate sip of her hock.

She was how we all thought of Sweden in those days. Like the Swiss and the Irish and the Portuguese, the Swedes had been neutral in the Second World War, leaning slightly towards the Nazi cause – in which they were only human, as German power surrounded them on three sides, while Russian power seemed to threaten them on the fourth. We thought of them as smug, fortunate, rich, efficient, socially trendy, spared the anxieties of greater States, with complacent ideological preferences and a high suicide rate, which served them right. No wonder, I thought that evening, the juvenile social worker drank her wine with such prissy calculation – I can see her now, removing a minute segment of cork from her tongue with the tip of a well-manicured little finger.

## 18  *Imperial Swedes*

After that initial visit, however, I soon came to realize that Sweden had once been a Nation-State of a very different kind: presumptuous, swanky and aggressive, the Terror of the North – another of those damned Powers, in fact, which have so often snarled up Europe's progress. I think my perceptions were changed by a statue of King Karl XII (1682–1718) which stands in the Kungsträdgården in Stockholm. The gardens themselves are almost exaggeratedly Swedish. All around them is a bustle of restaurants and cafés, and the bulk of the Opera House stands above. In summer, when the sun shines and the sky is a theatrically northern blue, the air is filled with the slapping of ropes from the harbour and the snapping of flags in the wind (Sweden is a terrific place for flags, most of them in the national blue and yellow, and all of them apparently brand-new). At the foot of this agreeable place stands old King Karl. He does not look in the least like a Swede in the contemporary kind. He looks demonstratively imperial, and he is holding out his right hand in a peremptory fashion in the direction of St Petersburg, as if to say, 'On, on, you noble Swedes,' adding something about gentlemen in Sweden now abed. This is not just sculpted histrionics, either. The Swedes really have invaded Russia more than once, have sent their armies storming across half Europe and their colonists to the Indies East and West – where on the French island of Saint-Barthélemy, years after my conversion, I came across the extremely Swedish mansion of the island's quondam Swedish governors, clean and trim as could be beside the tropic sea.

Forty years ago one occasionally saw in Stockholm representatives of the old imperial class. The King of Sweden was still a proper king in those days, living in his vast palace beside the harbour, and sometimes there stalked the streets late representatives of the Swedish aristocracy. They looked slightly oriental – Finnish blood, no doubt. Their greatcoats were Junker-like, almost down to their heels as they strode through the snow, and their boots were patently made of supple deerskin by family cobblers on ancestral estates. Were they corseted, or was that just their masterful bearing? Did they wear monocles, or am I making that up?

## 19  Beyond the archipelago

I never see them now, and I look in vain for their images in the Stockholm gossip pages. The King and Queen no longer usually live in that great palace beside the harbour, but at the sweeter, softer palace of Drottningholm, leaving behind the helmeted dragoons of the royal guard to blow their trumpets and wheel here and there in the courtyard. The longer I have known the Swedes, though, the more jejune I realize my original paradigm to have been. No longer one of the Powers, there is still something rather heroic about them. They are certainly not the most beloved people in Europe, but that is perhaps because they have so successfully looked after their own interests throughout a century of general uncertainty. For years after the Second World War they kept their warships in huge excavated sea-caverns, from which they emerged into the daylight with vastly echoing rumbles of their engines: there is no denying heroism to that!

Besides, if their country is hardly an earth, a realm set in a silver sea, it really is epically situated. Its northern territories protrude into the frozen North; its southern peninsula commands the entrance to the Baltic, to my mind the most ominous and eerie of Europe's waters. Fearful things happen in the Baltic. Wars embroil it. Ice freezes it. Unidentified submarines prowl it. Empires storm this way and that across its shallows. Predatory Powers one after the other covet its control – now the Germans, now the Russians, now the Swedes themselves. An archipelago of small islands protects Sweden from this sea, and although nowadays it is largely the province of affluent second-homers with yachts and saunas, it always seems to me to be protecting, too, against all the threats and mysteries of the wider world. Behind the archipelago Sweden stands plump, confident and well-armed beneath its bright new flags, a Power no longer, a threat to nobody: beyond the archipelago anything may happen.

## 20 *Ibsenesques and Griegisms*

Norway next door has never been a Power at all, and has been a State only since 1905, when it broke away from Sweden's rule. Back in the 1950s it seemed to me magically northern, provincial and introspective, like a *mise en scène* from Ibsen. I was invited to lunches of perfect bourgeois decorum, to eat gravlax and boiled potato in decors of heavy velvet, white-painted panelling, polished wooden floors, paintings of stern ancestors and stormy seascapes. Writers still looked wonderfully writerly in the Norway of the 1950s, painters were like painters then, middle-aged ladies properly middle-aged and cardiganed. I happened in Oslo one night to see some members of a theatre cast assembling for a post-performance supper in a restaurant, and watching their meticulously staged arrivals, their accomplished greetings and their mastery of incidental business was almost as stimulating as seeing the play itself. Nothing then seemed to me more absolutely of the country than Edvard Grieg's suburban house in Bergen – not a showy house at all, but homely and full of bric-à-brac, secluded in a garden, with a wooden pavilion among the trees in which the composer, warmed by a big iron stove in the corner, had settled at his worn old table to write his melodies. And what grand Norwegian themes had come to him through the trees, from the still water of the fjord in front of his windows, from the wooded hills behind! Norway was just the place, I concluded, for writing A-minor piano concertos.

## 21 *New Norway*

Forty years later, primed by North Sea oil, richer than most countries, Norway showed every sign of cosmopolitan modernity. One day, as I sat on a bench in Oslo, I jotted down in my notebook all that I saw about me, and here is the register. A man with a pigtail pushed a baby-carriage along a pavement. A young executive talked into a car-phone. A Eurobus set off on a holiday trip to Andalusia. An interracial procession of raggle-taggle students marched by holding ecologically protesting banners. There were shops with names like Ambiente and Marc O'Polo, a Pakistani corner store and a Bulgarian tourist centre, a sushi bar, a pizza counter and a graffito on a wall claiming Norway for the Norwegians. There were statues of playwrights, animals, nude and preternaturally athletic children. The yellow-brick Stortinget, the national parliament, looked more interesting than lovely, I thought – like an aardvark perhaps. The National Theatre looked unmistakably national and theatrical. The university looked, with its classical columns and sandwich-eating students, indisputably academic. All in all, Oslo had become a little epitome of modern Europe.

Even in more utter parts of the country there seemed to be nothing very insular or introspective to Norway any more, even in reaches of the bleakest North, where all is desolate sea and tundra, the wind howling off the Arctic and the little fishing-towns, hundreds of miles from one another, huddled beneath their rocky bluffs in the half-light. By the 1990s hardly a one of those towns was without its modern chain hotel, with Country and Western Music on Saturday Nite. At Bergen by then there was a Gay Disco at weekends. At Skjervöy, far above the Arctic Circle, they were advertising package tours to the Canary Islands. At Trondheim I came across two whole-hog Rastafarians drinking hot chocolate in a café, together with a genuine punk couple, complete with Mohican haircut and ethnic jewellery. Mexican restaurants were all over the place, video shops, soft-porn magazines, and wherever you looked there was likely to be an infant drinking Fanta through a bent straw. I did once see a scrawl on a wall, in Ålesund, which seemed to speak of that older Norway. 'TELL ME ONE REASON FOR LIVING,' it said, and I was tempted to add another: 'IBSEN RULES, O.K.?'

## 22 *From* An Enemy of the People, *1882, by Henrik Ibsen, translated by Peter Watts*

DR STOCKMANN: I feel so indescribably happy at being part of all this teeming, flourishing life. It's a wonderful age we're living in – it's as though a whole world were springing up around us!

THE MAYOR: Do you really think so?

## 23  *The Lucky Country*

Years ago at the airport in Leningrad, as they then called St Petersburg, I chanced to see an acquaintance of mine from the British Embassy in Moscow, waiting for a flight to Finland. It was winter, and he was dressed in full paraphernalia of fur hat, fur coat and heavy boots. I thought he looked like an English Muscovy merchant in an old painting: lean, clever, ready to drive the hardest of sealskin bargains, or arrange a cruelly advantageous shipment of amber. What was he really going to Finland for? He was going to the dentist.

It used to be thought that there was something magical about the Finns – lightfooted, high-cheeked, speaking a strange language, addicted to mystic folklore: it was claimed that the very word 'Finn' meant 'magician', and even at the end of the nineteenth century British sailors were reluctant to sail with Finns because they thought they had unearthly powers. Magic or not, certainly throughout my fifty years Finland has been the Lucky Country of Europe, maintaining a brilliant equilibrium through all history's convulsions. The Russian invasion of 1939 was Stalin's one example of restraint in military expansionism. The German alliance which followed it was soon forgotten. Nobody holds grudges against the Finns, unless there are inherited Scandinavian grievances that I know nothing of; the Finns are respected by one and all, if only for the slippery skill of their diplomacy. In the days of the Communist Empire, whose dominion it so narrowly escaped, Finland was like a safety-valve on the edge of Russia. Not only young men from the British Embassy went there for their comforts: Communist apparatchiks, you may be sure, knew their way across the frontier, or over the narrow waters of the Gulf of Finland, to the dentists, the restaurants, the dressmakers, the fleshpots and the bankers of Helsinki. 'o to be in finland,' wrote e. e. cummings in 1950, 'now that russia's here.'

Going there from Leningrad then was a tonic. The wind out of a Russian sea was like a death in the family, but the same wind in Finland was just a tingle in the cheek. An hour in a Finnish sauna, after even a week or two in the Soviet Union, seemed to scour some miasma from your person, to leave you clean, brisk and ten years younger. Nobody could possibly feel pity for the Finns, as I often felt pity for the Russians. Besides, you could do anything you liked in Finland! You could take a ride in a pony-sleigh across a frozen harbour without being watched through binoculars by suspicious policemen. You could drive a car at a proper pace – in Russia in those days they never seemed to go more than thirty. You could go to a French film or an American play, and read the English newspapers. You could march around with a placard demanding currency reform or forecasting the imminent end of everything. You could satisfy your every craving. My own particular desire, when I first flew into Finland out of the Soviet Union, was for raw carrots, and when I arrived in Helsinki I went straight to a grocer, bought half a pound, washed them in my hotel bathroom, and ate them luxuriously with a glass of schnapps. Gogol once wrote that in the land of the Finns 'everything was lost, flat, pale, grey, foggy . . .'. He should have tried carrots with schnapps.

## 24  *Lucky still*

Thirty years or so after those long-ago visits, when the Soviet Union had disintegrated, I went back again to Helsinki. I arrived by sea this time. Hoisting my bag on my back, I walked around the south harbour towards the centre of the city, and found the whole place *en fête*. It was Helsinki Day, and I was greeted at the Kauppatori market-place, where the daily mart of the waterfront was already in full swing, by a uniformed band playing from the first floor of the City Hall. Flags were everywhere, the café tables were hedonistically crowded, and Senate Square, the handsome focus of all Finland, was taken over by an extremely merry marching ensemble – a military band which undertook such hilarious convolutions of march and countermarch, the drum-major sometimes leaping in the air with his baton, the bandsmen often breaking into a puffing trot to maintain the pattern of movement, that I found myself laughing out loud in appreciation. Helsinki seemed flushed with success and self-esteem – well-dressed citizens promenading, tourists from all over, androgynous youths distributing brochures, trams trundling, bands playing, yachts scudding, musical marchers strutting, shops opulent, hotels fully booked, and nearly everyone smiling.

The Lucky Country! Actually it was not quite as lucky as it looked, there being an economic slump at the time, and 20 per cent unemployed. It seemed lucky to me, though, and I felt almost as fortunate to be there as I had all those years before when it had given me most of the relief of an escape from jail. I tried hard to re-enjoy my happy sensations of the 1950s, and succeeded with most of them – the freshness, the newness, the liberty, the variety, the colour. When it came to satisfying that old craving of mine, though, for the life of me I could not remember what the craving had been.

## 25  Luck changes

Only fifty miles from Finland, across a narrow gulf, is Estonia: an independent State before the Second World War, a Soviet republic for fifty years, since 1991 an independent State again. Tallinn, its capital, has been the very opposite of Helsinki. It has been the Unlucky City, repeatedly fouled by the historical detritus of our times. Grabbed by the Russians in 1940, by the Germans in 1941, by the Russians again in 1944, it entered Estonia's post-Communist independence burdened with an incubus of unwanted Russian settlers that formed a third of the entire population. Luck could not come much worse. Yet by 1995, when I got there, you would scarcely have known it. Tallinn's Old City, scarcely damaged by these events, had evidently determined to make itself one of the great destinations of mass tourism. All was ready for the rush. The cobbled streets were in good order. Piano music sounded romantically from upstairs windows. Baubles gleamed fresh-gilded on church steeples, and the grand central square, Town Hall Square, was done up like something from a medieval picture-book, with ice-cream stalls and cafés added. The Festival Grounds on the edge of town were ready for the next All-Estonian Song Festival – 200,000 people usually came: the biggest concert audience in Europe, so I was told a hundred times if I was told once. In multitudinous cellars and crannied storage-places the antique salesmen, bistro chefs and boutique proprietors were eagerly at work, and tandoori kebabs were sizzling at Sanjay's. I had heard that the Estonians were famously taciturn – asked why he had spoken for the very first time only at the age of twenty, a deaf-mute of Estonian legend replied that he'd had nothing to say until then – but in 1995 Tallinn seemed to me downright talkative. I had lunch at one of those cellar restaurants with an Estonian academic, and she was almost as amazed as I was by this capitalist transformation of the capital – only four years before mired apparently interminably in the Communist bog. We ate crayfish, and they reminded her loquaciously of her childhood in the Estonia of long before, before the Communists had come at all, when she had fished for them with her parents in limpid streams among the birch trees, and boiled them in cauldrons on the river-bank.

Unfortunately it turned out upon inquiry that the crayfish came from Louisiana, but that did not spoil the spirit of the occasion. Nor did all the standard post-Communist complaints I later heard about lost jobs, low wages, rising prices, crime, sleaze, housing shortages and all those wretched Russians – some of whom were pointed out to me skulking about in a Marxist manner in one of their insalubriously Stalinist suburbs. No unpalatable truths could alter the fact that in 1995 Tallinn, the Unlucky City, had struck a lucky streak at last.

## 26 Esoterica

When I was a child, and spent much of my time tracking the ships that came up the Bristol Channel, the most esoteric of the vessels I saw through my telescope were the small freighters, with high deck-cargoes of timber, that flew the flags of Latvia and Lithuania. I was vague about the localities of those countries, and entirely ignorant about their histories; and when long afterwards I set foot in them I was not much the wiser. Together with Estonia they were the only States of my Europe that were actually absorbed into the Soviet Union as constituent republics, after having been occupied by the Nazis in the Second World War; and although I reached them only after the collapse of Communism, when they had regained their interwar independence (more or less, because as in Tallinn Russians of one sort or another were still influential in their affairs), they remained for me the least familiar of all the countries of the continent. The process of de-Sovietization was more difficult there than anywhere. By 1996 the two capitals of Riga and Vilnius had gone a long way down the free-market road, and were becoming recognizably normal European cities; but looking for somewhere that would more truly illustrate the halfway condition of the republics, still emerging from Stalinism, I came to the Lithuanian industrial town of Šiauliai (Schaulen to the Germans) – particularly suitable to my purposes because in Soviet times it had been forbidden to all foreigners as the site of a strategically important base of the Red Air Force. I had never heard of it before.

I checked in at the main hotel, a dowdy high-rise that was built in Soviet times, might well be still Soviet-owned (nobody seemed to know), and had doggedly stuck to those old ways that I had begun to find nostalgic back on page 78: which is to say, streaked concrete, no heat, derelict telephone booths, dismal food, receptionists muffled in greatcoats, a Moscow chat show on the television, and a notice on the wall quoting different rates for Lithuanian citizens, citizens of the former USSR, and the rest of us. 'Just what I wanted,' said I to myself as the terrifyingly jerky lift carried me in spasms to my room. It was almost as though Lithuania had never achieved its independence at all, and when I went out for a morning walk I thought I might well be in some relatively prosperous township of the USSR ten years before, except that there were no statues of Stalin or Lenin.

Everything else was there. There were the monumental square office blocks of State, overlooking spacious squares with parks in them. There was the statutorily ornamental pedestrian highway, Vilniaus Street, running through the city centre, with various cultural institutions on it, and many benches for the well-earned refreshment of happy workers, and babushkas selling bananas. The crowning church of St Peter and St Paul, with its tall polygonal steeple, had been handsomely rebuilt – as a museum of atheism, perhaps? – and there were many manifestations of the whimsical humour that was meant to give a human face to Soviet Communism, like funny statues of rabbits, a stone shoe on a pillar, and a cat museum. Most of the factories, on the outskirts of town, were disused, deprived of their Soviet markets and left to languish. The former airbase was being turned into a free economic zone, but it gave me a shudder nevertheless, as I wandered among its shabby half-dereliction, its hangars and abandoned guardhouses, to imagine what kind of reception I would have had if I had strayed through its barricades in Stalin's time.

But gradually, very gradually, the little Baltic States were finding an identity again, and so was Šiauliai. Here and there along Vilniaus Street very different institutions were arising. Cappuccino was available. Rock music blared from boutiques. Foreign businessmen ate expense-account lunches at smart new restaurants. Credit cards were accepted. Ravishing girls in miniskirts would never grow up to be babushkas. There was a bowling alley in the basement of Vilniaus 88, and you could eat quite a decent hamburger at 146. The Universaline department store still looked a bit Stalinist, but as the Business Advisory Centre's *Šiauliai At Your Fingertips* indulgently suggested, it was 'a good place to visit for nostalgic reasons'. Up at St Peter and St Paul five masses were celebrated every day.

At the end of the street, nevertheless, irreconcilably loomed my hotel. No cappuccino there, no country-and-western music. It was, in *Šiauliai At Your Fingertips*'s snide classification, 'where most people stay if the other hotels are full'. At breakfast a long table covered with a brown velveteen cloth was occupied by twenty young Russian males, like visiting technicians from the old days, while at the end of the dim-lit room there sat alone in silence at her victuals a woman who might be typecast as a lady commissar: severe, spectacled, muscular, her hair in a bun, and her skirts long and heavy. A solitary waiter in shirtsleeves served us – thick black coffee (they were out of milk), fried eggs with peas, black bread and very good cheese. Halfway through the meal we were each given a bottle of Coca-Cola. Most of the men drank theirs there and then, in tandem with the coffee: but I noticed that when the lady commissar left the room, wiping her mouth fastidiously with her paper napkin, and studiously not looking anyone in the eye, she took hers with her.

## 27  *At the pleasure gardens*

My acquaintance with Denmark has been slight, and unsatisfactory. It is another of the small States that were once great Powers, and long ago I walked the streets of Danish imperialism in Tranquebar, on the Coromandel coast of India. There in the seventeenth century the Danes had founded a fort and trading colony, and although the plaster was peeled and the pilasters were crumbling, I could still discern the remains of Danesborg and Prins Christian Gade dreaming the centuries away. My introduction to the Danish motherland was scarcely less curious. In 1952 I attended a North Atlantic Treaty exercise designed to demonstrate how instantly the West could come to the support of the Scandinavian countries if ever the Soviet Union attacked them. Its climax was a landing by marines on a beach at Skagen, at the very tip of Jutland between the Kattegat and the Skagerrak, between the North Sea and the Baltic. This was my entry to Denmark, and I remember it largely because the battalion of the Danish Home Guard assigned to receive the landing went to the wrong place and appeared far too late, merrily huffing and puffing in its long greatcoats along the strand.

It is unfair, I know, but I suspect that this ridiculous episode was always subconsciously to colour my view of Denmark. It was a pleasant country, that was undeniable. Its landscape was genial, its architecture handsome, its people were generally honest and friendly. The things it made were beautiful. Its butters and bacons were tasty. Its National Museum was one of the best in Europe. Lego was a blessing to harassed parents around the world, and so were the tales of Hans Christian Andersen. Denmark's behaviour during the

Second World War had been exemplary (though there was no truth to the well-known legend that good King Christian X had appeared in public, during the Nazi occupation, wearing a Star of David on his sleeve – Danish Jews were not obliged to wear them anyway). Yet somehow it always seemed to me a *foolish* place, and if this feeling was first inspired in me (I was young and somewhat militant in those days) by the spectacle of those part-time soldiers jokingly shambling along the beach, too late for the action, it was particularly reinforced over the years by the central position that the Tivoli Pleasure Gardens in Copenhagen appeared to occupy in the national psyche. Mention Copenhagen to almost anyone, Danish or foreign, and they would mention the Tivoli Pleasure Gardens in return. The gardens themselves were certainly agreeable, with their Chinese lanterns and flowered terraces, their swings and slot-machines and rifle-ranges and jolly orchestras playing far into the night. I have paid happy enough visits to the Tivoli Pleasure Gardens. But I have always found it childishly demeaning that they should stand at the very centre of Denmark's life and reputation – Denmark, home of the Vikings, the country of Gorm the Old and Harald Bluetooth, which once sent its colonists to India and Africa, and its conquerors all across the icy northlands! That it should all come down to this, I used to think: tinkly music, clowns and fairy lights in the Tivoli Pleasure Gardens!

Besides, the public style of Denmark has never allured me. Nothing could be much more footling, in my view, than the daily changing of the royal guard at the Amalienborg in Copenhagen, after the Tivoli the central Danish tourist spectacle. Most military displays appear pretty childish to me nowadays, but the Amalienborg ceremony seems deliberately designed to be absurd. The unfortunate men of the guard look as though they are officially trained to impersonate toy soldiers, with their white cross-belting, striped blue trousers, heaps of buttons and preposterously exaggerated bearskin hats. The bandmasters stamp about like parodies of sergeant-majors. When some of the more diminutive officers, dwarfed by their bearskins, march in an embarrassed way around the ranks, or fiercely draw their swords in salute, I find it hard not to think of them as comics in a farce.

Something sugary, something whimsical about this culture turns me off. Jazz, which seems silly in the hands of most Europeans, seems silliest of all in the hands of middle-ageing Danes. The chain of Copenhagen pedestrian streets called Strøget, the most famous shopping precinct in Denmark, is dominated by a tawdry-glitz sort of capitalism and frequented by the trendiest kind of street performer – the sort that plays Peruvian pipes or performs incomprehensible mimes. The very titles of Denmark's favourite fairy tales say it all for me – 'The Little Matchgirl' – 'Little Claus and Big Claus' – 'The Steadfast Tin Soldier' – 'The Rose-Elf'. I sympathize with the vandal who climbed out one day to the statue of The Little Mermaid, sitting prettily on a rock in the harbour, and sawed her head off. But there we are: perhaps I am not made for Hans Christian Andersen. Perhaps I am the Brothers Grimm type! Danish humour has never much amused me. I do not respond to the national taste for japes and winsomeness, or its reliance on charm and pixie-lore. I have repeatedly tried to make myself enjoy Denmark, but have failed so far: such is the power of unfair prejudice – and the unfairer, perhaps, the more powerful.

## 28  No owls in Iceland

I feel very differently about another of Denmark's former possessions, Iceland. I have felt happily at home in Iceland. I certainly do not mean at home in its landscapes, which are almost hallucinatorily alien, scarred with terrible glaciers, spouting all over the place into hot springs and volcanoes – an eighth of Iceland is one immense snowfield, and down the years I have myself watched the island of Surtsey, off the south-east coast, maturing from a plume of fiery smoke in the sea to a sizeable piece of new Icelandic territory. I mean I have felt at ease with the national outlook. Iceland is not in the least insular, in any pejorative sense. Nor does it seem, when you get there, particularly remote. Reykjavik feels just up the road from Edinburgh, where many citizens go for their Christmas shopping. I arrived once on the same aircraft as a well-known Swedish tenor, who had come to perform in an oratorio and would be popping back to Stockholm again next morning. The harpist of the Iceland Philharmonic is traditionally recruited in Wales, and on my very first visit to the republic, when I dined with the British Ambassador, he told me that the night before he had thrown a whisky bottle at the Icelandic Foreign Minister – as though they had been enjoying a rather too rowdy evening at the Students' Union.

The Icelanders are something like the rest of us, but not much. Descended about equally from Celts and Vikings, sometimes they look gently poetical, sometimes so loutish that they ought to be wearing horned helmets. Beauty and the Beast is a true Icelandic allegory. I have repeatedly been stopped short in Iceland by some totally unexpected dead end of behaviour or comment. Years ago I bought in Reykjavik a copy of Horrebow's *Natural History of Iceland*, published in an English translation in 1758. For the most part it is an archetypal work of the Age of Reason, arranged in chapters uniformly named and rationally argued – 'Concerning Earthworks in Iceland', 'Concerning Forests in Iceland', 'Concerning Horses', 'Concerning Butter and Cheese' – but Chapter 17 is a more characteristically Icelandic entry. 'Concerning Owls in Iceland' is its heading, and it consists in its entirety of the following minimalist analysis: 'There are no owls of any kind in the whole island.'

## 29   Which was the illusion?

I loved this odd streak in the Icelanders from the start. Many peoples suppose themselves extraordinary, and boast of being 'quite, quite mad', but the only ones who really seemed to me nationally, generically eccentric were the people of Iceland. Perhaps the long northern winters were the cause, or the cage of the winds above. Gargantuan toasts, awful hangovers, free love, sexy high spirits, gallons of coffee, throwing bottles at one another, sleeping round the clock – all these things I came to associate with the Icelanders. Their ancient language, the core of their nationality, was surrounded by a mystic exaltation, not without comedy. Bards abounded, people launched themselves without warning into poetic declamation, and strangers spoke of characters in the sagas, Grimur Goatbeard or Leif the Lucky, as though they were neighbours up the road.

One evening in Akureyri, on the northern coast, I heard the sound of solemn singing emerging from a restaurant, and peering through the door I saw that a large party was in progress. There the Icelanders sat in ordered ranks, their arms linked around the long tables, and as they sang what sounded like some sort of sacramental anthem they swayed heavily from side to side in a rhythmic motion. It gave me a queer impression of private solidarity – Iceland all over. Everybody knew the words of the song, and the whole assembly seemed to be in arcane collusion. I noticed that if ever I caught an eye, as the celebrants sang and swayed there at the tables, after a moment's puzzled focusing it abruptly switched away from me, as if to dismiss an illusion.

## 30 *Labyrinths*

I suppose the Romanians are *almost* as odd as the Icelanders. I did not get to Romania until 1994, but I felt I knew them well already. They were Frenchified Latins, peculiarly implanted among the Slavs of the East, and they were famously raffish, intriguing, high-flown, unpredictable and unreliable. At first it seemed to me that most of their conversations concerned *tunnels*. Tunnels apparently played a large part in Romanian history, as they figured largely still in their affairs – tunnels of love, tunnels of escape, rumoured conspiratorial tunnels. Tunnel-talk was everywhere. The whole Romanian mind-cast, it seemed to me, was tunnelly. The appalling dictator Nicolae Ceauşescu and his no less frightful wife had been dead for five years, but many of their associates were still in the Government, and every manner of twist and mayhem still complicated the corridors of power, making them feel subterranean too.

Ignorant as I was, I was dazed by the complexity of Romanian allusions. Which was Moldova and which Moldavia? What was the difference between Iron Guardists and Legionnaires? Was the Trans-Dniester issue the same as the Trans-Istria question? What was the Romanian Orthodox attitude to the matter of Bessarabia, and how did Catholics feel about the return of King Mihal? Was King Mihal the same as King Michael? Who were the Szekels? Louche but devout, often elegant in a feline way – with women tram-drivers smoking on the job, and headscarved babushkas sweeping leaves – with vulpine sellers of medicinal roots and peasants in high fur hats – with cinematic rogues, coats over their shoulders, trying to cheat you with financial transactions – with slyly evasive bureaucrats and delightfully cynical historians – with conversations bafflingly opaque, and memories almost fictionally improbable – the Romanians struck me as a cavalcade of everything I thought of as most unchangeably Balkan. While I was in the country the head of the national intelligence bureau declared Romania to be under threat from Legionnaires, Iron Guardists, international terrorism, organized crime, extreme leftists, Hungarian autonomists and the secret services of Russia, Ukraine, Hungary and Moldova. The fate of all Europe, he said, depended upon the solution of the Trans-Dniester issue.

## 31  *Six reasons*

One day I was given six different reasons why I might not enter Peleş Castle,
the former palace of the Romanian kings and queens at Sinaia:

(1) It was being rebuilt.
(2) There had been a robbery in it.
(3) An inventory was being conducted.
(4) It was about to be visited by President Hosni Mubarak of Egypt.
(5) It had lately been visited by President Saparmurad Niyazov of
    Turkmenistan.
(6) It was closed.


## 32  Nico o problema

Nevertheless the Romanians, who are lived among by large communities of
Hungarians, and are all wound about by Gypsies like a plant enmeshed in
the tendrils of a parasite, despite their neuroses are charmingly welcoming
to the stranger. Walking one day past the gloriously baroque Central House
of the Army in Bucharest, a marvel of elaboration in the very heart of the
Paris of the Balkans, I noticed that its ground floor appeared to be a restaurant.
I breezed in through the revolving doors and asked if I could bring some
guests to dinner. '*Nico o problema,*' they said at once with the well-matured
smile Romanians specialize in, and sure enough that night, with a jolly crew
of acquaintances, I found myself sitting there, to the deafeningly amplified
thump of a band, eating pike-perch from the Danube and drinking a happy
Riesling from Moldavia (as against Moldova, I think). And when I once
blundered into the headquarters of the Romanian Writers' Union, for decades
a tribunal of Communist orthodoxy, I was allowed to wander as I wished,
bemused and unhindered, through the accumulated cigar-smoke of a thousand ideological debates, amiably nodded at now and then by marvellously
literary-looking confrères.

## 33 *Psychotocracy*

Romania's Communist despotism had been different in kind from those in Warsaw, Budapest, Sofia, Prague or East Berlin. It was a Latin autocracy, it was often at odds with the Soviet Union, and it was presided over by a pair of psychotics, Ceauşescu and his all-but-illiterate wife being more like crazed tyrants of the old Orient than normal Stalinists. They had destroyed whole villages by the hundred. They had planned to drain the marvellous Danube delta, one of Europe's great havens of wildlife, uproot all its vegetation, and turn it into paddy-fields. Even more than the recidivism of Hungarians, even more than historical grievances or Ottoman legacies, even more than the Trans-Dniester issue, even more than the Gypsies! the ghosts of this appalling couple still muddled and muffled the affairs of the country. An entire generation had grown up under their twenty-two-year aegis, and it showed.

I had assumed the fall of the Ceauşescus to be something definitive in Romanian history, like the collapse of the Berlin Wall – the end of dreams and nightmares, the opening of the road to the prosaic. Once in the country, I was not so sure. Ceauşescu's follies seemed to have become organic to the place: perhaps it was the nature of Romania to absorb everything, spewing out nothing, simply adding even the wildest excess or improbability to its historical repertoire, or storing it away in a tunnel. For example, an immense boulevard, two or three miles long, had been intended to form the central axis of Ceauşescu's infamous new Bucharest, one of the supreme megalomaniac monuments of history. It was still unfinished in 1994 (all its myriad fountains were dry), but already parts of it were being humanized by trees, shops and the general flotsam and commotion of city life, so that I could imagine it in another twenty years being as essential to the flavour of Bucharest as the boulevards of the city's Francophile past. Even the vast palace which crowned Ceauşescu's capital was becoming familiar, if hardly homely. Its scale and ugliness was inexpungible, of course. If the Vittorio Emanuele monument in Rome were to be magnified twenty or thirty times, it would have no more civic clout than Bucharest's Parliament Palace (née Palace of the People, a.k.a. Palace of the Ceauşescus). In living and working space the building was surpassed only by the Pentagon: in sheer volume only by a rocket-assembly hangar at Cape Canaveral and the Pyramid of Quetzalcoatl in Mexico. It wasn't finished, either, yet it seemed to me that people were already accepting it as part of the municipal furniture. Tourists were taken

there, conferences were held in its immense salons, and both houses of
Parliament were expected to move in one day. When I left the building one
afternoon I noticed curled up beside the ceremonial doors, which were
guarded by milling soldiers and security people, an elderly dog snoozing in
the chill sunshine. It looked perfectly at home.

## 34  *Shrines and symbols*

Over the Danube is Bulgaria, whose recent history has been, by and large,
one long record of difficulty and frustration, geography having placed it
between two of the most uncomfortable neighbours on earth. Russia was
traditionally Bulgaria's protector – 'Grandfather Ivan' – finally bestowing
upon it a particularly distasteful Stalinist regime; Turkey was traditionally its
oppressor, occupying the country for several centuries and intermittently
indulging in massacres. In the twentieth century Bulgaria has experienced
nothing but trouble – despotisms of one kind and another, defeat in the
Balkan War of 1913, humiliation in the First World War, unfortunate alliance
with the Nazis in the Second, the Russian 'liberation' of 1944, the long years
of Communist autocracy, remembered by the world at large in eerie images
of poisoned umbrellas, hired assassins and the brutally forced Bulgarization
of minorities.

It was only during the 1990s that the Bulgarians, a charming people that
nearly everyone likes, achieved the freedom to be themselves. When I
travelled around the country during the hiatus between Communism and
whole-hog capitalism – when the collective farms lay in ruins but the battery
hens had not yet arrived, when the party headquarters had been turned into
a cinema but the mausoleum of Georgi Dimitrov, the father of Bulgarian
Communism, had not yet become an art gallery – when I made my journey
then it became a journey from one national shrine to another, through rings
of pride and defiance. Such monuments of fortitude and National Revival!
Such images of brave Bulgarian lions! Such museums of sacrifice and revolution! Such cenotaphs, mausoleums and tombs of poets and soldiers! Such
monasteries of patriotic faith! Such statues of heroes, churches of thanksgiving,
sites of brief-lived constituent assemblies! No patriot on earth is more patriotic
than a patriotic Bulgar, and nothing is more symbolic than a Bulgarian
symbol.

An enormous hilltop cenotaph, the Freedom Monument, commemorates the most fateful event in modern Bulgarian history, the battle of the Shipka Pass. It stands high in the Balkan Mountains in the very heart of the country, embellished with the mightiest and best-fed of all the Bulgar lions. The battle was actually an episode in the Russo-Turkish war of 1877, but it resulted directly from the great Bulgarian rising against the Turks in the previous year, which was put down with such savagery that all Europe was horrified. The Russians went so far as to intervene on behalf of the Bulgarians, and the victory won among the snows of Shipka led eventually to the independence of Bulgaria. There are plenty of memorials to the Russian sacrifices of the battle, but the Freedom Monument easily caps them all. Was it not the Bulgarian contingent, after all, which really won the day, 'supported', as my Bulgarian history bravely says, 'by not very many Russians'? An almost constant stream of schoolchildren climbs the 894 steps to the cenotaph of Shipka, a little vague I dare say about the strategy and even the participants in the battle, but left in no doubt that it was a famous victory of their own.

## 35 *Loyalty in the rain*

One day I was caught in a torrential rainstorm in the very heart of Bulgaria, Aleksandâr Nevski Square in the capital, Sofia. How the rain pelted down, making the green gardens soggy, making the paving-stones shine, dripping off the leaves of the trees all around, streaming down the gaudy ceramic tiles of the Holy Synod building and the golden domes of the cathedral! In a flash the pedestrians vanished into shelter, and only a few cars cautiously navigated their way through the downpour in the streets around the square. I fled myself, this way and that in search of somewhere dry, until I reached the doors of the church of Sveta Sofia. This is a very holy little place. It was built in the sixth century, and gave its name to the city itself. Inside I found two nuns and a young priest, chatting there in the shadows, and they dragged out a kitchen chair for me, and invited me to join them. Icons shone around us. The old brick church was dark and echoing. The rain drummed on the roof and splashed against the doors. I spoke no Bulgarian. The nuns and the priest spoke nothing else. We sat there benevolently smiling at one another, now and then nodding or shyly laughing, until the rain seemed to be dying away at last. I said my thanks and goodbyes, and walked back into the square.

The storm was passing away towards the mountains, rumbling. Around the corner, soaked to the skin, his clothes hanging dank around him, his hat all floppy with water, an elderly man was standing still and silent before the Tomb of the Unknown Soldier.

## 36 Nazdrave!

Cherishing a decided weakness for the Bulgarians myself, I heartily sympathize with all these emotions, and am as stirred as anyone by the Freedom Memorial, the Tomb of the Unknown Soldier and all the tales of patriotic derring-do. Every people needs its moments of romantic ecstasy, to make up for its miseries, and even in the late 1990s Bulgaria's troubles did not seem to be over yet. The countryside looked lovely, the wine was delicious, flowers were everywhere, waiters shyly smiled, geese, goats and donkeys roamed the purlieus of picturesque villages, truckers' halts served nourishing soups, the package-tour resorts on the Black Sea thrived; but most people were extremely poor still, politics sounded murky and economics unreliable. Of course the Bulgarians wanted shrines and symbols! Who wouldn't? Often enough they went far back into their history to find them, into the rich hazy world of proto-Bulgars, Thracians and Bogomils, and the most apposite of all their patriotic icons, to my mind, was one of these. Above the village of Madara, with a railway station that suggested to me something to be blown up by Lawrence of Arabia on the Hejaz Railway, in the cliffs above the dusty hamlet there was carved an antique figure. So old was it, and so eroded, that you could discern it only when the setting sun caught its outline, and no more than vaguely even then. But in photographs you could see more clearly the Horseman of Madara, and realize how relevant he was to the condition of his country. There he rode, indomitable if only just recognizable. He had a jolly greyhound at his heels, and appeared to have lately slaughtered some wild beast. With his right hand he grasped the reins of his prancing horse, but his left hand was raised exuberantly high above his head, and in it he was holding a wine-cup. 'Nazdrave!' the Madara Horseman cried to history – 'Cheers!' And 'Nazdrave!', down the centuries, Bulgaria had loyally cried back.

## 37  *The wrong story*

Just as I drove away, on page 68, to my war in the Middle East, the people of Budapest rose in arms against their awful Communist Government. As we said heartlessly at the time, two great stories broke simultaneously, and I went to the wrong one. The Suez adventure turned out to be hardly more than a squalid and ignominious expression of pique: the Hungarian Rising was the most tragically heroic event of the entire Cold War between capitalism and Communism.

Budapest was just the place for it. It does not seem to me a very lovely city, as the tourist brochures claim, but it is made for glory. On the right bank of the Danube is piled the old capital of Buda, with its royal castle and cathedral resplendent at the top; on the left bank extends the mass of Pest, all grand boulevards, parks and church steeples, running away to the horizon in a flatland of suburbs, and fronted on the river bank by the grotesque and mighty Parliament. Six bridges connect the two halves of Budapest, and the whole city suggests to me a figure of lapidary pride, commemorating always the sieges, battles, rebellions and miscellaneous splendours of its history. By and large modern Hungarians may look about as ordinary as the rest of us, but in my romantic way I like to fancy in them the spirit of the Magyar horsemen who ride in sculpted bronze about the national memorial in Heroes' Square: haughty magnificent noblemen, ineffably proud on their caparisoned horses as they ride at a leisurely pace into the city, their kingly leader looking majestically in front of him, his companions glaring this way and that from beneath their feathered helmets like presidential security men. And in 1956, as it happened, my fancy proved to be true: the people of Budapest, ancients to schoolchildren, rose in fury against their oppressors as to the Magyar manner born.

How I would love to have been there! Within a month a thousand Soviet tanks had viciously suppressed the Hungarian Revolution, and a whole-hog Communist Government was reinstalled. But, though the battle was tragically lost, it was the start of the winning of the war. By the time I did get to Hungary, in the 1970s, it was the first of the Communist countries of eastern Europe to be flirting with the idea of a market economy. There was talk already of a Hilton Hotel! Russian soldiers were still all over the place, still pouring off the Moscow train, still strutting about in their preposterous officers' hats, but by the standards of Poland, Czechoslovakia or East Germany

the regime was enlightened. I was astonished by the conversations of the
citizenry, so risky it seemed to me then, blatantly subversive, apparently
confident that life was going to get better. The diktats of Communism were
brazenly disregarded. I was taken to a privately owned holiday home on
Lake Balaton which might almost have been in Switzerland, and for the first
time I experienced the bitter pleasure of choosing between State-owned
shops and private enterprises – the first so abjectly disagreeable, the second
already full of smiles and salesmanship.

Twenty-five years on again, and I was back in Budapest for Christmas.
Now the war was won. Apart from a memorial or two, there was almost
nothing to remind me of the Communist years. The Hilton, so wild a
promise in the old days, had been joined by four or five other international
hotels, all equally luxurious. The shops were vivid, and, hard though I tried
(for I missed them rather), I could find none of those grumpy white-aproned
women, congenitally unable to smile, who had represented the triumph of
Marxist-Leninism behind the counters of Communist Budapest. And that
old air of heroism? Had it evaporated? I went to a performance of operetta
pieces at the Vigadó concert hall, and for a time I thought it had. There was
plenty of froth, of course, to the old melodies, plenty of Gypsy charm, but
the young gentlemen of the dancing chorus seemed to me a little effete as
they waltzed around the stage in white ties and tails. Presently, though,
having slipped into something looser, they broke into the violent stamp and
strut of the *csárdás*, that old display of everything most theatrically Hungarian;
and then as they threw their heads back, drummed the floor, slapped their
thighs, flung their arms into the air and sometimes wildly shouted, while the
audience clapped to the accelerating rhythm – then I saw in them, benignly
mutated, the cold sneer of the horsemen in Heroes' Square, and the reckless
style of the boys who had swarmed over the Red Army's tanks in 1956.

## 38  Bringing back the style

One symptom of Communist relaxation, in the Budapest of the 1970s, was
an emphasis on historical continuity. It is true that an official history of the
capital I was given then casually dismissed the 1956 rising as counter-
revolutionary, and claimed that almost at once 'a resolution of the Hungarian
Socialist Workers' Party analysed its causes and laid the foundation of new
political measures and economic decisions'. True too that part of the Great

Boulevard, Budapest's monumental ring road, was still named for Lenin. But I was struck by the surprising attention being paid to the memory of the Habsburgs, whose kings and queens had ruled Hungary until the collapse of their empire after the First World War. Part of the Boulevard was named for Vladimir Ilyich indeed, but part was named for the Emperor Franz Josef; the yellow paintwork so characteristic of the Habsburg domains was assiduously renewed; my party cicerones made a point of directing me to cafés and restaurants which preserved some of the old imperial atmosphere – the New York Café, ineffectually renamed the Hungaria, Gerbeaud's patisserie, the old resort of the sweet-toothed aristocracy, or Gundel's restaurant, which had started life as the zoo restaurant but had become the very epitome of Habsburg Budapest around the turn of the century.

In 1996 the Habsburgs and their era were even more fulsomely remembered. The New York Café and Gerbeaud's had become among the city's best-known tourist sites. Most of the Great Boulevard once more honoured the old monarchy. Gundel's, for so long a fief of the Communist State, had been taken over by rich and imaginative Hungarian Americans, and was frank in its gastronomic loyalties; I did not in fact try the soup identified simply as Franz Josef's Favourite, but I did indulge myself in a marvellously courtier-like meal consisting of Wild Suckling-Pig Soup Flavoured with Tarragon, and Count Széchenyi's Roast Breast of Pheasant Stuffed with Hungarian Goose Liver. I felt the presence of archdukes around me as I ate, and was not surprised to read a testimonial from Otto von Habsburg himself, the dispossessed heir to the imperial monarchy, declaring that Gundel's revival showed Hungary was 'on the way to recovery from years of oppression, and moving towards a glorious future'. Precisely, said I to myself, indelicately burping.


39  *From* The Budapest Sun, *19 December 1996*

### HEIR PROMOTES EU BID

To help promote the country's bid to join the European Union, Hungary appointed royal heir György Habsburg Ambassador for European Integration.

The Habsburg family, heirs to the Hungarian throne since the fifteenth century, have used their dynastic and diplomatic network to lobby for Hungary in European organizations since the political transformation of 1989.

Habsburg is the director of MTM Communications, the largest movie production and distribution company in Central Europe.

## 40  *Hellenic disillusionments*

On a lovely spring day I climbed the Mouseion hill in Athens, all among the olive trees, to see the celestial view of the Parthenon from its summit. The morning smelt delectably of pines and flowers and dust, and my mind was full of Hellenic glories: halfway up, a Greek sprang from the bushes, opened his mackintosh wide, and revealed to me his manly equipment.

Well, I suppose, why not? Greek art has been displaying masculine glories to us for a few thousand years. Nevertheless, on the Hill of the Muses, within sight of the Acropolis itself . . . I felt betrayed. My generation was brought up to think of things Greek as particularly pure and radiant, down to the Greek soldiery which had, apparently in pompoms and ballet skirts, so courageously defied both the Italians and the Germans during the war. Were the Greeks not the inventors of democracy? Were they not the fathers of poetry? To find a representative of this noble race flashing his cock to innocent tourists on the Mouseion was a sad disillusionment.

But actually Athens had long been a come-down itself. I fear in retrospect that those Hellenic fragrances I relished on the hill were fragrances purely of the mind, because already the capital was habitually veiled in a greenish smog, swirling up from the industrial quarters of Piraeus and so thickly masking the city that sometimes the Acropolis, protruding above its vapours, looked as though it was levitating. The sentries outside the royal palace, too, were something of a disappointment to anyone of romantic fancy. Goose-stepping up and down in their full and famous finery, they looked less like soldiers of Greek myth than farm boys in drag – bulging, rather sweaty young men who might easily, I could not help thinking, in their off hours mount a performance on the hill of Mouseion.

## 41  *The Quandary*

Do the Greeks, I once asked a Greek acquaintance of mine, consider themselves a Western or an Eastern people? 'That,' he replied, 'is our Quandary.' He said it with a palpable capital Q, and with reason. By the 1990s Greece had become a full member of the European Union, but for myself I still doubt whether Greeks are temperamentally, instinctively, even stylistically Europeans. In the days of classical education John Murray's *Handbook to Greece*, 1884, could observe comfortably that any visitor 'with the usual knowledge of ancient Greek' might read the Athenian papers with ease. The knowledge is not so usual now, and the universal links with Greece, fostered by generations of teachers, theologians and art historians, have long since weakened. For every Winckelmann or Byron, devoted to the ideas of Hellenism, there are a dozen scholars and artists dedicated to the culture of Africa, the Incas or the Australian aborigines. As for me, there are few places in Europe where I feel abroad these days, so intimately related are this continent's languages, histories, approaches to life and love, but in Greece almost everything is foreign to me, from the script to the cuisine to the manner of thought. In Greece I feel hardly more among ethnic relatives than I do in Bangkok or Zagazig.

## 42  *A pasha*

'Is the hotel open?' I innocently asked in the deserted off-season lobby of the posh Xenia Palace in Nauplia. 'It seems to be,' said the receptionist unpleasantly, 'since you're inside it.' Greek functionaries can be very disagreeable, and even in the 1990s I take this to be an echo of the long centuries of Turkish occupation – we were within sight of the castle of Bourdzi, where the executioners whiled away their old age back on page 64. The Xenia receptionist was like one of the obstructionist pashas one reads about in old travel books, perpetually making things as difficult as possible, and there is a good deal in Greece which smacks to this day of Ottoman orneriness, together with those suggestions of slyness and conspiracy that now seem as native to the country as ouzo.

## 43  *Europe or not?*

Let us visit any run-of-the-mill provincial town in the last years of the twentieth century in Greece. The sea is in front of it, the hills are behind. Architecturally it is mostly pure Balkans: flat roofs, flowered concrete, busts of national heroes, and rival cafés across a cement-flagged square. Technically it seems to be in a condition of semi-suspense, so that we can never be sure whether any given traffic-light is working or not, and half the buildings appear to have been abandoned before completion. Our brand-new hotel smells of cement, and we are woken in the morning by a rhythmic banging from the quayside outside its windows, where a fisherman is slapping a large octopus on the ground to soften it for the pot. The town's manners vary unpredictably from the sweet to the curmudgeonly. In the least forbidding of the restaurants we are given the choice of mutton, fish stew and thick pasta, all bubbling in their cauldrons in the kitchen. The beach, pictured in brochures pristine as anything, is in fact scummed with rubbish, pecked over by carrion crows and scavenged about by cats. In the evenings the cafés are taken over by the Greek Army, hundreds of uniformed conscripts sitting about doing nothing in particular, while up at the market quarter all is a souk-like vividness of commerce and vegetables, lightly touched with tourism. The voices of this town are very loud. The air is exhilarating. The temper is generally cordial. Are we in Europe or not? It is a Quandary.

## 44  *The charm of it*

But it can be a Liberation, too. The easy individualism of the Greeks is fine – if there is anything the contemporary Greek is not, it is downtrodden or standardized. For one of my tastes the general sense of incipient anarchy is a stimulant, and the effervescent variety of life, the feeling that you never know what is going to show up round the corner, is a welcome antidote to the growing homogenization of everything elsewhere. One minute there is the spectacle of a scudding hydrofoil out at sea, thundering in a blur of spray towards some Homeric isle, the next a dissonant clanging of bells fixed to the axle of a horse-drawn cart. A hurrying truck blows a horn like a fairground carousel. From the little glass-fronted shrines that line the highways there is an atavistic glint of trinkets, coins and bottles. There must be more beehives in Greece than in the rest of the world put together, and at Delphi they sell the honey in tins, with peel-off tops like beer cans or cat food. On the Byzantine slopes of Mistra I once encountered a nun picking olives halfway up a tree, attended by her goat at the bottom.

Sometimes it seems to me astonishing that anything works at all in Greece, so slap-happy does its populace seem, but this is perhaps as much a matter of personality as of capacity. More often I feel that if it comes to an emergency a kind of makeshift efficiency will prevail – Levantine guile combined with the chewing-gum-on-the-carburettor improvisation that used to characterize the resource of rural America. One night at a hotel in Euboea I found myself without my passport, carelessly left behind several hundred miles away in the Peloponnese. A few extremely loud telephone calls, a complex mobilization of taxis, buses and family contacts, and somehow or other by the next morning it had found its way to Khalkis. 'I am going to make you very happy,' said the hotelier as he produced it like a conjuror from beneath his desk, and he knew of course that I was about to contribute to *his* happiness, too.

## 45 Drunk in Monemvasía

I have only twice been properly drunk in Europe – tipsy ten thousand times, really sozzled only twice. The first time was at Catterick Camp in the north of England, when I was just eighteen. The second time was at Monemvasía, in the Peloponnese, when I was fifty-two, was working on a book and should have known better. I had taken a room in a private house on the outskirts of the village, and in the evening I walked a mile or so to a tavern for my supper. It was very full, and very lively – local people mostly, with some merry Americans. We drank large amounts of furiously resinated draught retsina out of metal mugs, and I seldom had a happier evening. In the small hours I staggered up the road again to my lodgings, and I can still see the face of my landlady, in a flowered housecoat over her nightdress, as she pulled back the bars and undid the chains of her front door to let me in. I expected her to be tight-lipped and disapproving: instead she greeted me with a sly and knowing smile of collusion, very nearly a wink, as if she had been enjoyably up to no good herself. I went to bed incoherently whistling, and awoke in the morning fresh as a daisy.

## 46 Euro-Hellene

Europe? Would my landlady have been so conspiratorially forgiving if we had been in Germany? Do Greek truck-drivers really keep to the European tachometer rules? Are the scrawny Greek sheep of the mountains really dipped and vaccinated to Brussels standards? Do any Greek fishermen, thumping their octopuses on the quay, take any notice of European laws about keeping their hair covered while processing seafood? But there we are, the Greeks are officially Westerners now, and their admission into the comity of Europe suggests to me something raw and vital put into a vat to help the fermentation: a rough organic agent, with plenty of bacteria in it. This is a different metaphor indeed from the classical visions of my youth – gone from the Greek image is the bounding grace and elegance, the gravitas of the philosophers, the style of the clean-limbed athletes with their curls and chiselled noses. But who knows? Perhaps the people of ancient Greece were really Levantine all the time – dark-skinned, stocky and evasive like second-hand car dealers in Piraeus.

In 1993 I spent a day at Epidauros, where the temple of Asklepios once offered its cultists the hope of eternal life. The marvellous theatre, cradle of stage drama, was swarmed all over by visitors of a dozen nationalities. Sometimes people standing in the orchestra whispered, or rustled pieces of paper, to demonstrate the famous acoustics of the place. A tour guide mounted a block and quoted some verse, instantly recognizable to anyone with the usual command of ancient Greek. An Italian performed 'O Sole Mio'. A tall young man and an elderly lady half his height sang with much feeling and to great effect some kind of romantic ballad – a touching performance, in a tongue which none of us recognized, but which moved us all to applause.

What language were they singing, I hastened to ask the performers, there in the theatre of Sophocles, Aristophanes and Euripides? It was Finnish, they said, and the song was a folk-melody from Europe's remotest north. I was exuberant. 'Viva Europa!' I cried in my adolescent way: but nobody responded much, beyond a sheepish laugh or two.

## 47   Mirësevni në Shqipëri!

'Mirësevni në Shqipëri' is what it said on the immigration forms when I arrived in Albania – 'Welcome to Albania.' They must have been printed after 1992, because until then Shqipëri was the most inflexibly, disagreeably, alarmingly and indeed insanely unwelcoming country in Europe. For most of my fifty European years I had contemplated it in bewilderment from outside. Its blue-grey coast looked back at me tantalizingly across the Strait of Corfu, inaccessible as a bank vault. I gazed upon its silent mass, as upon a morgue, from the mountains of Montenegro. As I pursued the tracks of the British Empire in the Ionian Islands, I remembered with a shudder the hired executioner who used to come over from Albania (no Greek would do the job) wearing a face-mask and a particoloured costume like a jester. The case of the Corfu Strait, when Albanian mines sank two British destroyers with terrible loss of life, rumbled through my early years in journalism, and for decades I could hardly turn on my short-wave radio, wherever I was, without hearing the monotonous dogmatic voice of Radio Albania, telling us of Comrade Hoxha's latest achievements in revolutionizing chemical production, or eliminating religion. Comrade Hoxha – Friend Hoxha, as his subjects were supposed to call him! Of all the unhinged despots in the Europe of my time, Enver Hoxha was undoubtedly the most deranged. He was madder than Ceauşescu. His people were cut off from all outside sources of information whatever, and for years they were conditioned to think of him as all-but-magical. He could cause the rain to come! Flowers blossomed in his footsteps! Many of his subjects really did believe that he had made Albania uniquely successful and enviable among all the nations of the world, whereas in fact it was uniquely *un*successful and *un*enviable. Hoxha quarrelled successively with the Western democracies, with Yugoslavia, with the Soviet Union, with Communist China, with God himself ('the only religion in Albania is being Albanian'), until in the end his country was all alone, friendless, destitute and paranoically nasty to everyone.

## 48  *Hoxha lives!*

Hoxha had been dead for six years when at last I reached Albania, and his irrational brand of Communism had been rejected for four. Almost at once I made a pilgrimage to honour a far older champion, the warrior-chief Skanderbeg – Alexander Bey – who had famously held the predatory Turks at bay in the fifteenth century. For Albanians Skanderbeg was undoubtedly the No. 1 Albanian of history, and he was the one Albanian who, with his heroic beard and his goat-horned helmet, had been known to me all my life as a face on a postage stamp. The scene of Skanderbeg's most celebrated exploit was the ruined fortress of Krujë, in central Albania, epically sited on a mountainside looking across a plain to the distant Adriatic. The place was fine, I thought. The view was tremendous, shimmering with heat-haze down to the sea. The citadel was properly defiant in its wreckage. The bazaar down the hill sold fox-skins. But even then, even in 1996, even in the presence of Skanderbeg himself, Enver Hoxha lived! For all across that wide landscape, much the most compelling feature of it, were the thousands and thousands of concrete pillboxes, egg-shaped, like so many grey-white igloos, which the dictator had caused to be constructed throughout the length and breadth of his country. I was told there were 800,000 altogether, big and small, and there seemed to be no strategic or even tactical pattern to them – they just popped up wherever you looked, sometimes in twos and threes, sometimes in dozens, and only now that Hoxha was dead were they beginning to crumble. Some had been broken, or upturned, or were used as houses or hay-stores, and down on the holiday coast one or two had recently been turned into cafés.

## 49 *The great release*

When I asked whom these defences had been to defend Albania against, they said 'Everyone.' Having spent much of his young manhood as a guerrilla partisan, Hoxha apparently feared invasion by the Americans, the Russians, the Yugoslavs, the Greeks, the Italians, and for all I know the Libyans too. One man I asked about the pillboxes in Krujë merely put his finger to the side of his head and twisted it. I don't know how persuaded most ordinary Albanians had been by Hoxha's persecution complex, but now that he had gone it was as though they were awakening from some awful nightmare, shaking their heads to be rid of the memory. His was a fearful tyranny. Scores of thousands of Albanians had been murdered or worked to death in his prison camps – forty-eight of them, in a country the size of Wales or Maryland. Every kind of freedom had been abolished. Censorship had been absolute. Secret police and Government informers were everywhere. Beards, blue jeans and rock music were forbidden. Just as nobody could enter the country, so nobody could leave either. Babies' names had to be chosen from an officially approved list, changed each year.

Six years after Hoxha's death, when his body had long been exhumed from its tomb of honour, the sense of release was still palpable, and infectious. Poverty was still cruel in Albania, industry was ramshackle, politics were corrupt. The usual post-Communist mafia was rampant – Albanian gangs were a byword as far away as Germany. Nevertheless it seemed to me, in 1996, a remarkably exuberant country. All the symptoms of capitalism were sprouting then – Western-financed hotels, Arab-financed tourist developments, Italian restaurants, backstreet boutiques, service stations, car-washes, glossy propaganda magazines for visiting foreign executives. I went down to the coast one weekend, and the beaches around Durrës were jammed with cars and coaches, festive, noisy and sticky. All among the seaside pine-woods, full of picnickers, those pillboxes abjectly lurked.

## 50 *En fête*

In 1992, when the Albanian Communist regime came to an end, there were only fifty cars in the capital, Tirana, and pictures I had seen of Skanderbeg Square, the heart of the city, showed it all but empty, with only a few disciplined pedestrians crossing its enormous ceremonial space. By the time I got there 40,000 cars swarmed the Tirana streets (a third of them Mercedes, almost all of them second-hand, most of them stolen in Germany) and Skanderbeg Square was a sort of maelstrom. It contained a mosque, a clock-tower, a museum, a cultural centre, a functional-modernist hotel, a national bank, a fountain or two, sundry Italianate government offices, dozens of street stalls, an equestrian statue of Skanderbeg, and two extremely noisy funfairs. Countless men of all ages wandered around offering black-market exchange rates. Innumerable children rode the funfair rides. Around the edges of the place scores of cafés were in a perpetual kind of frenzy, and round the back an immense street market pullulated in a welter of fish-stalls, butcheries, vegetable-carts and stacks of old bicycles. It was rather as though the great square of Marrakesh had been worked over successively by Atatürk, Mussolini and Stalin, and then handed over to the management of the Tivoli gardens in Copenhagen.

In the evening the entire population of Tirana seemed to emerge for the twilight *passeggiata*, strolling up and down the main avenue, sitting on the edges of fountains, milling around the funfairs, wandering haphazardly across highways apparently under the impression that there were still only fifty cars in the city. The noise seemed to me then a supremely Albanian noise – the hooting horns of a thousand newly acquired and uncertainly driven automobiles, the whistles of distraught traffic cops, and the deafening beat of mingled rock, rap and Balkan folk-music. I loved the louche insouciance of it all, ever-ready smiles from the citizenry, inescapable suggestions of roguery, the immense hum over everything, the quirks and surprises. Sometimes I felt a small dry kiss on my arm, and turned to find a Gypsy child irresistibly importuning me for cash. When I testily shooed off a young man in a T-shirt and jeans, supposing him to be yet another currency tout, he shyly introduced himself as one of the President's bodyguards, trying to warn me away from the presidential front gate.

I walked one night into the huge pyramidical structure which had been designed to be a museum of Enver Hoxha – in his own lifetime! – and was now converted to more secular uses. It was strikingly lit up after dark, and swarmed all around by numberless crowds of idlers, up and down its ceremonial steps, in and out of its basement café, eating ice-creams and loudly talking. Irrepressible urchins climbed its smooth concrete buttresses in order to slide down again. What should I find in the main hall of this tumultuous building, this hilariously discredited monument of egotism, but four young people exquisitely performing Ravel's string quartet?

## 51  *Positive identification*

Poor old Hoxha! What would he think? Ogre though he was, I rather regretted his posthumous elimination from Tirana. For most foreigners, after all, Hoxha rather than Skanderbeg was Albanian No. 1. I did visit his house, in the formerly sealed-off official quarter known as The Block – a respectable suburban-style part of town from which, in Hoxha's day, ordinary citizens were entirely banned. Even in 1996, as I wandered the tyrant's garden paths I was followed always by an armed guard, and when I stooped to pick a flower from a bed of Michaelmas daisies I thought I heard behind me (though perhaps I was fantasizing here) the click of a safety-catch. Was it OK to take a flower? I asked the young man over my shoulder, just in case; but instead of shooting me he made an expansive gesture of permission. Take the lot, he seemed to be saying. They were only Friend Enver's.

I wished Hoxha's museum were still his museum, and in particular I wished that his immense bronze statue still stood in the main square (where its plinth did remain, beside one of those funfairs, and was tottered over by enterprising infants in need of parental guidance). So I was excited when somebody told me that the statue still existed in Tirana, preserved in the Monuments Factory where it had originally been cast. In a flash I was there, accompanied by a young Albanian engineer of my acquaintance. Like most Albanian factories the Monuments Factory had gone out of business, and at first the watchman took us to the wrong statue – that last public statue of Stalin, as it happened, which I noticed on page 79. 'Oh, you want *Enver*,' the watchman then said (everyone in Albania still called him Enver): 'Enver's in *there*' – and he directed us to a windowless warehouse apparently sealed off for ever. We circled this gloomy mausoleum searching for keyholes to look through or doors to peer under, and in the end I found a spyhole between the bricks.

There Enver Hoxha was, recumbent in the shadows, just his bronze thigh to be glimpsed like something not very interesting in Tutankhamun's tomb. It was enough. My engineer positively identified the old monster, and he should know. As a student he had been in the forefront of the rejoicing crowd when the statue was pulled down in Skanderbeg Square. 'I pissed on it,' he complacently recalled, and you can't get more positive than that.

## 52 *Normality returns*

So normality of a kind returned to Albania, if only for a year or two, but it had already long returned to the Czech Republic, which I first knew as part of Czechoslovakia, and which had imprinted its name and character upon the consciousness of all Europe since the day in 1938 when Neville Chamberlain, Prime Minister of Great Britain, fatefully described it as a faraway country of whose people 'we know nothing'. When I first went there, in the 1950s, it was a country of degraded servility, where everything seemed to smell of sausages. The slogans of Communist piety nagged from every hoarding, the drab emblems of State management were on every corner shop. The only foreigners around were approved comrades – Afghans and Syrians, come to buy arms or cars, ideologically correct delegations of Poles, Romanians, Hungarians and East Germans, or groups of square-shouldered Russians in baggy trousers and drab hats.

At that time I took note, for literary purposes, of an apartment block at the corner of Kaprova and Valentinská streets in Prague. A cross between baroque and art nouveau, it had a small onion dome on one corner, and was embellished all over with symbolic images. There were balconies, and window-boxes, and lace curtains in the windows. A tobacco shop stood on the ground floor, and at the end of the street, over the river, you could see the spires and battlements of Hradčany, the old stronghold of the Czech kings. I chose to describe this building as an allegorical hostel of Communism, and fancied it full of drabness, fear, longing, austerity, compulsory pictures of Lenin and nosy-parker informants. I saw it too swirled about, there at the

road junction, by the whole parade of European history. I saw the armies of
Franz Josef, Adolf Hitler and Joseph Stalin all marching past its doors. I
saw ecstatically courageous students shouting slogans and waving banners.
Commissioners, gauleiters and commissars drove officiously by. Franz Kafka's
faceless functionaries trudged past on their way to the interrogation rooms,
Jaroslav Hašek's Good Soldier Švejk, bless his heart, smiled ironically down
on the lot of them.

But years later I went back to the corner of Kaprova and Valentinská
streets to reimagine these matters, and this time I saw something quite new
on an upper balcony of the apartment block, above the potted geraniums.
It was a TV satellite dish, the universal emblem of market-force society. It
suggested to me the olive leaf that the dove brought back to Noah, when
the flood began to recede.

## 53  *History on the blink?*

Had history ended in the Czech Republic? Going back to the country a few
years after the Velvet Revolution which finally got rid of the Communists,
sometimes I felt it had: the one great thing that had happened since was the
voluntary separation of Slovakia from Czechoslovakia, and that had been
scarcely noticed by the world at large (although, by an irony worthy of Švejk
himself, it was the very separation which, when Hitler implicitly decreed it,
gave rise to the Second World War). In the 1950s Prague had seemed to me
the most oppressive of the Communist capitals of eastern Europe, but its fate
was tragic and tremendous. Forty years on, the collapse of the Soviet Empire
had left its own smouldering layers of sleaze and squalor, but the public
miseries of the place were miseries familiar to us all. Stalinist Prague was
sufficiently corrupt, God knows, but in institutional ways: at least in the
1950s one was not cheated by taxi-drivers or robbed by jostling pickpockets.
The secret policemen were everywhere in those awful old times, every
official was waiting to be bribed, but there were none of the beggars
sitting with bowed heads, sometimes with their eyes hopelessly closed, who
represented contemporary sadness in the 1990s.

In 1993 I went to a political meeting in Old Town Square, scene of heroic
demonstrations in the days of the oppression, to hear a speaker inveighing
against Germans, Gypsies, prostitutes and illegal immigrants; he was supported
by skinheads and miscellaneous layabouts, protected by mounted police,

assaulted by flying bottles and the odd rotten vegetable. Prague had joined the ordinary world, and history was at least on the blink. In 1957 I had been warned, by somebody who knew, that not only my room in the morose Palace Hotel but actually my table in its restaurant was likely to be bugged. Now the same hotel offered American cable television in its bedrooms, a lavish variety of soaps, lotions, bath salts and shower-caps, and such excellent little notepads beside its telephones that I helped myself to a few from the maid's trolley in the corridor. When the Czech journalist Karel Kyncl returned to Prague in 1989, after seven years of exile, he said it was like sleep-walking.

## 54   Three recitals

In the last decade of the century Prague became one of the great tourist destinations of Europe. It had tried to be one under the Communists, but in those days its drably printed brochures and smudgy programmes did little to counteract the dark reputation of the place, and not many foreigners responded. Now thousands came, and loved it – its buildings, its atmosphere, its beer, and perhaps most of all its music. When I was last in Prague I went to three musical performances which profoundly affected me in different ways.

The first was an impromptu jazz concert in Old Town Square, where that right-wing demagogue had said his piece. Throughout eastern Europe jazz had played an important part, almost a symbolic part, in the various risings which had put an end to Communism, and I thought it stirring to hear the blast of the saxophone, the wail of the blues, there in the heart of Prague. I sat drinking *borivicka* then, as the Good Soldier would have done before me, and Prague's glorious baroque skyline was silhouetted around me against a velvet sky. The horses of the pleasure-barouches stood chomping at their bits, attended by grooms in long cloaks and brown bowler hats; the performers played with immense ebullience; every now and then excited small children, encouraged by their fond parents, ran out to deposit coins in the band-leader's open trumpet-case.

My second performance gave me less benign sensations. One windy morning I chanced to arrive at the gates of Hradčany Castle, beneath the proud standard of the President of the Republic, just in time for the changing of the guard. This struck me as an ambivalent display. The soldiers, in their long grey greatcoats, wore white scarves like Americans but marched like Russians. The bandsmen appeared at open first-floor windows, rather like the holy figures appearing at that very moment in the little windows of medieval clocks all over Europe, and they played a series of lush fanfares that sounded bathetically like film music. The flag flapped heavily in the wind above us. The troops marched and countermarched. The filmic fanfares sounded. I could imagine it all turning rather nasty if ever history started up again in Prague.

And my third concert was a recital, in the battered gilded church of Our Lady of Týn, of six different settings of Ave Maria (Schubert, César Franck, Cherubini, Saint-Saëns, Verdi, Gounod). It was extremely cold in the church, and we were all bundled in our pews. The soloist, Zdena Kloubová of the National Opera, sang from the organ loft behind us, and now and then I turned to see her. She looked very small and brave up there – almost defiant. She was wearing a black leather jerkin against the cold, and as her lovely voice rang out among the altars I thought her a haunting reminder of more heroic days among the Czechs: bad times, cruel times, but times when history happened.

## 55  My first Poles

My first Poles were Poles of the diaspora. For years after the Second World War I came across them everywhere. Near my own home in Wales hundreds of officers and their wives, exiled in 1939, lived out their lives in a bleak camp of Nissen huts and institutional buildings: many had fought with distinction in the war, many had been landowners and professional people in pre-war Poland, but over the decades I watched them age in dignified impotence among the sandy scrubland, until only a few ancients were left to mull over their memories and tell tales of old glories for junior reporters preparing feature articles for the local press. A Pole rented the room upstairs from mine when I first went to live in the dismal, battered and frequently power-cut London of 1948: he had been a cavalry officer at the start of the war, and he still went off most elegantly, in a bowler hat and a well-worn dark suit, to his work as a hotel doorman. Years later, visiting a Royal Air Force fighter squadron in Egypt, I found that the oldest and most dashing of the pilots was a Polish veteran of the Battle of Britain. The young men called him 'Uncle'. All these people seemed to me, whatever their circumstances, to be stylish and vivid in their exile: some had perhaps been Fascists of a kind, many were undoubtedly anti-Semitic, but war had scoured them, and made their minds as lean as their bodies – for none of them seemed to be fat.

## 56  Poles at home

These were my original Poles. How different they seemed when, in the 1950s, I met them on their native soil. Poland then was sunk in Stalinist subjection, governed by a regime of puppet ideologues. At first I thought the country infinitely dispiriting, because nobody seemed to have much hope of ever changing things. Poland had so often been occupied by those damned Powers down the centuries that the people seemed punch-drunk. Some colleagues took me to stay at a writers' retreat near Zakopane in the southern mountains, and on the way we were stopped by the police, on some pretext or other. Our driver, a journalist of great charm and intelligence, about my own age, did not even speak when the cop tapped on his window. He merely took his driving-licence from his inside pocket, tucked a banknote in it, and handed it out. The policeman did not speak, either. He had no need to. He just took the note, handed the licence back, and walked away. My friend drove off without a word to me. He knew what I was thinking, and there was nothing to say.

  If such a lively, clever and delightful man, I thought, was so numbed by history and the system, what could I expect of the populace at large? They seemed to me utterly disillusioned. On my first day in Warsaw a waiter offered to change money for me at generous black-market rates, and I accepted. When I happened to mention the fact to Polish acquaintances they said I had made a foolish mistake. The waiter might well have been an *agent provocateur* – I would find out when I came to leave the country and had to produce my receipts. It might have been a trap. The penalties were extreme, especially for foreigners – especially for foreign journalists. On the other hand perhaps it was just another poor sod trying to make a bit on the side, like that policeman in the South. Who could know? What could I do about it, anyway? Who cared? Forget it, and hope for the best. They took me up to Krasiński Square to show me the manhole into which the heroic fighters of the 1944 rising, driven out of the Old Town at last by the Nazis, had escaped with their wounded into the sewers below: but it was just another manhole, just another reminder of national impotence, and we looked at it in silence.

Then on a very cold and slushy day I stood on the great square of Kraków to hear the *hejnał Mariacki*, the trumpeter's call of St Mary's. Every hour, night and day, a trumpeter appeared in a high window of the church of St Mary to blow a slow sad call north, east, south and west, the most plaintive of tocsins, breaking off always in the middle of a phrase as tradition demanded (a thirteenth-century predecessor having been shot dead by a Mongol arrow before he could finish his warning). This was an unforgettably haunting polonaise, a true catch in the throat, and it was a terrible thing, I thought, to hear it then in the vast, beautiful and desperately shabby square. Kraków had been the capital of the wartime German colony of Poland. The General-gouvernement Polen, the administration was called, and everything in Kraków had been forcibly Germanized – Adolf-Hitler Platz had of course been the new name of the square, and so established did the Germans feel their presence to be that Baedeker even produced a guidebook (*Das Generalgouvernement*, 1943). Just along the road was Auschwitz. Now the Germans had gone but the Russians were there instead, just as domineering, just as arrogant, apparently irremovable. Kraków had not been badly damaged during the war, but there hung over it that day, I thought, a miasmic sense of helplessness. There were very few people about: the trumpet sounded over a muffled city, muffled alike by snow and by history, and when it broke off so abruptly the silence that followed seemed to me absolute.

## 57  *The style flickers*

Surely, I thought, this enervated fatalism had once and for all blunted the vigour and optimism which made the Poles of the diaspora so irrepressible. But I was wrong, and especially in the capital I did sometimes sense it. Warsaw was indeed the saddest place imaginable in those days. Looming over it was the enormous Palace of Culture donated by the Soviet people to their unfortunate neighbours, and this stood there as an inescapable emblem of recurrent subjection to the Powers. Piłsudski Square was now Stalin Square. Most of the city was inexpressibly run down, much of it still in ruins. Yet there were flashes of the old spirit. They were rebuilding Old Town Square, a baroque ensemble utterly destroyed by the Germans, just as it was, house by house with meticulous accuracy, and this seemed to me a saving

grace of the regime – to be honouring the past with such diligence. I
remember a covey of merry schoolchildren sloshing through the snow one
morning, their high-boned faces peering through fur hoods like fox cubs
through bushes. A few beautiful women somehow managed, for all the
shortages and hardships and puritan interferences, to dress themselves stylishly
and walk with panache. Though the Poles might be hangdog in the general,
in the particular they were still amused and inquisitive. Polish drunks were
still cheerfully bawdy. Polish humour was disrespectful. The style of the
Poles, which I found so poignantly urbane in their exile, flickered too among
the miseries of home. The writer Neal Ascherson says (in his *Black Sea*, 1995)
that for 150 years 'the essential experience of every generation of young
Poles' had been drinking hot drinks in cold rooms, arguing about what
kind of Poland they wanted, singing and listening to poetry. They were
acclimatized, I suppose.

## 58  Yarning

In the 1970s I took home from Poland a record by a popular young Polish
tenor of the day, singing (in English) Songs That Swept The World. How
it touched me then, and touches me still! Out of that snowbound, unhappy
country, a programme of wishful schmaltz, a reaching-out as it were to all
the more fortunate rest of us. The singer's English was peculiarly imperfect
as he carefully enunciated the words of those now half-forgotten lyrics; the
slightly jazzed-up strict-tempo orchestra was like something from a radio
broadcast of the 1930s; and as the young man rode his sentimental melodies
– '*Be my larv, fur nowan ulse can ind this yarning!*' – as his voice rose heroically
and invariably to the tonic in the final cadences, he brought into my distant
sitting-room all the grand pathos and passion of the Poles.

## 59  Not Chopin

I went back to Poland again in the winter of 1996, when the Soviet Empire
had long collapsed, and was surprised to find my emotions much the same.
Of all the ex-Communist countries, it seemed to me to have changed least.
There were bright new shops enough, posh hotels, plenty of cars, a lively
*jeunesse dorée*, all the usual paraphernalia of capitalism: but still the place

breathed a spirit of heroic poignancy, the spirit of Chopin in fact, once characterized by Schumann as guns in flower-beds. The patina of Communism still lay heavily upon Warsaw. The Mongolesque Palace of Culture, though surrounded now by the stalls and parked vans of a fairly dubious free market, was still the dominant building; the tenement oblongs of the old ideology still marched gloomily away into the suburbs; even the famously restored Old Town Square looked to me unmistakably a pastiche now, and a little shoddy at that, whose doors did not fit as the originals would have fitted and might have been better made (it occurred to me with a pang) by the carpenters of Disneyland.

On the other hand when I returned to that manhole near Krasiński Square I found a plaque on the wall above it, and over the street was a huge monument to the heroes of the 1944 rising, emerging furious from their hiding-places with guns at the ready, finally disappearing in ever-glorious defeat into the labyrinth. The Communists remembered that insurrection equivocally, because the tanks of the Red Army, already in the suburb of Praga just across the river, had declined to come to the help of the Poles, whose fighting leaders were anti-Communist to a man. Now the terrific tale has come into its own again, and is recognized as one of the supreme episodes of Polish history. It was a heroic failure, of course, but then most of Poland's battles are heroic failures, and the glories of Poland are always tinged with sadness.

The trumpeter was still faithfully blowing the *hejnał Mariacki* down in Kraków, and although the great square was far from empty now, and the lovely city had come wonderfully to life again – full of students and tourists and foreign entrepreneurs – even so I found the long slow call as sad as ever. The Communists had built a huge steel plant on the outskirts of the city, and sometimes during my stay Kraków was so plunged in smog, like an old London pea-souper, that the top of the church tower was lost in murky vapours, and we could not see the trumpeter at his high window. But one morning it cleared, the sun came out, and up there the brass of the trumpet flashed against the shadows. A party of schoolchildren waved enthusiastically, and when the call broke off I could just make out the hand of the trumpeter waving back – like the hand I saw in the blockhouse in Ireland, back on page 70.

So Poland moved me still, and Warsaw especially. It remained the least *superficial* of Europe's capitals, the least suited to all our glitz and trendiness, still sullenly ablaze, guns among the flower-beds, with its memories of cruelty, love, courage, hope, despair and sacrifice. 'Nice car,' I remarked to the man who drove me to the airport in his big new Volvo. He shrugged his shoulders and looked at me with a dry smile. I knew what he meant. 'Well no,' I added in afterthought, 'I suppose it's not Chopin': and he knew what I meant, too.

## 60  *An ad-hoc State*

How anomalous that Belgium should have become the administrative centre of the European Union, my generation's attempt to make a unity of the continent! Belgium is certainly not a Power. It is decidedly not a nation, split as it is between two peoples, the Flemings and the Walloons, each with their own language, loyalty, history and territory. It has been a State only since the 1830s, and even when there was a Belgian Empire in Africa the Congo was no more than a personal fief of the King. It still seems to me a kind of ad-hoc entity. One day I walked up to the royal palace in Brussels, which is a sort of distillation of all the royal palaces that ever were, and just as I arrived a plenipotentiary emerged through its gates in a big black car after a diplomatic presentation to the King of the Belgians (the sixth to hold that title since its invention). A footling squadron of cavalry awaited him in the ceremonial square outside. Its officers wore romantic white cloaks. Its troopers, in slightly cock-eyed bearskins, as in musical comedies or fancy dress, included some sceptical-looking horsemen of the old-sweat school, and at least one rosy-cheeked woman. When they clattered and bounced away with the ambassadorial Cadillac, a municipal road-sweeping truck came trundling around the place where they had mustered, cleaning up the horse-shit. Its driver told me he spent his days doing it. There were so many embassies, missions and international institutions in Brussels, he said, that the palace cavalry was always at it – and, sure enough, as he spoke the horsepersons, having disappeared around the corner with their fluttering lances, came ridiculously back again with another couple of limousines.

## 61  *Nothing to lose but their dividends*

The Belgians endure as many unkind jokes in Europe as the Poles used to in the United States, or the Irish and Welsh in England, and I hate to bait them; but I have to say that even the very heart of this kingdom, the Grand'

Place in Brussels, which is frequently touted as The Most Beautiful Square in the World, has always seemed to me pretentiously unsatisfying. There is no grace to it, except when its flower-market blossoms, or they turn part of it into a Christmas skating-rink. Its centrepiece is the gloomily Gothic Hôtel de Ville, and all around it are pompous gabled mansions of old trade guilds. They are covered with gilding and curlicues, with statues and symbols representing Grain, Prospects, Abundance, Agriculture, Slaughter (for the Butchers' Guild), sea-gods (for the river-boatmen), quivers (for the Guild of Archers), St Nicholas (patron saint of haberdashers), Bishop Aubert (patron saint of bakers), St Barbe (patron saint of tailors), together with weather-vanes and ogee windows and bobbles and baubles and initials and elaborate gilded dates. Nothing, to my mind, can make them seem elegant. They are heavy aldermanic houses, rich, chain-of-office houses, and the only touch of irony to them is the fact that in one of the grandest, No. 9, Marx and Engels collaborated in 1847 on the Communist Manifesto – 'Workers of the world unite!' Nowadays the Grand' Place and the streets that run into it are chiefly devoted to Belgium's pre-eminent activity, eating, and the house where Marx and Engels worked is La Maison du Cygne (four red spoons and forks in Michelin).

## 62   *Where are the barricades?*

By contrast with Belgium the Netherlands (Holland as the world wrongly insists upon calling the country) is very much the real thing. Ninety-six per cent of its people are Dutch, which makes it decidedly a nation; nobody can dispute its potent Statehood; and in its time it has been a great imperial Power. It is an economic Power still. Dutch corporations ring the world: stores, bus companies, publishing houses, shipping lines in many countries are Dutch-owned; Japanese and American firms by the dozen prefer to base their European activities in the Netherlands, where things work well, people are reliable, and the meaning of hard cash is properly understood (I once saw a suburban house in Delft named 'Time is Money' . . .). In my time, nevertheless, the popular image of the Netherlands has been pre-eminently one of progressive if not outrageous tolerance, of a country where anything goes. In the 1960s a visit to Amsterdam, undisputed capital of the Alternative Culture, was one of the thrills of Europe. The whole world was variously fascinated and appalled by the allure of the place then, and almost anyone with a taste for anarchy made the paradoxical pilgrimage to this country of mellow colours, gentle façades and commonsensical businessmen.

It was curious to return to Amsterdam thirty years later. It was not like going back to Prague when the Communists had gone, but it was a sort of culture shock nonetheless. This was not the Amsterdam we had known and loved! Where was the shock of it? Where the barricades? There was hardly a drug pedlar or a squatter to be seen, not a protest procession, not a broken bottle, not a whiff of tear-gas, no heady suggestion of libertarianism or ungovernable youth. The triple-trams went smoothly by. The glass-topped tourist launches slid around the waterways. A hundred thousand bicycles sensibly came and went. The traffic was orderly. The noise was not excessive. Dear God, it was a different city when we were young!

Of course there were still echoes of Alternative Amsterdam. There was a Sex Museum. You could drift the waterways on a Smoke Boat Cruise (wink wink, as its organizers said), or sample a choice of cannabis in cafés. In the red-light quarter, down by the Oude Kerk, the whores still displayed themselves in pink and silken *déshabillé* behind their windows, and after dark there were plenty of men on street corners whom I assumed to be pimps, drug dealers or at least honest-to-goodness deviants. But then so what? By then you could find these things anywhere in Europe. By then pornography was all the rage in *Albania*! In the Amsterdam of the *fin de siècle* there was not much to disconcert your grandmother from the country; but then grandmothers were not what they used to be, either.

## 63  *The nature of modernity*

Besides, the Netherlands was a particularly modern country. Its 1960s-style permissiveness was very modern in its time, but over the decades it became a little *passé*. Thirty years on, Europe as a whole, astonishingly varied though it remained, was undeniably more *ordinary* than it used to be. It was the nature of modernity, and the Dutch were in the van of it. As an old seafaring and imperial people, they always had cosmopolitan sympathies, and now they easily accepted the gradual homogenization of Europe. Rotterdam was really as much a German as a Dutch port. Young and indistinguishable rentiers from a dozen countries emerged from the offices of Amsterdam at lunch-time. No need to speak the national language here: I once saw a man riding along on his bicycle with his baby daughter on the pillion behind,

and as they passed I was not in the least surprised (nor was the baby) to hear
him talking on his mobile telephone in the lingua franca of all Europe,
English. Another day I met a man so allegorically Dutch that I deliberately
engaged him in what I hoped would be allegorically Dutch conversation.
He was a tall man with military moustaches, deep-blue eyes and a proper
burgher's paunch, but he did not talk about Rembrandt, tulips, dykes,
Queen Beatrix, the new season's herrings, Admiral de Ruyter or what the
Concertgebouw was playing that night. No. He talked about unemployment,
too many Asian immigrants, keeping his weight down, and his hopes, earlier
in life, of being a professional footballer. He was a citizen of The Netherlands,
but I have met him all over western Europe, and that's what he always talks
about.

## 64  *Where they signed the treaty*

It is only proper then that Maastricht, an emblematic Dutch town, should
have given its name (whose emphasis should be on the *tricht*, by the way,
not on the *Maas*) to one of the seminal European treaties, the 1991 agreement
which gave a new structure to the European Union. It lies in the confusing
territory where The Netherlands, Belgium, Germany, Luxembourg and
France very nearly meet. Sometimes Aachen is spelt Aken on the road signs
around there. Luik and Luttich are both Liège. The very Maas of Maastricht
is only the familiar Meuse. Brussels, Dortmund, Koblenz, Lille, Eindhoven
are somewhere near, one way or the other, and are thundered between by
ceaseless thousands of trucks from every corner of Christendom. When I
woke up on my own first morning in Maastricht, and looked out of my
bedroom window through the mist, this is what I saw: a pair of early (or
possibly late) lovers embracing at the river's edge, a few bicyclists rattling
over the cobbles, and a long black barge throbbing downstream towards
Rotterdam; it carried a load of coal, a car was parked high behind its
wheel-house, and inside its bright-lit cabin a woman in a flowered pinafore
bustled about with a coffee-pot in her hand.

Everything, in short, paradigmatical. It was like Europe in filmic terms:
the cobbles, the lovers, the bicycles, the mist, the great river, the barge, the
lady with the coffee-pot, the towers, steeples and battlements of the old
town. Behind the quays too, I discovered when I got up, Europeanness was
everywhere. My hotel, an exhibition of Dutch charm and efficiency, turned

out to be British-owned, and in a brief walk down the exquisitely Low Country street behind it, ornamented with the hoary signs of crafts and guilds, I found the Cottage Café, the Nuance dress shop, something called Prima Vista, a graffito declaring 'FASCISME IS OVERAL – ANTI-FASCISME IS IN', and a car tantalizingly advertising Fair Play Perfect Amusement. I looked in at the Basilica of Our Beloved Lady, expecting a calm display of northern Catholicism; what should I find but the blaze of a thousand candles before an image of the Star of the Sea, glittering with such devotional bravura that I might have been in Sicily. But I wasn't – I was in Eurotown, The Netherlands!

## 65  *On the terrace*

A brief moment now in Bratislava (formerly Pressburg, a.k.a. Pozsony), the capital of Slovakia, still in convalescence after the long malaise of Communist rule. On the terrace of the Parliament building there, one day in 1995, a plump and youngish Government Minister presides over a little luncheon party in the sunshine. The Danube flows below; the castle stands behind; the terrace parasols advertise Coca-Cola. The Minister's principal guests are a visiting pony-tailed artist of some kind, perhaps a Slovakian rock star, and an entrepreneurial whiz-kid complete with mobile telephone, each accompanied by a svelte, minimally skirted, heavily made-up and virtually indistinguishable woman. A few attentive bureaucrats sit lower down the table. My, how the party swings! Once or twice the wunderkind's telephone rings, and he turns away from the table to talk urgently into it; otherwise the Minister is in absolute genial command. He is the image of your post-Communist democrat – shiny, popular, easy. Sometimes a pair of shirtsleeved security men look out of a door, to see he is all right, and he exchanges a few jocular words with them, as a modern politician should. He is full of stories, full of generous bonhomie. How the bureaucrats laugh at his sallies! The two women say very little, but laugh more than anyone. The star guests contrive to be at once languid and respectful. Across the terrace I am eating mushrooms and potatoes, with white Slovakian wine, and once His Excellency, in mid-joke, raises his glass to me.

## 66  *Two Austrian princesses*

I first went to Austria in 1946, travelling there by train through the Brenner
Pass, when my regiment was stationed in the Po valley of Italy. Vienna was
then occupied by four armies: the American, the British, the French and the
Soviet Russian ('four elephants in a canoe,' said Karl Renner, the Austrian
head of State). It was an agreeable place for a few days' leave. As it happened
one of my fellow officers, German by origin, had two aunts in the city,
elderly Austrian princesses, he said, of gamy instincts. I never met them, and
they may have been half-mythical, but they did allow us to use an agreeable
apartment in the heart of the city.

   Vienna had not been too disastrously damaged in the war, although the
Staatsoper was wrecked and the cathedral was roofless, but the atmosphere
was curiously ambiguous. The victorious Powers had decided, in 1943,
that when the war was won Austria would be treated as a victim of Nazi
Germany rather than an ally. This was a fortunate decision for the
Austrians, who had given the Nazi cause some of its most fervent
supporters, and was not very convincing to us: one of the leading figures
in Vienna at that time, Cardinal-Archbishop Theodore Innitzer, had not
only celebrated a thanksgiving mass for Germany's surrender in the previous
year, but had enthusiastically welcomed Hitler to Vienna when Austria
became united to Nazi Germany in the *Anschluss* of 1938. I am a child of
my times, and I have had mixed feelings about Austria and the Austrians
ever since.

   In 1946 one of the capital's most famous hotels, the Sacher, had been
requisitioned as a British officers' club, and it was there that I first developed
a distaste for the snobbery and pretensions of the country. In the hotel's
lobby we were often greeted by a *grande dame* in a wide picture hat and many
pearls, whom I always took to be Madame Sacher herself, until I discovered
forty-nine years later that the latter had died before the war. This lady was
frightfully grand anyway, and has remained my presiding Austrian image;
for although she was always welcoming and courteous, one had the nagging
feeling that she might be more courteous still to a titled colonel of the
Coldstream Guards, say, or for that matter a Wehrmacht officer with the
right aristocratic introductions; just as our old princesses (who were alleged
sometimes to peep through the bathroom keyhole, to see the young Britons
at their ablutions) were doubtless relieved to know not only that we were

recommended by their dear Otto, but that we came from a decent enough armoured cavalry regiment.

Not until 1993 did Austria's President Thomas Klestil express 'dismay' that the Austrians had participated in the Nazi persecution of the Jews and had failed to oppose the *Anschluss* (i.e. had supported it by a popular vote of 99.75 per cent, Jews having no franchise).

## 67 *Dying like a tailor*

It is the sycophancy of older Austrians that I most dislike. It stems no doubt from the days of the Habsburg monarchs, who called themselves in all seriousness Their Imperial, Royal and Apostolic Majesties, and received obsequious flattery from all classes. Almost every Austrian gesture, it sometimes seems to me, is a salute to hierarchy; almost every conversation, among people of a certain age, finds its way to matters of rank or status. The tragic story of Crown Prince Rudolf and his seventeen-year-old mistress Baroness Maria Vetsera, who died in 1884 apparently in a suicide pact, is repeatedly told in Austria to this day, and it precisely suits the place, being snobbish, romantic, nostalgic, maudlin and rather cheap. The Emperor Franz Josef, informed of his only son's fate, said that the young man 'had died like a tailor', and ordered that the little Baroness should be buried obscurely in a village graveyard far from her lover. I visited her grave once, and was just in time to hear a Viennese lady of a certain age explaining the circumstances to some American guests. 'In any case,' I heard her say, without a trace of irony, 'she was only the daughter of a bourgeois . . .'

Mind you, it works in many ways. It helps to make of Austria a kind of national family – the Emperor used to be called the Father of his People – and the love of hierarchy means that, if the Austrians fawn to their superiors within the family, they cherish their inferiors. E. M. Forster suggested 'Only connect' as a text for living: the Austrians would say 'Only belong.' I was walking up Kohlmarkt in Vienna one morning when there stalked beneath the carriage arch of the Hofburg a well-known local eccentric. He was extremely thin, spectral almost. Dressed all in white, as in a toga, he wore an imperial laurel around his brow, and he carried a long staff to which streaming banners were attached. As he walked he shouted high-pitched slogans, slip-slopping in his sandals out of the great archway into the sun. Nobody seemed surprised. A policeman chaffed him, a youth on a bicycle

slowed down to pat him affectionately on the shoulder. He was one of their
own, with his own slot in the pattern.

A crank is a crank; a cop is a cop; a Professor is decidedly a Professor. In
1977 the Viennese erected a monument to Sigmund Freud, with the following
inscription: 'Here, on 24 July 1895, the secret of dreams revealed itself to Dr
Sigm. Freud.' Revealed itself to a Jew, one notes, but at least revealed itself
to a Dr.

## 68  *Blue Danube*

At a ball in Vienna Brahms autographed a lady's fan with a few bars of 'The
Blue Danube' and the inscription 'Not, alas, by Johannes Brahms.' I can
hardly believe that Brahms really wished he had written that tiresome waltz,
but there is something about Austrianness which affects almost everyone.
The Austrians are the most incorrigible of the Europeans, but still one's feet
tap blithely to their melodies, and even for me there are few conditions more
agreeable than to be revising a typescript on a sunny day of early summer in
a Viennese pavement café.

Sometimes on such a morning I still see that lady from the Sacher,
figuratively as it were. She wears a brown tweed suit, without the hat but
with the pearls. If I smile at her she responds at first with a frosty stare, as if
to remind me that we have not been introduced, but if I engage her in
conversation she lights up with a flowery charm. Inextricably linked with
the preposterous social consciousness of the Austrians is their famous *Gemütlichkeit*, their ordered cosiness, and though this can sometimes be enough to
make a Welsh anarchist's flesh creep, at other times it is most endearing. In
those coffee-shops I welcome it when the people at the next table smile or
flutter their greetings at me and wish me well with my writing. I am touched
despite myself by the Austrian ability to reduce the grandest expressions of
art, especially music, to a domestic scale – the conviction, for example, so
often revealed in the faces of elderly concert-goers, that Father would have
played that adagio with rather more finesse. At the grave of Beethoven, in
Vienna's central cemetery, I even found myself becoming by osmosis a little
Austrian myself: for the gilded lyre upon its headstone, its Old German
lettering and its generally metronomic or Edition Peters manner only made
me think of piano practice.

## 69  *The kiss*

Driving through Vienna once in a rented car, I slowed down uncertainly to decide upon my route. Instantly the driver in the car behind blasted his horn most rudely. I gave him a vulgar two-fingered sign which I would never have dreamt of using had I not recently learnt that it was merely a gesture devised by Welsh archers to prove to opponents that their shooting-fingers were intact. When the other car overtook me its occupants both looked eagerly in my direction. The stout tight-buttoned horn-rimmed burgher at the wheel shook his jowls at me in affronted astonishment. His wife blew me a kiss.

## 70  *An interlude on flags*

Let us now give ourselves a break, in our fitful march across Europe, and contemplate a few matters that are common to the whole continent but at the same time illustrate its infinite variety. First, flags. All these States and Powers, and some of the nations, have their own flags. Political progressives used to dislike them – 'rags to be planted on dunghills' – but they remain emotive symbols for most Europeans. Although none of them are treated with the superstitious respect that old-school Americans accord Old Glory (which may not, under Public Law No. 623, touch the ground, the floor or water, and should never be carried horizontally except when draped over a casket), the flags of Europe are full of meaning. Some of the oldest display the Christian cross in one form or another – testimony to this continent's founding unity, or perhaps to the fervours inspired in its people by their battles against Islam. The Danes were the first to adopt it: they had been saved from defeat in a thirteenth-century campaign against the Estonians when a red banner with a white cross floated miraculously down from Heaven, and they rallied round it. Today the British, the Swiss, the Greeks and all the Scandinavians still fly some version of the cross of Christ.

Most of the other European flags are tricolours, distinguishable from each other only by their colours, the arrangement of their colours or the way their stripes run. For this we can blame the French. The Dutch were the first to have a flag of three coloured stripes, and because of their long war of independence against Spain it came to symbolize libertarian principles

across Europe. But after their revolution, in 1797, the French adopted the
schema for themselves, turned the stripes vertical rather than horizontal, and
gave everyone the idea that the colours were intended to represent their
own ideals of Liberty, Equality and Fraternity. The pattern – the pattern of
nineteenth-century political correctness – has since been unimaginatively
copied, sometimes with minor embellishments, by at least seventeen European States, down to our own times: skilled indeed are the vexillologists
(from the Latin *vexillum*, a banner) who can match every flag to its country.

In the days of monarchical Powers the national flags, though fewer, were
much more fun, being gorgeous with two-headed eagles, golden crowns
and crossed sceptres. The minute sovereignty of Liechtenstein still has a
crown on its flag, and Vatican City has a papal mitre. Albania flaunts the
black double-headed eagle of the hero Skanderbeg. Bosnia-Hercegovina has
a blue heraldic shield on a white background. The Scots have a rampant
heraldic lion on a yellow background, and the Welsh have the most striking
flag of them all, the Red Dragon of Cadwaladr against a background of green
and white, claimed by some to be directly descended from the purple griffins
of Roman imperial banners. The colours of many other national flags
are the inherited feudal colours of vanished princedoms, archdukedoms or
margravates, but in design only a few are still distinctive. The Scandinavians
enliven their fairly orthodox ensigns by cutting them in swallow-tails. The
Swiss have the grand simplicity of a small white cross on a plain red background
(conveniently reversed for the most celebrated of Swiss institutions, the
International Red Cross). The Greek Cypriots have a map of the island –
the whole of it! – on their flag. The English combined their own cross of
St George with the Scottish cross of St Andrew and the Irish cross of St Patrick
to emblemize for ever, or so they hoped, the union between the three
countries, and called it the Union Flag (for a time it had a harp in the centre,
to symbolize not Wales but Ireland more emphatically). The elegant Breton
flag of black and white – *Gwenn ha Du* – is said to represent the linguistic
division of Brittany: black for the French language, white for the Breton.

Outside the European institutions, in Brussels, Strasbourg and Luxembourg, many of these flags bravely fly, and with them is the newest and not
the least handsome of the continent's banners: the deep blue flag of the
somewhat tentative European Union. It has twelve gold stars upon it, arranged
in a circle. This design will remain the same however the Union's membership
expands or contracts (as I write there are fifteen member states): not for the
convenience of flag-makers, but because the Council of Ministers long ago

decided that a circle of twelve was the definitive symbol, as their publicists put it, of 'perfection and entirety'.

## 71 *An interlude on anthems*

All the European States, and some of the nations, have their anthems. I am everybody's patriot, and many of them move me greatly, when properly performed in the right circumstances. Could anyone resist the call of 'La Marseillaise', played by the mounted band of the Republican Guard as it clops, plumes astir, down the Champs-Élysées? Napoleon himself said it was the Republic's greatest general! I am even stirred by 'God Save the Queen', that lumpish old melody of the British, when it is played with sufficient solemnity, or in Elgar's spectacularly grandiose arrangement.

Actually in historical terms 'God Save the King', as it was originally, is much the most distinguished of them all. Although it is apparently hard to put a definite name to either its author or its composer, it has certainly existed in more or less its present form since the 1740s, and has some claim to being the best-known tune in the world. It was the first national anthem, for one thing, being originally given that title in 1825, when most of the States of modern Europe did not yet exist. It is also much the most widely used. Beethoven wrote a set of variations on it to 'show the English what a blessing they have in "God Save the King"'. Twenty other countries have at one time or another adopted the tune for patriotic songs of their own. In Germany it was the tune of '*Heil Dir im Siegerkranz*' – 'Hail to Thee in the Victor's Crown' – which was the German national anthem until 1922 (though in the time of the showy and extravagant Kaiser Wilhelm II it was suggested that its opening words should be altered to '*Heil Dir im Sonderzug*' – 'Hail to Thee in the Special Train').

Half a century ago, wherever the British were, the playing of 'God Save the King' was always a formal occasion, most of the monarch's subjects standing ramrod stiff, even at the end of a movie, until the last chord died away. Concert-goers, it was said, were sometimes to be seen bobbing up and down whenever the melody sounded, as it frequently did, in Weber's Jubilee Overture. The years passed, people grew more fidgety during the anthem, and cinema managers took to playing only the first phrase of the hymn. And when it was found that more and more customers were ignoring it, gathering their hats and coats and creeping out of the cinema when the music began, generally speaking they stopped playing 'God Save the Queen' altogether. It is still broadcast in full gravity at the end of the day's transmissions on the BBC, and I dare say there are still a few devoted subjects who stand to attention, thumbs down the seams of their trousers, until the last chord fades and they can go to bed.

Other countries, other styles . . . The original Yugoslav anthem, when the Yugoslav kingdom was formed after the First World War, consisted essentially of Serb, Croat and Bosnian national songs ingeniously strung together: under Marshal Tito, after the Second World War, it was a lyric starting '*Hej, Slaveni!*' – 'Hey, Slavs!' – sung to a tune cribbed from the Polish national anthem. The anthem of the Corsican patriots is a seventeenth-century hymn to the Virgin Mary; they long ago changed its words slightly, from the dedicatory 'Give us victory over *your* enemies' to the inflammatory 'Give us victory over *our* enemies.' The Welsh national anthem is dedicated, uniquely, to the survival of the national language – '*O bydded i'r hen iaith barhau!*' – 'O, may the old tongue survive!'

The most beautiful and fateful of anthems is the glorious tune that Haydn wrote in 1797 to be 'The Emperor's Hymn', the first national anthem of Habsburg Austria, and eventually sung in ten official translations throughout the Habsburg Empire. It was consciously intended to rival 'God Save the King', and to answer the inspirational momentum of the French Revolution. Haydn based his melody on an old Croatian folk-tune, which he remembered from his childhood among the Croatian settlements of Lower Austria, and he loved it. He used it too as variations in the Emperor Quartet, and until the end of his days frequently played the tune on his piano – it was the last music, it is said, that he ever did play. It was only in 1922 that the German Weimar Republic adopted it as a national anthem, and gave it the unfortunately ambivalent lyric '*Deutschland, Deutschland über Alles*': a poem written in 1848, by Hoffmann von Fallersleben, as a plea for the unity of the German peoples, Maas to Memel, 'above all else in the world'. The Nazis adored it, almost as much as they adored the 'Horst Wessel Song', and so this lovely tune – the perfect melody, to my mind – came to represent all that was most ominous and arrogant in Germanness. It is still the national anthem of Germany, but only the second verse of the poem is used now, and contemporary Germans sing about striving for unity, rights and freedom 'brotherly with heart and hand'.

In 1823 Beethoven incorporated in his Choral Symphony the words of a poem by Friedrich Schiller – 'Be embraced, you millions! This kiss is for all the world!' He set it to a melody so tremendously inspiring, so simple in theme but so rich in orchestration, that it is generally judged to provide one of the supreme moments of symphonic art. It is the 'Ode to Joy', the anthem of the European Union.

## 72  An interlude on parliaments

All the States of Europe have their parliaments, because they all call themselves democracies. The worst police States of Communist Europe used to be called Democratic Republics, and it was a pretence even of the crazy Ceauşescu that he was the popularly elevated guide of his people. Like markets and law courts, for a taste of the national flavour the parliaments of Europe are always worth visiting, if you can get past the policeman at the gate. ('Anything interesting to see this evening?' I once asked the doorman at the Irish Dáil. 'There's always me,' he said – 'I'm interesting.') Most of the buildings are unexciting, generally cast in the neoclassical mode that was fashionable and symbolically explicit when the parliamentary system took hold in Europe in the nineteenth century, but one or two have flair. The British Houses of Parliament seem to me the most exciting buildings in London, all spikes, towers and serried windows beside the Thames. The parliament at Budapest, although for most of its career it has been hardly more than a creature of despotic masters, stands with a similar but more monstrous panache beside the Danube. They used to call it 'The House of Lies' in the Communist days, when its parliamentarians met for only eight days in the year, but one can forgive it a lot – it was the first European public building to be air-conditioned, and until 1839 all its proceedings were in Latin.

Most parliaments turn out to be fairly dull in performance, too, the delegates sitting chaste and ordered in their horseshoe ranks, but sometimes there are flashes of animation. London's House of Commons, which likes to call itself the Mother of Parliaments, can sometimes be interesting to watch, if only because the confrontational style of British politics brings out the worst and occasionally the wittiest in parliamentarians. If you are lucky you might come across a minor riot in one of the assemblies of southern Europe. But for national revelation I most recommend the infinitesimal parliament of the Icelanders, a modest little grey assembly house next door to Reykjavik Cathedral, at least as I knew it in the 1970s. No pomp and little circumstance attended the deliberations then. If it was winter, the

members' galoshes were parked neatly outside the chamber door, and in the
public gallery loungers cheerfully read newspapers in the warm. Icelandic
politics can be vicious, but the parliamentarians rarely burst into invective,
perhaps because they were nearly all each other's cousins, and often in
armchairs at the side of the chamber members comfortably smoked their
pipes together, for all the world as though they had dropped by for a family
discussion. Occasionally a page hastened in, with a quotation for the Foreign
Minister perhaps, or a statistic for the Minister of Finance, but he was likely
to be wearing a check shirt, a green jersey and corduroy trousers, and as
often as not he interrupted the flow of debate by banging the door behind him.
Nobody much minded. 'Drat the boy,' one seemed to hear the Honourable
Members murmuring. 'His father was just the same.'

## 73  *An interlude on food*

All the various countries have their own cuisines, too, and often flaunt them,
although fast and frozen foods are rapidly taking over in most parts – the Big
Mac is not just an American innovation, but springs from the human
heart. I am anything but a gourmet, but here are some of my conclusions,
observations and recollections after half a century of eating European.

¶ The Italians eat most sensibly. The British eat most unhealthily. The
Spaniards eat most abstemiously. The Scandinavians eat most fastidiously.
The Greeks eat most monotonously. The Belgians eat most indigestibly. The
French eat most pretentiously. The Germans eat most.

¶ Irish oysters are best. German asparagus is best. Dried cod is best in
Portugal, eaten with onions and scrambled eggs. Raw herrings are best in
The Netherlands. The richest dish I ever ate was a soup made of baby eels,
in Valencia. The worst food I ever ate was the salted beef, with thick fringes
of yellow fat around it, that was popular in England fifty years ago and was
probably horse-meat. The best food I ever eat is *pasta al burro* with a local
red wine and a mixed salad almost anywhere you care to mention in Italy.

¶ My favourite café in Europe is the Grand Café in the main square at Oslo:
this is dominated by a huge mural of the place identifying regular customers
of its nineteenth-century prime – Master of the Horse Sverdrup, Landowner
Gjerns, Writers Olsen and Ibsen, and many another – all of whom, *mutatis
mutandis*, are to be seen to this day eating prawns and smoking at its tables.

My favourite European restaurant is the Walnut Tree near Y Fenni –
Abergavenny – in Wales, one of whose famous specialities is Lady Llanover's
Salted Duck. My favourite European bar is Harry's in Venice, where sultry
Italian aristocrats swapping modish gossip confront self-conscious tourists
laughing nervously when they see the bill.

¶ In Cognac, France, they offer you soup, pâté and sausages for breakfast.
In Aachen, Germany, they sell twenty different kinds of liquorice. Belgian
specialities include deep-fried sausages stuffed with shrimps, and mussels with
potato chips. It used to be said (though I find it hard to believe) that at
Burnley, Lancashire, England, more Benedictine liqueur was drunk than
anywhere else in Europe, the Lancashire Fusiliers having picked up the habit
in France during the First World War. An advertisement for the Hostinec
u Kalicha in Prague says that its cuisine is Heavy, Fat and Unhealthy, but
Very Nice. In a little shop beside the canal at Colmar, in a part of France
that used to be German, the family of Jean-B. Werz have been selling fish
since 1686: they keep live crayfish in a tub, and their motto is '*Pensez Poisson!*'
– 'Think Fish!'

¶ A Lithuanian national dish is called a *capelinas*, a 'Zeppelin', because it
looks like an airship: it is made of tightly packed potato dough soaked in
bacon fat, with mushrooms or a sausage in the middle, and is the most
repulsive-looking food I have ever set eyes on.

¶ My guidebook to Helsinki in 1995 promised me thirteen cuisines to
sample in the city – Finnish, German, Greek, Hungarian, Irish, Italian,
Japanese, Russian, Mexican, Spanish, Swiss, Tex-Mex and McDonald's. My
guidebook to Paris in the same year said that Arpège, a restaurant famous
for its carpaccio of langoustines with caviare, and its lobster with turnips, 'is
not the place for a casual tourist, but for people who really understand about
food, such as the sophisticated and often most influential Parisians . . . who
fill the dining-room twice a day'. *Ugh!*

¶ I spent a week once at a pension in Haute-Savoie, France, eating gargantuan
breakfasts, ample picnic lunches and stout dinners every day: on the way
back to the airport at Geneva I stopped at the Auberge du Père Bise, then
one of the most celebrated restaurants in France, for a lakeside lunch of little
fishes with white wine. It was exquisite. The bill came to more than the bill
for all those breakfasts, all those packed lunches, all those dinners and a week's
accommodation at the pension, and I did not regret a franc of it.

¶ The most puffed-up restaurant in Europe seems to me the Wierzynek in
Kraków, Poland, which claims to have started its career with a dinner-party

in 1364 attended by King Casimir the Great of Poland, the Holy Roman Emperor Charles IV, King Louis of Hungary, King Waldemar of Denmark, King Peter of Cyprus, princes from Austria and Pomerania and the Margrave of Brandenburg. It has been entertaining kings, emperors, shahs, presidents and prime ministers ever since, and is hung all about with courtly trophies. ¶ 'In numerical order,' said a taxi-driver to me in Stockholm, 'what are the chief attractions of Wales, first, second, third?' 'I don't know,' said I, 'but I know what's forty-eighth.' 'The food,' he instantly and perceptively replied.


## 74  *The least Power*

So, recuperated, we come to the Powers. In the last decade of the twentieth century there are still five States in Europe which see themselves as Powers – only a united Europe could claim to be a super-Power, and it hasn't come to that yet. Of the five, Spain is the least convincing in its pretensions, which are based less on present circumstances than on past glories (in the Rambla at Barcelona stands the Palace of the Viceroy of Peru!) and on the continuing and growing importance in the New World of the Spanish language.

I went to Spain in 1960 because I had been commissioned to write a book about the country. I had only been there once before. I bought a Volkswagen camper and a Spanish language course on records, and drove there over the Pyrenees. Spain was still in the grip of Franco's dictatorship, smouldering with the hatreds of its Civil War twenty-five years before, and separated from the rest of Europe not just by geography but by deep gulfs of history, habit and ideology. I still remember with a frisson the moment when, dropping down from the high pass of Roncesvalles (guarded by surly Civil Guardsmen in their patent-leather tricorn hats), I found myself among the Spaniards. The very first town I reached was Pamplona, where the bulls famously run through the streets on the feast of St Fermin, and in 1960 nowhere could have been more quintessentially Spanish. The people in the streets seemed to me dark, brooding, glowering people. Church bells clashed all night long. In the morning I drank hot chocolate tangy with cinnamon out of little cups. In the evening I hung around my sombre hotel until at ten o'clock dinner was served at last. My fellow guests seemed excessively grave and formal, and their children should have been in bed hours before. I remember the whole city as dark and clenched. I found it extremely exciting.

To some degree I was right in my romantic responses. Of course I was influenced by Spain's red-hot reputation – the familiar legends of violence, towering sensuality, dukes, castanets, raging bulls and all that. But I was to discover that much of the traditional flair of Spain really had survived the years of autocracy, and even the unforgiving recriminations of the ex-soldiers, Royalist or Republican, Fascist or Communist. Spain then was almost an island, so rigidly had history cut it off from the rest of Europe, and within its frontiers marvellous things survived from earlier times: customs and crafts, ways of thought and manners of speech, all the high drama of Andalusia and Castile. Across the wide landscapes of Spain, in those days, bullocks pulled ploughs across apparently interminable fields, and fierce dogs marched about with long sticks in their collars, to keep them out of the house. How poor were the poor of Spain then, how lordly the aristocrats, how ubiquitous the priests, how infinitely remote seemed the whitewashed villages of the mountains, where women in black sat around sewing, and flocks of goats scampered between the doorsteps! I hardly thought of Spain as being part of Europe at all: it was like another continent, astonishing to discover.

## 75  A melancholy capital

Madrid in those days seemed to me infused with melancholy. A quarter of a century after the Civil War, which had placed it at the heart of all the world's preoccupations, it felt lonely, stagnant and neglected. The warring armies had fought at the very gates of the place; now, when I sought out the correspondent of the London *Times*, to pick his brains, I was told that the paper no longer had a correspondent in the city. Madrid struck me as a capital out of an Orwellian past, animated only by elderly disputes – Left against Right, Liberals against Fascists, agnostics against the Church, anarchists against authority, even Spaniards against Foreigners. Foolish headlines announced, day after day, the Caudillo Franco's latest unparalleled triumph of policy. The new Air Ministry building was said to have more doors than the Air Force had aircraft. The Minister of Public Information, when I went to call upon him, gave me as a memento a book called *Death in Spanish Painting*. Very few new ideas seemed to be knocking around. I went to the Prado to see Giorgione's marvellous picture of the Virgin, St Roch and St Anthony of Padua, which had been in that museum since 1839: and as I stole once more into Giorgione's bewitched silent world of unanswered inquiry, where something mysterious or portentous is perpetually on the brink of happening, I felt the picture was a proper anagram of the city outside the gallery, where for a third of a lifetime history had been holding its breath.

## 76  *That's where!*

In the country too, though in a nobler way, time seemed to have been suspended, and perhaps reality too. I once stopped my camper in the colourless expanse of La Mancha, Don Quixote's homeland, and asked a couple of ploughmen which of the villages I could see around me was the Knight's birthplace. 'Don Quixote de la Mancha?' said they, for they always gave him his full title then, out of respect. 'Why, he was born just outside Argamasilla de Alba. They've pulled the house down, but you can still see the place – over there, beyond the church tower, that's where Don Quixote de la Mancha was born!' I half expected them to say they remembered him well.

## 77  *The sense of oppression*

When I look back at it now, over the motorways and supermarkets of modern Spain, over the high-rises of the Mediterranean coast, over the fizz and urbanity of Madrid, what lingers most in my memory is a sense of second-rate oppression. The Civil Guardsmen at Roncesvalles were only the advanced patrols of a Philistine army, dedicated to keeping Spain in the condition that Generalissimo Franco had decreed for it, and they were inescapable. Church and State were supreme, supported by all the forces of reaction and revenge – for Franco had never forgiven his enemies of the Civil War, and the place was heavy still with suspicion and accusation. Emblems mysterious to me kept the memories alive: names of heroes familiar only to the Spaniards, badges of lost divisions with high-flown mottoes, memorials to forgotten battles or atrocities. Dark secrets were kept still. Some people were better left unmentioned – La Pasionaria, García Lorca. Terrific tales were told and retold, of sacrifices and massacres and epic defences. One day in Madrid I saw the old dictator himself, deep in the back of his limousine, surrounded by the prancing splendour of his Moroccan cavalry. I thought he looked as though he would live for ever: when, years later, he lay on his deathbed, his doctors desperately kept him alive with infusions and injections, week after week, as though when he went Spain would go too.

## 78  New Spain

So it did, in a way. By the 1990s Spain was another country, a full member of the European Union, a democratic kingdom, a leader in the movement towards political regionalization – a sort of Power, in fact. It was an odd anomaly that there were still Spanish colonies on the north coast of Africa, where those resplendent cavalrymen had been recruited, and from where Franco had begun his rise to power – the only European possessions left in all Africa. Madrid had become one of the sprightliest and most exhilarating of capitals: when the Olympic Games were held in Barcelona in 1992 they were hailed as a brilliant exhibition of Spanish modernism.

Spain is a big place, though, still devoted to its own ways, and it will be a long time before it is all like other countries. In the very year of those Olympics, I made an experimental return journey to one of its most traditionally backward and isolated regions, the Alpujarras. This is mountain country between the Mediterranean and the Sierra Nevada: when the writer Gerald Brenan went to live there after the First World War its people combined their Catholicism with a lively paganism, and his neighbours were under the impression that Protestants had tails. But it is perilously close to Málaga, the awful Costa del Sol and the other nightmare littorals of Andalusian tourism, and I was not surprised to find the chief road into the area proclaimed a Ruta Turistica, or to pass on my way the tourist super-train called the Andalusian Express, sweeping down to Seville.

All the standard conveniences of our time have penetrated the Alpujarras, and I very much doubt if today's local prostitutes, like their predecessors in Brenan's time, would be satisfied with half a dozen eggs as payment for their services. A helicopter pad, a solar energy panel, several Citroën agencies, a Disco Pub, rap music and a total non-appearance of priests – these were among the symptoms of the new Spanishness that I took note of as I rambled through. I also noticed a vast amount of rubbish, from the hulks of discarded cars to beer cans and plastic bags. Somehow, though, this did not offend me. Just as in Spanish cities the tapas bars contrived to be welcoming despite the almost ankle-deep litter of their floors, so here in the back-country the least biodegradable trash managed to seem organic, and was so mingled with the rocks, the brown soil, the gravel and the scrub that it became part of the landscape.

And, as the Alpujarras seemed able to live with the new physical garbage, the excreta of progress, so they were apparently rising above cultural trashing too. Modernization was evidently happening on the Alpujarras' own terms, and there was still never a moment, I thought, when I could be anywhere else but Spain. There were mules about, carrying women to market or simply tethered, as they had always been, mysteriously alone to wayside posts. There was mutton and roast partridge still to eat. There were folk-healers, if not witches. Women in flowered pinafores brushed their front yards with besoms, watched by cats. Old men propped their crooked sticks against walls while they pissed beside the highway, and prickly stalwarts with guns slung across their shoulders struck into the mountains in search of game, attended by gambolling dogs. Spain, 1992 – Olympic Year!

## 79  *Among the Italians*

Three things were true of Italy, when I first arrived there, that now seem almost inconceivable. (1) Some marks on the pavement in the Piazzale Loreto in Milan were shown to me as bloodstains from the corpses of Benito Mussolini and his mistress, suspended there heads-down not long before. (2) The most prominent politician of the day, Alcide de Gasperi, had begun his career as a deputy in the Austro-Hungarian parliament in Vienna. (3) Another two years were to pass before espresso coffee was invented (by the Milanese barman Achille Gaggia).

Fifty years ago the British popular image of Italy was less than flattering. Propaganda had persuaded most of us that the Italians were a nation of buffoons, their soldiers incompetent, their organizational powers laughable. Few of my generation had been to Italy before the Second World War, and when elders went on about beakers of the warm South it sounded to me like maundering sentimentality. The glories of Italian art and literature seemed altogether of the past. Modern Italy had been summed up for us by Winston Churchill, when he dismissed Mussolini as Hitler's jackal – a metaphor enthusiastically adopted by the dutiful London cartoonists of the day.

Hundreds of thousands of British soldiers, including me, found our attitudes changed when we set foot in Italy itself. Some, having been stranded behind enemy lines for one reason or another, told heart-warming tales of Italian kindness and sacrifice. Others, having fought with the partisans, gave us startling new insights into Italian fighting capabilities. And nearly all of us, I suspect, were impressed by the Italians' apparent lack of xenophobia. That the population had probably been as welcoming to German soldiers as they were to us may have initially disturbed me (for I was very young and callow, and my ideas of patriotism were elementary), and I was doubtless arrogantly scathing about the fact that Italy had started the war on one side and finished it on the other, but I soon perceived a maturity to these attitudes that we perhaps lacked ourselves.

## 80  'He will never know'

I was an anarchist manqué, and I was impressed too by the average Italian's disrespect for authority in all its forms. Once, having illegitimately purloined my colonel's jeep for a jaunt into the mountains, I bashed it into a wall in the valley of Cadore. At all costs it had to be back in camp next morning, as though it had never been out. What to do? 'No worries,' said my Italian mountain hosts. 'We'll fix it.' They took me to the village garage, only a stage removed from a smithy, and through the night its solitary mechanic hammered and painted. In the morning, swathed in complicit smiles, they returned the jeep to me just as it had been – not *too* pristine, or my colonel might have smelt a rat. 'He will never know,' they said in delight: and he never did, for the dear man is dead now.

## 81  The Italian infection

I was bowled over, even then, by Italian design. I had supposed the nation's visual genius to have been atrophied, or at least to have coarsened into the trumpery of Fascist art, but the contemporary objects I saw around me seemed of an elegance I hardly knew. What a world separated the lumpish Austin Seven of home from the delicate little Topolino, Mickey Mouse, which hardly looks archaic half a century later! The only typewriters I knew were heavy industrial-looking Underwoods or Remingtons: here for the first time I saw the Olivetti portable – sleek, light, strong and graceful – and I was to stay with it in its various forms until I entered the computer age. ('What's that?' demanded an American customs officer in the 1960s, when

I took my adorable bright-red Olivetti Valentine into New York, for it did not look like a typewriter at all. With an Italianate gesture I swept it out of its integral case, and the officer, marvelling at its neatness and beauty, thanked me courteously for the demonstration.)

And, like everyone else, I gradually realized that in Italy, more than in most countries, the past and the present overlapped. Leonardo might have devised that Topolino, or Michelangelo designed the Valentine. The old grace of Italy had its benign effect on me, and I recognized that the memoirs of those pre-war travellers had not been the mere nostalgia of ancients. Italy infected me, as it infected countless young Britons deposited there by war and history then. Long before opera was reinvented as a popular art form by the brilliant publicists of the 1994 world football championship, innumerable British soldiers of all backgrounds had learnt to enjoy it. My own very first opera was at La Scala itself. It was *La Traviata*, and I remember still the delicious frisson of hearing for the first time Alfredo's off-stage aria '*Amor, amor è palpito*' – soft and distant, half-muffled, from somewhere deep behind the scenery, out of Italy's heart.

## 82  *A benediction*

Italy was a benediction: and the greatest blessing of all came when one morning my commanding officer summoned me to his tent and told me commiseratingly that I was to be detached for a time to help run the motor-boats of Venice, all then requisitioned by the British Army. We were shortly to be transferred to Palestine, and he assured me that I would be back with the regiment in time for that: in the meantime, while he was extremely sorry to do this to me, for organizing motor-boats seemed a plebeian sort of task to such a professional cavalry colonel, still he hoped I would make the most of the opportunity, and gain something from it.

It was the best present anyone had in life. Getting to know Venice changed everything for me. Fourteen years later I wrote a book about the city, and my association with the place was to be a continuing joy to me. One of my duties then was to welcome visiting generals and conduct them into the city in one of our boats. As time passed I developed a proprietorial pride in this activity. Few of those senior officers had ever been to Venice before, and I felt myself almost *in loco parentis*, adolescent that I was, as we chugged up the Grand Canal, and I watched the shifting expressions of astonishment and delight that passed over their grizzled warlike features. Venice was a dream then, hushed and empty in the aftermath of war, still imbued with the melancholy that so captivated its Victorian visitors, and which bewitched me too. I was billeted with a friend in a house on the island of Giudecca, looking over the waste lagoon, and in the evenings especially, when the island was silent except for the lapping of water in our boat-house, or a sudden peal of laughter, perhaps, from somewhere over our garden wall, I found the wistful loveliness of the place almost orgasmic – my first intimation that love for a beautiful place could be more than simply sensual, but actually sexual too.

## 83 An Italian dog

Remember that Scottish dog, following its master to the corner pub? Here is an Italian dog. It is a fat spaniel waddling along a quayside, plod, plod, tail wagging, and it stops at a big wooden warehouse door and gives a throaty bark. In a moment the door opens and a man virtually identical with the animal, except for his two rather than four legs, broadly beams down at the spaniel, and over it at us. Then he kneels on the pavement and embraces it. The dog pants affectionately, tongue lolling. So does the man.

## 84 Black Italy

There were black sides to Italy too, which haunted me down the years as the sunshine and the ripple enchanted me. The black economy, which used to sound engagingly libertarian to one of my temperament, turned out to be generally not free at all, but mercilessly governed by the brutality of the Mafia. The charm of Italian medievalism, its narrow winding lanes and eccentric towers, often gave a specious veneer to a world of squalid ignorance. Join me now one evening in 1961, when as a literary voyeur I followed a couple of lively girls up the hill to their home in Cagliari, the capital of Sardinia. Downtown Cagliari, where we first set eyes on them, is a vivacious cosmopolitan seaport in the 1960s, and the girls seem full of confidence and fun. Sailors wink at them, youths whistle. The cafés, spilling across the pavements under the street lights, are properly crowded and animated. Squadrons of Fiats and Vespas scurry up and down the boulevards. The girls saunter through with easy aplomb, here greeting an acquaintance, there stopping to gaze in a shop window, until, not very late, while the Via Roma is still pulsating with zest and enjoyment, they walk home to the Dark Ages.

Passing through a gloomy gate tower, they return to the mazy dim-lit quarter of the city called Castello. Instantly modern Europe is forgotten. In that dark jumble of alleys, tunnels and cramped courtyards the pressure of poverty is all around, and the hiss of superstition. It is a place for beggars and bandy legs, dwarfs, shibboleths, old wives' tales, and it is full of babble – the rasping of crones, the wailing of tired children, the sibilance of gossip, raucous laughters, voices raised in shrill quarrel or reproach. Into this place those girls return, their footsteps growing slower and more laggardly the closer they get to home, until at last they reach their native alley. A scraggy cat gnaws an intestine outside their door. A baby is screaming somewhere. Their mother greets them with eldritch imprecations from the back quarters. There is a smell of cooking-fat, cats, tobacco, damp stone and bad drains. The girls take their shoes off, reassure their mother with a kiss and a chide, and return to – where shall I place them? – the fourteenth century, say. In some parts of Sardinia, in those days, they still talked a kind of Latin, and so tight-knit were the communities that in nine neighbouring villages the wagtail was called by nine different names. The Sardinians never thought of pruning their olive trees, until they were introduced to the practice after the Second World War, and I have been told that only just before the time of our walk through Cagliari, at the end of the 1950s, did they learn to accept the edibility of the carrot.

## 85  *A gas in the air*

Sometimes I have been inspired by the dogged Italian devotion to the old order of things, coming as I do from a kaleidoscopically shifting kingdom of the North, but sometimes there is something eerie and threatening to it, like a gas in the air. In Sicily especially I have felt this, and particularly in its dusty and blistered countryside – the 'remote unchangeable landscape' that simmered so oppressively in the background of Giuseppe di Lampedusa's *The Leopard*. In the 1960s I stayed for a time with friends outside the town of Partinico, south of Palermo. In the early mornings, when I strolled on my balcony, the prospect before me seemed altogether delightful – innocent, exotic, fresh. The mottled vineyard plain ran away to the distant metallic blue of the sea, and all around the villages sprang into pictorial clarity as the sun caught them. Farmers clattered down the lane beneath the house, their horses gay with feather tufts, their carts gaudily painted, and when they caught sight of me perched there above them they would give me a discreet flicker of the hand and the glimmer of a smile. But in the evenings, when I returned to my balcony at the end of the day, a very different sensation used to overcome me. Then a drear disquieting mood seemed to fall upon that landscape. The hills now seemed to crouch menacingly above the plain, and the villages, so charming in the morning sun, now looked huddled and forlorn. When the sun went down the whole place was silent, clamped and empty, for old legacies of fear and malaria sent the Sicilian country people home with the dusk.

These chill suggestions were not all fancy. It really was a countryside of ominous complexity, webbed and secretive and potentially dangerous. My hosts were active in a movement to give more economic independence to the local peasants, chiefly by building irrigation works, and they were genuinely under threat from the dark forces of Sicilian reaction, secular and sacred. In the very next year, I was later to learn, the Franciscan monks of a nearby monastery were found guilty of extortion, embezzlement, theft and murder. The holy work of the monastery had continued unaffected by their criminal activities, its abbot being the *capo* of the gang, and one brother admitted to having said a funeral mass, and preached a sermon, over the corpse of a man whose murder he had himself ordered.

## 86 *So it is supposed*

Throughout the subsequent decades, though much did change in the Mezzogiorno, southern Italy was to remain for me a sinister and alarming place, tinged always with the macabre. 'Are there Mafiosi in this village?' I once asked a Sicilian. '*So it is supposed*,' he said, and he said it in unmistakable italics. I remember with a shudder straying into a festival mass in one of the remoter and more introspective hamlets of Calabria, a place apparently discarded, like a pile of old rubble, high in the stony goat-chewed mountains. The church was packed. There were five priests in attendance, and two policemen by the door, and myriad thin and restless children, and beggars in tattered black cloaks, and withered men clearing the phlegm from their throats, and hundreds of arthritic rat-faced women. The church stank of incense and indigence; beside the altar the golden-robed priests moved

purposefully to and fro; and so strangely trance-like did the atmosphere feel
that day that I felt I had strayed into some alien plane of existence.

## 87  *Futuristic*

Once I sailed into Naples out of its calm celestial gulf to find the notorious
traffic of the city magnified to the power of hell by a protest march of the
unemployed. The whole place seethed and fumed, and although my hotel
was almost within sight of the ferry pier, and I never even set eyes on the
march, it took me an hour in a cab to get there. You might suppose this to
have been a dispiriting experience, but in fact it was like a shot in the arm.
The taxi-driver, an elderly enthusiast for his trade, treated the event as a
challenge to his virtuoso skills, and so we progressed through a sequence of
short cuts and private diversions, wildly the wrong way up one-way roads,
heedlessly squeezing between the stalls of shopping alleys, sometimes obliged
to reverse by the sheer pressure of public opinion, sometimes making desperate
three-point turns in virtually impassable backstreets. We laughed, we shud-
dered, we shut our eyes. Now and then the driver wiped his brow in a
theatrical way when we momentarily emerged into the relief of a piazza,
before putting his foot down again and hurtling us through a line of flapping
washing into yet another labyrinth of the slums. Outside our windows –
'*Keep them closed!*' cried the driver, '*bad people here!*' – the Neapolitan legend
was displayed as in a theme park, or perhaps an aquarium. Suddenly children's
faces would appear runny-nosed an inch or two away. Bad people eyed our
luggage with predatory sneers. Old ladies gave us what I took to be the evil
eye as we scraped against their fruit-stalls. On the Via Partenope even we
stood stagnant for a time in the helpless congestion of the traffic, but all
around us, like howling imps, motor-scooters shot in and out between the
cars, on to the pavement and far away, demonically belching exhaust smoke.

The people of Naples appeared to be living in a condition of perpetual
motorized cock-up; but they were evidently far from defeated by it. Tempers
did not seem to be fraying. Horns were seldom hooted. Whenever we caught
the eye of an adjacent driver, in some evidently terminal gridlock, he seemed
more amused than exasperated, and those devilish motor-scooters weaved their
insouciant way between us all for all the world as though they were surfing, or
playing with Frisbees. It seemed natural to the Neapolitans to be in this fix.
They were the masters of motorized disorder. It occurred to me that they were

ahead of sober, sensible Northerners in these attitudes. They were readier to accept the inevitable awfulness of modernity, had already adjusted to it, and this put them well ahead of the Swedes, say, in the futuristic stakes. Where do you suppose a UFO would choose to land, Naples or Gothenburg?

## 88 *Old and very tough*

Later I reached rather similar conclusions in Rome, for me the focus, summit and distillation of all things Italian. At the end of 1991, thinking properly sententious thoughts about the turn of another year, I leant on a Roman balustrade to watch the sun set behind St Peter's. Unfortunately the sun never reached the horizon that evening, instead finding itself glaucously absorbed into the thick pall of smog which lay like a curse over the city. I could almost hear the noise it made, I thought – not a fizzle, more a kind of glurp – and imagine the sulphurous smell of microwaved exhaust fumes as it disappeared into the murk. The symbolism of that sunset struck me as powerful. It had been an unlovely year, and the corrosive pollution of Rome seemed to me like an allegory of some more general decay. The atmosphere was fearful, the congestion was appalling, squalid litter lay everywhere, blown across glorious piazzas, festering in fountains, lining the Appian Way. Abandoned and unlovely the poisoned Tiber flowed between its concrete quays. Buildings that used to seem picturesque now seemed dingy almost beyond redemption, pavements were cracked and potholed, all over the city restorations and excavations were in abeyance for lack of money.

For a time the conclusion I drew, as I wandered the city, was that the European civilization, having once reached here so exquisite an epitome, was now running irrevocably down, so that the glittering shops of the Via dei Condotti, the gorgeous rituals of St Peter's were no more than cruel anachronisms. Gradually, though, this notion was replaced by one more invigorating: that if the environment of Rome was invalid, by God, the inhabitants of Rome were robust as ever. Smog or no smog, they remained precisely as they had always been, displaying just the same mixture of swagger and simplicity, cunning and compassion, that visitors had discerned in them down the ages. The guard at the Vittorio Emanuele memorial was not above a brief exchange of greetings as I passed by. The Gypsy children only giggled when I thwarted their transparent efforts to rob me. The taxi-driver cheerfully gave in when I declined to pay him half my worldly wealth to drive me from St Peter's to the Spanish Steps. The black boys did nothing worse than laugh and dance when motorists angrily declined to have their windscreens cleaned at traffic-lights. If the whole city were suddenly to be transformed, I came to think, all its buildings spick and span, all its traffic ordered, all its corruptions cleansed, the Romans would hardly notice. One afternoon I observed motionless upon a buttress of the Ponte Sant'Angelo a very small and curious-looking lizard. I examined it closely, thinking it might have been mutated in some way by the stinks and chemicals perpetually swirling all about it: but no, it was just immensely old, inconceivably old, and tough.

## 89 'C'est moi!'

More insidiously seductive, I think, is the glory of France, perhaps because it has always struck me as being perfectly humourless. One cannot laugh at the swank and strut of it, just as it would have seemed unkind to snigger at the gaunt solemnity of General de Gaulle, to whom all life seemed so tragically in earnest, and to whom the idea of France not being a Power would have been preposterous. I was in Paris once when for festive reasons the Champs-Élysées was cleared of all traffic, allowing pedestrians to stroll the length of it from the Place de la Concorde to L'Étoile. I undertook the walk churlishly, for I have always disliked the pomp and monotony of Haussmann's boulevards. As I walked the gentle slope of the great street, however, through the green parks, past the line of rich buildings, towards the Arc de Triomphe revealing itself at the end of it – as I strode up there along the very centre of the avenue, with thousands of Parisians in high proud spirits all around me, minute by minute I found myself falling into a genuine Sun King or Gaullist swagger. One can never be indifferent to France, Alexis de Tocqueville said. It was the most brilliant and dangerous country in Europe, he said. Besides, to my mind French glory is true glory.

## 90 *The Hundred and One Days*

After the Second World War glory soon became *passé*, though, and by the 1990s it seemed to me that for four decades France had been trying to drag it out – living, as it were, an illusory and unconvincingly stretched Hundred Days. In my lifetime French martial prowess had not, to be frank, been very

notable. Shamefully defeated in the Second World War, thrown unceremoniously out of Indo-China, ignominiously obliged to leave Algeria after indulging in every kind of jingo claim and military brutalism, the French had had
their military reputation redeemed only by the dash and bloody-mindedness
of individual gallants, plus the Foreign Legion. Yet more than any other
people in Europe the French clung to the forms and illusions of military
power. Long after the age of the Dreadnoughts I remember seeing towering
above the dockyards of Toulouse the great superstructure and peculiar funnel
of the *Jean Bart*, the very last European battleship, extraordinarily expensive
to maintain but still on the active list as an embodiment of French self-esteem.
She was a magnificent-looking ship, one of the most powerful conventional
weapons of war the Europeans had ever built, and I imagine French people
still viewed her with patriotic complacency – it was public opinion that had
compelled her completion after the war. To me she already looked forlorn,
if not actually pathetic, a mere symbol of grandiosity: I could think of no
circumstances in which the French Republic could ever put the *Jean Bart* to
sensible use, and sure enough six or seven years later the French Republic
reached the same conclusion, and she was scrapped.

I was spending the night once, in 1956, at a country inn near Chamonix,
in Haute-Savoie, and heard sounds of revelry from the bar. I went down to
investigate, and found that the local class of conscripts was having a celebratory
reunion and binge before going off to the doomed colonial war in Algeria.
They were extremely soldierly young soldiers, all in the camouflage gear
which the French presently made *de rigueur* among armies throughout the
world. Their heads were cropped, they were bursting with the vigour of a
few months' basic training, and their voices got louder, their songs bawdier,
as the night wore on. They were like characters in a movie, *les poilus* playing
it up before going off to Verdun, perhaps, and seemed to me to be consciously
playing their parts. They seemed to have been born out of their time, enacting
out-of-date heroics, seeking a glory nobody much cared about in a war that
should not have been fought.

## 91   *In character*

But then the French are born character actors, and wonderfully fulfil their
own stereotypes. I chanced to arrive in Paris in 1968 when the student
rebellion of that year was reaching its climax, and was astonished to find

myself in the middle not of an old newsreel but of a historical re-enactment. This, I thought, is just how the cinema of the twenty-first century will reconstruct European student demonstrations of the century before. Never were riot police more loaded down with helmets, truncheons, shields, hoses, gas canisters, goggles and guns. Never did their vans, lined up nose to tail along the quays, look more theatrically sinister. And the students, surging to and fro between their makeshift barricades, handkerchiefs over their mouths, throwing things now and then and shouting slogans – ah, the students! They were all that old people dream they were themselves when they look back to the days of their liberty, the days when they had causes to throw bricks for, when to be alive was grand enough, but Heaven itself was to be young, radical, brandishing a stick and shouting a slogan in Paris.

## 92   *End of a grudge?*

Before they completed the Channel Tunnel, when I was queuing at Dover once to board a hovercraft with my car, two young French people came around with a clipboard, conducting a poll or survey. Was I pleased at the prospect of a tunnel under the English Channel at last? I told them I was (for Welsh nationalist reasons, actually), and I remember still the delight with which they recorded a tick in the appropriate box. It was almost their first tick. In Dover they had experienced almost nothing but negatives, they told me, sometimes rudely expressed, and they had found this most disheartening, because they themselves believed passionately in the project.

Why? The building of the tunnel would affect France far less than it would affect Britain, and in theory at least might indeed be culturally harmful. The French are among the most nationalistic of all Europeans, but they suffer the disadvantage of sharing frontiers with eight other States, if you count Monaco and Andorra. Maintaining their Frenchness is a constant struggle. Their only modern Maginot Line is their language, and the spectacle of the immortals of the French Academy preserving it against all comers suggests to me some indomitable band of elders mustering with antique guns and pitchforks to resist invaders. Even so, they have been unable to prevent inroads: in a hundred yards of a Paris shopping arcade, in 1987, I jotted down the following shop signs: Paris Basket, Tie Break, New York New York, Scoop, Blue Way, Awards Academy, Yellow, Bubble-Gum and Lady, together with the nearby graffiti 'Fuck Off Skinheads', 'Kill the Cops' and 'Crack Snack'.

The Channel Tunnel, one might think, would surely admit many more foreign vulgarisms under the water: yet the French in general were far keener on the idea of it than the British ever were. I think this was because they felt it would bring the ending of an old, old grudge. They thought it would mean that the British (or the English, as they would certainly say) no longer had the moral and psychological advantage of being different – not simply islanders, but different in other ways, a different kind of people, only twenty-five miles from France yet detached from the preoccupations common to all the rest of Europe, and saved from so many of the miseries that the continent had suffered. This was my own theory. What those pollsters said, when I asked them why they wanted the tunnel so badly, was, 'All nations should come together.'

## 93  *The Frenchest man*

The Frenchest person I ever met was Yves Saint-Laurent, the couturier. He was utterly French. He told me that the only books he ever read were eleven volumes of Proust's *À la recherche du temps perdu*, over and over again, but that the twelfth and last volume he had never read at all – saving it up, I supposed, for a last splurge of Frenchness on his deathbed *chaise longue*. Everything that was French seemed to be embodied in him, even a bit of the old *gloire*, for there was a distinctly grand manner lurking behind his melancholy shyness, and he lived in a grand style too. The student protests that had seemed to me so quintessentially French had fired his imagination as well. He had translated their images into a cult of unisex shirts and jeans, radical, cheap, which was to change the lives of women everywhere, and long afterwards, when his clothes had taken a classic turn again, he used to say that true elegance was 'to forget what one was wearing'. Saint-Laurent liked to call himself an artisan, and the little world of craftspeople he had built up around him, the dedicated world of cutters, shoemakers, milliners and tailors, seemed to me a true ornament of French civilization, and a vindication of French pride. I asked him if he was consciously contributing to the splendour of France, and he smiled rather distantly. He was, he said, he was. When they called him up for the army, he had a nervous breakdown.

## 94  *In the country*

The French countryside of my youth often looked (at least in my memory now) like a slow ballet of horse-drawn ploughs – ploughs wherever you looked, some going one way, some another, serenaded by soaring songbirds and watched by rich fat cattle. France seemed to me then permanently old-fashioned. It was still a peasant country, I used to think. The Alpine village I settled in for a while in the 1950s was several generations behind the times. In the autumn it used to be visited by an itinerant steam distillery, and with much chuffing and hissing its apple crop was turned into a powerful kind of schnapps, to be tasted in back kitchens beside steaming cauldrons of soup more or less permanently simmering on the stove. I collected our mail each day from the village bar, for there in mid-morning I knew I would find the postman enjoying his cognac.

I doubt if a single Percheron draws a single plough in France now. Most of the birds seem to be of the invisibly chirpy persuasion, twitching about in copses, and the cattle are mostly anaemic Charollais, which look as though they have been drained of their blood for the making of black puddings. Even in our village of Savoie the ski culture has fallen upon the old ways, the high cow-chalets have been turned into holiday homes, and I doubt if the postman has time for his mid-morning brandy. For me the lost innocence of Europe, itself no more than the product of a romantic imagination in its youth, will remain always a memory of long ago in France.

## 95  *An invitation*

Allow me to invite you to Sunday lunch at a French country restaurant of the old kind, *circa* 1955. Neither fast food nor gastronomic pretension has yet corrupted the establishment, which is in one of those ancient towns of central France where the streets wind upwards from the railway track, through scowling walls of medievalism, until they debouch in the square outside the cathedral door, surveyed by huge stone animals from the cathedral tower and prowled around on Sunday mornings by cats and desultory tourists. The restaurant displays its menu in a large flowery script in a brass frame, and in most respects remains more or less as it has been for several centuries. Madame the proprietress looks an epitome of everything false and narrow-minded.

One waiter seems to be some sort of duke, the other is evidently the village idiot. At the table next to ours sits a prosperous local family out for its Sunday dinner, well-known to the proprietress and esteemed throughout the community – solemn, voluminously napkinned, serious and consistent eaters who eye us out of the corners of their piggy eyes as they chew their veal. The veal is, as a matter of fact, rather stringy. I do not doubt the bill will be erroneous. I am sure Madame despises us as much as we distrust her. But what a contrary delight it all is, is it not? How nourishing still the vegetables, fresh from Madame's garden! How excellent the wine, from the vineyard down the hill! How stately that duke! How endearing the idiot! How mollifying the farewells of the family at the next table, when with bows and cautious smiles they fold their napkins and leave us! How persuasive, after all, even the steely charm of Madame herself! With real gratitude we wrap the old-fashioned Frenchness of that luncheon around us like a cloak, and return cherished to the world of the 1990s. *Ah, où sont les déjeuners d'antan?*

## 96  *All is not lost*

But all is not lost! More successfully than most countries, France has achieved an equilibrium between the old and the new. As the twentieth century draws towards its close the French are indeed a very modern people. I first really felt in touch with cyberspace in the 1980s when, calling at a French country inn somewhere, I found the chef punching up his day's luncheon menu on a computer, from some central database of gastronomy. Today nothing seems to me quite so elegantly futuristic as the solar-powered telephones which gently revolve, like sunflowers, beside French *autoroutes*. No capital in Europe is more smoothly organized than Paris, and a true image of our *fin de siècle* is the spectacle of the great Paris–Lyon–Marseille *Train à Grande Vitesse* sweeping down the Rhône valley at 180 m.p.h.

Yet by most standards life in the French countryside still seems amiably and enviably close to the soil. The songbirds may have gone, but the swallows still whirl around on summer evenings. Widowers shout greetings to each other as they wobble home on their bicycles, long loaves protruding from their saddle-bags. Gentlefolk stroll in the autumnal gardens of their villas. At the wood's edge the logs are still chopped and Vergilianly piled. Aromatic smoke lingers. The buzz of the *vélomoteur* merges comfortably – well, fairly comfortably – with the buzz of the bees. Picnic parties spread their cloths beside dragonfly pools as in painters' fancies long ago. More happily than anywhere else trees and rivers, cities and motorways, seem to coexist by mutual arrangement, a harmonious balance between the natural and the invented.

For me one of the most comforting components of this arrangement is the continuing French attitude towards animals. French people seem to recognize what Montaigne, the patron saint of animal equality, called 'a certain obligation and mixed commerce' between man and beast. We may force-feed you for your liver, they seem to say to their fellow creatures, boil you alive, snare you on migrations or bottle you in brine, but at least we will deal with you man, so to speak, to man. I raised the matter once at a café beside whose door a very fat and surly Golden Labrador lay sluggishly where everyone would trip over it. It was a very old dog, said the proprietor, one did not care to disturb the animal: but when I mentioned Montaigne's notion of commerce and obligation he seemed to think it mere sophistry. 'I owe the dog nothing, it owes me nothing, one day it will die and then – *pfft!*' The dog did not budge an inch as, precariously balancing my coffee-cup, I stepped across it to find a table on the patio outside: but, remembering where I was, I restrained myself from giving it a good kick as I passed, to hasten the *pfft*.

## 97  A fling of France

What I love to do is to drive on a bright sunny day, with the roof of the car open, at a scudding speed around the Périphérique, the ring road that surrounds the city of Paris. The scudding speed is advisable, or awful French drivers will more or less run you off the road. The sunny day is essential, because it turns an expedition that could be dismal, exhausting or even alarming into an exhilarating fling of France. The road snakes around the capital, rather than circling it, and offers jerky flashes of Frenchness as in an avant-garde silent movie: now a drab industrial quarter, now a pictorial row of poplars – a tedious white housing estate, barges chugging down a canal – a grand boulevard for an instant, a cluster of medieval houses, the sudden swoosh of a tunnel, a couple of vast juggernauts deafeningly overtaking you – and always present, brooding but radiant, just off-stage, the most magnificent capital in Europe.

This is not only France encapsulated: to my mind it is 1990s France all over. For most of us by now, for most of the time, France is a sequence of flashes, a kaleidoscope repeatedly shaken as we hurry across its varied landscapes to the particular French spot that means most to us. When the milords travelled this way in their creaking high-wheeled carriages it must have been more of a continuum, and the slowly passing scenes had a classical clarity, shaped and ample despite the frightful bumps in the road. Now we are all surrealists, and as France hurtles through our windscreens and away through our rear-view mirrors its images are disjointed and contradictory. You want tragedy? It hangs to this day over the elegiac trench-landscapes of the north. You want hedonism? Napkinned tables beckon to us through the windows of snug and steamy restaurants as we rush by, wine awaits the tasting in a thousand hospitable *caves*. Wildness? Bleak bare places are around us now: granite places, moorland, heroic monasteries, uninviting hotels on mountain passes. Romance? Here is the sweet creeping in of violets, ochres and tawny browns that speak of the Mediterranean. Marsh country of the Gypsies, pale estuaries of oyster-men, windy grasslands where menhirs stand and Celtic names jump out at us from roadside signs in the rain – all this, all this grand fling of France, comes into my mind as I drive around the Paris ring road: and now that France itself is so relentlessly, so furiously on the go, I sometimes feel that the grand old nation itself is pounding, head down, foot on the floor, radio blaring, around its own historical *périphérique*.

## 98  *The English*

Ambivalently unique, at the start of my half-century, used to stand the English. They were governed by aristocrats (or so their reputation said), but they were a nation of shopkeepers. They were law-abiding, but famously funny. They were reserved, but had thrown themselves across the world in an irresistible frenzy of greed, ambition and do-goodism. They had won the Second World War, as much by their notoriously cunning diplomacy as by their fire-power. And they were altogether unmistakable, whether they were haughty patricians, up-tight bourgeois or bawdy and good-humoured working people. Everyone knew, at least in theory, the Hertfordshire lord, the Oxford scholar-sportsman, the City gent, the Lancashire mill-owner, the Somerset yokel, the cockney Tommy. As late as the 1950s the clubmen of London still sauntered down St James's in their uniform pinstripe suits,

black bowlers tipped elegantly over the eyes, carrying their tightly rolled
umbrellas like the leather-covered swagger sticks which, only a few years
before, so many of them had carried as army officers. London taxi-drivers
then were cockney almost to a man, often elderly and grumpy, very like
hansom-cab drivers in old *Punch* cartoons. The English in fact were still
themselves: so incorrigibly themselves that they generally talked about their
whole State as being 'England', forgetting all about Scotland, Wales and
Northern Ireland. Some of them still think that way. When they laugh at
Scottish, Welsh and Irish objections, I try to be kind: for I know their
laughter is only an inherited relic of their own glory days, when they were
briefly the Power of Powers and could laugh at anyone with impunity.

## 99  *How they talked*

The divisions of class in England then were indexed almost precisely by the
way people spoke, and we can still hear how the upper classes talked from
the dialogue of old movies: with an accent almost unbelievably affected, in
vowels amazingly distorted, and with a particular flatness of emphasis, as
though not only emotions but actually vocabulary were clenched by the stiff
upper lip of convention. This strange dialect was more pronounced among
women than among men, and we hear even the best of actresses trying to
express undying love or patriotic passion through its medium: Celia Johnson,
for instance, on the railway platform in David Lean's *Brief Encounter*, a
suburban Anna Karenina, her strained protestations of infatuation marvellously countered by the lush Slavic cadences of Rachmaninov. Queen
Elizabeth II herself talked in it, until iconoclasts made fun of her delivery
(the brave Lord Altrincham likened her to 'a priggish schoolgirl with a voice
that is frankly a pain in the neck'), and her mother was to be one of its very
last exponents, speaking it almost into the twenty-first century.

The language itself was full of nuances long since forgotten. Americanisms
had been assaulting it at least since the 1930s (the upper classes were especially
vulnerable to the appeal of jazz and Hollywood), but as late as 1956 Nancy
Mitford was able to enter the best-seller lists with her analysis, borrowed
from the philologist Alan Ross, of words and usages that were U or non-U
– socially proper, that was, or unacceptable. The phrase 'not very U' went
briefly into the language itself. I must confess that some of Mitford's absurd
prejudices I shared. God knows why, but I would never have dreamt of

calling a mantelpiece a mantelshelf (and wouldn't even now). The English language was as subtly and rigidly stratified as English society itself, and the wrong use of a noun or an unfortunate choice of idiom could indelibly brand its speaker.

Since then the language has been transformed, semantically by the flood of Americanisms, socially in particular by changes in the way of speaking. Even the standard accent-less English which used to be the lingua franca of the educated is fast disappearing, to be replaced by a flat neo-cockney. Regional accents survive, against all predictions, but you can no longer place every Englishman in his social class, as Bernard Shaw once said you could, the moment he opens his mouth. In television commercials old-school educated English, only slightly exaggerated, is reserved for comic effect: and stand-up comedians slip into it for implications that are perfectly understood by everyone, except I suppose bemused foreigners.

## 100 *How they looked*

There used to be a specifically English look, too. I used to be able to recognize an Englishman anywhere in the world, not simply by his bearing or his manners, but actually by his face. Now I am never so confident. The English Gentleman, one of the most easily identifiable people on earth, is virtually extinct, and the rest of the nation has lost its distinctive appearances. This is partly biological. The English are no longer the homogeneous Caucasian islanders who stood so complacently in island isolation, and hundreds of thousands of Asians, Africans and Latins have contributed their genes to the stock during my half-century. Turn on London television in the 1990s and you would get the impression that half the population were immigrants. Although this is partly the distortion of positive discrimination, still there are not many parts of England that do not have their immigrant residents, some of them as English as anyone in everything but look.

But the changed appearance is not merely ethnic. Even the purest English face is different now. It is more blurred, less northern-looking. Diet has contributed, and wider education, and the changing manner of speaking, and central heating (considered sissy fifty years ago, and still a bit wimpish to me), but I think it is chiefly a matter of history. Fifty years ago the English were enormously proud of themselves. They had won a fearful war in epic style, led by a statesman of charismatic genius, under the aegis of a royal

house which was universally admired and believed by 40 per cent of the
population, so surveys showed, to be divinely chosen. The English knew
themselves to be special. When I went to London in the 1940s I felt I was
visiting the heart of an immense historical organism, spread around the globe,
to which hundreds of millions of people of every faith and colour looked in
something approaching reverence. When I was abroad the grave sound of
Big Ben on the BBC World Service, and the resonant, almost ecclesiastical
way in which the announcer declaimed 'This is London' over the often
crackling and fluctuating air-waves, made me feel that England was somewhere permanently unique on the planet. London might be battered and
impoverished, but it was still in most British minds the centre of all things,
the best, the biggest, the oldest, the eternal.

No wonder the English face was so distinctive, and no wonder that in the
half-century since then it has lost its edge. It was the face of confidence,
whatever its class. One can imagine a citizen looking at it in a mirror in
those days, when people still knew their Gilbert and Sullivan, and thinking
with horror that it might have been the face of a Rooshian, a Frenchman
or a Prooshian. Thank God he had resisted all temptations/To look like
other nations! It remained unmistakably the face of an Englishman.


101  *From 'A Stranger in Venice', 1906, by Max Beerbohm*

Often, passing through the streets of London, I have wondered what on earth the
inhabitants would look like if they had no longer the thought of their pre-eminence
to sustain them.


102  *The Wakeman and Harry's Challenge*

Here, nevertheless, are two glimpses, from as late as the 1990s, of an England
that was still England. The first concerns that favourite English abstraction
Immemorial Tradition. I arrived one evening at the little cathedral city of
Ripon just in time to hear the Wakeman blow his horn. Around the façade
of the City Hall, in Market Square, is written in large letters 'EXCEPT
THE LORD KEEP YE CITTIE YE WAKEMAN WATCHETH
IN VAIN', and below it, at nine o'clock on every night of the year, wearing
a tricorn hat, the official Wakeman of Ripon blows an admonitory blast

upon his African ox-horn at each corner of the town obelisk. He has been doing so, it is said, since the eighth century. Many cities of Europe observe the custom of the watchman's call, but few if any can boast such an uninterrupted record. I thought it might be an embarrassing affair, an Old Tradition succumbing, as Old Traditions so often do, into tinsel pastiche, but it turned out that evening to seem perfectly organic. The stalwart horn-blower did his job in a stately but untheatrical way, while the cars came and went around him, citizens walked impassively by, and Yorkshire conviviality sounded from neighbouring pubs. I asked the Wakeman if impertinent adolescents ever mocked him as he blew his ox-horn in his antique hat, but he said not. He was bigger than they were, he said.

My second resilient survivor of the English identity I also found in Yorkshire. By now there are Harry Ramsden Fish and Chip Shops all over the world, but the original shop still thrives, at Guiseley, and as a reminder of what used to be, has become a kind of pilgrim shrine. At the back of it is preserved Mr Ramsden's first shack-shop, from the 1930s, and this reminds me of St Francis's woodland chapel preserved within the mighty basilica of Assisi; nearby a souvenir shop sells bottled sweets and comic plaques as substitutes for votive candles and pictures of the Virgin; the restaurant itself is all carpets, chandeliers and stained-glass windows, with many icons of the late Harry Ramsden (died 1963) and a menu dominated by the grand sacrament of Harry's Challenge – a fish-and-chips dish so gigantic that if you get through it you are given a free pudding and a signed certificate as absolution.

I had a pre-Christmas luncheon at Guiseley in 1995, and England was certainly English then. All the customers were the real thing – not an outsider among them (except me), only celebratory office parties hilarious over Harry's Challenge, and amiably extended families with grandmothers in hats, and burbling children with hand-held video toys, and not a few stout parties who would have done better to cut down on the Steamed Ginger Pudding. At one o'clock precisely there arrived outside the front door the Scissett Youth Band of Huddersfield, to serenade us lustily with all the good old carols – none of your fancy ecumenicals – setting many a sensibly shod foot tapping to their rhythms, and inciting me, as an inveterate whistler, to join in messily over my mushy peas.

## 103 *From* Harry Ramsden: The Uncrowned King of Fish and Chips, *1989, by Don Mosey*

> Harry stood at the Pearly Gate,
> His face was worn and old.
> He meekly asked the man of fate
> Admission to the fold.
> 'What have you done,' old Peter asked,
> 'To seek admittance here?'
> 'I owned a Guiseley Fish Shop
> For many and many a year.'
> The gate flew open sharply, as
> Peter touched the bell.
> 'Come in old man, and take a harp,
> You've had enough of hell.'

## 104 *Doubts*

Rationally, people even half a century ago knew that England was not really a Power of Powers any more. The vastly superior strength of America was apparent to anyone who cared to think about it, and I remember the subalterns of my regiment, when we were still in Italy, fantasizing about a ceremonial end to the island kingdom, becoming the forty-ninth State of the American Union perhaps, or marching four abreast, all 40 million, off the peninsula of Land's End into the oblivion of the Atlantic. For the most part, though, the nation put its decline out of mind, and in this it was helped by the continuing jingoism of the media and by a wistful tendency to dream: when Queen Elizabeth II was crowned in 1953, the event was generally hailed as the dawn of a new Elizabethan era, in which an England recovered from the traumas of war would resume its triumphant panache.

I suppose I shared some of that fantasy when, in June of that year, I went to Buckingham Palace with the members of the British expedition that had just achieved the first ascent of Everest – I had been the news correspondent with the team, and my dispatch reporting the success of the climb had reached London on the night before Elizabeth's coronation. It was my only meeting with the Queen. She was just my age, and although I was already something of a republican, I would have been less than human if I had not been moved by the meeting. I asked her how the news had reached her, and she said it had been brought to her in her bedroom in a red dispatch-box. How marvellous it was, I thought, to imagine the progress of my little message – in my own hands down the slopes of the mountain, into the lowlands in the pouch of a Sherpa runner, winged across the continents, and finally delivered into what I imagined to be the heavily gilded, curtained, eiderdowned and doubtless four-postered apartment of the Queen of England!

Not long afterwards I was walking down the Mall in London, the capital's one ceremonial highway, when the Queen came by on a tall charger. It was the day of Trooping the Colour, a splendidly obsolete military manoeuvre which was performed simply for the show of it every summer. Flags flew, a band played somewhere, jangling cavalry processed, three strange old gentlemen rode past, weighed down beneath fat bearskin hats, with huge swords bouncing at their side. The street was lined with those fresh-faced troops, apparently younger than any others, who used to give a touching sense of innocence to the British Army. Jolly women thronged the pavements, waving little flags, while policemen figuratively rocked on their heels. When the young woman herself passed on her lofty horse the crowd watched her with a kind of exalted compassion. But I already thought it had lasted too long. The Queen herself looked tired, and the whole panoply of the parade, all that starch and polish, all that unchangeable ritual, seemed to me the dying display of an exhausted tradition: year after year, century after century, the same beat of the drums, the same fluttering plumes, the same bent old courtiers on their horses lurching generation after generation down the Mall.

## 105 *The coachman*

A friend and I were driving one day along a quiet Oxfordshire road when we saw a picturesque sight in front of us. A fine old four-in-hand was running along at a spanking pace, driven by an elderly gentlemanly-looking coachman on his high box. There were passengers behind him on the rooftop, and it looked a perfectly workmanlike, everyday equipage. 'D'you see the man driving it?' said my companion. 'That's the most hated Englishman alive.' It was perfectly true that if the Germans had won the Second World War that coachman would probably have been smuggled out of the country by underground routes to Australia or the Falkland Islands. Not only his enemies hated him, either. Thousands of his own countrymen considered him a war criminal. When I heard who he was, I myself looked up with distinctly mixed feelings as we overtook his coach. Should he have done it, I asked myself? Had he any choice? Was the slaughter justified? Had his men, who had come from the world's four corners to serve under him, wasted their courage in an evil campaign? Did the cause of a righteous victory justify the means of murder? Even Winston Churchill had doubts.

That coachman was Sir Arthur Harris — 'Bomber' Harris. He it was, during the Second World War, who had unleashed his vast fleets of black thudding aircraft, manned by crews from every country of the old British Empire, to devastate scores of German cities and kill hundreds of thousands of German civilians. I stared rudely at him through our rear window as we left those trotting horses behind, but he looked a jolly enough old fellow, up there behind the reins.

## 106  *The lost kingdom*

There is a statue of 'Bomber' Harris in London now, at the tail-end of the century, but although the Queen of England still attends the Trooping ceremony, she no longer rides a horse there. The courtiers and the drum-majors ride by, but the police have a meaner look these days, the soldiers look more loutish, the crowd is no longer like the flutter of neighbours around the church gate at a wedding, and it is no longer heretical to think the whole royal charade a symptom not of pride and unity but of decline. The national characteristics of the English had been universally recognized in the 1940s and 1950s. By the 1980s the English *had* no national characteristics. They had been obliged to think of themselves as multi-ethnic, multicultural, so that the very word 'English' had almost lost its meaning. They had been taught to be ashamed of their lost empire. They had been so bewildered by incessant legislation that they had almost forgotten the basic principle of their own law – that when the law is silent the citizen is free. One by one their most cherished institutions had been deliberately discredited, if not by politics, then by satire. They were almost comically subservient to American models: every youth craze, every semantic or artistic trend was copied, and from the passion for litigation to the style of television news-reading, in foreign policy as in social attitudes, slavishly the English tracked the footsteps of the

Americans – whom, at the same time, in a grotesque echo of old supremacies, they all too often professed to despise.

The English, in short, were in a transient limbo. It could actually be said that they were suffering from an inferiority complex – who would have believed it possible when I was young? Actually I think they had lots to be proud of. In the arts, in show business, in popular fashion, in horribly brilliant tabloid journalism, in finance and commerce, even I suppose in the brutal kind of undercover soldiering that the British Army had made its own – in all these things the English were still pre-eminent. Their new racial mix, as a melting-pot State, often made them seem more modern than most of their continental peers – as though, chrysalis-like, they would presently emerge as a new sort of nation. But to most of the English themselves England seemed to be supreme at nothing any more, except when now and then some American magazine decided that London was swinging or cool, momentarily raising the islanders' morale. Yearning for the great days of their Powerdom (vicariously, for there were few alive to remember it), they had always viewed the prospect of a more integrated Europe, still more a federal Europe, with suspicion and distaste. Within a European union, they feared, they would no longer be special. They would be one among many. They would be losing their sovereignty. Continental trickery, the profoundest national conviction seemed to say, would gang up to humiliate them. The Nation-State, the Nation-State!

But they would doubtless get used to the idea of a united Europe, if it ever came about, just as they very soon got used to the existence of the Channel Tunnel, for years opposed by English opinion as being an obvious thoroughfare for hostile armies, nasty foreign ideas, noxious beetles and rabies. When I telephoned London from Wales to book a ticket on the Eurostar train to Brussels, almost as soon as the service had begun, the booking-clerk at the other end sounded to me almost stagily English – middle-aged and motherly – but not in the least surprised or excited by the revolutionary nature of her job. A ticket under the English Channel! 'Oh, you'll have a lovely trip, dear,' she said in the homeliest way, and after suggesting that I might travel first class, just to give myself a treat, she said goodbye to me for all the world as though she had just sold me an excursion ticket to Weston-super-Mare. One gets used to anything.

## 107  *The fulcrum*

Germany is the only place to end such a random tour of Europe's States, through fifty years of time, 10 million square kilometres of space. 'Europe,' as one of Dostoevsky's characters puts it – 'the everlasting Germany!' Germany is the fulcrum of this continent; my entire European generation, and my father's and grandfather's too, has lived in response to the energies of Germany. As German patriots have so often argued, unfortunately for the rest of us, their country occupies the continent's commanding position, bang in the middle, the richest, the most powerful, the most persistently dynamic of the European States, sharing frontiers with France, the Netherlands, Luxembourg, Belgium, Denmark, Poland, Austria, the Czech Republic and Switzerland. It is like a generator, or alternatively an incubus. As we reach the end of the twentieth century, which the Germans themselves did so much to make dreadful, it is also a powerfully cohesive country, a federation of semi-autonomous *Länder* but a community still assertively conscious of its national and racial unity. Before the Second World War Germany was claiming rights of sovereignty over territories inhabited by Germans anywhere in Europe: since then Germans of the diaspora have returned to the Fatherland in their hundreds of thousands from Poland, from Czechoslovakia, from Lithuania, from Romania, from the Ukraine, from Russia, and the 16 million citizens of Communist East Germany have been reabsorbed into the unified Federal Republic. It has been a mighty feat of adaptability, on the whole stoically performed.

Yet in some ways Germany still strikes me as being more vulnerable than most of the European States. 'Germany, where is it?' asked Schiller in 1797, and to me there is something orphan-like about it still. Sometimes even now it feels almost pitifully detached from the greater world, the world in which other peoples have moved so profitably and comfortably. The Germany into whose baleful presence I was born (only eight years after the First World War) was a State already humiliated and soured by history. The British, the French, the Dutch, the Italians, the Swedes, the Danes, the Spaniards, the Portuguese had all in their time possessed big overseas empires, long accustoming them to the wide horizons. Even the Russians had a Pacific coast. The Germans had entered the imperial competition, with fretful interventions in Africa and China, only when the imperial idea was almost dead. Not for them the scented shores of Malabar, or Carib palms and strands!

The Germans were dissatisfied with destiny, and their energy curdled into malice. In neither world war were they beaten in straight combat, by equal force of arms: in a symbolical way it was power out of the sea that had frustrated them – the power and wealth that had been amassed by more fortunate peoples, organically more free, with more friends, collectively demonized by the Germans themselves as those old bogies of Christian Europe, the Elders of Zion.

Fifty years of peace have calmed the German neuroses. The Germans are now as familiar with the rest of the world as anyone else – they may never have ruled those distant shores and strands, but they sell their products there more successfully than any other Europeans, and sunbathe there as assiduously (though, by an inhibition that I take to be a remnant of old uncertainties, disproportionately seldom staying in the best hotels). The overseas empires are dead and gone, and by a paradoxical change of fortune Europe now looks back to Germany's own kind of imperium, an older kind – the days good and bad when Germanness was the master-force of Europe itself.

## 108 *The scene of an accident*

My goodness, I certainly did not feel this way on my original visit to Berlin. I thought then that never in my lifetime could it be a great capital again. Such terrible things had lately been ordered there, such nightmares almost beyond imagination had been concocted, that it seemed less like a city than a chamber of horrors. It was mostly in ruins still, but among the shambles fearful monuments remained. Hitler's bunker was pointed out with a shudder, an indistinct mound among the rubble. Goering's Air Ministry still stood, and the headquarters of the Gestapo, and I stayed in the last rickety remnant of the burnt-out Adlon Hotel, where once the Nazis had mingled insidiously with the *haut monde* beneath the potted palms, and a thousand corruptions had been arranged. Down by the Wannsee was the villa in which they devised the Final Solution, the mass murder of the Jews of Europe. What an awful city! Even among the shattered palaces and broken churches, the streets blocked with rubble, the gaping Reichstag and the boarded-up wrecks of theatres, a fearful potency seemed to linger. Until the very last shades of Hitler's capital were exorcized, I thought then, Germany could never be easy again.

Then the Berlin Wall went up, and the city seemed unreal in a different way. Now it was like a dual exhibition. East of the Wall Communism paraded itself in mammoth boulevards, gigantic apartment blocks, State shops and propaganda posters, all the grim paraphernalia of autocracy and secret police. On the tall mast of the television tower a bulbous observation capsule looked down like an eerie eye on everything below. West of the Wall all the gallimaufry of contemporary capitalism pranced and preened itself: neon signs, jukeboxes, *Time* magazine, pony-tails, paperback thrillers, dry Martinis. One side was dour and relentless: the other side mercilessly glittering. In those years the city seemed to have little to do with Germany. Its two halves were implants of distant Powers: the one of America, the other of the Soviet Union. The hideous ghosts of Nazism gradually receded, but nothing indigenous had come to replace them, only those drear or tawdry exhibitions of other nations' values.

## 109  *O Berlin!*

Only when Communism failed, and the Wall came down, did I come to feel that Berlin was a proper city, like any other. Then year by year I watched with pleasure its revival. I took to staying on the eastern side of the old divide, in one of the hotels which attended the Unter den Linden and which, while hardly up to the sinister pre-war dazzle of the Adlon, at least aspired to the standards of the capitalist West. From here I could walk out into the very focus of the awakening city. Bit by bit the crumbled and blackened boulevards were restored; smile by smile (I sentimentally like to fancy) the spirit of the old Berlin came to life again. Eating *Apfelstrudel* and cream in the Operncafé, while the sparrows played at my feet and the students laughed beneath the trees, I felt at one with all the generations of happy Berliners who had fattened themselves on the same spot. And once, hearing celestial music sounding through a basement window at the back of the Schauspielhaus, I peered inside and met the preoccupied eye of a young violinist of the Berlin Symphony Orchestra, jacketless in his white tie as he warmed up for that evening's concert. He seemed to me Berlin eternalized: but many years would pass before the Germans decided what kind of city they wanted their new Berlin to be, the new capital of a united democratic Germany, and recruited all Europe's architects to plan it.

## 110  *Executive prisoners*

The first Germans I met myself, in any numbers, were prisoners of war employed as mess servants and general handymen by their captors, the British Army. There were thousands of them in Egypt. They seemed to me almost servilely disciplined, but they also seemed at once simpler and better educated than our own soldiers. On the one hand they were often excellent craftsmen, and could mend things, or build things, in a way British soldiers seldom could: on the other hand they seemed intellectually more confident, as though a German private could read a map, for instance, or devise a timetable as competently as any British officer. I got the feeling that a large proportion of those prisoners were what the British would call 'officer material': and, since they seemed much like our own men in physique and temperament, I could only assume that education had made them so. Their Germany, the Germany that disappeared in flames in 1945, was a country still of aristocrats and peasants: at the one end scores of petty princelings still on their ancestral estates, at the other a large agricultural proletariat living in the old way even into the 1940s, ploughing with horses, dressed in quaint costumes. Yet those soldiers seemed like educated men, liable I dare say to atavistic excesses of cruelty as of courage, but quick to learn and reason. When, decades later, Germany had once again become the wealthiest and most powerful State in Europe, I sometimes remembered those diligent and clever prisoners of ours, so humbly serving us our dinners in the mess, and wondered how many were now sitting amply in swivel chairs at corporate desks in skyscrapers.

## 111  *An oblation*

It was the Germany of the Kaisers that my mother had known. Like many Britons at the time, her father avidly admired its culture, and halfway through my mother's time at Leipzig he eagerly went out to visit her, taking with him a brace of Monmouthshire pheasant as an oblation to Robert Teichmüller, her eminent professor. Eighty years later I went there myself, to see just where she had spent those happy years of her girlhood. I imagined her arriving, excited but a bit scared, on the platform of the great railway station – in her time the biggest in all Europe. I relived her merry student evenings in open-air cafés. I heard as she did the strains of Bach ringing from Bach's own Thomaskirche. I walked through her parks and gardens, and fancied her hurrying to the concert hall when, forbidden to attend a performance of Richard Strauss's unsuitable opera *Salome*, she jumped out of a window to go anyway. Finally I found my way to the Conservatorium itself. It looked to me just as it did in the engraving on my mother's graduation diploma – the very acme and epitome of a German music academy. In I went, and there were the statutory bearded busts of famous musicians, and students hurried past with cellos and music-cases, and notices of recitals or rehearsals fluttered from noticeboards as they had doubtless fluttered constantly since my mother's day.

Nothing had changed, so far as I could see, through two world wars, the end of the Kaisers, the birth and death of Nazidom, the coming and going of Communism. Beside each door was a list of the Herr Professors, and I would not have been in the least surprised to see the name of Teichmüller among them. When we went into one of the practice-rooms, where a student was hard at it with a Chopin prelude, just for a moment I thought it was my mother, young and smiling, looking up at us expectantly from her keyboard: on the window-sill, I am almost sure, lay a brace of pheasant, wrapped in a copy of the *Monmouthshire Beacon*.

## 112 *By the lake*

Through the window of a lakeside restaurant at Mölln I watch four German children playing. Their families are having lunch inside, and I would guess the children to be between six and ten years old. The two boys are always in the lead, dashing here and there, throwing stones into the water, waving to passing boats. The girls follow dutifully but enthusiastically behind. One is slim, blonde and pretty, and wears a long floral dress which she likes to flounce about. The other is very plain, short and fat, and wears a blue anorak, with sleeves too long for her, over a short tartan skirt. The plain girl is always last. She can never quite keep up. When they run out to the end of the jetty, she is always left behind. When they rush helter-skelter into the restaurant to speak to their families, who are lazing over beer and pipes at the end of the room, the door closes behind the other three and there is a long pause before, panting heavily, the short fat girl opens it again with difficulty and stumbles in. I like her best of the quartet – she tries so hard, smiles so gamely, struggles so constantly to tuck up the sleeves of her anorak. I feel for her, too. Her family take little notice of her, and the other children treat her as one might treat a puppy-dog. However, when they all scamper out again once more, and I offer her a smile as she passes my table, she returns me a most malevolent glare.

## 113  *Sorry for the Germans*

Sometimes I have felt sorry for the Germans – notably at Passau in northern Bavaria, a delightful town which stands on the Danube at its dual junction with the rivers Inn and Ilz. With a number of literary colleagues I was once kindly entertained there by a young German professor of English literature. He posed us on his balcony while he ran down to his garden to take our photograph, and this gave me a chance to look around his apartment. It was Schubertian. Simply furnished, spare and sweet, it was decorated with artists' proofs and littered with paperbacks, and still on the roller of an old manual typewriter there was an uncompleted poem. Through the window the light of the river palely gleamed. 'Ready!' cried the young professor. There he was below us, beneath the flowering cherry of his little garden, on a lawn thick with dandelions. He focused his lens, we braced ourselves, a blossom fell at his feet, and suddenly I felt sorry for the Germans.

We were five of us up on the balcony – two from England, one from South Africa, one from Scotland, one from Wales – and it felt to me as though we were visitors from some altogether freer, easier, fundamentally happier world. Passau stands very near the heart of Europe, profoundly landlocked. The Alps block its way to the Mediterranean; the whole expanse of Germany stands between it and the Baltic. Even as the crow flies it is some 700 miles to the Bay of Biscay. The steamers on the river sail to Bulgaria, Romania, Russia – mile upon mile among the flatlands, through the Iron Gates of Illyria, before they reach the Black Sea. That day I felt some of the sense of unfairness that the Germans used to cherish. The charm of Passau, the flowers on the cherry tree, the young professor with his poem and his typewriter – all suddenly moved me. When he looked out from his balcony, I thought, he saw only the enclosing ramparts of Germany, and the river-boats sailing away into loveless territories of the Slavs. When we looked out from ours, we looked out across the continents, and when our ships slipped away from port they were bound not for the Iron Gates or the awful Sea of Azov, but for all the world's wide oceans. Hitler lived in Passau for a

time, and I found it easy to suppose him brooding out of his window over
the river with some of the same thoughts. How remote New York or Sydney
must have seemed to him, and how gloriously enviable the spectacle of the
British Empire, ranging the hemispheres with such arrogant ceremony!

'Smile, please,' said the young professor. We all smiled, but my smile was
the sickliest.

## 114 *From* Buddenbrooks, *1901, by Thomas Mann, translated by H. T. Lowe-Porter*

'We want freedom,' Morten said.

'Freedom?' she asked.

'Yes, freedom, you know – Freedom!' he repeated; and he made a vague, awkward,
fervent gesture outward and downward, not toward the side where the coast of
Mecklenburg narrowed the bay, but in the direction of the open sea, whose rippling
blue, green, yellow, and grey stripes rolled as far as eye could see out to the misty
horizon.

Tony followed his gesture with her eye; they sat, their hands lying close together
on the bench, and looked into the distance.

## 115 *'The world will notice us'*

In 1995, with the blessing of the German Government, the Bulgarian-
American artist Christo Jaracheff performed one of his transformation displays
at the Reichstag in Berlin – which is to say, he covered the entire building
in a grey plastic wrapping, bound with blue ribboning. This struck me as
not simply foolish but actually degrading – imagine the US Capitol, for
example, being similarly muffled – but I was astonished to discover that the
Germans loved it. They treated the whole thing as an entertainment, the
unfortunate building being surrounded by food stalls, hot-dog stands, picnickers, performance artists, buskers, bands and a tented restaurant, like a
fairground. Biplanes and helicopters circled overhead. Hardly anybody I met
found indignity in the spectacle of the historic old structure wrapped up like
a Christmas parcel, with odd protrusions apparently threatening to break
through the plastic. Indignity? Dignity was the last thing they wanted of
their rulers. They wanted Governments that would be close to the people,

not lofty or distant, not dignified. They wanted fun. They wanted modernity. They had been brought up, after all, to suppose the tinsel capitalism of the old West Berlin a civilized epitome, and they thought it was good for Germany that the national assembly should be made to look silly. 'It will make the world notice us.' But I was sorry for them, again.

## 116 *Feeding the ducks*

Foreigners can still feel very foreign in Germany, especially I imagine if they are Asian. Through the windows of a riverside restaurant at Lüneburg we watch one now feeding the ducks from a bridge nearby. He looks Iranian, perhaps: his eyes are dark and his face is sad. With tender melancholy gestures he throws his crusts of bread into the water below, out of a white plastic shopping-bag, against a background of a hefty medieval tower and a row of half-timbered Hanseatic inns – as German a background as could be. His every movement seems to speak of isolation, mingled with a yearning for affection. He is like a prisoner feeding his only friends, quacking and squab-bling in the brown water below. The townspeople, crossing the bridge behind his back, take no notice of him. When all the bread has gone he scrumples up his bag and prepares to go, but finding one last fragment inside he tosses it to a solitary pigeon which has been hanging about hungrily at his feet. Then, lighting a cigarette, he disappears into the gateway of the tower, and we shall never see him again.

## 117 *Happy hour*

Because of Wagner, Hitler's favourite artist, I always used to think of Bayreuth as a Lourdes of Germany, a place of pilgrimage for those in search of the German soul. Here had been put into music all the Germanic grandeur and mystery. Here the heroes and demons of German myth came face to face with the triumphs and despairs of German reality. I did not get to Bayreuth, though, until the early 1990s, by which time the tragic Germany of my youth had been brought back from the abyss: and what I found then in the famous town was less like a divine immolation than a Happy Hour.

The longer I sat in Maximilianstrasse, the main square, the harder I found it to imagine Wagner lording it in these streets, still less Hitler and his minions sweeping through in their black convertibles. The square was grand enough, and handsomely embellished with baroque fountains and façades, but there was certainly nothing Wagnerian about it. There was a McDonald's on one side, and the shopping street that led away to the west had been pedestrianized and taken over by chain stores. I had my coffee in a standard café that might just as well have been in Holland or England, and very likely belonged to the same conglomerate. A few miscellaneous louts messed about the place, and a drop-out lay feet up on a bench, and rock music thumped somewhere, and there was a general prevalence of well-disposed middle-aged women doing the family shopping. Yet here the gods had seen their twilights! Napoleon passed through here, and Ludwig II of Bavaria, and Hitler, and then the United States Army stormed in, and for forty years the Iron Curtain was slammed down a few miles to the east, making this a frontier town between the ideologies. And by then Richard Wagner himself had come and gone, so that almost anyone in the world, asked to think of Bayreuth, would think of thundering harmonies, flaming Brünnhildes, heart-rending Tristans, helmets and breastplates and Hitler himself, with his hair slicked down and swastikas on his arms, wild-eyed in the stalls.

Now the Happy Hour had come. Bayreuth could afford to linger over its beers at the trestle tables in the square, while the shadows lengthened towards McDonald's. It was a rich little town, well-run, well-fed, proud of its famous festival. It had not forgotten its gods and demons, all the same. I stayed at an old post-house whose previous customers, the landlord told me, had included Napoleon, Ludwig and Hitler. And which of the three, I asked him, would he most like to have as a guest again? He did not smile. '*Alle shit*,' he said.

## 118  *City of Culture*

What a pleasure to stroll through the streets of Weimar, a little German city whose distinction has traditionally been elegantly cultural! In the late eighteenth century the young Duke Carl August made his capital a happy retreat for artistic geniuses, and ever since Weimar has basked in the memory of their names. There is a pleasant restaurant, you will be told, behind the Liszthaus. Turn right at the Goethehaus to get to the bus station. You want the Schillerhaus? That's easy: just go straight down Schillerstrasse from the Goethe and Schiller statue. And agreeable indeed it is to amble around the town among these illustrious shades, now and then taking an ice-cream beneath its trees. The streets are mostly quiet and gentle. Small boys wade across the little river Ilm with fishing-rods. Street musicians agreeably play. Delectable parks and gardens are everywhere. It is easy to imagine young Carl August promenading with lyricists on each arm, bowing right and left to his affectionate subjects.

But here's a terrible thing. As the literary capital of Germany, the repository of its immortal poetic spirit, a retreat of nature-worship and mythic dreams, Weimar became beloved of the Nazis, and it loved the Nazis in return. Its mixture of Hitler and Goethe, wrote Thomas Mann fastidiously in 1932, was 'particularly disturbing'. In the market square stands the Elephant Hotel, and all the waters of the Ilm cannot wash the taint from this unfortunate hostelry. It is a handsome 1930s building, but redecorated inside in a glittery, chromy style that irresistibly suggests the imminent arrival of swaggering gauleiters and their women. This impression is all too true. Hitler and his crew were particularly fond of the hotel, and more than once the Führer spoke from its balcony to enthusiastic crowds in the square outside.

So enamoured were the Nazis of Weimar, in fact, that they erected there one of their most celebrated and characteristic monuments. The site they chose was on the lovely hill of Ettersberg, just outside the city, which Goethe himself had long before made famous – he loved to sit and meditate beneath an oak tree there. One evening I paid a reluctant visit to this place, now a popular tourist site well-publicized in the town. My taxi-driver, a gregarious soul, chatted cheerfully to me all the way. Had I enjoyed my stay in Weimar? Did I visit the Goethehaus? What did I think of the food? Did I know that Weimar was to be the European City of Culture in 1999, at the end of the millennium? 'Congratulations,' I said. 'Recognition once more for the city of Goethe and Schiller.' 'Exactly,' said the taxi-driver, and just then we turned up the side-road to Buchenwald.

## 119  *Country style*

In the days of the Communists, East Germany seemed to me one of the most terrible places of all, and the legacy of industrial pollution was to linger for years and years. On the other hand, the Communists having been less than advanced in their agricultural methods, the wide plains of the Brandenburg countryside were mercifully unsterilized by chemicals, which left them wonderfully fresh and natural – unkempt, since half the fields had gone to seed, and half the trees needed trimming, but still gloriously organic. All day long the skylarks sang above my head when I travelled among those lovely landscapes, and there were meadows full of poppies, and long avenues of fruit-laden cherry trees, and now and then storks' nests, those fairy-tale emblems of old Europe, comfortably on chimneys above cobbled hamlets. Once I saw three storks flying high and majestically over Berlin itself: I suspect mine is the last generation ever to see such a sight.

## 120 *Ashamed*

One day in the 1980s I found myself a trifle lost when driving through Rostock, on Germany's Baltic coast, and I faltered and swerved as I tried to find my way on the street map. Immediately there was an irritable blast of the horn from the car behind. Rostock was notorious at that time for recent racist attacks upon Turkish immigrants, and my blood boiled. 'Damned Germans,' I found myself saying, 'they never change. Can't the brute see I'm a stranger here?' – and I turned around in my seat prepared to give him that rude gesture of the Welsh archers, as in Vienna. *Gott in Himmel*, he was a very intemperate Asian! I blushed, even to myself, especially as I have myself experienced almost nothing but kindness from Germans of all sorts, under Communism as under capitalism, during my fifty years of Europe.

I am a child of the wars, though, and have not always been so generous in return. With a pang I remember still the young Germans I met at a party in Baden-Baden in the early 1950s, when the nation was still sunk in shame and disillusion. They were about my own age, bred by Hitler Youth out of defeat, and our conversation was wary. We skirted around recent history, we evaded questions of morality, but even so I found, when we parted company at last, that one woman was in tears – tears of mortification, to compare her self-doubts, her guilt and her sense of undeserved bad luck with the unabashed pride of nation which in those days I could not help displaying. Thirty years later I made a television film with a German television crew, travelling through several European countries. Strangers often asked us what we were up to, and I always made a point of saying that, while the director and his crew were German, I was from Wales. 'You are ashamed to be thought one of us,' the director accused me mournfully one day: and, though I declined to admit it, so I was.

These are people of God, too. More than any other European people they have been the instrument of the most divine of the arts, music, perhaps because of the special rhythms of their language, perhaps because Martin Luther, their greatest prophet, made music intrinsic to his religion. Even at their most degraded they have honoured this spark within themselves – even sadistic officers at concentration camps felt the necessity, whether in truth or in charade, to show themselves lovers of music. Out of the tormented and often cruel national psyche have come the glories of Bach and Beethoven – a cliché indeed, but still a mystery. Nothing moves me more than to enter one of the great German cathedrals, very likely in its day a positive cauldron of racialism, and to hear one of the tremendous Bach chorales thundering down the nave – an ultimate expression, to my mind, of human aspiration, and a supreme glory of Europe.

I went to Berlin in 1991 for the two-hundredth anniversary of the Brandenburg Gate, an anniversary of awful possibility. The Gate was a triumph of Prussian vainglory, undeniably an arch of hubris. It had been restored at last after the mutilations of war, and its shining quadriga was once again equipped with the Iron Cross and Prussian Eagle pointedly absent during the Communist years. Through it overblown victory parades had passed, and the plumed pageantries of State visits, and the railway coach from Compiègne was towed in vindictive triumph. The long anniversary celebrations ended with a performance of '*Deutschland über Alles*', and what a nightmare that might have been! I prepared to scowl. But it was played by a string quartet, in Haydn's delicate last version of the melody: and its gentle cadences, drifting over the silent crowd, through the lights of the great reviving city, were enough to melt a Junker's heart.

# 4
## THE INTERNET

*

*Trieste exists as a city only because it is on the way to somewhere else. From any vantage point in the surrounding hills you can see its raison d'être. Here roads out of the European interior reach the Mediterranean; here they meet highways running to Italy one way, to the Slav countries the other; and here ships sail away down the Adriatic to the world outside. Trieste is the very epitome of a port, standing at the point where essential trade routes converge upon a deep harbour. It has been a great entrepôt in its time, and a great exchange, an emporium free of customs duties, a permanent trade fair. Fond Trieste tradition claims that the Argonauts, having sailed up the Danube from the Black Sea, carried their ship across the hills and came down to Trieste on their way home with the Golden Fleece. Certainly the Romans founded the port of Tergeste here, and nineteenth-century Trieste historians loved to say that it was depicted on Trajan's Column in Rome (a hypothesis, declares one more recent scholar, 'without the least appearance of probability'). An oil pipeline still runs from the port of Trieste to Ingolstadt in Germany, following more or less the route the medieval traders followed, when they carried earlier products of the East to the marts of Augsburg and Ulm.*

*The city reached its apogee with the railway age, when trains linked Vienna directly with its waterfront, and made it the chief outlet for all the Austro-Hungarian Empire, so that its interests extended far into central and eastern Europe. The first modern port of Trieste, in fact, was built by a railway company under the patronage of the Emperor Franz Josef II, who graciously came down from Vienna to inspect its progress, and eventually three separate railway lines connected it with its hinterland. I can remember when steam trains still puffed along these quays (keeping Gustav Mahler irritably awake at the Grand Hôtel de la Ville), and sometimes, in the blazing Adriatic sun, they had snow on their wagons – snow of the North, snow of the mountains! Nothing could have exemplified more clearly the shape and meaning of Europe, ranging from the subtropical to the Arctic, and pulled together down the centuries (when it was not tearing itself apart) by a myriad highroads and waterways, along the great river valleys, through and under the mountains, up the coasts from the balmy to the ice-bound.*

*These were bonds, as often as not, that had existed before history, ways followed for so long that they had become matters of instinct, like the tracks of animals through forests. They formed an immemorial internet. In the days soon after the Second World War when the new Communist Yugoslav federation was all but closed to the West, and lay beyond Trieste's hills like a menacing and forbidden limbo, a small steamer sailed regularly from the Maritime Station down the Istrian coast to Dalmatia. I can see it still in my mind's eyes, the straggle of its black smoke petering out across the bay as it chugged off into the South. It pottered humbly down the coast, heedless of ideology, almost without thinking, or so I fancied. I used to watch it go with sympathy, as one might watch a ferry crossing the Styx, but it invariably came safely back again a day or two later. It had always sailed that way, it was part of the pattern of life and history.*

*Now the bonds are tighter still. Each year trade, finance, transport, tourism, communications and mass travel make Europe more familiar with itself, and nearer a whole. Trieste was the first city I knew with an Internet Café, where unengaged customers, between their cappuccinos, could idly surf the Web.*

## 1  *On the roads*

For me one of the excitements of Europe is the immense cavalcade of trucks which perpetually criss-crosses the continent, night and day – growing from a tentative trickle at the end of the 1940s almost to saturation fifty years later. I love to watch the passage of the leviathans at one of the great continental crossroads. The very names on their canopies carry a thrill for me, and the varied majesty of the vehicles themselves is marvellous to see – trucks from Madrid with sun-visors over their windscreens, mighty trailer-trucks out of Germany, weather-beaten Irish trucks, Italian trucks in racy colours, English lorries travelling in brotherly pairs, on their way to Sofia or Bucharest, Hungarian trucks *en route* to Portugal, Polish trucks bound for Holland, or Lithuania, or Liechtenstein: and when, in the truck park of some motorway café, they pull in with roaring engines for the night, it is like seeing a great caravan in laager, surrounded if the weather is warm by a thin shimmer of heat, and bivouacked all about.

## 2  *Truncations*

I cherish this euphemistic view (which is certainly not shared by Europe's environmentalists) because I see the trucks as fulfilling historical schedules. The roads they take nowadays are mostly freeways, but often enough they keep to the tracks of ancient trade routes, along the same valleys, over the same passes, between the same centres of commerce and industry, crossing the same rivers high above the passages of prehistoric fords or ferries – as long ago as the fourteenth century couriers established a daily overland service between Bruges and Venice. Sometimes they follow roads that are holy, like the roads through Brittany which once led cultists to the mysteries of Carnac, or the grand route that for centuries took pilgrims across France and northern Spain to the shrine of St James at Santiago de Compostela. Sometimes they are following still older footsteps: the famous parabola of Oxford's High Street, in England, along which the occasional skulking juggernaut still finds its way, is said to reproduce precisely the curve a man naturally follows when he walks across a meadow.

They frequently drive along Roman roads. If they are taking a load through southern Italy to Brindisi they are following the route of the Appian Way, the most famous of them all. If they then take a ship over the Adriatic to Durrës in Albania, and rumble away towards Tirana, they are on the Via Egnatia, which once connected Rome with Constantinople itself. On the old road from Bad Ragaz to Zurich, in Switzerland, they pass through villages whose very names remember the numbered Roman way-stations along the highway – Prümsch, Siguns, Terzan, Quarten, Quinten. We all think we know a Roman road, even the children in the back seat, when the wandering European country road suddenly turns for a few miles into a dead straight military highway, clinical and commanding. Actually it is often not Roman at all, but a former railway track, perhaps, or just an abnormally easy stretch of modern construction. But sometimes it really is a work of the Romans, the first builders of modern roads in Europe, and then there is a legitimate historical frisson in travelling upon it. Over most of Europe, every now and then, these ghosts of an old order greet one with a special promise of efficiency and punctuality. Where there are no Roman roads at all – notably in Ireland – to this day I still feel an extra suggestion of anarchy. Where they exist, I think of them as a measured pattern of Europe, linking not just Rome with its old colonies, but Romania with Portugal, Sicily with Germany, Poland with Wales, where one of the westernmost Roman highways of all came to an end among my recalcitrant tribal predecessors at the village called Caersws.

South from Caersws, in the lee of the Brecon mountains, there is a stretch of Roman road along which the wagon-trains of the legions carried loads of lead and gold out of the hills. Its original paving-stones are unimproved and unsurfaced, and along it one can still drive a car. The road leads nowhere nowadays, and a modern highway runs nearby, taking the trucks towards Ireland, but progressing bumpily over those ancient slabs in a state-of-the-art automobile seems to me to truncate the centuries wonderfully.


## 3  Toutes Directions


It is in France, though, that I feel myself most gratefully in the presence of the road-building Romans. The country roads there are so long and straight, bounded so neatly by avenues of poplars, that back-seat children assume they are Roman every one: half of them are – until the eighteenth century nearly all proper French roads were Roman. The road numbering of France, introduced by Napoleon, seems positively Caesarean. All the clarity supposed to characterize the Roman mind, all the logic of the Latin language, is expressed in those brilliantly straightforward *Toutes Directions* signs which, welcoming you as you enter the purlieus of any French town, engaging your entire trust, guide you so infallibly through the backstreets, around the squares, over the flyovers, towards – well, very likely towards *Théâtre Romain*.

## 4 From 'A Song of French Roads', 1923, by Rudyard Kipling

Now praise the Gods of Time and Chance
    That bring a heart's desire,
And lay the joyous roads of France
    Once more beneath the tyre –
So numbered by Napoleon,
    The veriest ass can spy
How Twenty takes to Bourg-Madame
    And Ten is for Hendaye.

## 5 The dogs

Long ago, on a cold day when I was young, so long ago and so cold that my memories have become rather dream-like or hallucinatory, I drove a car over the Great St Bernard Pass. It had just been opened to traffic after the long winter, snow was still intermittently falling, and I was all alone as I wound my difficult slippery way out of Switzerland towards Italy. I was buoyed up by the significance of the journey. The greatest of all European barriers has always been the line of the Alps, extending in a great arc from France to Yugoslavia, separating the Mediterranean from inner Europe, the Latins from the Teutons, the bitter North from the warm South – Cisalpine, in fact, from Transalpine. The Great St Bernard was the most famous and fateful of the passes which pierced them. The Romans made the first paved road over it, building a temple to Jupiter at the top, and countless pilgrims, traders and conquerors had passed that way before me.

Up and up I went, then, through the still-shuttered villages in the lee of the pass, until at last I reached the Hospice of St Bernard at the top, two massive blocks beside a frozen lake, with a cross on a protruding rock in the middle of it. These were then said to be the highest occupied buildings in Europe. They looked forbidding, but for centuries they were the most fervently welcomed buildings in Europe too, in the days when foot-travellers struggling over this pass, in the terrible stormy weather of the high Alps, were often saved from death itself by the Augustinian monks of the hospice and their St Bernard dogs, brandy-flasks at their collars – dogs that were all meekness and gentleness, thought the poet Samuel Rogers in 1842, 'though large of limb'. Hardly a traveller crossing the pass can fail to have stopped at the hospice, and when I myself went inside out of the now driving snow, and was shown around by an obliging monk, I found its rooms full of *ex votos* and tributes – touching little messages from medieval wayfarers, books in the library presented by monarchs and dignitaries. 'And of course,' said my cicerone, 'we still have the dogs.' The dogs! After 900 years, after all those multitudes of passers-by, they still had the dogs! Around the back he took me, and there luxuriating in what I remember as a kind of stable, sweet-smelling of straw and warmth, there were two of the noble dogs, looking up at me kindly with soft grey eyes out of the half-light.

Nearly fifty years passed before I drove over the pass again, in high summer this time, and I was not surprised to find it very different. Scores of tourist buses were lined up by the hospice. Hundreds of people swarmed all around, in and out of souvenir shops, drinking pop at café tables, wandering around the lake. A large sign said, 'TO THE DOGS', but they were no longer in the straw-fragrant kennels of my memory, but on display, whole families of them, in big wire cages like breeders' showcases. The dogs themselves, though, had not changed: they were meek and gentle still, and at least as large of limb.

## 6 *The most exciting pass*

The most exciting of all Europe's mountain highways, in my experience, is the road over the Lombardy Pass, one of the highest motor-roads in the continent, running from the Italian town of Vinádio over an outlying ridge of the Maritime Alps into the valley of the Tinée in France. It has never been of much significance except to pilgrims making for a holy place, the Sanctuary of Sant'Anna, which stands in a high lonely site just on the Italian side of the frontier. The road is extremely winding, steep, rock-strewn, potholed, bumpy, with scores of zigzags and hairpin bends to negotiate and sombre rocky cliffs all around, streaked with gold-green lichen. I met no other cars when I went up there one autumn day, saw no sign of human life except the huddled group of buildings that is the sanctuary. At the summit abandoned fortifications mark the frontier, some of them forgotten outliers of the Maginot Line, and among them flocks of grey-white cattle nibble the meagre grass in a distracted way; but what gives the pass its excitement is the legacy of its countless pilgrimages. All the way up the last steep stretches of that road, laboriously put together every few hundred yards, are the cairns of the supplicants and penitents of Santa Anna down the centuries. Sometimes they are quite carefully made, substantial piles of rock with rough crosses on the top; sometimes they are just small mounds of rubble which look as though they have been thrown there by people at the very last extremity of exhaustion. Occasionally groups of cyclists hurtle hilariously down the steep winding road of the Lombardy Pass, and at the French end of it, when you tumble through forest-land towards the Tinée, there is a ritzy ski-resort, built in the 1970s to cater for a different category of palmer.

## 7 *Through the Alps*

Relatively few travellers labour over the high Alps these days, except for fun. Most of the traffic goes under them, by the tunnels which pierce the range between one country and another. These prodigies of engineering have been built by several States over many generations, and repeatedly updated; but they always suggest to me one immense concerted operation, like the American space programme perhaps. Sometimes birds fly through the tunnels, and in the days before Europe's frontiers were relaxed long, long lines of trucks used to wait to make their passage, massed there along the approach roads and in the truck parks like so many migrating creatures themselves. It sometimes happens that, entering the Mont Blanc Tunnel in France in drear and drizzly weather, you emerge into Italy in brilliant sunshine, and then the Alpine tunnels seem to be true metaphors for Europe itself, in all its contrasts, contradictions and surprises. Napoleon Bonaparte, having had the first road built over the Simplon (in 1806), thought the pass so special, and so important to his European scheme of things, that he created the Republic of the Simplon around it.

## 8   *The new Roman roads*

I first set eyes on a freeway, motorway, *autoroute, autobahn, autostrada, autoput* in Italy at the end of the Second World War. I was driving eastward in a jeep along Route 11 from Milan (I have just looked up the road number in my magnificent old Touring Club Italiano atlas, which is dated XIII E.F. – Year 13 of the Fascist Era). Across the fields of the Brenta valley I saw, striding bizarrely towards the horizon, a series of tall billboards in pairs, every few hundred yards as far as one could see. They were the advertising source of revenue for the Padova–Venezia Autostrada, not only my first motorway, but the first true motorway anywhere – the first road, that is, dedicated expressly to high-speed motor-traffic. It had been one of Mussolini's earliest and most successful initiatives, started in II E.F. It ran absolutely dead straight for twenty miles, linking up with the causeway which crossed the lagoon to Venice itself, and all the way along it, as I presently discovered, those billboards stood garishly on either side, advertising not (as one might suppose) ideological ideals, but homelier things like washing-powder or cornflakes.

I don't know why the Fascists decided on Padua–Venice as the first route for an *autostrada*. Perhaps it was just a practice run, so to speak, but in the event it was only after the fall of the regime that Italian *autostrade* were built to the places one would have expected them to be built – to the Alps in the north, to the French frontier in the west, together with the glorious Autostrada del Sole which sweeps nobly from one end of the country to the other. In Germany, conversely, the *Autobahnen* were conceived specifically as strategic routes, enabling German armies to be moved swiftly to one frontier or another just as the Roman legions marched to their stations along those straight and level roads (although Hitler believed, as a matter of fact, that roads were destined to supersede railways in general). In England, where the movement of forces from one shore to another was seldom a preoccupation, no motorways were built until well after the Second World War, when I remember a Minister of Transport ushering a bus-load of foreign guests along a few miles of undistinguished highway as though it were the start of a new age.

Nowadays the motorways, reaching as they do most parts of Europe, give the continent their own suggestion of comity – or uniformity, according to your taste. We are all more or less at home on a motorway. We all know our way around the motorway cafés, whatever country they are in. We can ring home from there. We can pay for lunch with a credit card. We can probably put a bit of plastic in a slot and get a few Deutschmarks or a few thousand lire instantly debited to our bank account in Thessalonika, Graz or Bruntingthorpe. One hardly feels abroad anywhere on a motorway in Europe.

## 9 A step that wasn't there

My prime revelatory moment of European travel, all the same, came not on a road but on a railway – a seminal moment, a moment of historical shock. It occurred when for the first time in my life, for the first time in all the millennia of my paternal forebears' residence in the isles of Britain, I set foot on the Continent of Europe without having set eyes on the sea. The passenger train through the Channel Tunnel had just started its operations, and welcomed me blue and silver in its custom-built London terminal, attended by multi-ethnic staff with well-instructed smiles. It was all smooth, padded, cosmopolitan, humming. I had booked my passage from that kindly soul on page 219, but I might have been boarding a space module.

The Eurostar was obliged to saunter rather between London and the coast, the track not being up to the train's potential 180 m.p.h., but I didn't mind that. I rather liked the sensation that we were in no particular hurry, as we ambled through the Kentish hopfields, but viewed the whole 180 m.p.h. business as a trifle *arriviste*. In the same way the train seemed to take the tunnel itself casually in its stride. I hardly noticed it. One minute we were loitering through the Garden of England, the next we were sprinting through Belgium, eating lunch. It hardly seemed worth making a fuss about.

It was only when we debouched in Brussels that it all came home to me. *I hadn't seen the sea!* This was a peculiar and ambivalent feeling. I didn't know whether to be exhilarated or deflated, to be here in a foreign city, after so many thousands of ancestral years, without having seen salt water on the way. It was like treading on a step that wasn't there. The young Evelyn Waugh felt rather the same when, in 1930, for the first time he flew across the English Channel, instead of going by ship – 'when one has got accustomed to a certain kind of approach . . . a new route seems very unconvincing'. But as a historical revelation I don't think his experience matched mine.

## 10  *Some resonances*

Generally the big trains of Europe, even the newest, lack the immense
magisterial authority of American trains, which crawl over their enormous
landscapes as though they own the prairies. European trains never have so
far to go, and their wagons are smaller, and their locomotives less grandiose,
and their whistles pettier. It is true that if you are French, seeing from your
motorway one of the *Trains à Grande Vitesse*, the TGV expresses, hurtling
through a countryside two or three times faster than you can drive, is likely
to make you proud of your country, like L. R. Bultoen in Antwerp's
cathedral; but for me the romance of the European railroads lies less in the
trains themselves than in the grand roll-call of their destinations. The network
is staggering, and some stations have machines by which you can, at the press
of a button or two, plan spectacular trans-European routes. You can get on
a train at Constanţa, on the Black Sea, and, give or take a few changes, get
off again at Thurso at the very northern tip of Scotland. A train from the
Peloponnese will eventually unload you in Lapland. It is theoretically possible
to travel on a single ticket from Lisbon to Tallinn. Pack a picnic hamper for
the journey in Thessalonika, and you could finish it off in Cork. In the days
when Europe was still divided by the Iron Curtain, the international expresses
could carry with them more disturbing resonances. I remember seeing a train
that had arrived at Berlin from Moscow, on its way to Paris: and sensing, as
I walked down the platform along the length of it, suspicious or bewildered
eyes staring out at me from stuffy overcrowded sleepers – as if I might
somehow have the power to send the whole train back again, sullenly to
return to the dark side of the continent.

## 11  *Little trains*

The little trains of Europe, on the other hand, beat anything in America,
and were properly celebrated by Charles Aznavour in a French song greatly
popular in the 1960s. Europeans, it seems, have a weakness for old steam
trains, which is perhaps why a schoolchild's silhouette of an old puffer is still
the conventional warning sign of a level crossing. In Spain in the 1960s I
used to see excited parties of aficionados from Germany, Sweden or Britain
waiting camera-slung beside the railway tracks to see the mighty brass-bound

steam locomotives which then hauled the Spanish expresses. No such leviathans are still in regular service, but all over the continent small steam trains
are affectionately operated. There are delightful narrow-gauge trains in North
Wales: for years, in that region of chapel austerities, the only place one could
buy a drink on Sundays was in the bar-car of the little Ffestiniog Railway
passenger train. Through the streets of the spa town of Bad Doberan, on the
Baltic coast of Germany, an antique steam train routinely trundles, picking
up housewives with their shopping-baskets, dropping salesmen with their
briefcases. In Leipzig there still stands the magnificent railway station that
my mother knew, all twenty-six tracks of it; but down the road they cherish
the quaint steam trains which irregularly come and go from the modest
castellated depot of the old Bavarian Railways. As for the network of steam
trains that operates in the Harz Mountains, in the days of the Cold War these
proved so popular among spenders of hard currency from the West that the
frontier was especially eased to allow entry to their admirers.

In French Haute-Savoie we lived near a village called Sixt, at the end of
a valley which had been, until the present century, particularly remote and
insignificant (when John Ruskin found his way there in 1844 all he said was
that its wild strawberries tasted of slate). In 1858 an English family built a
chalet in the foothills above, for the sake of the Alpine climbing, staying
there for several generations; and besides taking a grand piano up there, and
a billiard-table, and producing a book about the place (*The Eagle's Nest*, by
Alfred Wills, 1860), they were instrumental in connecting Sixt with the
outside world. This they achieved by sponsoring a little electric train, which
ran all the way up the middle of the road from the Swiss frontier, and when
we lived there it was still working. It was half a train and half a tram, I
suppose, its rolling-stock looking like a couple of superannuated streetcars
from some distant metropolis. Nothing could be more charming than to see
this little equipage, on a white wintry day, bustling up from Annemasse with
its complement of shoppers, farmers and schoolchildren, blowing a whistle
sometimes in rather a wistful way. It was not a steam train, however, and
when I returned to Sixt long afterwards I found it had bustled its last.

## 12 *The hush of the platform*

At the start of my fifty years the steam trains were not curiosities or tourist
attractions, but were everyday means of transport. What I remember best

about travelling on branch lines in those days is the sudden quiet which seemed to descend whenever the train stopped at a country station, day or night – not the eerie silence of the frontier that we experienced at Dôle, but a gentle rustic stillness that I associate in my memory with the rolling of milk-churns. Often nobody joined the train and nobody left it, and we simply waited for a moment or two, to fit the timetable, I suppose, or load the churns. The little engines did not snort and cough, like the locomotives of big international expresses, but just stood there amiably hissing, and sometimes one heard murmured rustic exchanges on the platform outside, or a couple of railwaymen conversing as they walked by with their lunch-boxes, before the guard blew his whistle and the train almost imperceptibly moved on again. In his poem 'Adlestrop' the Anglo-Welsh poet Edward Thomas immortalized this sense of hiatus – 'The steam hissed. Someone cleared his throat./ No one left and no one came' – and I do not doubt that everywhere in Europe, wherever the tank engines took their three or four coaches down winding lines to rural places, people knew that hush of the down platform.

### 13  *From* When We Dead Wake, *1882, by Henrik Ibsen, translated by Peter Watts*

MAJA: Why did it stop like that, if there was nothing there?

PROFESSOR RUBEK: I don't know. No one got off and no one got on, but the train stood there, silently, for what seemed like hours. And at every station I heard two railwaymen walking along the platform – one of them carrying a lantern – and they mumbled quietly to each other in the night, without expression or meaning.

MAJA: Yes, you're right; there are always two men talking . . .

### 14  *Near-calamity on the old Orient Express*

We used to take the old Orient Express to Venice, in the days after the war, when travel by car was a more demanding alternative, and I had a disagreeable experience on it once. My partner and I, leaving our two small boys sleeping peacefully in our compartment, made our way to the dining-car, two or three coaches back, and ate our supper. When we started to return to our beds and our children we found a communicating door had been locked, and we were unable to get through. Presently the train stopped at one of those high Swiss stations, just before a tunnel, so we jumped out and ran along the platform to get to our own coach. Just as we began to climb the steep iron steps to the carriage door the train started to move off again. It was very dark. It was very cold. The tunnel entrance was very near, and we could not open the door to get in. The corridor of the coach was jam-packed with standing passengers, blocking the door and looking out at us in stunned astonishment as we gesticulated at them through the night. They seemed paralysed by our appearance there. We shouted – we banged on the window – we hung on desperately – the train gathered speed – the people gaped – the dark hole of the tunnel approached – *calamity on the Orient Express!* In the nick of time two dark unshaven men forcefully pushed their way through the corridor crowd to open the door and hoist us inside. They were Turkish migrant workers, they told us, returning to Istanbul from Germany for their holidays. Our children slept through it all, and for twenty years and more loved to be told the story.

## 15  *Pathos and banality on the new Orient Express*

Later I travelled more than once on the tourist-dedicated Orient Express of the 1980s. I found it sad. It had been intensely hyped as the last of the classic travel experiences – 'Stepping back into the Golden Age of Travel': gleaming Pullman coaches, courteous waiters, ladies in evening gowns, gentlemen in black ties, sophisticated Americans from the 1930s, cocktails in the piano bar before dinner, such were the suggestions of its publicity. But it was not really like that. The coaches certainly gleamed, but lacked air-conditioning or showers, rolled about a lot, and were heated in an all too classical way by a coal-burning stove at the end of each corridor. The music of the piano bar was electronically amplified. The Americans were scarcely Cole Porters or Scott Fitzgeralds (two of them missed the train at Innsbruck, on one of my journeys, having gone into town in search of hamburgers). The poor ladies from Harrogate or High Wycombe, who had won their trips as prizes in office competitions, perhaps, or had been given them as diamond-wedding presents, were certainly dressed to the nines with wraps and patterned stockings, but must have been disconcerted to find the Cocktail Hour dominated by the sort of men they might just as well have met at Rotary dinners. Here are three conversational fragments I jotted down, during my steps back into the Golden Age of Travel:

¶ 'I've always said,' observed one American matron to another, 'I'm not going to be a possessive mother, because *his* was' – and she jerked her head towards her husband in the next seat. For a moment or two, as the train ploughed on, rattling the soup-spoons, the two ladies eyed him speculatively. 'He'll be no good to us in Venice,' said the first.

¶ Young English wife, on her honeymoon I guessed: 'Oh, look at the castle. Isn't that a lovely castle?' Young English husband: 'It's a castle. A castle is a castle. You've seen castles before.' She relapsed into a thoughtful silence. He returned to his thriller.

¶ An American man, to me: 'You gotta read this book, I've been reading it all the way since London. It's called *God Owns My Business*. *God Owns My Business*, that's the title. This guy who wrote it, he's a very low-key man, but he's got a sign above his store, "Christ Is My Manager". When do we get to Innsbruck? We might get a hamburger there.'

So we proceeded, not terribly fast, towards Italy. The banality and pathos was all inside the train. From the outside the Orient Express really did look a paragon of wealth and urbanity. People in the fields seemed to watch us pass without envy or resentment but only in simple pleasure, waving enthusiastically now and then to see such an exhibition of style sweep by. *Well, you've seen people waving before, haven't you? He'll be lost with those gondolier people. 'Christ Is My Manager', in big letters there above the door.*

## 16 *Into the space age*

Years ago, when the TGV trains were new to me, I stood on a platform at Dijon in Burgundy admiring the Paris express which, vibrating slightly with the whirr of its generators, stood there waiting to leave. I had never seen one before. It was like something out of the future, with its big snout-nose slightly battered by the elements, like an airliner's, and its air of brooding power. As I stood there two elderly women stepped into one of the coaches, taking not the slightest notice of the bulbous space-age ambience as they found themselves seats well-placed, I suspected, not for observing the landscape, still less for inspecting the equipment, but for eyeing other passengers. I walked to the far end of the platform to watch the train leave, with a jerkless and inexorable rumble, and as the great thing accelerated swiftly past me, its wheels gently humming, I caught sight of the two old ladies at their window. They did not seem in the least anomalous. They were talking hard, looking speculatively around the coach, and knitting.

## 17 Over the hump

If you stand on the summit of the hill called Tryvannshøgda, near Oslo in Norway, and look directly north, you seem to be surveying a limitless wilderness. In winter everything is white with snow, and the ridges, lakes and valleys stretch away apparently trackless towards the Arctic Circle and the Pole. The country looks more or less uninhabited, and by most European standards it is. Yet even as you stare aghast at the uninviting scene, one of the most heroic trains in Europe is chugging its way clean over those mountains from Oslo the capital to Bergen the second city, passing through 189 tunnels on the way. You can make the journey far more easily by air, but a ride on the Bergen Express is worth doing anyway. It is no TGV, being a sedate handful of carriages which, if not actually made of wood, feel as if they ought to be, drawn at a moderate speed by an electric engine. It is amply supplied with food and drink, pressed upon you by a solicitous lady attendant, and it gives you glimpses of the whole Norwegian spectrum.

At the start, as you climb out of Oslo into the hills, and the attendant brings you a preliminary coffee, everything out there looks neat and ordered: neat little gardens, neat little houses, laundry hanging apparently frozen stiff from washing-lines, delightful children scrabbling about in the patchy snow or leaping over garden fences to invite their neighbours out to play. In no time, though, you are in that wilderness. The attendant offers you a ham sandwich. The train climbs very steeply, and soon it looks as though everything has been permanently abandoned. Houses lie up to their eaves in snow. Bumps in the snow seem to indicate buried cars. Huge snowdrifts rise all around the track, and if there are any roads out there there is nothing at all to be seen of them. 'Please O God,' you may find yourself saying, as the attendant wonders if you would care for a piece of cake, 'don't let the train break down!' Almost at the highest point of the journey an alarming branch line suddenly peels off and appears to plunge headlong into the void, hurling itself catastrophically towards the fjord you can just see, a splash of deep blue, far down there at the foot of the precipice. 'More coffee, then?' says the attendant.

Very soon you are on the way down again, on the other side of the Norwegian massif. The snowdrifts shrink, houses emerge again, there are touches of green, the first cars appear, the first tidy suburbs, the first children clambering over garden fences to invite their neighbours out to play. The neatness comes back, the orderliness, the reassuring ordinariness of life, and punctually on time the train pulls into the station at Bergen, where it is almost certain to be raining, because in Bergen it always is. 'Don't hurry,' says the attendant. 'Finish your coffee.'

## 18 *Tail-lights*

Roads down the border between Germany and Poland sometimes cross railway lines. Some are big main double tracks, but some are branch lines, and in my memory at least these always seem to run away into dark forests. What a shudder those rails give me! Hardly more than half a century ago the extermination trains passed this way out of Germany towards Auschwitz and Treblinka: I seem to hear still the moans of the poor Jews crammed in their filthy cattle-trucks, and the laughter of the men of the police battalions in their guard-vans behind, and the hollow snorts of the steam locomotives as they plodded away into the woods. I have never seen a train on one of those lines, but I have often imagined red tail-lights swinging away into the darkness.

## 19 Funiculì, Funiculà

I cannot begrudge myself one short paragraph about the funiculars, cog and rack railways of Europe, because I love them – not the myriad daring mountain trains, but the modest usually old-fashioned mechanisms which give a special cachet to a few privileged towns and cities here and there. At Zagreb a minute funicular connects the lower and upper towns: it is only a couple of hundred yards long, steeply rising towards the baroque towers above, and if you saunter too idly up the street towards its waiting carriage the conductor will tap urgently on his glass window, to tell you to hurry up. At Salzburg a train whisks you operatically above the Mozartian domes and gilded towers of the city, preferably encrusted in snow and glinting in winter sunshine, precipitously to the Hohensalzburg Fortress. At Budapest a meticulously reconstructed Victorian funicular travels from the Chain Bridge almost to the gateway of the Royal Palace on the Buda hill, and makes you wonder if Franz Josef himself, just for the fun of it, ever rode in its bottom car to see the city retreating so spectacularly below. At Bridgnorth in England a track with a gradient of two in three, connecting the lower town with the High Street on a ridge above, is comically matched by the tower of the castle, which was blown up during the English Civil War and is now slumped at an angle three times greater than that of the leaning tower of Pisa. And at Venice, where there is certainly no rack railway, you may well be reminded on an August evening of the most famous of them all; for echoing down the Grand Canal, around a little fleet of gondolas, through the sultry city come the strains of one of its favourite melodies, sung with quavering gusto by an elderly tenor to doting groups of tourists – Luigi Denza's paean to the old Vesuvius railway, faintly at first, out of sight, until the flotilla turns into a *rio* to pass beneath the very bridge over which you are sentimentally leaning. Then the veteran serenader, catching sight of you above, offers you a courtly bow, possibly blows you a kiss between phrases, and lets loose, just as he passes into the shadow of the bridge, upon the grand chorus of the piece – '*Iamme, iamme, via montiam su là. / Iamme, iamme, via montiam su là. / Funiculì funiculà funiculì funiculà. / VIA MONTIAM FUNICULÌ, FUNICULÀ!*'

## 20 *From Baedeker's* Southern Italy, *1893*

The WIRE ROPE RAILWAY (Ferrovia Funicolare) is 900 yards long, and the upper end is 1300 ft. higher than the lower. The gradient varies from 34:100 to 63:100. The ascent or descent in the train takes 12 minutes. At the upper station guides with numbers on their caps are in waiting (others should be dismissed).

The thanks of tourists are certainly due to Messrs. Thomas Cook & Son for the energy with which, in face of serious difficulties, they maintain order and discipline among the guides and others, who have been accustomed for generations to practise extortions upon travellers.

## 21  Achtung! *Comes the tram!*

'*Achtung!*' several Viennese ladies screamed at me. '*Achtung!* Stop! Comes
the tram!' Trams are essential to the nature of Vienna – hefty, responsible
vehicles, with flags on their roofs, and Cyclopean headlights, and sundry
pipes and couplings connecting their carriages – but there are some places
in the Ringstrasse where they run against the direction of the traffic, and are
all too likely to murder you. They once almost murdered Dr Kurt Waldheim
himself, although that was, so several people hastened to assure me, before
he became President of the Republic.

After the Second World War several shattered tram systems of the continent
were re-equipped with discarded streetcars from the United States, but I
always think of trams as quintessentially European things, especially trailer-
trams. It was while sitting in a tram at Berne in Switzerland that Albert
Einstein, one of the greatest of Europeans, is supposed to have conceived
his theory of relativity; and it was only proper that perhaps the most celebrated
photograph of the Second World War, showing a Soviet soldier raising the
Hammer and Sickle above the ruins of the Reichstag in Berlin, should
include in its background a couple of burnt-out streetcars in the rubble-strewn
street below. European cities without trams (like those foolish English muni-
cipalities which gave them up in the 1940s and 1950s) seem to me somehow
incomplete: 'Bremen without trams,' says one book about that eminently
sensible city, 'would be like Venice without gondolas,' and the same is true
of many another place. Is there any sensation more absolutely of this continent
than the sudden jerky lurch, accompanied sometimes by a clanging bell and
a shower of sparks from the lines above, which happens when a tram embarks
upon a corner? Some of my fondest memories of London concern the antique
open-topped trams, garish with advertisements, which used to run along the
Embankment there, carrying me shivering but expectant on the upper deck
towards some happy youthful rendezvous. Nowadays, of course, many trams
are streamlined, modern and computerized; in some Swiss and German cities
they seem downright cybernetic, and accelerate with thrilling whining noises;
but they are still often colourful with publicity, and slide through their city
streets with all the old matronly assurance. Amsterdam is a great place for
trams – psychedelically painted, as often enough, and apparently running
every other minute; when I first went there some of them had postboxes
beside their doors. One of the most delightful of tram-scenes is offered at

Riga, in Latvia, where little pairs of trams trundle neatly, like toys, across the immense modern bridge over the Daugava, often all alone upon its great span. But Vienna is my tram-city *par excellence*. There used to be a Vienna city tramline which ran all the way to Pressburg, now transformed into Bratislava and the capital of a different country! I think the Vienna trams impress me most because they are so proudly at odds with the character of the city itself. It is a place of endless pretension: they run not only against the flow of the civic traffic, but against the flow of the civic temperament too, being stolid, plain-spoken, down-to-earth kinds of mechanism. When I nearly lost my life to one of them that day in 1983 – '*Quick! Comes the tram the other way!*' – they seemed to me to play an almost metaphorical role in the city of Freud. As I stepped back from the track just in time to avoid extinction I looked up at the passing tram and distinctly saw there, just for a moment, my own face in its slightly steamed-up window. We exchanged distant smiles, as between Id and Ego.

## 22  An allegory

Once when I was driving through Sofia, in Bulgaria, I saw a woman step directly into the path of a tram – not on purpose, but simply in a hurry. She was heavily loaded with bags and parcels. The tram was probably full of passengers, but through the city's morning smog I could see none of them, nor a driver either. It was like an allegory. The woman was the very essence of humanity – loaded with burdens, flustered, anxious, hurried: the tram looked blankly mechanistic, a hefty iron thing moving mindlessly along its tracks. There was a peculiarly metallic kind of noise, half scrape, half skid, as the two collided and the prostrate woman was pushed in a litter of shopping-bags fifty yards or so along the track. A moment of dead quiet followed, as the tram stopped, the woman lay there unconscious, and the bystanders looked on silent and appalled.

## 23  Through the linings

Even the passage of the trams, though, is not so utterly of Europe as the coming and going of the water-traffic along its rivers and canals, flying the flags of half a dozen venerable States, taking vast quantities of materials and manufactures from quay to quay of the continent – from the North Sea clean to the Black Sea, from the Baltic to the Mediterranean. I love to watch the boats go by: so did Mendelssohn – 'I came here with great plans to work,' he wrote from his room beside the Main at Frankfurt in 1836, 'but now a week has passed and I have done little else . . .'

Powerful big craft roam the waterways of modern Europe. Tremendous engines heave vessels from one level to another. Down the Rhine the barges surge, one after the other, at high speed between the bluffs, their engines echoing, their flags streaming. On the Danube strange white tourist craft surge and circle, like big water-insects. Almost anywhere in France you may come across a barge chugging down one of a hundred unsuspected water-routes. Even in the England of the 1990s, where commercial barge traffic had nearly all given way to tourist pastiche, there were visionary proposals for a commercial canal to link the Irish Sea with the North Sea; in the meantime one of the curious sights of northern England was that of a barge loaded with rolls of newsprint regularly making its way up a little waterway to the offices of the *Yorkshire Evening Post* in the medieval heart of York. Nowhere else has water-traffic quite like Europe's, at once so formidable, so varied and so homely – for often, as a mighty barge ploughs its way across the hundreds of miles to Rotterdam or Hamburg, Budapest or Marseille, you may see the captain's wife hanging out her laundry on the poop, watering the massed pots of geraniums which ornament the wheel-house, washing the family car that is carried on the foredeck, or making the coffee as at Maastricht.

The boat-people of the inland waterways form an inner community of Europe, for ever on the move, crossing the old frontiers constantly and meeting colleagues from all over the continent at the big river ports and junctions. At my home in Wales there is a German businessman who, having come to Britain as a prisoner-of-war, married a Welsh girl and has spent the rest of his life in Wales. He was born into a barge-family of eastern Germany, and one afternoon he spent half an hour with me tracing on my atlas his childhood journeys among the waterways of Silesia and Brandenburg, and out to the west into the Elbe and the Mosel. He had seen much of the continent, but from an altogether different perspective from mine. As he talked about those immense half-hidden voyages of long before, far from the railways and motorways, through countryside most travellers seldom see, he reminded me of the Venetian epithet for backstreet walking: *per le fodere* – 'through the linings'.

## 24  *Father Rhine*

The supreme European river is the Rhine – far more than a mere frontier, as we considered it earlier, but a majestic communication. Rüdesheim in Germany is one of the most famous towns along its banks, being an archetypal half-timbered, tourist-frequented, vineyard-backed German beauty spot just upstream from the Lorelei, but it is also one of the best (or worst) places to gauge the importance of the river and its valley as a conductor of traffic. Try sleeping a night in a hotel somewhere on its outskirts, and the geographical meaning of the Rhine will be made horribly plain to you. Every quarter of an hour or so a distant angry murmur, like a wind rising, warns your poor nerves that in a few moments another freight train will shortly come rushing down the east bank on its way to Mannheim. When it has passed you may hear the echoing clatter of its opposite number on the west bank, speeding northward to Rotterdam or Hamburg. And in the brief spells when a train is not passing, one way or another, or a truck driving by on this bank or on that, ceaselessly sounds the deep chug-chug of the barges, swiftly downstream, laboriously against the current. There is seldom a silent moment on the Rhine at Rüdesheim, scarcely a moment without the plod, hurtle or judder of the river's purpose. The Rhine is the busiest of all waterways. As a highway it begins at Konstanz, on the frontier between Switzerland and Germany, where a large figure o on a riverside board tells the barge-captain that he has 1,165 kilometres to go to the North Sea. By the time he gets to Rotterdam he will have passed beneath some 150 bridges, sailed along the littorals of six nations and helped to define a continent. The Rhine, said Thomas Carlyle, was his 'first idea of a world river', and a world river it is, because the goods it carries across Europe to the sea are distributed across all earth's oceans.

## 25  *Pilgrims to the sea*

I once joined a Dutch barge for the last phase of its journey down the Rhine, through the Low Countries to the river's mouth. I had lately made a voyage on a towboat on the Mississippi, and I thought this might be the same sort of experience – the Germans, after all, speak of Old Father Rhine rather as the Americans talk of Old Man River. It was not at all. The Mississippi voyage had been above all purposeful and calculated, but in my memory at

least the Rhine voyage had an exaltatory feel. It was like the end of a
pilgrimage. For most of the time I sat on the open deck of the barge, and
all around me other vessels streamed with us towards the ocean, as to a
shrine. The further we went, the thicker the traffic, and the faster we seemed
to sail, and the more feverish the beat of our engines, and the fiercer our
bow-wave, until at last we burst into the sanctuary – the port of Rotterdam,
the greatest port on earth, where a hundred deep-sea freighters loomed all
around us, tugs scurried, sirens blew, lock-gates opened and closed, trucks
hurried along the quaysides, and we took our string of barges in as though
we were bringing tributes out of the East for the water-gods.

## 26  Should I have genuflected?

The River Maas joins the Rhine not far from Rotterdam, and is another
great channel of Europe's water-trade. At Maastricht, where the barges sail
by night and day, I walked one morning to the St Servaas Bridge, the oldest
bridge across the river and the city's *raison d'être*. As I crossed its footpath a
tall-masted tug approached, and beneath my feet I felt the bridge begin to
move to let it pass. With a discreet shudder of mechanisms the structure
levitated horizontally into the air, taking me with it; and so stately and gently
was this motion, so priest-like the figure of the bridge-master in his cabin
above, that there too I felt I was taking part in some immemorial ritual of
the waterways, and ought perhaps to genuflect as the tug sailed below me.

## 27  To the East

The Rhine is a Western river, but the Danube looks to the East, and
undergoes many a metamorphosis on its journey to the Black Sea. Sometimes
it is a busy thoroughfare, sometimes it runs lonely through desolate wastelands.
It is called the Duna here, the Donau there. Three hundred lesser rivers join
it on its course, and nine European States stand upon its banks. It formally
begins at Donaueschingen in the Black Mountains of Germany, where two
small streams unite below a symbolic statue in a park: I thought it very apt
that when I asked a man there which of them was more properly the original
Danube, he plucked a small branch from a laurel bush and explained the
hydrography by means of its tributary twigs.

The Danube can let one down, especially at Vienna, the home of its romance and reputation, where it is not visible at all in the city centre, having been canalized to the north in 1875 – a circumstance which does not prevent the waltz orchestras of the city from playing Johann Strauss's serenade to the stream several hundred times in every working week. Elsewhere it is full of surprise and excitement. In Bucharest, which stands on a Danube tributary, I found on a second-hand bookstall a booklet about the Romanian Danube Flotilla, which was full of marvellous images of antique river gunboats fighting their way up and down the river in the course of one war or another, desperately low in the water and sometimes so weighed down with camouflage branches that they looked like floating piles of brushwood. Upstream at Bratislava, forlornly on the Danube waterfront stands a memorial to the river boats of the Soviet Navy which, now forgotten by all, helped to drive the Germans back to Germany in the Second World War. One of the strangest of Danubian sights is an enormous empty space of reclaimed land, on a bend of the river near Esztergom in Hungary, which is all that remains (at least as I write) of an abandoned dam: the Hungarians and the Czechoslovakians had embarked upon a monumental joint project to exploit the river, but in 1994 the Hungarians pulled unilaterally out of the enterprise, aborting what had already been done at astronomical expense, infuriating the Slovaks, upsetting the Austrian building contractors, embroiling themselves in endless international litigation, and leaving only this desolate memorial to mark the spot.

The Danube is all it ought to be at Budapest, big, brassy, consequential. It is gloomy at Belgrade. It is suitably thoughtful as it passes under the Stone Bridge at Regensburg, beneath the city's fabled hundred towers. It seems to me properly suggestive at Passau, where, reinforced by the Inn and the Ilz, it assembles itself to leave the German world for the lands of the Slavs and Magyars. It separates the Bulgars from the Romanians in a calm judicial manner, moving in wide curves between wooded banks. It subsides mysteriously and gloriously into the Black Sea through the waterlands of the Danube marshes, amid the squawks of a thousand seabirds and the splash of fishermen's nets. I enjoy it most through the windows of one of the numberless hydrofoils, mostly Russian-built, which run scheduled passenger services here and there along its course. Then one swooshes exuberantly along the river, past castles and fishing-platforms and monasteries, overtaking barges, swerving around shallows, from one ancient city to the next.

## 28  Flops and 'istory

Sometimes, like the Danube at Vienna, the greatest rivers of Europe can be sadly disappointing. They can be romantic enough at their sources, and imposing at their estuaries, when they turn into majestic ports or shipping channels. But the supreme episodes of their passages, when they arrive at the famous capitals and metropolises to which they have given birth, often turn out to be anticlimactic. Setting the river of the capital on fire has been a proverb in several European countries for the excitement of achieving a great ambition, becoming celebrated, powerful, or at least notorious, but all too often the river turns out to be non-combustible. 'What!' I can still hear myself exclaiming, when I first went to Rome. 'That's the *Tiber*!' That was the river which flowed with blood, whose bridge Horatius guarded, which Popes and emperors and conquerors had been proud to survey, and poets and painters since the start of history anxious to immortalize – the river which, 'sung so often in poetic lays,' as Addison put it, 'with scorn the Danube and the Nile surveys'! What a flop to find it was no more than a sluggish stream, lovelessly dyked and foully polluted. Then there is the Seine at Paris, which tourists conventionally gush over, and excursion boats sail expensively in the twilight, but which always looks to me less like a real river than a not very beautiful segment of a canal (and which, as a matter of fact, geographers now say is not really the Seine at all, but only some undistinguished tributary). The Rhône is not half so memorable at Lyon as it is when it passes under the bridge at Avignon, or meanders to its fate beside the grasslands of the Camargue. As for the Spree, which has given its name to several languages as a synonym for a good night out, even in the 1990s nothing could be much less festive than its course through the heart of Berlin, viscous with fearful memories, past the great gloomy hulks of museums and dead palaces, under bridges decorated with the faces of mercifully extinct emperors and the crests of fortunately vanished Powers.

Still, on the right day the broad Tagus, sweeping under its magnificent suspension bridge, provides a glorious boundary and belvedere for the city of Lisbon; the Guadalquivir still speaks of great navigators and treasure fleets as it says goodbye to Seville; the Arno is lovely but does not count, because all that anyone knows about it is the fact that it flows through Florence and Pisa; the river which apparently provides a stately centre-line for the architecture of Edinburgh, dividing the medieval from the Georgian, does not count either, because it turns out on closer inspection to be a railway track; the Vltava at Prague honourably reflects the stately buildings all around; the dear old Liffey is all one could ask for Dublin – a river of Guinness, along whose quays James Joyce forever shortsightedly strolls, together with Mr Bloom, the Yeats brothers, Dean Swift and several intoxicate poets. Best of them all, though, to my mind, is the River Thames as it strides through London. English people constantly reproach themselves with having neglected the London river-banks, but I do not agree. I love their piecemeal mixture of the consequential and the trivial, the squalid and the luxurious, the old and the new, and I think Europe still has few things to show more fair than the view of the Thames at night from one of its bridges – the dazzle of the West End lights, the great glow that is the dome of St Paul's, the dark patches that suggest the old and mighty consequence of the place, the clumped blocks of the financial quarter, the tower of Big Ben like a sentinel – which even then, if you are lucky, resonantly booms out the time across the water. 'Liquid 'istory', as the politician John Burns famously put it, looking out from the terrace of the House of Commons.

## 29 Crossing the rivers

Great European rivers have generally decreed the situation of great European cities, founded where there was a convenient ford, or an easy bridging site, or at the highest point of navigation, or at the estuary. Run your eye upon a map of the Rhine, and you find upon its banks Rotterdam, Düsseldorf, Cologne, Mainz, Mannheim, Strasbourg, Basle. The Rhône has given birth to Geneva, Lyon, Avignon and Marseille, the Danube to Regensburg, Vienna, Bratislava, Budapest and Belgrade. Many a famous battle, too, has been fought around the river crossings, from Horatius holding his bridge against the Etruscans to Montgomery aiming a Rhine bridge too far at Arnhem. Who has not stood upon a bridge parapet, above some famous stream, and sententiously marvelled at all the history, wasteful and productive, sad and joyful, that it has sponsored on its journey, through so many centuries, to the sea? I do it often myself on the little stone bridge across our river Dwyfor at home, which has been tumbling for so many thousand years the full nine miles between its source in the mountains and its fusion with the Irish Sea! No wonder the course of the river is the most familiar of all pulpit metaphors.

But the crossings themselves, too, can be metaphors of another sort, illustrating mankind's own energies. The bridges of Europe are among the most suggestive of all its structures, especially when they form links between nations, States or Powers: the fateful Rhine crossings, or the fine pair of modern bridges, over the Severn, which separate England from Wales, or the Glienecker bridge over the River Havel at Berlin, which is where they used to swop the spies of East and West during the Cold War, or the bridge between Hungary and Slovakia, below the basilica of Esztergom, which Patrick Leigh Fermor immortalized by ending his masterpiece *A Time of Gifts* bang in the middle of it.

On the Danube there is only one bridge along the whole frontier of Bulgaria, from the Yugoslav border almost to the Black Sea. It is a monstrous iron thing at Ruse, built jointly by the Communist Governments of Bulgaria and Romania in the 1950s, and called (of course) the Friendship Bridge. When it was built it was the second longest bridge in Europe. It springs from the Romanian shore at Giurgiu, and subsides on the Bulgarian side in a welter of oil-tanks, pipes, gas stations, railway lines and truckers' cafés. Ruse itself has always been a cosmopolitan river-crossing town. The novelist Elias Canetti, who grew up there in its once thriving Sephardic Jewish community, wrote that everything he experienced later in life had already happened to him in Ruse. Through all the vagaries of Bulgarian history, and despite much heavy industry, and drear chemical pollution from the Romanian shore, it has remained surprisingly elegant – rather Viennese, with well-proportioned boulevards, and lots of sidewalk cafés. However, from the water-meadows along the river-bank a few miles downstream you would hardly know the city existed at all. The river flows placidly by down there, the banks are gently wooded, cattle graze the meadows, an occasional boat chugs by, bucolic sounds emerge from the village behind your back, and all you can see upstream is that bridge – an enormous cantilevered structure with pompous towers at each end.

Different metaphors indeed entered my mind when I stood in the sunshine in 1995 considering this object, for it looked to me a very conduit of skulduggery. It was the principal route of traffic out of central and eastern Europe towards Turkey: trucks came to it from many countries, trains from Bucharest, Prague, Berlin, Kiev, Moscow and even St Petersburg. I imagined I could see all the villains of post-Communist Europe flooding across it into Bulgaria, driving stolen Mercedes (every self-respecting Balkan villain had to have a Mercedes, preferably with the plates of some far-away country).

Romanian rogues, Hungarian con men, Gypsy thieves, opportunists from
Moldavia, Russian crooks – there they all were, I thought, rumbling between
the cantilever girders with crates of contraband, packets of cocaine, bundles
of money to be laundered, introductions to flexible Government ministers
and handguns secreted under the floorboards. There is nothing like a big
river bridge for stimulating the fancy.

## 30  *A bridge transformed*

In my time few European cities have been more startlingly revivified than
Prague, and the prime symbol of its metamorphosis is the Charles Bridge
across the Vltava river. One of the most beautiful and celebrated bridges in
the world, in Communist times it used to strike me as a froward edifice,
leading between its bowed and crumbled statues over the river to Hradčany
Castle, where dreadful things looked as though they might happen. When
I went back after the fall of Communism I found it had become, almost
overnight, one of the liveliest river crossings in all Europe. Here, where the
tutelary saint of bridges, St John of Nepomuk, was thrown into the river by
royal command, and the old kings of Bohemia processed in arrogant glory
towards their coronations, the whole gallimaufry of tourism now assembled
beneath the sacred images: sellers of etchings and leather purses, mime artists,
instant portraitists, folk-musicians with bagpipes and wheezing gourds, merry
little dogs running here and there, the inevitable classical violinist, and an
accordion-player who looked exactly like the Emperor Franz Josef himself,
and who thanked me with a truly sovereign bow when I congratulated him
upon the resemblance.

## 31  *Changing the geography*

The myriad canals of Europe, often linking one river with another, have
changed the arrangements of the continent – it was Charlemagne who first
artificially connected the Rhine with the Danube. The two most famous of
them have actually changed its geography. One is the Corinth Canal in
Greece, opened in 1893 after several thousand years of false starts, which
links the Ionian and the Aegean Seas and makes the whole of the Peloponnese
an island. The other is the Kiel Canal, née the Kaiser Wilhelm Nord-Ostsee-

Kanal, which was opened in 1895 to connect the Baltic with the North Sea. No two works of engineering could be much more different of manner or allusion.

The Corinth Canal is only about three miles long, but runs in a deep ditch, straight as a die, from one gulf to the other. Its banks are so steep that from the deck of a ship you can see nothing of the passing countryside, so that a voyage through it is more an imaginative experience than an episode of travel. I have traversed it twice on ships from Venice, on my way to and from Piraeus, and I found the presence of the lion of St Mark, bold and noble on the funnel above me, wonderfully conducive to historical fancy. The Venetians themselves must often have crossed this isthmus in the course of their imperial adventures, travelling overland between their colonies, or finally sending their armies to the siege of Athens itself, when they blew up the Parthenon. But more suggestive still, for me, was the thought of the classical goings-on out of sight over those high banks – vaguely conceived comings and goings of Spartans, Corinthians and Athenians, armies from Persia with strange beasts, philosophers declaiming in town squares, sculptors working away at immortal figures, mathematical geniuses in their baths, javelin-throwers and tragedy-actors in full display – all happening up there above the thin drift of vapour from our smokestack, like a dream-show.

But think of Kiel and you think of Kaiser Bill, and all the mighty works of German threat and enterprise that led up to the First World War. The Kiel Canal linked the great Baltic naval base of Kiel itself with the North Sea, through sixty miles of pleasant pasture land, and, quite apart from its commercial convenience (scores of ships used to be wrecked every year in the treacherous navigation through the Danish Belt), it meant that the German High Seas Fleet could now sail from one sea to another without having to pass through foreign waters at all. How the Kaiser and his admirals gloried in it! At the opening ceremony a hundred warships sailed through, led by the Imperial yacht *Hohenzollern*, and the Kaiser delighted in showing off the wonders of the canal to eminent foreign visitors. When King Edward VII of England sailed through it in 1908, along its banks gorgeously uniformed German cavalry trotted in escort all the way. The building of the canal was a deliberate spit in the eyes of the British, enabling the entire German fleet to be easily concentrated against them. In 1906 my friend Admiral 'Jacky' Fisher of the British Navy built his 17,000-ton battleship *Dreadnought*, obliging the Germans to build to a similar size; the Kiel Canal had to be widened and deepened at immense expense – an annoyance Jack boasted of ever afterwards.

The best place to see the Kiel Canal is at Rendsburg, about a third of the way along from Kiel. Three ancillary marvels there make the great canal seem even greater, and, since the place is an old garrison town, there is an apposite plethora too of barracks and parade-grounds and streets named for kaisers, kings and crown princes. The first wonder of Rendsburg is the tremendous four-lane tunnel which takes Route 77 under the canal, a work of terrific power and elegance. The second is the high-level bridge over the canal. This not only has a transport-carriage for cars always swinging backwards and forwards under its span, but is so lofty that when its railway tracks descend to Rendsburg station they can do so only in an immensely wide-swinging curve, enclosing an entire quarter of the town as within a rampart. The third wonder is the longest escalator in Europe, which plunges deep beneath the canal to take pedestrians to the other side. I stood one morning looking down this dreadful shaft, which was all empty and rumbling, wondering if anyone ever used it, when a cheerful girl rode up behind me on a bicycle. Without a pause she tucked the bike under her arm, as it were, and launched herself upon the moving staircase. I stood there watching her go: and down and down she went, all alone, smaller and smaller, clutching her bicycle, until she disappeared altogether into the hole beneath the Kiel Canal. Above her the ships sailed on through the green countryside.

## 32 Sea-route

Europe is three-quarters an island, with a wide isthmus between the Baltic and the Black Seas, and all around it sea-traffic is still active, ferries crossing gulfs and channels, coasting vessels nosing into fjords and river estuaries, not to mention fishing-boats and dredgers and pleasure craft sailing ever more ambitiously from country to country. Among the surviving sea-routes, the most resilient is the Hurtigruten, the coastal shipping service of the Norwegians. This was not what I imagined when I went to board one of its ships at the quay in Bergen in the 1990s. I had half expected to see an old black-and-white steamer with a tall smokestack, with those big trumpet-like ventilators that steamships used to have, and hefty derricks fore and aft. Instead I found a kind of cruise liner towering there, like something out of Miami, humming, with cargo going on board via fork-lift trucks through a huge side-hatch, and a coachload of Norwegian-American tourists at that moment gregariously embarking.

'Hurtigruten' means 'Fast Route', and stands generically for the Coastal Express, the service of ships which has for more than a century linked the ports of the Norwegian coast from Bergen around the North Cape to Kirkenes on the Russian border: part working passenger and cargo ships, part pleasure-vessels. The coastal service is a national institution, part of the Norwegian way of things. 'Just wait till tomorrow,' cries Ibsen's Professor Rubek (again in *When We Dead Wake*). 'Then the great comfortable steamer will put into the harbour, and we'll get on board and sail northward all round the coast – right up into the Arctic.' In his day a couple of ships a week made the voyage. By the 1990s eleven vessels maintained a daily service all the year round, putting in at thirty-two ports along the way. It was an epic and an elegant enterprise. The ships sailed 500 miles above the Arctic Circle, and in winter they were the only links with the rest of the world for many of the isolated communities of the North.

I should have known better, of course, than to expect that tall-funnelled old steamship. That was the kind my grandfather sailed on, when he made this voyage soon after the turn of the century. My Hurtigruten ship, the *Kong Harald*, 6,270 tons, was modernity exemplified. Nevertheless our progress up the long coast faithfully followed the pattern of the steamboats that had gone before: the same route, the same mooring-places, the same manner of familiar service. Time and again the old and the homely intervened, with a suggestion of simpler times. When we were warped into some lonely quayside, with a grey scatter of houses around, a few fishing-boats, a warehouse or two and a pile of crates to be loaded, often down on the wharf there would be a Norwegian Gothic couple, waiting with their bags to take passage to Tromsø or Hammerfest. And once there came aboard, to disembark at the next port, an entire brass band. Its musicians were of all ages, down to small boys and girls, and they were festooned with medals, of musicianship I suppose, dangling from ribbons on their breasts and arms. As we ploughed on through the twilight they earned their passage by playing marches in the forward lounge on Deck 4 – solemn but rousing stuff, speaking to us I thought directly out of the bandstands of Professor Rubek's Norway. The younger members of the ensemble, when the performance was over, swarmed into the cafeteria to eat ice-creams, but this did not spoil the effect at all, because their faces were quintessentially Norwegian – pale, long, incurious, handsome faces. One boy asked me where I was from, and when I told him he said, 'I have a grandmother in Wales.' 'You don't mean it,' I exclaimed. 'No,' he said, 'I was only joking.'

## 33 *The Via Baltica*

Another busy sea-route is the crossing between Helsinki in Finland and Tallinn in Estonia, fifty miles across the Gulf of Finland. All day long ferries are working this route, and they are almost always full. Thousands of Finns cross every week in search of bargains of one kind or another, to make deals or perhaps conclude skulduggeries on the other side. Flotillas of housewives with shopping-bags sweep on board in festive mood, as if they are off to a holiday camp. Businessmen get their heads down to work the moment they find a seat, like commuters. Two fortresses guard the sea-crossing. On the Finnish side there is the tremendous island fortress of Seaborg, now called Suomenlinna, for generations one of the crucial works of the Baltic, built by the Swedes, captured by the Russians, bombarded by the British, ceded to the Finns, and now kept in repair by squads of inebriate motorists, performing their community service. On the Estonian side is the medieval castle of Toompea, battered but proud upon its hill. It is only an hour's run from one stronghold to the other, and although Helsinki was originally founded in rivalry with Tallinn, in the 1990s they suggested to me a couple of old business colleagues passing the traffic confidentially between them. This was the Via Baltica, linking the far North with central Europe and the Mediterranean. For more than half a century its traffic was interrupted by war and ideology, but by the time I made the crossing the power of the market had restored it.

## 34 *A fellow traveller*

Half way to Tallinn I looked out of the cabin window and saw a big grey goose flying alongside us, at almost the same speed, and not much higher. I take it that bird had been flying the Via Baltica all its life, unimpeded by politics, and I would like to be able to describe it as winging an effortless, graceful, timeless way towards Estonia. The fact was that it was showing every sign of strain, flapping its wings with evident difficulty, and with an expression on its face, I fancied, of weary disenchantment. We overtook it gradually, and as it disappeared astern I could almost hear it panting.

## 35  *On the ferries*

Hydrofoils work the Helsinki–Tallinn route, which is why we could overhaul
the goose. Although hundreds of the old ferries still sail across the narrows
and straits of Europe, one by one they are giving way to more modern kinds
of vessels – rattly hovercraft, svelte hydrofoils, futuristic catamarans with vast
galleried cabins like the insides of fictional spacecraft. The most enjoyable of
these, I think, are the Italian hydrofoils which skim about the Mediterranean,
because they go so fast, and are so swirled about by spray and buffeted by
wind, that they give a kind of stylized or impressionistic view of the world
around you. Take the hydrofoil to one of the offshore islands in the Gulf of
Naples, and if it is a blustery day they will probably not allow you to stand
on the narrow open deck, where you might fall off and sue them, so that it
is through a scummed and sea-sprayed cabin window that you watch your
progress through the archipelago. If it is a misty day too, so much the better.
Then everything out there seems an opaque synthesis of Mediterraneanness –
islands, white villas on headlands, fishing-boats, surf around rocks, lighthouses,
brown-skinned children playing immemorial games on beaches, olive trees,
castles, that sort of thing, until an indistinct sign on a jetty, announcing a
disco club, Zimmer Mit Deutsch Spoken or a Special Touristic Restaurant
tells you that you have reached your destination.

But in my own view there is still no substitute for the big-ship ferries. It
is a fine thing to see their hulking white shapes, one after the other, churning
a passage across the English Channel; and nothing in European travel can
beat the thrill of the first sight of the white cliffs of Dover, seen from an
open deck on a fine blustery day, with Dover Castle standing like an ancient
defiance above them, and the inviolate line of the English coast stretching
away to the west. Could anything be more delicious than to prop yourself
against a ventilation shaft on the foredeck of a little ship from Piraeus and
watch the isles of the Aegean rise up in magical succession out of the sea?
What could be more satisfying than to sail away in a snug cabin to the islands
of the Scots – Orkney or Shetland or the windy Hebrides?

The biggest and grandest ferries of them all are the huge liners which sail
back and forth, night and day throughout the year, between the European
ports of the Baltic, half of them owned by those island shipmasters of page
88. For reasons I forget, I was once given the most luxurious stateroom on
one of these ships, and went to sea early one morning all alone in what I

remember as a vast glass-walled suite quite near the bows of the ship, below the bridge. Aft of me, I knew, multifarious restaurants, gambling-saloons, bars and floor shows already pulsated, to the beat of rock music, the scamper of excited children and the constant clink of money-tills (for many of the passengers on these vessels sail just for the shopping). In my stateroom all was infinite calm, with only a distant tread of engines, and I felt myself to be all alone in my plush eyrie above the pale but sunny Baltic. I rang for breakfast (there were four telephones in the cabin, and two television sets).

## 36 Watching the ships

Cuxhaven, a small port and resort at the mouth of the Elbe in Germany, is the best place in Europe for ship-watching, because all the multifarious sea-traffic of Hamburg passes it by. It is a pleasant town, with green promenades, a few hotels, and restaurants offering all possible varieties and combinations of herring. Beside its docks, which are lively with small freighters and fishing-boats, there is a viewing-pier at the river's edge where old salts with binoculars and well-wrapped tourists (it can be very chilly on that North Sea shore) hang around hour after hour watching the ships go by. In stately procession, day and night, the vessels come looming down that fairway – tankers, coastal freighters, vast container ships like floating fortresses, a police launch occasionally, sometimes a cruise liner, ferries to Heligoland, trawlers, sometimes a lean grey warship pounding out to sea. Often it is misty at Cuxhaven, and one cannot see the opposite bank of the river very clearly: but dimly one can discern, along the low sandy shore of Schleswig-Holstein, a row of modern windmills slowly whirling, as the ships tread grandly by.

## 37 The old ships

Luckily for people like me, many Europeans have a sentimental affection for old ships, and there are lots of veterans still to be seen, and some still to be sailed in. Oh, the ships I have seen with my own eyes in Europe! I have seen the behemoth *Jean Bart* (1945, 38,000 tons), awaiting her end at Toulon, and Queen Victoria's own royal yacht, the *Victoria and Albert* (1899,

4,700 tons), like an elegant old dowager among the destroyers at Portsmouth Dockyard, and the *Queen Elizabeth* (1939, 83,000 tons), the greatest of all passenger liners, decidedly showing her age, and the *Aquitania* (1914, 45,000 tons), last of the Atlantic four-stackers, apparently as sprightly as ever, and the *Rex* (1936, 51,000 tons), the pride of Mussolini's merchant fleet, wrecked outside Trieste, and the *Great Britain* (1845, 3,500 tons), the first iron steamship, being towed home to Bristol on a pontoon after decades as a hulk in the Falkland Islands. I have walked the deck of Nelson's *Victory*, and inspected Amundsen's *Fram*, which in 1912 went further north than any other surface vessel before or since, and stood on the forecastle of the *Cutty Sark*, the most famous of all the clipper ships.

I never did see the legendary Nydamboot, an oaken rowing-boat of the ancient Germanic tribes, because its museum-house in Schleswig was closed for the season, and I could only make out the dark mass of the vessel, shrouded in tarpaulins, by jumping up and down to look through the windows, like women touching the lucky owl at Dijon. I did see the black fragments of the Kyrenia Ship, 'the oldest trading vessel known to us', still with its cargo of amphoras in northern Cyprus, and I peered through the bullet-proof glass portholes of the sealed container, at the German Maritime Museum at Bremerhaven, in which a fourteenth-century Hanseatic cog was spending a few years immersed in preservative liquid. All these venerable vessels are among the ornaments of Europe, and best of them all, one of the continent's magical sights, is the stupendous seventeenth-century warship *Vasa* at Stockholm. To enter its huge museum hall beside the harbour and see this ancient marvel for the first time, towering there above you in the half-light, shadowy, glistening, immensely old, powerful, strange and beautiful – a first glimpse of the great ship *Vasa* is an almost mystic revelation.

### 38 *From 'The Old Ships', 1914, by James Elroy Flecker*

> It was so old a ship – who knows, who knows?
> – And yet so beautiful, I watched in vain
> To see the mast burst open with a rose,
> And the whole deck put on its leaves again.

## 39 Still working!

Less tremendous old ships are still working in several parts of Europe. On Lake Mjösa in Norway the oldest operating steamship in the world, the *Skibladner* (1856), gamely cruises in the summer months, and on many of the lakes and rivers of Germany and Switzerland (the French seem less susceptible) steamships and paddle-steamers are still earning their daily living. Half the river-boats of the Dresden *Weisse Flotte* are still steam-propelled: the oldest of them, the paddle-boat *Diesbar*, whose tall skinny funnel and green paddle-boxes make it one of the familiar sights of the city, has engines built in 1857 that are officially listed as monuments. The most endearing of such vessels, for my tastes, are the venerable paddle-steamers which maintain a scrupulously efficient service around the shores of Lake Lucerne in Switzerland. There are five beautiful old ships, and when I stay at Weggis, on the foreshore, it is largely for the pleasure of seeing them. A blast of the siren heralds the arrival of one of these indefatigable champions, the oldest of which was built in 1901, the youngest in 1928. Then there is the heavy plonking of the paddle-wheels, and sundry gasps and hissings. Finally the ship appears around the point, graceful as a sea-horse, punctual to the minute. Its prow is wonderfully gilded, its brasswork gleams, its paintwork is spotless, only a thin sliver of vapour escapes from its elegantly raked funnel, and on the wing of its high bridge its master stands, guiding it effortlessly into the jetty in all the splendour of captaincy. I think it would be as satisfying to command the *Uri* (1901) or the *Schiller* (1906) as it would be to command one of those blockbuster container ships we watched looming up the Elbe at Cuxhaven.

## 40 Par avion

When, in September 1938, Neville Chamberlain, the British Prime Minister, flew to Germany to negotiate with Adolf Hitler, he had never been in an aeroplane before. Now, of course, *par avion* is a norm for Europeans great and small. Most people fly. Most letters go by air mail, and it is a telling anachronism, in the late 1990s, that the British Post Office still recommends a blue air-mail sticker on letters for the European mainland. Almost anywhere over Europe one may see the vapour trails of the airliners, as they quarter the continent night and day. The very code-letters of the airports have

become familiar – VCE for Venice, CPH for Copenhagen, FRA for
Frankfurt, LHR for London Heathrow, ZRH for Zurich, CDG for
Paris Charles de Gaulle (though not everybody would recognize SKG for
Thessalonika, or VXO for Växjö). For people of my juvenile tastes, it is a
grand thing to watch the parade of the airliners at one of the great hubs –
Frankfurt, Rome, London or Paris – in all the splendid variety of their
liveries, the crests and logos, flying dragons and rampant lions, gnomic
folk-devices or insignia of long-dead feudalisms. Air travel has made my
generation unprecedently familiar with the geography of Europe. Who has
not crossed the snowy Alps? Who has not looked across the Straits of Gibraltar
to the African shore? We have observed for ourselves the Skagerrak and
Kattegat, and seen in one more-than-Homeric sweep all the islands of the
Aegean.

I once flew between the Alps, rather than over them, with an airline that
operated small Swedish turboprop airliners between Geneva, on the north
side of the range, and Lugano on the south. This seemed to me an eerie
experience. It was winter, and the mountains were filmed in a veil of cloud,
through which I could only just make out hills and forests, gullies and gorges.
We were skimming over a sea of vapour, a Caribbean in reverse, as in a
negative rather than a print. Sometimes a rift ran away crookedly through
the cumulus, like a deep-water channel. Sometimes the clouds were rippled
and piled like surf. Sometimes islands showed – the sharp grey crags of
mountain-tops, misty Grenadines, protruding through the white. And presently almost on a level with us there slid past our windows, lapped all around
in cloud, fired in sunlight, the rocky snowdrifted summit of Mont Blanc. So
absolutely empty and inaccessible did that mountain-top look, as though it
really were floating there upon its white silent ocean, that I found it hard to
imagine any human being ever setting foot upon it. It seemed close enough,
as we flew steadily by, to step out of the aircraft door and take a jump into
its snows: but that would have been, I thought with a shudder, like jumping
on to a passing asteroid.

## 41  *At the airports*

Sometimes the airports of Europe seem busier, even bigger, than the cities
they serve, and in less-developed countries the best roads serve them, in
order to provide salutary first impressions. By the nature of things their

buildings are modern too, or are so constantly in a condition of development that they offer a suggestion of national vigour. Most of them are never actually finished, because technology is always overtaking them, and no country is sufficiently modest to build them entirely of temporary, disposable or enlargeable buildings. Every airport has to be a monument. At the end of the twentieth century the busiest of Europe's international airports was London Heathrow (LHR), with four big terminals and a fifth on the way – partly, I assume, a matter of habit, because not so long ago aircraft crossing the Atlantic found it expedient to refuel there. Fifty thousand people went to work at Heathrow every day, besides the odd quarter of a million who passed through it. Yet I can remember when the single terminal was nothing more than an assembly of huts and tents beside the Great West Road: a couple of customs men, as I remember it, sat at a trestle table, and we were all weighed at a big pedestal weighing machine, like something on a seaside pier, and sat about in wicker chairs drinking tea out of enamel mugs before boarding a converted bomber for our flight. Now Heathrow is a permanently unfinished city, known to some insiders as Terminal Bore, complete with one-way streets, subways, dozens of hotels of various nationalities, scores of restaurants, shops from the poshest of emporia to the junkiest of souvenir stalls, a chapel, a jail and an oyster bar, all put together in a kind of nightmare labyrinth, as though conceived in revenge by some insanely disgruntled town planner.

These are a few highly subjective assessments of other European airports I knew, during fifty years of varied experience:

¶ The most delightful was Dublin, where long ago they kindly cooked me scrambled eggs when they weren't on the coffee-shop menu – 'Ah well, the chef's a kindly man.'

¶ The most beautiful was Barcelona, a thrilling thing of steel, glass and cool vistas especially built for the 1992 Olympics.

¶ The smoothest was Frankfurt, where countless million pieces of baggage were transferred this way and that, to and from every part of the world, but only 0.0002 per cent, so it was claimed in 1995, ever got lost.

¶ The most awful was Athens, where nothing ever went right.

¶ The most exciting was Aberdeen, where the helicopters took off for the North Sea oil rigs, and went clattering away with their thousands of workers – American, English, French, Dutch, Spanish, Italian, Greek, Norwegian, Swedish, German – to wild windy destinations with magical names – Cormorant, Piper, Active King, Dogger Shore . . .

¶ The most promising was Venice, because there you could board a motor-boat which would take you directly, across the desolate lagoon, into the canals of the most beautiful city in Europe – ravishing you with fulfilment when, having pottered slowly through the northern back-canals, the boat suddenly gathered speed and burst into the glory of the Basin of St Mark.

¶ The sleaziest was Kirkenes, in northern Norway, because in the late 1990s it was always full of dubious Russians from Murmansk, on their way to steal things from the local shops.

¶ The most surprising was Bucharest, because there, if you smiled nicely at the official lady, she might well let you off your entry tax.

¶ The most amazing was Tempelhof in Berlin, because the Nazis had built it bang in the middle of their capital.

¶ The most misleading was Nice, because its runways were on the edge of the Mediterranean, and made you feel, as you swooped down there out of the grey North, that you were already surrounded by the peace and sweet scents of the South, whereas in fact it would be several sweaty hours before you finally checked in at your characterless concrete hotel on some hideously developed stretch of polluted Riviera shore.

¶ The most brazen was Manchester, which had a large illuminated sign in its forecourt, generally a scene of shabby chaos, announcing it to be The World's Best Airport.

¶ The most welcoming, in my memory, was Munich one sunny day in the 1950s: for actually beside the tarmac as we landed a rustic brass band was playing, in brass-buttoned uniforms, glowing with pleasure, beer and exertion, and led by a bandmaster who turned from his performers to wave us smilingly with his baton, one-two-three, one-two-three, down the steps from our aircraft door.

## 42  *The Hansa*

When I first walked into the Schiffergesellschaft, a famous old restaurant in the German Baltic seaport of Lübeck, I felt unmistakably that I was walking into Consequence. The restaurant is not particularly smart, or gastronomically remarkable, but it is housed in the ancient headquarters of the sea-captains' guild, and is fully equipped with the heavy beams, high-backed benches, long wooden tables, copper lamps and pendant ship models that sailing-ship captains seem to have preferred when they came ashore. And these, in the medieval heyday of the Schiffergesellschaft, were no ordinary sea-captains. They were maritime swells of one of the great European trading networks, which extended its influence over much of northern Europe, had its factories and its agents all over the place, and became, through the skill of its traders and financiers, very nearly a Power in itself.

The Hanseatic League was born in Lübeck in the thirteenth century, when the European States were still in embryo, and it became so wide, powerful and aggressive an association of trading cities that it has left formidable traces to this day. Some 200 mostly German towns were members in the prime of the League, and between them they established for themselves near-monopolies in many commodities in many countries, besides maintaining peace and order wherever they operated. Every three years they sent delegates to a peripatetic assembly, and they built up a common body of law concerning commercial, maritime and financial matters. All around the coasts of northern Europe, far to the south along the ancient trade routes of the continent, the sailors, merchants and fixers of the League were at work – selling and swapping timbers, furs, honey, tar, cloth, copper, iron ore, salted herring; bribing susceptible foreign statesmen; establishing factories; imposing embargoes on unfriendly States; putting down pirates; founding their own churches (sometimes in rivalry with local bishoprics) – even engaging in a war once, against the Danes. By the time it came to an end in the seventeenth century, outclassed at last by the rise of the Nation-States, the Hansa had permanent semi-autonomous outposts in Bruges, Bergen, Visby, Novgorod, London and many another port and mart.

I have always been excited by the idea of the Hanseatic League, a Power that was not a Power, without a constitution, without a central Government, without a permanent assembly, generally without armed forces, created entirely for the protection and pursuit of trade ('Hansa' simply means 'association'). When I first sailed into Bergen, in Norway, in the early 1950s, I was truly thrilled to find the long gabled row of the Hansa's headquarters, looking as ancient as anything, still dominating the Tyskebryggen, the German Quay. Many of the buildings have been burnt down since, but in those days, standing there crooked, black and planked beside the harbour, they might still have been populated by the German businessmen, seamen, goldsmiths, shoemakers, tailors, furriers, bakers, bankers, cutlers who had worked away there for three centuries and more, as self-contained and separate from the indigenes as a European trading settlement in eighteenth-century China.

Even now the traveller in northern Europe can hardly help crossing the tracks of the Hansa. For instance in the walled city of Visby, in Gotland, a great Hanseatic centre in the fourteenth century, there are some terrific old Hanseatic offices, part warehouses, part dwelling-places – high tottering structures, with upstairs storage rooms for grain and salted fish, and family quarters for the merchants and their wives, occupied now by workers in silver or stained glass, and one or two restaurants offering saffron pancakes to tourists. At Kaunas in Lithuania, at the other end of the Baltic, the elaborately redbrick Gothic headquarters of the Hansa stands beside the German merchants' church, around the corner from their comfortably mercantile homes. The most imposing churches in Tallinn are the two steepled churches of the Hansa – far larger than the Estonian bishop's cathedral on the top of its hill.

Even away in Shetland, in the Viking seas of Scotland, I like to fancy the businessmen from Hamburg, Lübeck and Bremen who built themselves booths upon the foreshore, and did their trade and bartering in the wind: hooks and nets, corn and flour, mead and linen, in return for wool, sealskins, beef, and fish for salting. The local Stewart earls were the patrons of this trade, and sometimes it seems the Germans grew to like life in those inhospitable parts: Segebad Detken, burgess of Bremen, lived for more than half a century on the inconceivably uncomfortable island of Uist, and is buried there. When I stood, near the start of this book, with my back to the London Stone, looking towards Cannon Street station, I felt a modest historical excitement there, too, for I was looking at the site of the Steelyard, the Hanseatic factory in England. There the all-male company of Hanseatic merchants lived richly aloof from the English, electing its own aldermen in its own guildhall. It had been there since the twelfth century, issuing its own currency, gradually enlarging its property in Upper Thames Street and docking its ships at a private jetty protruding into the River Thames. I do not doubt that my maternal great-great-grandfather, who himself died in Hamburg during a business trip in 1826, must have done business here too: for, although the Steelyard was closed in 1598, German merchants worked on the very same site on and off until the middle of the nineteenth century.

The three chief Hanseatic cities of Germany, Lübeck, Bremen and Hamburg, remained stoutly independent and internationalistic long after the end of the Hansa. When in the 1890s Kaiser Wilhelm II set about arousing public enthusiasm for a German national navy, he was advised not to expect much support from the Hanseatic seaports, 'because of their particularist tendencies and parasitic standpoint about foreign trade'. They kept a sort of nominal independence, and were officially known as Hansa towns, until the Nazis abolished their ancient privileges in 1934: Bremen and Hamburg are still self-governing *Länder* within the German federation, and all three carry the letter H on their car number-plates to this day.

## 43   Cities of trade

Of course traders criss-crossed Europe long before the birth of the Hansa, and long before the emergence of Nation-States, too. Near Schleswig in Germany there is a Viking settlement which powerfully illustrates the meaning of trade in ancient Europe. Hedeby was the greatest trading centre of the Vikings, their principal entrepôt. It was built at least 1,000 years ago on the very narrowest point between the Baltic and the North Sea, allowing portage for Viking trade routes that extended eastward to Russia and the Black Sea, westward to the British Isles, Iceland and Greenland – just thirty miles north of the site of the Kiel Canal which performs the same service now. For security it was tucked away beside a fjord within a fjord, in a lonely, safe and reedy place, and you can go there today by ferry from the old city of Schleswig. This is a haunting experience. A semicircular rampart surrounds Hedeby still, on the landward side, and within it at the water's edge all the paraphernalia of a trading city arose as early as the ninth century – the warehouses and the jetties, the offices and the dwelling-places, the shipyards, doubtless the taverns and brothels, and even a church for Christian merchants. You can imagine it all as your boat sails in. Though empty and marshy now, with a Baltic wind often whistling through those reeds, it still suggests to me a confident, self-sufficient and outward-looking sort of place – an archetype, in fact, of the great mercantile cities built by traders and merchants down the centuries across the continent.

## 44   Euro-cities

Europe is littered with such cities, and often they seem more compatible with each other than political capitals do. The twinning of European cities, which sometimes seems mere sentimentality and sometimes little more than an excuse for aldermanic bingeing, and is sometimes so profligate that it becomes civic quintupling or even sextupling – this late twentieth-century practice rings more true than usual when one venerable trading centre reaches across the frontiers to proclaim its affinity with another. In 1996 sixty of them were members of a kind of pseudo-Hansa called Euro-city, dedicated to the maintenance of civic rights and responsibilities. For centuries the trading fairs which thrived in such places were a prime unifying force of Europe. They brought merchants from all parts of Europe into contact with one another: Ulm, Venice, Augsburg, Frankfurt, Leipzig formed a familiar working circuit for businessmen of the time. Some have remained international fair-cities to this day. Through all the fluctuations of history, Leipzig in East Germany, Plovdiv in Bulgaria, Zagreb in the old Yugoslavia were still frequented by Western entrepreneurs during the chilliest stand-offs of the Cold War. Venice, in the Middle Ages one of the most dazzling of exchanges, as the home of the Biennale is still one of the world's main centres of the art trade. And Frankfurt am Main, the greatest fair-city of them all, draws hundreds of thousands of businesspeople to the international exhibitions in its vast modern fair-grounds.

Frankfurt is the business capital of Germany, and it seems only proper that the modern buildings of its ancient fairs, the foundations of its prosperity, should stand in the lee of the skyscraper blocks that are the headquarters of the Deutschmark. The traditions of the fairs, which were first held in the eleventh century, are never forgotten here. The chief square of the Altstadt is still called the Römerberg, after the travelling merchants from Rome who used to set up shop there; at official receptions foreign delegates are given a pretzel, descended from the welcome-offerings that were given traders in medieval times (though now wrapped in Cellophane). This is the apex of European commerce. Frankfurt's Book Fair has been held since 1480! Shylock bought his diamonds at Frankfurt! Schopenhauer loved Frankfurt because there were so many English businessmen about! The grand old Frankfurter Hof Hotel, in the middle of town, is the epitome of a merchant caravanserai, always full of complacent elder tycoons and eager youngish executives: when I once sat down in one of its lounges to write a lyrical essay on my laptop I was assumed to be a Toshiba demonstrator.

## 45 City-States

Some of these big provincial cities, built upon commerce, feel like City-States still – more so, some of them, now that they are fenced in by ring roads, as by city walls. Bremen really is one, as a German *Land* of its own, and everything about the place breathes a spirit of merchant independence – the civic motto is 'Far away or at home, risk or win!' Bremen's prime image is the huge fourteenth-century figure of Roland, Charlemagne's nephew, which stands in the main square, thirty feet tall and brightly belted, with a sword in his hand, an eagle-headed shield and a decapitated head at his feet. He is Bremen's symbolic champion against the overpowering authority of Church or State, and for six centuries he has looked with a slightly sarcastic smile across the square to the cathedral – smiling more ironically still, I don't doubt, when in 1989 the Bremen municipality removed from inside him a time-casket of propaganda documents inserted by the Nazis in the 1930s. Bremen is full of quirks and old traditions, tales and fancies, and has a long tradition of merry radicalism. I relish the egalitarian, opportunist spirit of it. Beside the cathedral there stands a pompous equestrian figure of Bismarck, the antithesis in every way of Roland down the way. The Iron Chancellor is unnamed on his plinth, and in 1995 I asked every passer-by to identify him for me. Not a soul could, and how we all laughed, all of us, as one after another those loyal citizens, looking up at the grim old statesman on his charger, had to admit they had not the slightest notion who he was. Roland laughed too.

Venice, for a thousand years a sovereign Power, still feels unmistakably like a City-State, and in Croatia the little city of Dubrovnik, ex-Ragusa, though knocked about a bit in the Yugoslav wars of the 1990s, bears itself within the glorious circuit of its walls as though it still rules its own fortunes. Milan is almost its own capital. Barcelona hardly feels subject to the Kingdom of Spain. Hamburg retained its liberal Hanseatic outlook throughout the Nazi period. Antwerp is the most truly polyglot city in Europe, and its people are called, uniquely in Belgium, *sinjorenz* – signors. Bruges, too, seems to me more consequential than Brussels. Riga in Latvia, seen from across its river, wonderfully suggests a City-State in an old engraving – castle, cathedral, spires and towers laid out in proud esplanade along the quays. Lyon and Marseille are far more than just French provincial cities, and the rugged old Scottish city of Glasgow, once the second city of the British Empire, always feels as though it ought to have its own Government, conducting its own foreign relations and flying its own flag (in fact in 1919, when radical discontent flamed there, it did fly the Red Flag above its City Chambers).

When I first went to Glasgow, soon after the Second World War, it was grimy, slummy, bombed, crime-ridden but high-spirited, and was still building the world's greatest merchant ships on its River Clyde; when I was there in the 1960s it was in a state of profound economic depression, its industries in decline, its buildings all blackened and decaying; when I went again in 1990 it had been declared Europe's Cultural Capital, and had been transformed into a kind of glitzy reincarnation of itself in its glory days. Through it all the city had remained colossally proud and fond of itself. The bookshops were always full of books about Glasgow, the museums were stacked with Glaswegiana, there were songs about Glasgow, poems about Glasgow, acres of Glasgow paintings, and more than one dictionary of the impenetrable Glasgow dialect. It was as though the place were altogether separate from the events that swirled about it, making it sometimes rich, sometimes poor, sometimes famous for its shipyards, sometimes for the slinkiness of its boutiques or the trendiness of its art scene. 'Glasgow's Miles Better' was the civic slogan in 1990, 'Glasgow Belongs to Me' was a sort of civic anthem in the 1940s, but they both meant much the same: as a Glaswegian lady said to me on my last visit, when I remarked upon the vast publicity the city was getting then, 'Ay, well, they talk a lot, but they haven't changed much really.'

## 46 *Hear, hear*

I always thought the best municipal text for such a City-State would be an enigmatic medieval slogan that is incised on the walls of the ancient Marischal College at Aberdeen, another pawkily independent Scottish burgh. 'THEY HAIF SAID,' announces this gnomic graffito, and answers itself: 'WHAT SAY THEY. LET YAME SAY.' But the very name of Nehaj, in Croatia, is perhaps better still. It is simply a contraction of '*ne hajem*', which means 'I DON'T CARE.'

## 47 *The brothers*

Sometimes private people, rather than statesmen, conquerors, cities or institutions, have contrived to tighten the internet of Europe. Stand with me
now with our backs to the river beside the Untermain Bridge in Frankfurt
am Main – not far from the Römerberg, where the medieval merchants
gathered. In an elegant terrace before us, facing the river, we may see a large
white house. It is a fateful house. Over the rooftops behind it rise the
stupendous towers of the Westend, the financial quarter – spiked, black,
mirror-glassed. In front of it a busy road runs, and before that again are the
lines of the freight railway which connects one part of the river docks with
another. Yet in my mind's eye, anyway, the house, which is substantial but
hardly a palace, seems to command the view, like one of those personalities
upon whom every eye is turned when they enter a room. It is the Jewish
Museum of Frankfurt, once among the great Jewish cities of Europe; also
the house from which the Rothschild banking family extended its activities
and influence with such skill, wisdom, cunning and tenacity that it became
one of the supreme economic forces of Europe.

Until 1848 the Rothschilds lived and worked in a more modest home, a
rambling half-timbered house in the Jewish ghetto, which stood over there,
behind the Deutsche Bank, but is now all but entirely obliterated. Meyer
Amschel Rothschild moved into Untermainkai 14 only when he was
sufficiently powerful and respected – sufficiently *salonfähig*, drawing-room-
worthy, as the Frankfurters used to say – to move among the Gentile ruling
classes on their own terms. 'Money is the God of our age,' wrote Heinrich
Heine, observing this progression, 'and Rothschild is his prophet.' Having
made the family bank the richest in Germany, the patriarch sent out his four
sons to establish branches elsewhere in Europe: in Vienna, in Naples, in Paris
and in London. The network they established came to stand above diplomacy,
above monarchies, above States and even Powers, and the Rothschilds
became all but royalty themselves. They had before them the example of
the Florentine Medicis, who had dictated the fortunes of seventeenth-century
Europe by their financial acumen. The Medicis' simple motto was '*Semper*',
'Always', and the Rothschilds too aimed at eternity.

They were immensely influential all over the continent (though the Naples
branch was presently closed, the Kingdom of Naples proving to be of
insufficient clout), and their incomparable courier service, as an agency of

intelligence, proved invaluable to many Governments. In nineteenth-century London, then the richest of capitals, their power was greatest of all. It was to his friend Baron Lionel de Rothschild that the Prime Minister Benjamin Disraeli turned when in 1875 he needed money to buy the Khedive of Egypt's shares in the Suez Canal – a colossal sum of money, to pull off one of the greatest political coups of the century. Disraeli's private secretary, Montagu Corry, was sent to Rothschild's office to ask for a loan of £4 million – more like £400 million by today's values – and left his own famous account of the occasion. 'When?' asked Rothschild. 'Tomorrow,' said Corry. Rothschild paused to eat a grape and spit out the pip – not perhaps a very *salonfähig* gesture. 'What,' he then asked, 'is your security?' 'The British Government.' 'You shall have it,' said Rothschild, and that was that.

To this day the Rothschilds are a European clan of legendary financial and intellectual eminence, with their banks still in London and Paris, their titles bestowed by France, Belgium and England, their vineyards in France, their family members distinguished in many callings. Even the Nazis were never able to humiliate this mighty Jewish dynasty. If you would like to see what heights history brought it to in the end, come with me now to the house called Waddesdon Manor, in the English shires, which was their English family headquarters until in 1957 James de Rothschild bequeathed it to the National Trust. 'Manor' is really hardly the word for Waddesdon. A long, long drive leads through parklands, past estate houses and handsome stables, past fountains mythologically spouting, past statues and ornamental urns, until it comes into the straight, as it were, and approaches the house itself.

Which really *is* a palace, or a château in the Loire manner – not gigantic, but tremendously, exhaustingly grand, with all the statutory cupolas and mansard roofs and turret windows of its kind. Nothing would induce me to live in such a house, but by the time it was built, in the 1870s, the Rothschilds had become, as it were, honorary royalty: and sure enough even today there flies from the highest rooftop of Waddesdon the family ensign – against a blue field, five arrows, representing those five original banks, in Frankfurt, Paris, London, Naples and Vienna.

## 48 *Academe*

The universities of Europe used to constitute a network of their own, so that medieval scholars like Erasmus could move easily with his ideas from one to another. They still do, I suppose, but to the outsider it does not feel like it. Intellectually Europe's myriad places of learning may still be meshed; stylistically they seem to have little in common any more. They used to share not merely a religion and a language, but a sense of taste and history. Only in a few of the most ancient and conservative foundations do I sense any aesthetic kinship now: Salamanca, Coimbra, Oxford and Cambridge, Uppsala, St Andrews, Vienna, Heidelberg, Bologna, Padua – all places where old buildings are lovingly preserved still, rituals have survived the homogenizing of scholarship and the interference of politics, and scholars and students may wear peculiar costumes from olden times and obey their own strange rules of conduct. Does it matter, anyway? If the power of thought is strong and free, a university can be as important in a concrete blockhouse, conducted in dishevelment, as ever it was in a lovely Renaissance palace, stalked through by men of learning all in gold and crimson. The Sorbonne in Paris is probably the most influential university in Europe at the end of the twentieth century, the one whose ideas have been most eagerly absorbed throughout the continent; and, although it is among the most ancient of them all, anyone who has wandered through its purlieus on the Left Bank knows what an unlovely mess it is.

But then conceptions of higher education itself have drastically shifted in my time. When I edited an undergraduate newspaper I wrote to various famous people asking them if they thought that in the world of the 1940s it was still worthwhile going to Oxford. Field Marshal Lord Wavell, lately Viceroy of India, replied that 'the traditions of Oxford, the dignity and beauty of the Colleges, the associations of the place must have a deep and lasting effect on all who go there – quite apart' (he added, more or less as an afterthought) 'from the education'. Fifty years later, how many of Europe's educationalists would dare express such a view?

## 49  *Monsters of the sea*

Despite all these ancient links, civic connections and scholarly interchanges, fifty years ago most of the peoples of Europe scarcely knew each other, except in war. Only the rich could travel for pleasure then, and nothing has changed the continent more, or made its nations more mutually familiar, than popular tourism. Familiarity does not always breed content, and there are parts of Europe where indigenes and tourists, however fulsomely they address each other, really loathe each other's guts: but they are no longer total strangers. They have learnt to speak each other's languages, if only a few words of them, to eat each other's foods, if only with suspicion or indigestion, possibly even to learn a little of each other's history. Some people are more diffident than others in their approaches to foreign parts, and so far it is only the people of western Europe who travel *en masse* across the continent for their holidays. But at least, during my half-century, a continent of warring soldiers has been metamorphosed into a continent of pleasure-seekers.

The ultimate European tourist destination, by the 1990s, was probably Disneyland outside Paris, an apparently irresistible American implant, but traditionally the fulcrum of international tourism has been Venice, where the horrors of mass travel can be extreme. At the height of the summer the dark entrance to the Basilica San Marco, all but impassably jammed with sightseers, is like a narthex to hell, and the thousands who swarm along the Riva degli Schiavoni are enough to squeeze obscenities out of a saint. It was always so. One of the very earliest paintings of Venice, from the early fifteenth century, seems to show a tourist bending backwards to photograph the crocodile of St Theodore on his pillar in the Piazzetta; a medieval chronicler marvelled at all the Turks, Libyans, Parthians and other Monsters of the Sea who then, as now, sauntered here and there about the Piazza San Marco. In 1959, when I was living in Venice, I compiled a kind of critique of the most numerous European tourists, partly from my own observations, partly from the responses of the Venetians themselves. For example the Germans, I reported, were loud, pushy and moved in regiments – the French were nearly all delightful – the British provided the best of the men and the most dispiriting of the women – things like that. None of it is true now, I think. Europeans have become harder to distinguish. The Germans are less noisy than they used to be, the English less gentlemanly, the French a little less delightful. I used to flatter myself I could tell the nationality of a European tourist group almost at a glance, but now it is only the language of their guide that tells me – and even that, expressed as it is likely to be in the parroting sing-song of the package holiday, is beginning to be unreliable.


## 50  One gets used to anything

It is the accepted wisdom that mass tourism, by and large, is dreadful. Certainly it has physically ruined many a coastline (for it is essentially a seaside phenomenon) with its second-rate buildings, its marinas and caravan sites. It has degraded many an ancient culture by making profitable parodies of its immemorial attitudes and customs. So ubiquitous has it become, though, so inescapable a part of European society, that probably in the end we shall hardly notice it. Phoney folk-costumes will be more real than real ones. The truest purpose of ancient buildings will be to be shown off to visitors. The theme park will seem as genuine as the historical site. 'Going to Land's End?' a man asked of me in Cornwall one day. 'Whatever you do, don't miss the labyrinth.' But when I got there, hoping for some surf-sprayed maze of caverns within the cliff, I found he was referring to The Legendary Last Labyrinth, The No. 1 Multi-Sensory Experience, which pulsated with wind machines, subsonic audio and twenty-eight picture projectors at the very western tip of England, on one of the supreme allegorical headlands of Europe, one of the most wildly epic of coasts. Huge car parks attended it, I found; ingratiating girls directed me to the admissions office. There was a mock galleon for the kiddies, and the inevitable trolley train. From The Mariner's Chest seeped out that sickly sachet scent peculiar to Gift Shoppes everywhere, and in the heart of it all was The Unforgettable Experience that Defies the Everyday Limits of Time and Space.

But one gets used to anything. When I walked to the edge of the complex, away from the crowds, I could still feel myself on the edge of the world, as a fierce Atlantic wind whipped out of the sunshine and seemed to bleach the very air of the place. Ships sailed by, a lighthouse stood on a rock, and inland the rocky waste of the Penwith peninsula, seamed with the stone patterns of Celtic farmlands, seemed utterly aloof from the Last Labyrinth. An American woman I met out there appeared to have forgotten about the theme park already. As we stood together in the blast of the wind, with our backs to the Multi-Sensory Experience, she turned to me ecstatically and said, 'My, it's like nobody ever stood on this spot before.'

## 51  *Nothing new*

Theme parks are nothing new, but in the old days their exhibits were the
real thing, not electronic substitutes or plaster casts. At another of Europe's
great headlands, the North Cape at the top end of Norway, far from human
habitation in a more or less perpetual maelstrom of winds out of the Arctic,
they have lately built an observation chamber, a restaurant, a museum and a
few other theme-park essentials, but in fact tourists have been going there
for generations. In my grandfather's time they disembarked from their
steamers with some difficulty in small boats below the headland, and then
climbed for a few hours up a steep shaly track to the Cape itself, where
nothing whatever awaited them except the sensation of being there. By my
day we stepped ashore comfortably on a jetty and were driven in warm buses
up an excellent road to the headland, stopping on the way for souvenirs at
an Authentic Lapp Village. I felt a little guilty, actually: especially when,
looking out through thick plate glass at the grey cold sea, with a cup of hot
coffee in my hand, I thought of my poor old grandad, queasy I expect from
the small boat, clambering gamely up the windswept cliff outside.

## 52  *A beach revived*

In the 1960s, when I was writing a book about Spain, I lived for a few weeks
in a former fisherman's cottage on the beach in a small hangdog village called
Fuengirola, on the southern coast, the Costa del Sol. All around me was
poverty, euphemized in my mind as simplicity. It was the easiest thing in
the world to find somebody to do the cooking – everybody wanted a job
in Fuengirola. Sometimes I went out on the beach to watch the fishermen
pursuing their primitive calling. It could be heartbreaking to watch. They
worked like slaves, wading into the sea with their huge net and laboriously
hauling it in, inch by inch, hour by hour up the sands: so much depended
on that catch, so much labour and good humour had been expended,
so many hungry children were waiting to be fed at home – and when at
last the haul appeared, a dozen small sardines in the mesh of the net, the
fishermen carefully cleared up their tackle and dispersed to their homes in
weary silence.

When I was in Fuengirola last I could not even make out where my cottage had stood. High-rise apartments and hotels dominated that once empty beach, no fishermen slogged away at their nets on the sand, and my guess is that if I had needed someone to help with the cooking I would never have been able to afford her fee.

## 53 *The resistance*

Of course there is much to be said for tourism in Europe; but naturally there is resistance, too, to touristic spoliation. Even the most avid of tourist authorities sometimes stand back and consider whether enough is not enough. Even Venice closed itself to tourists for a time, a few years back, when the holiday traffic seemed about to overwhelm it, and in 1996 Florence limited its tourist coaches to 150 a day. Elsewhere in Europe there have been sporadic attempts to reconcile tourism with conservation and demonstrate that a holiday resort need not necessarily ruin a landscape. In southern Spain, and in the South of France, there have been attempts to stop the rot by building tourist villages in local styles, mock pueblos, sham fishing-villages, which have a certain pathetic heroism to them.

By the 1990s the Balearic islands of the Mediterranean were especially horribly degraded by tourism – so horribly that the Spanish themselves used the verb '*balearizar*', to Balearize – but in Majorca, half a lovely mountain island, half a tourist nightmare, one development had successfully bucked the trend. The peninsular estate called Formentor, at the northern tip of the island, had been acquired in the 1920s by an Argentinian millionaire, who built upon it a hotel conceived in the first place especially as a retreat for poets, painters, philosophers and other sensitive vacationists. It became a fashionable resort of the 1930s, and remains today an enclave of calm and restraint in an often frenzied archipelago. Nearly everyone who is anyone has been to Formentor at one time or another, to attend Count Keyserling's famous pre-war Philosophy Weeks, to listen to chamber music nowadays, or just to hide away among the pine forests on the edge of the silent bay. I spent a few days there once, and found it all so relaxing, so quiet and reserved, so utterly unspoilt and environmentally sympathetic that I ran away to Barcelona.

Much more fun is the most light-hearted of these anti-tourist tourist places, the artificial hotel-village of Portmeirion in Wales. This was started by the architect Clough Williams-Ellis in the 1930s, to demonstrate that tourism need not be unsightly and profit need not be heedless. It is a highly entertaining *mélange* of architectural styles, some of its buildings rescued from demolition elsewhere, some indigenous, some the architect's own creations, part Welsh, part Italianate, with a Portofino campanile and a Gothic town hall, a camera obscura and a colonnade, the whole put together in a whimsically self-amused way on a peninsula rich in rhododendrons overlooking the Irish Sea. The cunningly arranged vistas are delightful; the architectural embellishments are endearingly excessive, as though Williams-Ellis simply could not keep his exuberance in check. From across the water Portmeirion looks like some rich man's folly, towers and high-pitched buildings disposed happily at the water's edge as if for pure amusement, and in a way it is: but its original intention was serious too, and it remains an elegant and humorous plea for civilized values in the holiday trade.

In the middle of Bremen another man of vision built, in the 1920s, the alley of cultural tourism called Böttcherstrasse. Ludgwig Roselius had made a great fortune by inventing decaffeinated coffee, and he invested it by buying up, one by one, the properties along the former Street of the Coopers, and having the whole thing redesigned under the inspiration of the art-nouveau sculptor Bernhard Hoetger. It is a street of infinite surprise, all built in handsome red brick and enlivened by every kind of nook, courtyard, quaint sculpture, curious allusion, joke and Germanic grace-note. There are art shops, bookshops, restaurants, a hotel, a cinema, a concert studio, a casino and a museum dedicated to the memory of Robinson Crusoe, whose family came from Bremen. The street is only a hundred yards long, but you never know what you will find next. Goldsmiths, potters and glass-blowers ply their crafts. Buskers play Bach on the violin. Here a carillon of porcelain bells rings a selection of sea-shanties, here there is displayed the silver treasure trove of the Company of the Black Heads of Riga. The Nazis hated Böttcherstrasse.

In a small courtyard halfway down the street Hoetger placed a Fountain of the Seven Lazy Men. These well-known Bremen brothers of legend were too bone idle to fetch water from the river, to chop wood in the forest, or to pull their carts out of the mud; so instead they sank a well, planted trees, and cobbled the village street. It is an apposite place to ponder the moral of the tale, because scornful as they have been of all the tourist orthodoxies, down the years Formentor, Portmeirion and Böttcherstrasse have one and all made heaps of money.

## 54 *Taking the waters*

The first sort of European tourism, I suppose, was travelling to take the waters, which has been happening at least since Roman times. Taking the waters enabled people to enjoy themselves and improve themselves at the same time. The first of the spas was Spa itself, a small town in the Ardennes mountains of Belgium, whose curative springs the Romans originally discovered, and which used to be known simply as The Spa: later spas have always been among the most cosmopolitan of European towns, where people of many nations have met in common valetudinarian pursuits – 'spaing', as the English used to say in the nineteenth century, or 'getting spa'd'. They have often been culturally distinguished. Celebrated architects have been proud to design their buildings – Karl Schinkel built the pump-room at Aachen in Germany, Friedrich Weinbrenner the magnificent Kurhaus at Baden-Baden, the two John Woods made their names at Bath. The art-nouveau virtuosi Ármin Hegedüs and Artúr Sebestyén designed the Géllert spa hotel at Budapest – the only capital city, by the way, to be a spa as well.

Writers, composers and artists have frequented the spas, novelists and film-makers have used them as settings, and they have often been centres of fashionable life, especially when their facilities have included gambling casinos. Bad Homburg in Germany gave its name to the Homburg hat. Vichy is where vichysoisse was invented. The spas have also played peculiar political roles in European history. At Vichy, for instance, the humiliated French Government of 1940 set up its headquarters; to Baden-Baden the neutral embassies were compulsorily withdrawn when Germany faced defeat in 1945; Aachen was Charlemagne's capital; at the original Spa, in 1918, the last Emperor of Austro-Hungary held his final meeting with the last Kaiser of Germany; half the political leaders of Europe, and many of the crowned heads, hobnobbed at one time or another over the Bohemian cures for their rheumatism or obesity. At the spa hotel of Bad Kreuznach, in 1917, the generals of the German High Command had their headquarters, and were visited by their ally Atatürk: thirty years later Adenauer and de Gaulle met in the same building to lay the first foundations of the European Union. There are hundreds of active spas in Europe still, and until well into the 1990s every taxpayer in Germany, where spa treatments have been most popular of all, was entitled to a free four-week *Kur* every three years.

## 55  Mirrors of history

The spas have often been historical mirrors or indicators. One of the most historically charged of elegies is an Anglo-Saxon lament about the ruins of Roman Bath, Aquae Sulis: on the other hand an oddly comforting European phenomenon is the ability of the spas, Bath included, to ride the tides of history. Two of the most resilient of them have been Carlsbad and Marienbad, which in this century alone thrived in one name or another under monarchical, Fascist, Communist and democratic systems. They stood agreeably forested in the part of Bohemia known as the Sudetenland, populated largely by Germans, and in the prime of the Austro-Hungarian Dual Empire the fashionable classes of all Europe enjoyed themselves there.

After the First World War the spas became part of the new Czechoslovakia, between the wars they were annexed by Germany, after the Second World War they were subject to the Czechoslovak Communist People's Republic. By the time I got there, in the late 1950s, one could hardly recognize them as places of pleasure at all. They were called Karlovy Vary and Mariánské Lázně then, all the Sudeten Germans had been expelled, and they were the preserves of Communist Party officials and labour unions, gloomily in the Stalinist thrall. Workers' Groups morosely sampled the health-giving waters. Girls of Youth Associations sauntered in frumpish crocodile. Comrade Doctors and Curators ran museums and administered colonic treatments. The Grandhotel Pupp at Karlovy Vary, probably the most famous of all spa hotels, was renamed the Hotel Moskva.

Twenty years later the two old resorts began to emerge once more into the democratic daylight, and when I drove there again in the 1980s I was delighted to find that some of the road signs had taken to calling them Carlsbad and Marienbad once more. By the mid-1990s they were very nearly back to their old gaiety. Bands played beneath their colonnades. The Pupp was the Pupp again. You could drink hot chocolate on Edwardian terraces, looking up at roofs rich in bottles, turrets and whirligigs. The Emperor Franz Josef himself, I thought, might easily come hobbling down the river boulevard at Carlsbad, with his white-jacketed sword-clanking aides; Admiral Tirpitz or Edward VII of England might well be staying at the old Weimar Hotel in Marienbad, emancipated from its long impersonation as a trade-union hostel. Long before, the old world of Germanness had reached a serene apotheosis here, and now as the century closed the spas offered its sensations in wistful echo.

The Germanness of Sudety had been one of the causes of the Second World War, enabling Adolf Hitler to advance his claims upon Czechoslovakia (and the Poles and Hungarians to retrieve other bits of it). By 1995 the very name of the Sudetenland was largely forgotten, and there were virtually no German residents. Lots of people, however, understood German still – the German frontier was close – and nearly all the foreign visitors were German. I went to the Casino Marienbad hoping for a blackjack flutter, but found to my consternation that its cavernous central salon had been taken over by hundreds and hundreds of middle-aged German tourists, sitting at long benches, laughing, talking hard and eating largely. The woman at the reception desk was amused by my dismay, and her own response was a kind of historical commentary itself. 'A whole trainload of them,' she said in mock consternation. 'Imagine, one whole train of Germans! Good business. Think what they eat.'

## 56 *From* The Ruin *(circa AD 700), translated from the Anglo-Saxon by R. K. Gordon*

Wondrous is this wall-stone; broken by fate, the castles have decayed; the work of giants is crumbling . . . the place has sunk into ruin, levelled to the hills, where in times past many a man light of heart and bright with gold, adorned with splendours, proud and flushed with wine, shone in war-trappings, gazed on treasure . . . Stone courts stood here; the stream with its great gush sprang forth hotly; the wall enclosed all within its bright bosom; there the baths were hot in its centre; that was spacious . . .

## 57 *'That was spacious'*

Bath may have been a sad ruin in AD 700, a memorial to the giants of Rome, but it recovered to become one of the most beautiful of the European spas, and one of the chief English tourist destinations. I had an apartment there for a time in the 1970s, and came to find its inescapable Georgian elegance a little monotonous, but I do recognize its splendour. There is a revelatory moment in Bath that I particularly used to enjoy. It is among the most famous of English architectural surprises, and I liked experiencing it best by car, with the roof open and something blithe and brilliant on the tape – Mozart, Mendelssohn, or Astaire singing Cole Porter. Then I would swing exhilaratingly around the Circus, the architectural centre-piece of Georgian Bath, and head down the short straight link road called Brock Street. I used to pretend to myself that I had never been there before, and for visual reasons drove slap down the middle of the street. At the end of it there seemed to be a vacancy – cloud, trees, a snatch of green in the middle distance, a transverse terrace beyond. A park? A football ground? A demolition site? The street-plan gave nothing away; the vacancy remained vacant; only that sense of impending space grew as I approached the end of the street; and then, narrowly avoiding the milk-van which, in a less exuberant condition, emerged aghast from Upper Church Street, I would top the barely perceptible rise, ease myself around the corner, and find before me one of the most splendid *tours de force* of European design, John Wood the Younger's Royal Crescent, which is really no more than a terrace of speculatively built houses, but looks like a magnificently symmetrical palace. I have seen visitors stopped in their tracks when, reaching that same spot on Brock Street, they have discovered this glorious scene in front of them: but they may only have been stunned by my own simultaneous passage around the corner, blaring joyous music on the wrong side of the road.

## 58  *Little spas*

There are little spas all over Europe, and some of them are charming. For example west of Rostock, on the Baltic coast of Germany, there stands the small watering-place called Bad Doberan, where we saw a little train chuff by back on page 245. This was once a summer retreat of the Grand Duke Friedrich Franz I of Mecklenburg, who at the end of the eighteenth century built the first of all German sea-bathing resorts on the coast a few miles away. 'The idea of a fashionable Bathing place in Mecklenburg!' ironically scoffed Jane Austen – 'How can people pretend to be fashionable or to bathe out of England!' But both the Bathing place and the spa flourished, and are delightful still. Bad Doberan is the classic spa in miniature. Graceful little pavilions ornament the civic park, and the Kurhotel, two doors away from the Grand Duke's own palace, is a very sublimation of a spa hotel. I had an attic room when I was there in 1993, low-beamed and cosy, and when I opened my window upon the spire of the minster among its great trees, and the rose-gardens of the palace along the road, I felt I could almost see His Grace himself, with his ladies and his friends, promenading in the evening down below, serenaded by a string quartet perhaps, and gossiping about inessential courtly scandals.

For in their heyday most spas had their own style or class of clientele. Baden-Baden in Germany has always cultivated the grand manner, and is still a resort of the very rich, who can alternate between the baths and the casino, and sometimes weigh themselves before dinner to see how much they can allow themselves to eat. Bath, having been the centre of all things modish in the eighteenth century, was in my childhood an exemplar of dingy respectability, where aged assistants in black suits waited with hooded wheelchairs at the railway station for their patients to arrive. And no spas were more specialized in custom than the minute watering-places which thrived in Victorian Wales: if Llanwrtyd Wells and Llangammarch were the favoured resort of Nonconformists, no self-respecting Welsh Anglican hypochondriac would go anywhere but Llandrindod.

## 59  At the seaside

In earlier times going to the seaside, too, was seen primarily as a health cure, and sea-bathing as a kind of therapy. 'Dr Brighton', they used to call the first of the salt-water bathing-places, on the Sussex coast in England, and Abbazia, now Opatija, the Habsburg Empire's own Brighton on the Adriatic coast of Croatia, was founded by a medical entrepreneur and officially proclaimed a Health Resort by a congress of doctors in 1885. Even in my time people used to go to Weston-super-Mare, on the English coast of the Bristol Channel, specifically because it was believed there were health-giving qualities to the ozone that came out of its mud. The Communist Governments of eastern Europe thought in the same way: the modern concrete hotels that were built for trade unionists and their families along the coasts of the Black Sea, the Baltic and the Adriatic were built not just to give them fun, but to make them healthy for further exertions in the factories. 'Strength Through Joy', as the Nazis had put it – and the ultimate pleasure-plant would have been their own never finished development called Prora, on the German Baltic island of Rügen, which would have housed 20,000 communal holiday-makers in one huge block, and, having been converted into a barracks, remains today a ghastly memorial to totalitarian tourism.

Whatever the reason, seaside towns, like spas, were often places of fashionable resort – San Sebastian indeed, one of the most handsome of them, became the summer residence of the Spanish court. If they have mostly become less modish now, as mass tourism overwhelms them, and are one and all dismal out of season, often enough they remain architecturally pleasant. Of all the European seaside resorts, Clifton in Ireland to Zlatni Pyasâtsi in Bulgaria (a.k.a. Golden Sands), I think my favourite is Trouville in France. The English invented the modern salt-water resort, but the French turned it into a genre of art, and it was at Trouville in Normandy that Monet and Bonnard first realized the beauty in the stoop of the child beside his sandcastle, and the preen of the promenading ladies. Trouville has long been overtaken by racier resorts, and diminished rather by the oil tanks and apartment blocks of Le Havre across its estuary, but that old aesthetic of the seaside is still recognizable there in all its tangy charm. Exuberantly the old hotels and villas still cluster around the beach, like so many jolly old gentlefolk in lace and grey toppers, out to enjoy themselves. Some are encrusted with coils, domes and classical flourishes. Some are half-timbered. There are houses built like castles, like fairy palaces, like Persian caravanserais. The rooftops of old Trouville are punctuated with golden birds, pineapples, crescent moons, spindles, metal flowers and urns, and all the way up the hillside behind the beach the mansions stand in majesty among their trees, unabashed by shifts of taste or society, and still looking, behind their ornamental gates and protective shady gardens, almost voluptuously comfortable. Trouville is wonderfully *composed*. When, in the years after the Second World War, unexploded mines and bombs occasionally turned up on the beach, the municipality officially classified them as '*Objets Bizarres*'.

## 60  *The ski-culture*

Another thing that brings Europe together is sport. Hundreds of thousands of people cross and recross the continent to watch games and contests from wind-surfing to car-racing, to have a go at water-skiing or tobogganing or playing golf or paragliding. They go to Switzerland for the Cresta Run, to the Isle of Man for the motor-bike races, to Italy for the Siena horse-race, to Spain for the Pamplona bull-run, and every single journey makes some part of Europe a little more familiar to the rest. The universally shared passion for soccer has not only cross-fertilized the nations by the transfer of professional players, but has accustomed many parts of Europe to hooligans from else-where. And the late-twentieth-century ski-culture has made what is almost a manner of life equally familiar to the people of many nations. Fortunately it is to my mind an enthusiasm that beautifies almost everything it touches, down to the very sleaziest of après-ski discos, down to the most unprepossess-ing of jumped-up Hooray Henry enthusiasts, because of its innate elegance.

There is the almost unfailing elegance of setting, for a start, and there is the elegance of the apparatus: the skis look so supple, the helmets are so bright and shiny, and there is nothing more functionally proper than your modern toboggan, with its steering-wheel and its brakes. The sounds of the culture are very satisfying – crunch of snow beneath racing skis, clunk of chair-lift passing pylons, glug of Ovomalt on the sunlit decks of mountain restaurants, sweet laughter of babes-in-arms as they execute particularly demanding slaloms at Kinderland. The movements are lovely. I am invariably seduced by the passage of the young bravoes crouched double and rubbery as they slam themselves down the pistes, but the endless calm motion of the chair-lifts can also be beautiful, and I never tire of watching the peculiar walk demanded of people wearing the modern kind of ski-boot – a sort of spacewalk, part dance, part goose-step, which is accompanied by intriguing creaking and clicking noises.

Helicopters whirr by in ski-places, and paragliders, like pink, red or yellow eagles, float around the snow-slopes, or come swooping down the valleys casting their eccentric shadows below them. Sometimes they look almost transparent, membranous against the sun. Sometimes they give me the feeling that they must be circling always out of sight up there, night and day like angels.

## 61 *Inter-crime*

On page 28, you may perhaps recall, I was robbed of my possessions by motor-bike thugs in Palermo. The city police took me on a leisurely tour of thieves' quarters by patrol car, but admitted that it was a waste of time, because by then my passport and credit cards were almost certainly in the hands of the Mafia. So far as I know this was my only direct contact with the organized crime systems which apparently extend over most of Europe and form another potent layer of the internet. The very word 'Mafia', which used to refer specifically to the Sicilian criminal guild, has now become a generic term for institutionalized skulduggery in many parts of Europe, and especially for the tide of criminality surging out of the old Soviet Union. Since that incident in Palermo long ago I have fortunately stayed clear of this amorphous subworld, having no arms to sell, no currency to launder and no hunger for cocaine: but from Dublin to Vilnius, and down to Sarajevo, I have often sensed its agents prowling round me.

It was always so, so the French historian Fernand Braudel says. Even in the Middle Ages capitalist skulduggery transcended national boundaries, and smart practitioners could always rig the odds in their own favour. They manipulated credit, traded bad money for good, and 'grabbed up everything worth taking – land, real estate, rents'. There were godfathers about even then.

## 62  *Spheres of influence*

The phrase 'spheres of influence' was invented as an imperialist device, and during my time in Europe it has had baleful connotations as a euphemism for the impositions of the Cold War. However there have also been beneficent spheres of influence within the continent – realms in which nations have affected each other without brutality, by force of example or presence, and thus helped to make Europe a little more of an entity. Often, of course, it has been a rich or powerful nation affecting a poorer one. All over Europe to this day countless Hotel Bristols remember the lavish spending of the fourth Earl of Bristol, Bishop of Derry, scattering largesse, injecting wealth into the local economies while he trundled around Europe in his coach-and-six as the swankiest and most eccentric of the English milords. For centuries the French, as the most cultivated of the Europeans, distributed around Europe mementoes of their passing presence. And most of the greater European nations have launched into the continental consciousness works of art which are representative of their own particular culture but are now the property of all.

The greatest creations of art, music and literature rise above national identities, but are often rooted in them nevertheless. Like it or not, Beethoven is undeniably German, Shakespeare indisputably English. Everyone identifies Michelangelo with Italy, Chopin with Poland, Ibsen with Norway, Camoëns with Portugal, Rembrandt with Holland, Voltaire with France. Books like *The Good Soldier Švejk, Don Quixote, Buddenbrooks, À la recherche du temps perdu*, *Oliver Twist* represent for millions of readers the truest essence of their patron nations. Yet at the same time they are an undeniable part of the common European heritage, familiar to educated Europeans everywhere, and linking them in a stronger bond than any political arrangement. I remember once standing bemused before a theatre poster in Stockholm trying to puzzle out the name of the play it advertised – *Som Ni Behagar* by W. Shakespeare. A passing Swede caught my eye. '*As You Like It*,' he said – 'the one with the melancholy Jaques.'

## 63  *Italianate*

Shakespeare frequently took his plots from Italian originals, of course. For centuries Italy has been lodged in the imagination of all Europe, and in my time has constituted a special kind of influence. Football, food, clothes, shoes, cars, opera – innumerable aspects of life, all over Europe, are Italianately tinged. At Christmas-time the trains of Europe are full of Italians, going home for the holiday, because Italians have settled, too, in every corner of the continent. Although they generally assimilate easily, and soon become part of local communities, still they maintain their links with Italy, and often go back to live there in their old age. There can be no big city of Europe without its Italian restaurant, and Italian restaurateurs were always the first to open their doors when the Iron Curtain dissolved and foreign cuisines were permitted in the countries of the East. To homesick travellers who have eaten their fill of borscht and dried cod, exhausted themselves trying to speak Latvian or Polish, feel themselves hopelessly alien to the Croatian temperament or the Icelandic scale of values – to such weary wanderers stumbling upon a Luna Caprese, with its familiar decor of fishing-nets and pictures of Vesuvius, can be like crossing the threshold of home.

In South Wales the first Italians were a pair of brothers named Bracchi, who went from the Po valley in 1890 to open a café in the tumultuously booming South Wales coalfield. It was a great place to make money in those days, and opportunists were pouring in from everywhere to get their share of the pickings. The Bracchis were like saloon-keepers in a California gold rush. They prospered, were followed by many more Italians, and have left behind them a thriving progeny of café proprietors, ice-cream sellers, grocers and video-shop renters, almost all claiming descent, if not from the same family, at least from the same part of Italy. It is they who gave South Wales

much of its legendary fizz – perhaps some of its physiognomy too, for you
often see young men there who have a decidedly Mediterranean look, if not
in the bone structure, at least in the eye and the strut. To this day the South
Wales Italians and their shops are known affectionately as 'Bracchis'.

## 64  *Frenchified*

In my half-century the influences of France upon the rest of Europe have
been mostly pleasurable – and I write as one unbeguiled by the songs of
Edith Piaf, the boulevards of Baron Haussmann, the furniture of Louis XIV,
the vainglory of Napoleon, the conceit of Charles de Gaulle, people who
turn ideas into movements, and for that matter ideas themselves when too
pressingly articulated. Cultural Frenchness has generally been a blessing to
Europe. A glorious language which long remained the diplomatic language
of the continent (almost, as the phrase seems to imply, its lingua franca,
though actually the original lingua franca was mostly Italian). A cuisine which
was until recently the ultimate to which cooks of all European nations aspired,
until it lost many admirers by attenuating itself into the briefly fashionable
*nouvelle cuisine* – the best of all French cuisines, for my own tastes, but hardly
the thing for those hearty gastronomes who used to thrive on rich French
sauces, hearty French meats and heavy French red wines. Architecture which
cast its spell across all the nations, so that even Bucharest used to look French,
and loved to call itself the Paris of the East. Spacious town plans based upon
dominant boulevards, and copied by many militant regimes on the principle
that bullets do not go around corners. Furniture which spoke always of olden
courtly times, spindly gilded elaborations of woodwork which were copied
everywhere and were considered just the thing for weddings. Cars which
were boldly original – the Citroën DS with its hydraulic suspension, lifting
its chassis over awkward bumps at the touch of a button; the primitive little
2CV which became, in the 1960s, the livery-carriage of the ecological and
conservationist classes. Films which gradually found their way out of the art
cinemas of the continent into the general public awareness, and made some
of their actors household names throughout Europe. French poodles. French
letters, which is what an earlier generation of Britons used to call condoms
(and an earlier generation of Frenchmen called English umbrellas). French
kissing. French cricket, which is what English schoolboys used to play in the
schoolyard at break. 'Pardon my French', as an English apology for bad

language. French defence, in which Black replies with P-K3 to a White opening move of P-K4. French flu, which is what Arthur Koestler called an excessive fondness for all things French. And fashion.

## 65  *At the salon*

In my time the French fashion industry hasn't been quite what it was, having been challenged by upstarts of one sort or another in every part of the world, not least in Italy and Spain – and England, where the wild fashion of the streets in the 1960s not only offered a fresh way of dressing smartly, but also gave a new cachet to the hitherto fusty reputation of the English. *Haute couture* gave way to ready-made clothes even in many of the richest households. Even so, my one incursion into the world of Parisian high fashion was a fairly heady experience for me. I had been invited to write about one of the summer collections for an American newspaper, and sat in the front row among the condescending New York buyers and unbelievably ugly priestesses of American fashion journalism who could between them, I was assured, make or break any collection. How awful they looked, draped in their furs, red-taloned, emaciated to the point of grotesquerie, while all about them graceful exponents of the art of French allure glided silkily around the room and along the catwalk (it was before the day of the sullen strut and pout). The audience otherwise seemed to be mostly composed, to my bemused eye, of characters from Proust; around the doorways seamstresses and lovely models clustered; the room, which appears in my memory to have been fabulously hung with chandeliers, was also extremely expensively perfumed.

I thought it all seemed, like so many French influences, a trifle *passé* – over the hump, striving with great charm and delicacy to sustain the traditions of a greater past, while making obeisance to cruder times. The clothes were so sumptuous! The prices were doubtless so astronomical! The models were so aristocratic! It reminded me of the old *Jean Bart* at Toulon.

## 66  *Anglicized*

The British (or the English, as continental Europeans almost invariably call them) were riding very high indeed when my European experience began. Half-ruined though they were by the Second World War, they were more admired and popular in Europe than they had ever been since their triumphs in the Napoleonic conflicts. People did not realize how poor they had become, or how their importance in the wider world had declined. They alone had stayed the terrible course against Hitler, from the first to the last, and it had been their inspiration that had kept the hope of freedom alive in Europe.

During the next fifty years their prestige inexorably declined, and they showed themselves maddeningly uncertain whether they wanted to be Europeans or not: but it seems to me an odd truth that of all the European nations, well into the 1990s, they still cast their influence most potently upon the others. Their affairs seemed to be the most interesting to everyone else, so that the scandals and romances of British royalty dominated tabloid headlines throughout the continent. Their rock music set the pace. Their football clubs, though no longer the most successful, still attracted cult followings everywhere. Approximations of English pubs were popular all over Europe; 'As long as the sun shines,' said the official guide to Vilnius, in Lithuania, in 1996, 'The Pub will be THE place to be', and in the small city of Flensburg, on the border between Germany and Denmark, a saloon advertised itself as 'the best English pub in town'. The ambivalent allure of London, its racy street life, its harsh social glitter, its incomparable theatre and its music still brought thousands of continentals across the Channel in curiosity and excitement.

Odder still, there remained like an echo over Europe the reputation of the English as phlegmatic and self-controlled. There was still cachet to the old-school, upper-class English style. There were still men all over Europe who dressed in the supposed English manner, bore themselves in the allegedly English way, paid tribute to legendary English values (the stiff upper lip, for instance) which the English themselves had long mocked or abandoned. In 1996 one of the great French best-sellers of the year was a comic-strip compilation, *L'Affaire Francis Blake*, about a pair of pipe-smoking, gentlemanly English intelligence agents who saved the kingdom from ignominy in a setting rich in respectful butlers and old-school policemen – 'Good Heavens!' Englishmen still habitually exclaimed in this affectionate memorial, or 'My word!', or even 'By Jove!' An expensive English car still carried prestige in Europe, and, however despised were English football louts and drunken English soldiers, educated English families still found themselves, almost anywhere in Europe, greeted with respect.

Their language helped. It had become Europe's true lingua franca now, besides infiltrating many other languages with its idioms (*Le Weekend*, for instance, *Il Weekend, der Weekend*), but in many minds it also helped to confuse the English with the Americans – even worldly Frenchmen still talked about 'the Anglo-Saxons' as though the two people were more or less the same. In 1994 the most popular boys' name in France and Belgium was Kevin; in the Netherlands the most popular names were Rob, Rick and Tom. Whatever the reasons – real or specious, hard-headed or nostalgic – everyone knew the English still, and from their offshore island they cast their influences unmistakably across the continent. As for the English themselves, they were willy-nilly beginning to lose their inherited contempt for almost everything on the other side of the Channel.

## 67 *From 'Dover to Munich', 1861, by C. S. Calverley*

> Bed at Ostend at 5 A.M.
>> Breakfast at 6, and train 6.30,
> Tickets to Königswinter (mem.
>> The seats unutterably dirty).
>
> And onward thro' those dreary flats
>> We move, and scanty space to sit on,
> Flanked by stout girls with steeple hats,
>> And waists that paralyse a Briton; –
>
> By many a tidy little town,
>> Where tidy little Fraus sit knitting;
> (The men's pursuits are, lying down,
>> Smoking perennial pipes, and spitting).

## 68 *Imperial memories*

During many periods of history the English actually ruled parts of Europe beyond their own frontiers. They still rule, in a manner of speaking, Scotland, Wales, Gibraltar, Northern Ireland, the Channel Islands and the Isle of Man, but they once had imperial footholds in France, the Balearics, Heligoland, Malta, Cyprus and the Ionian Islands. In Corfu people still played cricket at the end of the twentieth century. In Valletta they still drank at the Britannia

pub. Even in the Republic of Ireland, which the English had found much
the most difficult of their overseas possessions in Europe, their ways were
still sometimes honoured. The Germans and Scandinavians who by then
owned big properties in Ireland eagerly conformed to Anglo-Irish patterns
of behaviour, and the American Irish who stayed in country-house hotels,
vociferously though they often claimed kinship to fiery patriots of the past,
were evidently unashamed to be cosseted in the halls not of Tara but of the
old evicting classes.

In Dublin only a year or two ago I happened to find myself in St Patrick's
Cathedral when they were holding a memorial service for Battle of Britain
Day. Above us the helms and banners of long-gone Knights of St Patrick
gleamed; around us coolly stirred all the rituals of Anglicanism, the surpliced
clerks, the bowing vergers, the sweet music of the anthem; and here and
there in the congregation stood the last veterans of the King's Irishmen,
medals heaving when they bravely belted out the hymns, shoulders back as
they turned to the East for the Nicene Creed – for all the world as though
they were declaring their belief not just in the Almighty but in the loyal and
heroic past. I could not help remembering that when Hitler committed
suicide the President of the Irish Republic sent his condolences to the German
Embassy in Dublin: but when I told my hotel porter about the service at
St Patrick's, he said tolerantly, 'Oh, they have all manner of things in
there – they're very ecumenical.' Even Guinness, after all, that glorious
black-and-cream icon of the Irish legend, was created by a family of impec-
cably monarchist and Anglican credential, rich in peerages.

## 69 *The Hill of Victory*

By now most people in Europe have probably forgotten that the English
ever had European possessions, and remember only the part that English
arms have played in the history of the continent – the long roster of wars
which has brought English soldiers across the Channel, English sailors around
all the seas of Europe, English airmen in all its skies, to fight in battles
disastrous and victorious – Salamanca to Narvik, Crete to Walcheren, North
Cape to Cape Trafalgar. The last and most honourable of the victories was
sealed on a sandy patch of heathland, in the lee of a low pine-forested hill,
within sight of the ancient towers of Lüneburg in Germany, on 4 May 1945:
the first great surrender of Hitler's armies, when Field Marshal Sir Bernard

Montgomery accepted the capitulation of all German forces in northern Germany, Denmark and Holland. Not many people seem to go there now, few guidebooks identify the spot, and all that marks it is a big boulder inscribed in German with the words '*Nicht Wieder Krieg*' – 'No More War'.

It was more than half a century before I myself got to Tiemeloberg, Montgomery's Hill of Victory, and there was not a soul around. The silence was absolute, but for the birds and the wind. All the easier was it to imagine the scene there when the blackly leather-coated German emissaries arrived at Montgomery's field headquarters to submit to their conquerors. I could see the battered British trucks parked this way and that around the rutted heathland – tanks, perhaps, littered about the laager – dust and sand everywhere, and those throaty coughs of tank engines – dispatch riders skidding and revving as they came and went along the sand tracks – not very smart British troopers watching the arrival of the enemy in his beflagged Mercedes as they might watch the arrival of the devil himself – and in the heart of it all, beneath a Union Jack, Montgomery's shabby caravan with the Field Marshal himself, in his old black beret, waiting at its steps with a clipboard in his hand. He had pursued these people, slowly, carefully and inexorably, seldom taking a risk, during three long years of war, from the borders of Egypt, through Sicily, Italy, France, Belgium and the Netherlands to this stern Baltic heathland of Germany. He was not in the mood for niceties. A brisk exchange of salutes; a short presentation of conditions inside the caravan; a session with the photographers in a hastily prepared tent; Montgomery finds his reading-glasses and the surrender is signed.

Was it like that? Perhaps not. I have imagined it all. The face I remember best from the pictures of the surrender is the face of Montgomery's chief intelligence officer, and he was not at all a victorious-looking figure in his spectacles and unbecoming khaki beret, looking less like a soldier than a university don – which, as it happens, he was. Tiemeloberg is not a very glorious kind of place. It is no Waterloo or Blenheim, and no grand obelisk remembers what happened there. The soldiers assembled there that day were hardly a heroic army, the crumpled troopers only anxious to get home, the plain teetotal Field Marshal in his rough battledress. None of them much wanted to be on Lüneburg Heath: but there, all the same, the homely British consummated the long and bitter duty by which, at the end of their epic insular history, they saved Europe by their example.

70  *How Montgomery greeted the German envoys when
they first arrived at Lüneburg Heath (from Martin Gilbert's*
Second World War, *1989)*

'Who are these men?' Montgomery asked. 'What do they want?'

If they did not agree [to his terms], Montgomery told them, 'I shall go on with
the war, and will be delighted to do so, and am ready,' and he went on to warn: 'All
your soldiers will be killed.'

71  *Expatriates*

I was walking one day along a path near Deya, on the west coast of the
Spanish island of Majorca, when suddenly there appeared out of a tributary
track an unmistakable figure - Robert Graves the English poet, who was the
best-known resident of the place, and who smiled at me a brief Gorgonzola
smile before striding off in the opposite direction (in case, I dare say, I was
going to ask him for his autograph). A familiar phenomenon of Europe since
the Second World War has been the settlement of English expatriates,
escaping their native conditions in Tuscany, Normandy, the Dordogne,
southern Spain and the Balearics, Ireland and even Wales. But there used to
be even more of them, all over Europe, including hard-working communities
of businesspeople in some unlikely places. The present Danish Embassy in
Riga, for example, used to be the English Club there, and so many English
lived in the city that Napoleon sneered at it as a suburb of London. The
Genoese Association Football and Cricket Club was founded by the local
English community; the city's famous soccer club still spells itself in the
English way – 'Genoa' rather than 'Genova'. Any old Baedeker will tell you
where in Lausanne or Copenhagen the English had their church, which
English doctor was available in Funchal, where to buy the London newspapers
in Cannes, or which was the most fashionably frequented English teashop –
thus covering, in small italic print, all the principal requirements of the British
abroad. For me the archetypal expatriate was dear old Max Beerbohm, 'The
Incomparable Max', that urbane and elegant epitome of the old-school
Englishman, who lived for years at Rapallo on the west coast of Italy; and
in 1993 I set out to pursue his memory there.

On the wrong day Rapallo offers a recognizable likeness of hell, especially when you have driven there by the most loveless road in Europe – the *autostrada* from the French frontier, down which a million juggernauts monotonously lumber through ill-lit rough-hewn tunnels, swarmed about by ill-tempered Fiats and idiot Porsches from Milan. All the more poignant it was to find on one of the noisiest edges of the place the villa in which Max lived and died. It was a large, oblong, yellowish, not very inviting building, hemmed about in a suburban way by others of the same kind, with traffic going past all day. Nothing could have been much further from the tranquil idyll, vine-trellised, peasant-soothed, olive-shaded, cicada-serenaded, that is generally supposed to be the expatriate destiny. Max Beerbohm had few Italian friends, and never did learn to speak good Italian. First to last, he remained the quintessential Edwardian Englishman, and as such his passage through Rapallo, though it lasted for nearly fifty years, has left few traces. A prophet soon loses honour, in a country not his own, and the sight of the Villino Chiaro, the commemorative plaque upon its wall to be read only at peril of Fiat-annihilation, seemed to me a very parable of exile.

In Max's time a ceaseless flow of English people passed through Rapallo, but when did a wandering Briton, I wondered, last knock on the door of the Villino Chiaro, confidently expecting a welcome? The house looked well-kept still, but there was nothing about it to speak of English connections. If there had been but a Penguin book on a *chaise longue*, or the merest suggestion of Earl Grey on the afternoon air, I might have knocked on the door myself; but as it was I skulked away, vainly hoping that some elderly Oxbridge voice, thin and silvery, would pursue me up the alley – 'I say, you look a little lost, can I offer you a cup of tea or anything?'

## 72 *The regime of Richard Burton, the explorer, as a resident of Trieste, from* The World *magazine, London, 1878*

We have formed a little 'mess', with fifteen friends at the *table d'hôte* of the Hôtel de la Ville, where we get a good dinner and a pint of country wine made on the hillock for a florin and a half. By this plan we escape the bore of housekeeping, and are relieved from the curse of domesticity . . . At dinner we hear the news, if any, take our coffee, cigarettes, and *kirsch* outside the hotel, then go homewards to read ourselves to sleep, and tomorrow *da capo*.

## 73 *Cultural colonists*

Sometimes the expatriate English have created genuine cultural colonies in
Europe. One such is the Portuguese island of Madeira, nearer Africa than
Europe but unquestionably a European island. The English connection was
originally economic, entrepreneurs having settled there, as they had settled
in Portugal itself and in the sherry country of Spain, to gain control of the
wine trade. Several English families remained important in the Madeira wine
business at the end of the twentieth century, but they had long before
extended their activities to be more general merchants and traders, and in
particular they had come to dominate the tourist business. They gave the
island an English veneer, very comforting to well-heeled English holiday-
makers, and although millions of tourists of other nationalities now come to
the island, the English influence is still potent. Whether you take a ride in a
sightseeing bus, buy a bottle of Madeira, or even spend a morning at the
island's magnificent botanical gardens, you are in some way paying tribute
to Madeira's English connections. Above all Reid's, the island's most famous
hotel, is English-owned, and remains assiduous in its Englishness. Afternoon
tea there is an archetypically decorous affair, served to piano music on the
veranda above the sea, and those un-English tourists who are brave enough
to experience it may often be seen trying hard to comport to English
convention, in their manner of crossing their legs, calling for the waitress,
spreading the cream on their scones, or deciding which ought to go into the
cup first, the milk or the tea.

## 74 *All the rage*

In my grandfather's time, before the First World War, Germanity was all
the rage in many parts of Europe, because of the distinction of German
scholarship, the genius of German musicianship, the energy of German
science and industry, the professionalism of German arms. What could be
more proper than the statue of Baron von Eschwege, architect of the crazy
Pena Castle at Sintra outside Lisbon, which portrays him standing on a
commanding ridge beside his masterpiece dressed in the full Teutonic armour
of a knight-errant? Only recently united in nationhood, Germany was the
emblem of European modernity, and the young Kaiser Wilhelm II was

widely admired. In Corfu there is a hill still called the Kaiser's Throne, because he loved the view from its summit, and one of the island's great tourist attractions is the Akhillion, his holiday villa there, rich in Wilhelmine statuary and decor, and equipped with one of the saddles he preferred to sit on when he was writing letters or doodling designs for battleships. When he paid a visit to Budapest in 1897 he expressed his admiration for the burgeoning city, but wished there were a few more public statues: in the next ten years thirty-seven went up, most of them still lording it there. Kaiser Bill left a pleasant memorial too in the little city of Ålesund on the Norwegian coast. Like many Germans he loved Norway, which he believed to be a natural German sphere of influence, frequented as it was by properly Nordic gods. In 1904, while he was cruising its waters in his white steam-yacht *Hohenzollern*, the centre of Ålesund was almost entirely destroyed by fire. The young Emperor sprang into action. He gave large sums of money for the civic reconstruction, and he recruited an army of young architects, most of them German, to rebuild the town and rehouse its ten thousand homeless people. They did the job in three years, and the permanent result is a delightfully incongruous city of the fjords decorated in lavish *Jugendstil*, Germany's own version of art nouveau. Turrets and gables ornament fish warehouses, dragons and water-chimeras enliven burghers' quayside houses, and although nowadays local guidebooks ungratefully fail to mention the sponsor of these happy surprises, at the time it was all thought to be a characteristically German gesture of enlightened generosity.

## 75 *Valhalla*

In those days many a foreigner made the pilgrimage to Germany's own Valhalla, a temple of pride in the Doric mode built on a high bluff above the Danube near Regensburg. It is still there, sparkling white and lordly above the great river, and approached by 358 steps of gleaming marble. It is a paean in stone and statuary to all the great figures of German art, scholarship, statesmanship and war – all sorts, all conditions, so long as they had contributed to the German tradition: for its builder, Ludwig II of Bavaria, believed that the German civilization, like the Greek, was something universal, to which anyone worthy could be admitted. Erasmus is here, for instance (born in Amsterdam). The Empress Maria Theresa is here (born in Vienna). There are Swiss holy men, and a couple of Dutch admirals, and several generals of the Russian armies, and the Venerable Bede. Whether or not they all thought of themselves as German, they are consecrated German for ever in this hall of the heroes (its floor lavishly tiled in marble, its sky-blue ceiling upheld by caryatids, its oak doors plated with bronze).

A century ago people like my grandfather would wander awestruck about this place, marvelling at the glories of German culture – 'noble, patient, deep, pious and solid', as the Scots historian Thomas Carlyle called it. Of course one would find the field marshals – Gneisenau, von Moltke, Blücher – and a sufficiency of grim Teutonic statesmen. But Mozart was there too, and Beethoven, and Schiller, and Goethe, and a host of philosophers and scientists and theologians: Germans every one, in the sense that the German culture produced them, and they enriched the German culture in return – and in enriching Germany, my grandfather doubtless thought, they enriched all Europe too.

## 76  Un-influence

But look what history was to do to the German reputation! Before he died my grandfather had lost his only son to German arms, and for years he declined to listen even to his beloved Bach; by the time I got to Valhalla my chief response was surprise to find that the latest recruit to the pantheon was Albert Einstein, a Jew. The Germany that had once seemed a model of liberal and generous progress, the patron of poets and musicians, the reconstructor of Ålesund, had long squandered its assets. Even in the 1990s, when it was once more the richest and most powerful State in Europe, nobody wanted to be like the Germans. The Germans might be the best footballers, make the best cars, produce the best tennis-players, have the strongest currency, but nobody wanted to be like them. Nobody suggested that German, spoken by 80 million people in the heart of the continent, would ever be Europe's lingua franca. Nobody could even identify a German style, except in war, economics and automobiles, and few foreigners chose to spend their holidays in Germany. Fifty years after the death of Hitler and the extinction of his mad regime, when a new generation of Germans had come to maturity and the German Republic had established itself as one of the stablest and most democratic States in Europe, still nobody wanted to be much like the Germans.

In Leipzig once I was standing near the front of a box-office queue, in a long line of courteous and well-disciplined citizens, when a tall young German walked bumptiously in, pushed his way to the front, and demanded tickets. He got them, too. My blood atavistically boiled, and as he swaggered past me on his way out I poked out my foot and successfully tripped him. The Leipzigers in the queue smiled collusively at me as he dusted himself down and aggrievedly withdrew: perhaps they did not much want to be like themselves.

## 77  I clapped too

More than most European peoples, when Germans travel abroad they prefer to stick together. Like the English, they have established cultural colonies in Europe – places that they peacefully dominate with the willing collaboration of the indigenes. Ischia, for instance, has been so enthusiastically adopted by Germans that German is its second language, and its very public attitudes have been half-Germanized. No doubt the island's native calm forms part of the therapy for the multitudinous *Hausfrauen* and their ample husbands who come here year after year for the volcanic cures: after a stimulating sauna in the morning, a day's undemanding hike in the hills, or a potter around the piazzas, returning to a soothing sulphurous bath or mud treatment at the hotel spa before dinner (with perhaps a quick call to Dortmund thrown in, to reassure the blood pressure that everything's all right at the office).

I had a very German experience when I was lunching one day at a little café on the central mountain of the island, Mount Epomeo. A dog was tethered above the café, on an uncomfortably short rope which kept its legs tangled and constantly kicking. The Germans at the next table were upset by this, and asked the café proprietor to give the animal a longer leash. When he did so they clapped their approval, and presently all around the place people were applauding. Half of them had not set eyes on the dog, and had no idea what the applause was for, but they were all fellow Germans, and as they clapped they nodded to each other and smiled in a comradely way across the tables. I clapped too.

## 78  Certainties

For if we fellow Europeans do not always wish to emulate the Germans, we
still recognize those patient, solid elements in the German character, and it
can still be a pleasure to come across pockets of Germanness left behind by
history elsewhere in the continent. Most of them were eliminated after the
Second World War, when the German minorities which had been among
the causes of the tragedy were repatriated, or shipped off to labour camps in
Russia. A few were so deeply entrenched in their settings, had been there
so long, were so much a part of the local society's fabric, that they survived.
One such forms a dwindling minority to this day in the Romanian city of
Braşov, ex-Stalin, né Kronstadt, which was founded by the Teutonic Knights
during their eastern adventurings in the thirteenth century. Braşov does not
look very German now, except for the remains of its city walls and a few
ancient buildings that have survived the wars, but it has one gloriously
Germanic monument, fine to come across in the 1990s in shambled and
unpredictable Transylvania. The Black Church, built in the fifteenth century,
is the largest church in Romania, and stands with stern Gothic confidence
in the main square of the city. Inside the church one memorial, in particular,
represents the nature of the Saxons who lived, worked and fought in this
city for so many generations. It is the tomb of a seventeenth-century German
soldier, in full armour like the architect von Eschwege in Portugal, magnificently moustached and bearing the uncompromising inscription 'I KNOW
AND I BELIEVE'.

## 79  There for the crack

Among the European nations in my half of the twentieth century, then,
these have been the great influencers, affecting the way the rest of the continent
thought, looked, dressed, ate, played, earned its living and entertained itself:
the Germans, the French, the Italians and the English. Others exerted
influences of other kinds. The Scandinavians, for a few decades, not only
introduced Europe to new ways of furnishing its rooms, but also seemed to
set the guiding example of social progress. The Dutch, by their astonishing
industrial and commercial acumen, dictated far more of what Europe did
than most of Europe ever realized. Customs and styles of the Spaniards were

taken across Europe by millions of returning holiday-makers, and so were the Greek habits of drinking resinated wine and breaking plates in celebration. The Irish became legendary among the guitar-strumming Aquarian youth of Europe – I once saw a young German couple standing on the threshold of a Dublin pub and gazing at the fiddle-drum-and-whistle band inside, with its Guinnesses at its elbows, as though they were seeing emissaries from paradise.

By the last decades of the century, in fact, the Irish were all over Europe. 'Look at all the new boutiques,' said my cicerone proudly to me as she showed me round the streets of Tallinn in Estonia, recently emancipated from Soviet rule, 'look at all the bright new shops. That's a new bookshop. That's a television store. And that' – she pointed to a building under reconstruction – 'that will be the Irish pub.' By the mid-1990s there was hardly a big city without one, generally in some less expensive part of town, with its statutory Guinness sign in its windows, its warm and fusty atmosphere within, its generally youthful and boisterous clientele, and genuine Irishmen often behind the bar. What could induce such people, I once asked a Donegal barman in Paris, to leave the fun and comradeship of the merriest country in Europe and try their luck in often dismal side-streets in remote foreign cities? He said sure you know the Irish – we're all a bit mad. And what made his own pub so attractive to its evidently well-satisfied customers, crowding every corner of the bar and talking loudly in exuberant French? You know how it is, he said, they come for the crack.

## 80   *Beside the swan-house*

Three great influences, though, fell upon Europe from outside the continent, and have left their symptoms still. For a start there was Russia – the Russia both of the tsars and of the Marxists. The best place to contemplate the cultural effects of Old Russia is Riga, the capital of Latvia, if only because for much of its history it was actually *part* of Old Russia – Russia's third city, in fact. In a park in the centre of the city there is a wonderfully Russian memento – a wooden swan-house beside a small lake, with wide eaves, painted in the bright crude colours that Russians used to love, and rather crooked with age. Just the sight of it makes me think of Russian lovers under the trees, Russian officers strolling the paths in fur-collared greatcoats, Turgenev, Pushkin, troikas, exiled intellectuals, impoverished landowners,

serfs, students with bombs, and everything else that the memory of Old
Russia conjures in the minds of romantic readers of Russian literature. Much
of Riga looks like a tsarist city still, with its handsome terraced streets, the
skyline of its towers and steeples, and the castle by the river that now houses
the President of Latvia but once housed the Russian Governor-General.
Strung along the coast a few miles away is Jurmala, in the days of the tsars a
favourite seaside retreat for the St Petersburg gentry. Clapboard villas shelter
there among the woods, with outbuildings for horses and servants, and there
is a long pedestrian street of shops for strolling along and gossiping, and there
are coffee-shops where the samovars used to bubble, and suburban railway
stations where Anna Kareninas could stand tragically in the steam. 'Next
door to the Kurhaus at Majorenhof,' comfortingly says my Baedeker *Russia*,
1914, 'is the Sanatorium of Dr Maximovitch.'

Helsinki is good, too, if you like this kind of thing. It was once the capital
of a Russian Autonomous Grand Duchy, and for all its differences with
modern Russia it has by no means abandoned its heritage. An elderly
steam-yacht that cruises its harbour is called *Nicolai II*, and has the white
eagle of the Romanovs on its funnel. Old-school Russian restaurants abound,
not to mention old-school Russian rogues. You can buy Russian icons in
antique shops, and old postcards of St Petersburg, and paintings of peasants
and snow-scenes. Many of Helsinki's institutions are housed in Russian
buildings to this day. The Presidential Palace, authoritative on the waterfront,
used to be the palace of the Governor-General. The City Hall used to be
*the* hotel for visitors from Russia. The chamber-music auditorium was the
House of Nobility. The city's ceremonial centre-piece, the great square of
Senaatintori, was the creation of Tsar Alexander II, and looks decidedly like
St Petersburg, with Alexander himself riding a bronze horse for ever in the
middle of it. Not far away the double-headed tsarist eagle roosts upon
Tsarina's Stone, an obelisk commemorating an imperial visit in 1833 – in
the later years of the Soviet Union it was the only such bird left at large in
the world. Ah yes, if you happen to be a Grand Duchess yourself, you will
still feel at home in Helsinki.

## 81   *The after-taste*

But then Finland, as we know, is the Lucky Country: tsarist Russia generally treated it kindly enough, and Soviet Russia never ruled it. There is one other European country – Bulgaria – that still feels a historical debt of gratitude towards Old Russia, but there is no European country at all that feels grateful for the influence of the USSR. At the end of the twentieth century Russia retains only one foothold in my Europe – the enclave of Kaliningrad, which used to be German East Prussia, and which is cut off from the rest of the country by Lithuania: but a blight still hangs over all those other parts of Europe once dominated by the Soviet Communists. Sometimes it is a measurable economic or administrative blight, but more often it is an indeterminate legacy of shabbiness, squalor and corruption, a lack of colour still, an unhelpfulness, a grumpiness. One day, I suppose, they will remove the vast and vainglorious Soviet war memorials which stand with banners, bayonets and stars in every capital of eastern Europe, Stalin's sphere of influence. They may even demolish the pinnacled Mongol-Gothic skyscrapers, the Palaces of Culture, the Houses of the Party, which figure in so so many skylines. The sculpted Stalins and the Lenins have already gone, and only a few monumental factory workers and statuesque agricultural labourers are left to ornament office blocks and bridges. It will be generations, though, before that miasma finally disappears, with its wastelands of dingy concrete, its last rude shopkeepers, its dubious politicians and its mafia. In the meantime the citizenries cherish their bitter and satiric memories. In Budapest in 1996 the pizzeria called Marxim's, fitted out with Soviet posters, bare benches and chicken wire, awarded busts of Lenin to high achievers in the field of anti-art. In Vilnius the surviving Soviet-style restaurants were nicknamed Golden Oldies, and they were about to open a nightclub named Iron Felix, after a notorious local-born Soviet police chief: all the pleasures of Communism were to be ironically re-created in it, down to a choice between newspaper or real toilet paper in the lavatories.

## 82  *Interlude with Russians*

In a small coffee-shop in Riga, near the Freedom Memorial, the only other
customers are three hefty well-wrapped people sitting over the remains of
their lunch at a corner table. A man in a woollen hat drinks beer. A woman
heavily befurred has a bottle of white wine to herself. A youth in jeans and
a leather jacket slouches over a bottle of vodka. All three are very drunk.
They talk to each other in erratic spurts of invective. Often they knock
glasses over, or drop things on the floor. The woman is totally unsmiling.
The man occasionally looks ingratiatingly across the room to me. Every now
and then the youth slumps forward on to the table, as though unconscious.
When the man finishes his beer he hoists his companions to their feet and
they leave the restaurant. The woman walks out as though sleepwalking, in
a positive parody of inebriation. The youth staggers disjointedly towards the
door. The man, pushing him out with both hands, turns to me with the
hazed and flowery suggestion of a bow. 'My apologies,' he says in a slurred
approximation, and tries to bow again as he disappears into the street outside.
When the waiter comes to clear the debris of their table he looks across at
me, too, with a sour smile. 'Russians,' he says.

## 83  *Out of the East*

No less significant has been the effect of Islam, whose old threat did so much
to make Europe what it is. Before the wars of the 1990s in Yugoslavia a truly
Islamic experience was to drink a coffee in the little café in a tower of the
bridge at Mostar. I was particularly vulnerable to the spell of Islam when I
first went there, having recently returned from residence in Egypt, and
everything about the place enchanted me. The coffee was the thick black
Turkish kind, with cardamom in it. The room was hung with carpets. The
skyline around was pierced with minarets, and when the sun went down
one heard the magical call of the meuzzin echoing over the town. Figs and
lemons grew in the gardens along the river-banks. There were fields of
tobacco, and orchards as in Persia. It was lovely! The sixteenth-century
bridge was a miraculously fragile-looking single span, said to have been
designed by a pupil of the incomparable Sinan, architect of the Suleiman
Mosque in Istanbul, and was attended by all the proper Islamic legends about

collapses, penalties and generous sultans. If this was Europe, I thought, it was a Europe delightfully mutated!

But it was only a grace-note, only a happy incidental to a fearful theme. For generations the hostile power of Islam was one of the great unifying forces of Europe, making the continent more than ever synonymous with Christendom. Islam had come to Bosnia in the fifteenth century, by the agency of the Turks, but its first footholds in Europe were far older. The Arabs of North Africa invaded southern Spain and Portugal in the eighth century, remained there for 600 years, and for a time advanced far into France too. Other Muslims occupied Sicily for 150 years, and later the Ottoman Empire, storming Europe from the east, reached the walls of Vienna itself before the tide was turned. All this profoundly scarred the psyche of Christian Europe, and even now you can hardly escape memories of the long and bitter struggles against the Antichrist.

Some of Europe's great champions were champions against Islam, from the Catholic Monarchs of Castile, Ferdinand and Isabel, who drove the Moors from Andalusia, to Don John of Austria, who beat the Turkish fleet at Lepanto, or Charles Martel ('The Hammer'), the victor of Poitiers. The Muslim threat is not forgotten. Each pleat in the starched skirts of Greece's evzone soldiers is said to remember a year of Turkish occupation. In the Museum of History at Vienna they still display the head of the Grand Vizier Kara Mustapha, who besieged Vienna in 1683 attended by 1,500 concubines, 700 black eunuchs, several cats and an ostrich. In Spain they have never forgiven the savagery of Franco's Moroccan troops in the civil war of the 1930s. In Serbian Yugoslavia a supreme day of mourning is still the day of Kosovo Polje, the Field of Blackbirds, when in 1389 the Turks slaughtered the flower of Serbian nobility. It is a victory over Islam that the Bulgarians celebrate in their most grandiose national memory. As late as 1986 a memorial was erected in Crete to the heroes of the 1866 Sfakiot rising against the Turks. As late as 1995 Christian soldiers in Bosnia were murdering Muslims simply for being Muslim.

## 84 *From* A Hunter's Sketches *by Ivan Turgenev, 1847–1851, translated at the Foreign Languages Publishing House, Moscow*

LUKERYA: And I'll tell you what I was once told by a student of the Bible: there was once a country, and the Muslims made war on it, and they tortured and killed all the inhabitants; and do what they would, the people could not get rid of them. And there appeared among these people a holy virgin; she took a great sword, put on armour weighing eighty pounds, went out against the Muslims and drove them all beyond the sea. Only when she had driven them out, she said to them, 'Now burn me, for that was my vow, that I would die a death by fire for my people.' And the Muslims took her and burnt her, and the people have been free ever since then! That was a noble deed, now!

## 85 *The return of Islam?*

Perhaps all that is why, in the last years of the twentieth century, Europeans look towards Islam with fascinated apprehension. An element of love-hate is involved, because wherever it settled Islam left something alluring. In Spain its influence has proved inexpungible, not only in glorious buildings, but in a whole climate of thought and manners, making Andalusia still one of the most seductive regions of the continent. Steam still drifts from the shallow copper domes of the Király baths in Budapest, once the garrison baths of a Turkish army of occupation, much later to be a popular gay rendezvous: up the hill behind, through all the centuries, Muslim pilgrims have come to the tomb of the holy man Gül Baba, who died during the thanksgiving service for the Turkish capture of Buda in 1541. In eastern Europe, in Greece, Bulgaria, Romania, Albania and the countries of the old Yugoslavia, Islam itself was to live on for centuries, and in some places lives still. Nothing could be more evocatively Islamic than the spectacle of the Friday worshippers thronging the terrace of the Mosque of Mahmud Dashi in Skanderbeg Square in Tirana: the constantly shifting crowd of men, the sense of grave devotion, the low hum of male voices, the beggars at the gate, the imam stalking through the crowd to disappear into the shadows of the mosque – all this in a country which was, only a few years ago, officially godless.

For in the last decades of the twentieth century, Islam has been resurgent in Europe, frightening the more nervous Europeans once again, and reinforcing in some minds the idea of the continent as a Christian bastion. North Africans in France, Turks in Germany, Pakistanis in Britain – all have brought with them a devotion to their faith that has fatefully affected the native cultures. The Islamic Centre is one of the most striking new buildings in Paris. The London Mosque towers grandly over Regent's Park. In Granada, once the capital of Moorish Spain, Islamic missionaries are at work once more. And one of the most surprising experiences of European travel is to drive out of the Yorkshire hills, out of the country of Harry's Challenge and the Ripon Wakeman, into the old wool town of Bradford, and to find it full of Muslims – respectable Muslim families, disenchanted Muslim youths, militant mullahs and rich entrepreneurs. It is an Islamic sphere of influence.

But as for the bridge at Mostar, the last time I was there it was just a pile of rubble in the river, surrounded by ruins: and many of the Muslims of the town had died in the course of ethnic cleansing.

## 86  *The full blast*

It was a Power from over the ocean, anyway, that really changed the manners of Europe during my own fifty years. Far more persuasive, far more revolutionary in its effects than anything before it, outclassing all the old examples of French finesse, English reserve, German efficiency, Italian style, Russian ideology, Islamic dedication, there arrived in Europe in full blast, just when I arrived on the mainland of Europe myself, the engine of the American Way. The Europeans would never be the same again. The fun, dazzle, violence, opportunism, energy, generosity, deception, idealism, swagger, push and inanity of American life would mark the peoples of the old continent for ever after, and paradoxically bring them closer to one another. All Europe's graffiti-artists now scrawled in the same style, derived from the street calligraphers of Manhattan, and no European could be altogether a foreigner to another when they were both munching a hamburger, wearing identical baseball caps back to front, knowledgeably discussing the works of Woody Allen, or talking California computer-speak.

EUROPE

# 5

## SPASMS OF UNITY

★

*It is possible to consider Trieste as a totem of European disunity. During the past couple of centuries it has been incessantly squabbled over by rival Powers, States, nations and factions. Churchill saw it as the southern end of his Iron Curtain, and it stands at the edge of the ever fissiparous Balkans, almost within sight of the battlefields of the twentieth century's last European wars. I prefer, however, to hang around at the Caffè degli Specchi, by the waterfront, down the hill from the castle and the cathedral, and to think of the city as a pledge of eventual European unity. I could go and feel Latinate by drinking a Campari at the bar; this morning I shall feel Germanic by having a hot chocolate with a sticky cake at a terrace table – across half Europe, at this very moment, ladies are ordering chocolate and strudel of one sort or another, undoing their coats, tidying their hair, and settling down for half an hour of self-indulgence.*

*The square I am sitting in, the Piazza dell'Unità d'Italia, was once a showpiece of that immense multinational organism the Austro-Hungarian Empire – and thus by descent, by way of the almost indestructible Habsburgs, of the Holy Roman Empire. Next door to the café is the ornate old palace of the Austrian Governors. Around the corner is the opera house, Teatro Verdi, one of whose first productions was an opera by Antonio Salieri, Mozart's rival. Over the way is the splendid former headquarters of the Lloyd Triestino shipping line (formerly Lloyd Austriaco), which once took the dual eagle of the Habsburgs into all the world's oceans. At the bandstand which used to stand in the square the band of the Austrian 87th Infantry was frequently conducted by Franz Lehár of* The Merry Widow, *and in a laboratory along the quay Sigmund Freud, with a research grant from the University of Vienna, tried unsuccessfully to discover the testes of the eel. In some lights, in some moods, Trieste is a living relic of the old Empire.*

*But then almost everyone who has hoped to make a unity of Europe, whether by hook or by crook, by force or by ideology, has left his mark in Trieste. A plaque on a house just out of sight from my table records the fact that Napoleon stayed there once. In the 1930s the Italian Fascists foresaw a grand future for the city as an imperial port of a new kind: an instrument of Italian expansion, an armoury and an emporium, as one Fascist official wrote, to sustain 'the armed emigrants on the Black Continent'. In 1944, following the Italian collapse in the Second World War, the Germans annexed Trieste and its surroundings as an integral part of their Reich, and along by the docks at San Sabba are the remains of their only extermination camp in Italy; Trieste would again know a time of splendour, declared the local Nazi newspaper,*

Deutsche Adria Zeitung – 'the European idea' would see to that. Communism very nearly got its hands on Trieste in 1945, to put it on a par with Belgrade, Bucharest, Sofia, Prague and the other cities of Marx's half-Europe. It is one of those places, like Memel (Klaipeda), Danzig (Gdańsk), Fiume (Rijeka) or Königsberg (Kaliningrad), which get their own inset maps in old atlases, signifying their especially flexible status in Europe's history.

The faces around me, as I crumbily eat my cake, are an ethnic muddle – heavily Germanic faces, lean Latin faces, Slav faces with blue eyes and high cheekbones – and among the Italian conversations I shall probably hear some in Slovenian, and some in Serbo-Croat, and perhaps some German too. This is a mélange-city, where things are seldom absolute: in Trieste one can experience Gemütlichkeit with a sting to it, calm Latinity and bourgeois Slavdom! If there is a public festivity of some kind, as there very often is – an anniversary of the Audace's arrival, for instance – there may well be a military parade in the square, with trumpet-calls, bersaglieri marching at the double, Italian flags everywhere, and perhaps a warship moored at the Molo; but it always seems to me that on these occasions the Italian Government doth protest too much, knowing as well as everyone else that Trieste is really far more than just an Italian city, but a city of many races, loyalties and histories.

So it is that I sit here, drinking coffee from Brazil (Trieste is still one of Europe's chief importers of coffees), looking across to Miramare (from where the doomed Habsburgian Archduke Maximilian sailed away to found an empire in Mexico), and thinking not about Europe's incorrigible instincts for quarrelling, but about its successive impulses to unite. The relics of five such varied spasms, in particular, I distinguish in my mind – the Carolingian, the Habsburgian, the Napoleonic, the Prussian, the Hitlerian. Before I pay my bill and make for my lodgings, I let my imagination dwell too upon a sixth: what we fondly like to call, at the end of my half-century, the European Union.

# 1 *Euro-dreams*

When I first set out for Aachen, I am ashamed to admit, I was not at all sure where it was. Was it the same place as Aken? Could it be Aix-la-Chapelle? Was it in Belgium, the Netherlands, or Germany? On the map all three countries seemed to meet about there, with France and Luxembourg just over the map-fold. All was soon made clear to me, however. As I walked into town from the railway station, I heard rollicking male voices singing '*Ach, Du Lieber Augustin*', as students used to sing it after duels at Heidelberg in romantic comedies. Between a McDonald's and Schinkel's spa buildings I found the source of it. There on a temporary stage twenty or thirty well-built burghers, dressed in elaborate and extravagant fancy dress – here a prince in a feathered hat, there a jester or a helmeted general – were celebrating the start of the Rhineland carnival, accompanied by a chorus of eighteenth-century soldiers in periwigs; and around them half the populace of Aachen was tapping its feet, swaying rhythmically arm in arm, convivially smiling and drinking foaming tankards of beer. Germany it was.

I had gone there as to a grail, for in Aachen had been born, eleven centuries before, the first modern expression of a European whole: which is itself, of course, only a facet of the universal instinct, among all mature people anywhere on earth, to form part of one community. In Aachen half the peoples of this spiteful continent had once acknowledged a political focus, and their leaders had come to pay allegiance to a common loyalty. I had a lunch at a beamy Rhineland pub (kept by Greeks, as it happened), and afterwards I walked over the square to the cathedral. Rumbustious songs still sounded from somewhere across the city, but the building was shadowy, silent and almost empty. Only a few visitors wandered around the famous octagonal chapel – the 'Chapelle' of Aix-la-Chapelle, and the first dome north of the Alps. A single tour group whispered in the glass choir, marvelling at the jewelled and golden reliquary that stood on a dais in the centre of it. I leant against a pillar, though, with my back to the altar, looking up to the gallery of the chapel: for there I could just make out, palely in the shadows, a rough-cut seat of stone. It looked at once primeval and indestructible. There was no elaboration to it, no ornamentation, none of the gilt, silver and gems that encrusted the treasures down below. It was like one of those holy rocks of the ancients, I thought: powerful, and simple, and magnanimous. It was the throne of Charlemagne, the First European, and so the stuff of Euro-dreams.

## 2 *Un-holy, un-Roman, un-imperial*

The Holy Roman Empire was institutionalized at Rome on Christmas Day 800, with the coronation of Charlemagne as Emperor: but it really began its career at Aachen. As Voltaire famously said, it was neither holy, nor Roman, nor an empire. It remained always a confederation of sovereign States, nearly all German by nationality, owing a more or less voluntary allegiance to an emperor elected by a panel of member princes and ecclesiasts. It assumed its resounding name because it professed to be not only the secular agent of that holiest of sovereignties, the Catholic Church, but also a legitimate successor to the Roman Empire. Its glory was essentially the glory of once upon a time, a mystical, lyrical glory: until the time of Louis XIV every king of France sent the funeral pall of his predecessor to be laid upon Charlemagne's tomb at Aachen. It was nevertheless the original attempt at a political union of Europe, extending out of the continent's Germanic heartlands – my first pan-European spasm.

Charlemagne – Great Charles – gave political meaning to the name 'Europa', hitherto hardly more than a character of Greek mythology, and he made Aachen Europe's original capital. He brought there Christ's swaddling-clothes and loincloths, which are in the cathedral still, and which together with his own remains (now upon that dais in the chapel) made the city one of Christendom's most famous centres. Amidst this holiness thirty-one successor emperors were crowned, and Aachen has never forgotten its glory days. A heroic figure of Charlemagne dominates the main square. The Town Hall opposite, built on the site of his palace, contains all manner of imperial reminders – swords, crowns, electoral portraits, dynastic mementoes, a Coronation Hall – and this is where they present the Charlemagne Prize, awarded to statesmen who have contributed notably to the peaceful unity of Europe. All this because, long ago, a charismatic Germanic chieftain chose this agreeable watering-place to be the centre of his imaginary empire.

Imaginary or not, after a hiatus following Charlemagne's death it was to survive in one form or another for a thousand years. To some it always remained a secular branch of Christendom; visionaries supposed that at the end of all things the last of the emperors would battle it out with the Antichrist! Others saw it as an embodiment of German civilization, something (as Ludwig II of Valhalla thought) that rose above mere States to have a universal value. All over Europe its influence potently lingers. At Frankfurt, where the last of all the emperors was crowned in 1792, they still proudly display the roster of sovereigns anointed in the cathedral there, and the forty-five imperial portraits in the Kaisersaal, and the stumpy sandstone figure of Charlemagne outside the Historical Museum, which had its head blown off during the Second World War but has been recapitated. At Regensburg, long the seat of the Imperial Diet, they love to explain the layout of the Imperial Hall, fitted out in meticulous protocol to seat the princes, dukes, counts, bishops and abbots of the assembly. The Empire's supranational orders of chivalry died a very slow death, if indeed they have died at all. When in 1872 Isabel Burton went to live in Trieste (under Austrian rule then), as wife of the British Consul, she thought it expedient to resume the honorific '*geborene Gräfin*', inherited from a remote ancestor ennobled by the Emperor Rudolf II in 1595; and the celebrated Irish tenor John McCormack called himself a Count of the Holy Roman Empire until the day of his death in 1945.

Many a European phenomenon has its roots in Charlemagne's imperium. The archdioceses of Mainz, Cologne and Trier assumed their consequence because for generations their archbishops were *ex officio* Electors of the Holy Roman Empire. The princely house of Thurn und Taxis got so rich because it operated the only officially licensed postal service in the Holy Roman Empire. The great inland port of Magdeburg, on the Elbe, was originally important because it was a frontier town of the Holy Roman Empire. For better or for worse the Holy Roman Empire, whatever it was, cast its spell across Europe for centuries, and after its demise it was to inspire both Napoleon and Hitler to have their own try at creating a European unity. The vulgar Napoleon crowned himself with a replica of Charlemagne's crown. The lunatic Hitler called his Nazi Empire the Third Reich – the Second was the Prussian kaisers' empire of the nineteenth century; the First was born in that dim-lit chapel in Aachen.

3  *From* Faust, *1808, by Johann Wolfgang von Goethe,*
*translated by David Luke*

ALTMAYER: Tra la la la la!

FROSCH: We're in good voice; commence!

[*Sings*] The Holy Roman Empire, we all love it so;

But how it holds together, that's what we don't know.

BRANDER: A filthy song! Shame! A political song!

A tedious song! My lads, thank God in daily prayer

That running the Empire isn't your affair.

## 4  *Clouded mystery*

That's what they sang in Auerbach's Leipzig pub (which still exists, by the way, and thrives upon the Faust connection). I agree with Frosch. I cannot keep up with the Holy Roman Empire. Dutifully though I visit its historic sites, examine its sacred relics, view the lists of its emperors, I cannot really grasp it. It had no permanent capital to explore. Its frontiers were too variable to follow. Its emperors often sound fictional, and sometimes its possessions too. Was there really a country called Lotharingia? Did Charles the Fat really succeed Charles the Bald? What was the cause of the rivalry between Barbarossa and Henry the Lion? When was Arnulf? Why was Berengar? Who fought the battle of Lechfeld? What was the Investiture Controversy? How many Counts Palatine were there? I have dreamt sometimes that I am being subjected to some frightful examination about the Holy Roman Empire. Like Frosch and his friends, I would calamitously fail such a test, but I do not give up. Nor do my kind cicerones all across Germany. 'It was in this very room,' they solicitously tell me (more or less), 'that the Princely Electors, led by the Margrave of Württemberg-Coburg, together with the prelates of lower Saxony and the delegates of Pope Pius IV, met with Arnulf the Good to discuss the extension of the Golden Bull to imperial territories beyond the Elbe.' 'Fascinating!' I gratefully say, looking around me at the gilded stalls, the dark imperial portraits and the jewelled candelabra that formed part of the dowry of the Princess Caroline of Lotharingia when she married the Berengarian Prince-Elector.

## 5  Among the Habsburgs

Things get a little simpler for the historical wanderer when the Habsburgs, a family with a power-base in Austria, take over the Holy Roman Empire in the fifteenth century, more or less combine it with an empire of their own, and largely by matrimonial manipulation extend its German lands to include not only Spain at one end but Hungary at the other – my second spasm of unity. We all know the Habsburgs. The pretender to the throne of the Habsburgs is, as I write, a well-known member of the European Parliament, as are his two sons, and anyway the very faces of the clan are familiar to us from a hundred paintings: those bulging eyes, that underhung jaw, that expression of pallid fatalism. We know them even when they disguise themselves with mutton-chop whiskers, like Franz Josef.

The Habsburgs enthusiastically became Holy Roman Emperors in 1437, after one or two false starts, and they kept the title ever after, largely because the imperial territories were so wide and scattered that they had the Electors in their pockets. 'Sit fast, Lord God,' the Bishop of Basle reputedly warned his Creator about the first Habsburg emperor, 'or Rudolf will occupy *thy* throne!' The family's cryptic cipher 'AEIOU' still occurs in many parts of Europe, and has been most commonly interpreted as meaning 'Austria Est Imperari Orbi Universo', implying I suppose that Austria was destined to rule the entire world. The Habsburg monarchs certainly saw themselves as universal monarchs, and for generations the family really did preside over most of the continent of Europe, with members on the thrones of Germany, the Low Countries, Spain and Portugal, southern Italy and Sardinia, Bohemia, Austria and Hungary. When the Emperor Charles V visited England in the sixteenth century, they called him frankly 'Charles of Europe'. Even Franz Josef, who died only a decade before I was born, could still be dubbed not just His Imperial, Royal and Apostolic Majesty, not merely Emperor of Austria and of Hungary, but also King of several kingdoms, Margrave of here and there, Duke of a score of dukedoms and Lord of numberless lordships. For generations the Habsburg regime in Vienna was known simply, all over Europe, as 'The Monarchy', and when I first went to the United States, in the 1950s, if you mentioned 'The Empire' people generally assumed you to mean the empire of the Habsburgs, so many of whose citizens had run away to America. The first Habsburg monarch was born in Switzerland;

the last died on the isle of Madeira; if any clan could claim to be a genuinely European family it was the clan of the Habsburgs.

The curse of the house, wrote the Austrian playwright Franz Grillparzer in the 1850s, was 'to strive irresolute, halfway, with half-deeds and half-measures', but that is not at all how the Habsburgs strike me now. For a thousand years they seem to have been animated by an insatiable ambition for power, deliberately veiled in a suggestion of sanctity, and so irrepressible that even in the 1990s there was talk of reviving the Habsburg Empire. I first came face to face with the family, as it were, in their vault at the Kapuzinerkirche, the Capuchin Church, in Vienna, where 125 of them (minus their hearts and viscera, which went elsewhere) lie in enormously grand coffins in the half-light, trailed among by still respectful Austrians. Above the door was inscribed that mysterious cipher, and this powerfully engaged my imagination – so elemental and powerful, so easy to remember, so regally enigmatic. AEIOU! I have since learnt that, although there have been more than 300 different interpretations of the cipher, to this day nobody knows for sure what it was intended to mean.

## 6 A beginning, a middle and an end

On the top of a hill near Brugg in Switzerland stands Habichtsburg, the Castle of the Hawk, which is where the Habsburgs began their climb to glory. The Rhine, the supreme European river, flows nearby, and both France and Germany are within artillery range, making it a thoroughly European monument. Today the castle is hardly more than a tower with a few ancillary ruins, much of it turned into a restaurant, but its significance is certainly not forgotten: in its little museum a panoramic map shows how the legacy of this small fortress was eventually to extend across the entire continent and halfway across the world.

The place where the Habsburgs reached the climax of their power is more ironically suggestive. Philip II, of the Spanish branch of the family, son of the Holy Roman Emperor Charles V, built the Escorial outside Madrid to be at once a palace, a monastery and a family tomb. On my very first visit to Madrid I had trouble finding a hotel room, and a friendly concierge suggested I might get accommodation out at the village of Escorial. Taking me to the door of his own hotel, he pointed out to me a faint blur on the distant hills. 'There it is,' he said. 'You're sure to find something there, and while you're there you can take a look at the Escorial itself. That's something nice.' Something nice! What I saw outside my window up there, when I had checked into my pension, was the greatest *memento mori* in the world, a terrible reminder that even the majestic pretensions of kingship, let alone the petty frivolities of commoners, can end only in tears. From here the Spanish Habsburgs ruled not only much of Europe but also much of what is now the United States, the Philippines, and islands and settlements from Sumatra to the Azores – Europe's first great extension of power into the wider world. There are a hundred miles of passages in the Escorial and more than a thousand doors, and in it Philip the Habsburg lived abstemiously in work and prayer, surrounded by all the dossiers of State, the code keys, the dispatches, the files of secret information. It gave me quite a turn when I entered this palace-mausoleum next morning. I thought I could almost see Philip there still, receiving ambassadors with a high brimless hat on his head and his foot upon a gout-stool. Something nice!

The place where the power of the Habsburgs came to an end, on the other hand, and with it the second of my pan-European spasms, seems to me almost pathetically inadequate. Karl IV, the very last of the Habsburg rulers, lost all his thrones and principalities in the First World War, and having made rather a nuisance of himself in the aftermath, was exiled by the victorious Western Powers to the island of Madeira. There he died, in 1922, and he was buried not in the Capuchin Church in Vienna, like so many of his forebears, nor even in the local cathedral of Funchal, but in the small pilgrimage church of St Nicolas, on the slopes of the hill above the town. Madeiran people still frequent this church to petition its miracle-working image of the Virgin, sometimes making the last part of the journey on their knees: foreigners chiefly know it because of the pleasant gardens of the district, the alfresco coffee-shops nearby, and the wooden transport sledges which here begin their grating voyages, loaded now only with tourists, down the steep cobbled lanes to the seashore. Only a few visitors, in my observation, spare more than a brief puzzled glance at the tomb of poor Karl, behind a grille in the left-hand aisle of the church. There is a plaque above its door, and various imperial mementoes are to be glimpsed within the grille, making it rather like a provincial annexe to that portentous vault in Vienna: but few strangers realize who lies there, or know that he was a last successor to the Holy Roman Emperors themselves.

## 7  *The internationalists*

The Habsburgs stopped being Holy Roman Emperors, actually, in 1806, when the Emperor Francis II abolished the title to prevent the jumped-up usurper Napoleon acquiring it. They had already lost, or were soon to lose, their family possessions in Spain, the Low Countries and Italy. But their own empire in the East remained astonishingly cosmopolitan. They were German themselves, or Germanic anyway, but their domains in eastern and central Europe contained people of many races, languages, creeds and customs – a hundred races and a thousand languages, James Joyce said complainingly. (He added that the Habsburgs were the most *physically corrupt* royal house in Europe, but I don't know what he meant by that.) Vienna was truly an imperial capital, and still is, its streets leading not just to provincial towns but to ancient satrapies and fields of action – the Oststrasse *Autobahn* striking grandly out for Budapest and Prague, Triestestrasse leading to the Adriatic, Metternich's Landstrasse marking the beginning of Asia itself. The tug between the German and the Slav was never really to be resolved, but for a couple of hundred years the races of the Austro-Hungarian Empire, the Dual Monarchy of the Habsburgs, were at least kept in equilibrium. The ramshackle imperial system remained an improbable demonstration of Europeanism: Mussolini said of one of its progeny, the post-Habsburgian republic of Czechoslovakia, that it ought really to be called 'Czecho-Germano-Polono-Magyar-Rutheno-Romano-Slovakia'.

Like the Holy Roman Empire, the Austro-Hungarian Empire still crops up all over the place. For example the Corfu villa of Kaiser Wilhelm II that we visited on page 305 was built not for the All-Highest but for the Empress Elizabeth, wayward and half-estranged wife of the Habsburg Emperor Franz Josef – who is herself commemorated on the quayside in Geneva where she was assassinated in 1898. In the Boboli Gardens, the grand pleasance of the Pitti Palace above the Arno at Florence, there is a delightful little café, housed in an elegant circular kiosk, with an oriental-looking dome and a weather-vane on top. This is another unlikely memento of the Habsburgs. How the clan came to rule in Florence at all is as puzzling to me as it probably was to the Florentines at the time: but it seems to have been the result of some tricky bartering between the Elector of Saxony and the King of Poland – characteristic European diplomacy of the time. It was the Archduke Leopold, later the Holy Roman Emperor Leopold II, who built this engaging caprice in 1776. He also opened the gardens to the public, and it is a reminder of his sensible attitudes that the kiosk is still called, to this day, the Kaffeehaus – one of the very few reminders, for the average visitor, that the Habsburgs were ever in Tuscany at all.

## 8  *Habsburg horses*

Here's another glimpse of Habsburgdom. In Vienna the imperial court was supplied with horses from Slovenia, one of the Empire's obscurer provinces, where a particularly splendid breed had been cherished since ancient times. These were the Lippizaner horses, glorious white animals, trained into impeccable dressage by the riding-masters of the court (and now performing for the tourists, most days of the week, in the Spanish Riding School – followed as to the imperial manner born, as they canter round and round their palatial ring, by a lackey with a shovel to remove their noble defecations).

In 1918, when the Habsburg Empire was dissolved, half the Lippizaner horses were taken to Graz, within Austria, but the other half remained at their original home, which became the village of Lipica, first in the kingdom of Yugoslavia, then in the Socialist Federal Republic of Yugoslavia, finally in the independent Republic of Slovenia. There one day I went to see their descendants. An imperial estate had been established around the breeding-stables in the days of the Empire, with its own Governor, its own hierarchy of officials, and a gentlemanly park. By the time I got there, long afterwards, a casino had been built, together with a couple of hotels, and people were having picnics here and there, and drinking beer on terraces; but the park survived, wide grassland speckled with somewhat scrubby trees, and in the heart of it dimly I could discern, like some spectral dispensation, the remnants of the Habsburgs' stud-farm. Here was the modest mansion of the Governor (not, after all, a very senior imperial functionary), and here was the riding-track where the horses had been broken in down the generations, and here in their long stables, fluttered through by swallows, were the horses themselves, the original Lippizaners, on their own soil. They were magnificent creatures still, born to a curious destiny: there in the Republic of Slovenia to spend their whole lives honouring the heritage of a vanished dynasty – disciplined to bear themselves always, to lift their hoofs, to hold their patrician heads in the exact way prescribed for them so long ago by the equerries of the Habsburgs.

## 9  *To the four corners!*

For myself, the most exciting of Habsburgian sites concern the coronations
of the emperors as Kings or Queens of Hungary. This happened generally
at the Danube castle-town of Pozsony, now Bratislava (where the spire of
St Martin's Cathedral is still topped by a replica of the Hungarian crown),
until in 1867 Franz Josef was crowned at the shortly-to-be-united capital of
Buda-Pest. In both cities they remember still the mound that was always
erected on the banks of the Danube for the culminating ritual of the ceremony.
It was made of soil brought from all parts of the Hungarian kingdom, and
there after the coronation service the King would proceed on horseback.
Dressed in his coronation robes, his crown upon his head, he would spur
his horse to the top of the mound, and drawing his sword from its scabbard
would flourish it defiantly towards the four corners of his kingdom. For
horse-mad extrovert Magyars it must have been easy – just their style: but I
find it hard to see the whiskered Franz Josef, a born desk-emperor, performing
the ancient rite with much conviction.

## 10  *K.u.K.*

What most people now associate with Habsburg government is the vast
bureaucracy and military system by which, in their latter years, the Habsburgs
administered their eastern territories – a rambling instrument of supra-
nationalism, mustered in infinite grades of protocol. It was defined by the
Viennese politician Viktor Adler as 'a despotism softened by muddle'. It had
its grim aspects – Kafka immortalized some of them in Prague – and its comic
aspects, which make *The Good Soldier Švejk* one of literature's funniest novels.
It preened itself in fancy uniforms and incessant military parades: Franz Josef
thought constant parading was a way of exorcizing war. It documented itself
in the 'chancery double', an exactly prescribed sheet of paper, available at any
tobacconist's, upon which every imperial transaction, even the most trivial
personal request to Authority, had to be written. But it survived innumerable
onslaughts of conflicts and nationalism to leave its living echoes behind when
the last of the Habsburg monarchs had long gone to his grave in Madeira. If
you want a taste of it even now, come and loiter with me along the Ringstrasse
in Vienna, at the very heart of Habsburgism in its last century.

The Ringstrasse itself, the wide ceremonial street which surrounds the old city of Vienna, was built in the nineteenth century as a deliberate declaration of imperial assurance. Like some megalomaniac's dream (Hitler's perhaps – he loved it), its buildings rise one after another preposterously into view, Gothic or Grecian or baroque, plastered in kitsch or writhing with classical allusion, here a titanic opera house, here a refulgent Attic assembly, a university more utterly academic than Heidelberg, Cambridge and Salamanca put together, museums as overwhelmingly museumy as museums could possibly be, and all appearing to curve deferentially, even obsequiously, around the immense pillared and rambling sprawl of the Hofburg, the imperial palace – where for nearly seventy years Franz Josef, the last Habsburg emperor that anyone remembers, toiled at his simple desk, dressed always in his severe military uniform and addicted to boiled beef and potatoes.

This was a Habsburg trademark: simplicity allied to total power, and not infrequently to total ruthlessness too. But just as the buildings of the Ringstrasse, grouped around that palace, certainly expressed no architectural modesty, so the immense army of officialdom which sustained the throne shared none of Franz Josef's homely style. The Austro-Hungarian Establishment adored its grades, ranks and honorifics, the myriad layers of social and official import, Excellencies and Herr Professors and guilds and orders and nuances of precedence. There were the letters 'K.u.K.', for instance, often to be encountered still in memorials of the old Empire, and in pastiche – a retro-café in Zagreb is called K.u.K. They unfortunately lent themselves to the derivative 'Kakania', devised by the Austrian novelist Robert Musil, which meant in effect 'The Kingdom of Shit', but they really stood for 'Kaiserlich und Königlich', 'Imperial and Royal', referring to the Empire of Austria and the Kingdom of Hungary. Infinite gradations of etiquette and formality formed an intricate measured ladder from the humblest clerk to the grandest councillor. Watch now – stand back – here, in the 1990s, come a couple of ministers down the staircase from the Council Chamber in Parliament, portly important men, deep in portly and important matters of State – and, swoosh, like a rocket from his office leaps the porter, buttoning his jacket, panting heavily, urgently smoothing his hair, down the steps two at a time to overtake them, in the peculiarly Austrian movement once described by Joseph Roth as being a leap, a bow and a stiffening all at once – 'Bitte, bitte' – just in time, my goodness, only just in time to open the door for Their Excellencies, who acknowledge his grovel only with slight declinations of their heads, so as not to interrupt the flow of their discourse,

as they lumber out between the figures of Minerva and her attendant sages
to their waiting limousine in the Ringstrasse.

That porter is abasing himself to a couple of petty politicians in one of the
smallest of republics: but down that very same staircase his great-grandfather
similarly leapt, bowed and stiffened his humility to the rulers of half Europe.

### 11  From the funeral service of the Habsburg Emperor Franz Josef I, St Stephen's Cathedral, Vienna, 1916

THE FATHER SUPERIOR: Who art thou? Who asks to be admitted here?

THE GREAT CHAMBERLAIN: I am His Majesty the Emperor of Austria, King of
Hungary.

THE FATHER SUPERIOR: I know him not. Who asks to be admitted here?

THE GREAT CHAMBERLAIN: I am the Emperor Franz Josef, Apostolic King of
Hungary, King of Bohemia, King of Jerusalem, Prince of Transylvania, Grand
Duke of Tuscany and Kracόw, Duke of Lorraine.

THE FATHER SUPERIOR: I know him not. Who asks to be admitted here?

THE GREAT CHAMBERLAIN: I am Franz Josef, a poor sinner, and I implore the
mercy of Lord God.

THE FATHER SUPERIOR: Then thou mayest enter.

### 12  The wedding list

The Habsburgs achieved their hegemony over Europe with a minimum of
bloodshed and a maximum of advantageous marriages. '*Bella gerant alii*,' it
was famously said of them, '*tu felix Austria nube*' – 'Let others go to war,
lucky Austria, you get married.' Queen Mary I of England was married to
a Habsburg. Marie Antoinette *was* a Habsburg. Here is a list of the European
sovereignties which appeared on the matrimonial records of the Habsburgs
between 1415 and 1740: Portugal, Burgundy, Brittany, Bavaria, Castile,
Aragon, Savoy, France, Denmark, Bohemia, Hungary, Mantua, Austria,
Poland, Ferrara, The Netherlands, Tyrol, Palatinate-Neuburg, Lorraine,
Brunswick, Saxony, Tuscany, Parma, Saxe-Teschen, Spain, Naples, Cologne,
Württemberg, Sicily, Nassau-Weilburg, Salerno, Sardinia, Belgium, Bra-
ganza, Liechtenstein, Saxe-Meiningen, Mecklenburg, England.

## 13  *Marriage plans*

Such was the web of the dynasts, a powerful theoretical factor towards the uniting of Europe, and the Habsburgs were only the most formidable of a plethora of families that plotted, flirted, dowried and diplomatized towards useful matrimonial alliances, linking the most improbable States in cousinhood. The eighteenth-century Prince Eugène, the archetypal European commander – so famous that the Germans of the Second World War named both a division and a cruiser after him – Eugène the perfect European general had Spanish, French, Bulgarian, Czech and Italian ancestors. Almost into our own times princesses of one house or another were whisked around the continent, for betrothal to dear cousin Otto, or marriage to some totally unknown margrave, rather as footballers nowadays are transferred from Manchester United to Real Madrid. The complications were endless, and reached far back into European history. King Canute the Dane was the grandson of Mieszko I of Poland! Jan III Sobieski the Pole was great-grandfather to Bonnie Prince Charlie! In 1914 the King of England was cousin both to his ally the Tsar of Russia and his enemy the German Kaiser! In 1941 the Duke of Savoy, as nephew to the King of Italy, became King Tomislav II of Croatia! Lord Palmerston, the British Prime Minister, once said that only three people had ever known the solution to the dynastic complexities of the duchies of Schleswig and Holstein: the first had gone mad, the second was dead, and the third was Palmerston himself, who had forgotten what the solution was. As the *Encyclopaedia Britannica* observed in its 1976 edition, 'The House of Bourbon-Brazil, or of Orléans-Braganza . . . is not to be confused with the House of Borbón-Braganza, a Spanish branch originating in the Portuguese marriage of the infante Don Gabriel (a son of Charles III of Spain: see Table 5).'

## 14  *The crown itself*

All this seems absurd to me, but as a republican with a taste for swagger, with a weakness for ritual too, I have always thought that the future of monarchies might lie in emblemization. As the soul of the Ashanti people is contained in their Golden Stool, which floated down from heaven rather like the halberd of Trieste, so the virtue of European nations might be projected into that most venerable symbol of kingship, the crown. They could do without mortal monarchs altogether. The golden crown itself would be the emblem of their Statehoods, and stand at the centre of their rituals as royalty alchemized. When on some ceremonial occasion a regal coach passed by in all its gilded splendour, attended by flunkeys and outriders, followed by helmeted cavalry, through its windows the wondering crowds would glimpse only the national crown, flashing with gems, reclining on a crimson cushioned dais.

The Hungarians have come closest to this consummation. The supreme symbol of Hungarian Statehood is the marvellously Byzantine crown of St Stephen, their canonized original king, which is amazingly old, heart-rendingly beautiful, and attended by a profound and mystical significance. Legend says it was presented to the King, for his coronation at the end of the year AD 1000, by Pope Sylvester II, and augmented by later precious acquisitions: certainly during the next nineteen centuries it was used to crown fifty-two later monarchs, acquired the soubriquet 'The Apostolic Crown', and was kept in various fortresses and palaces throughout the Hungarian domains, ending up, when the monarchy collapsed in 1918, in Veszprém near Lake Balaton. Maria Theresa wore it when she rode side-saddle up the coronation mound at Pozsony in 1741, Franz Josef when he waved his sword to the four corners at Budapest in 1867. When in 1945 the Germans were driven out of Hungary by the Russians, they took the crown with them, and with other treasures it was buried beside the Mattsee in Austria, not far from Salzburg. There it was unearthed by the United States Army and taken away to America, to be kept for twenty-seven years among the gold reserves of Fort Knox.

Throughout its absence, throughout the long years of Communist rule, the Hungarians continued to revere the holy crown of the Saint-King. When I went to Budapest in the 1970s a mere replica of it, displayed in the National Museum, was surrounded by armed soldiers, as though just the memory of the real thing, even in a People's Republic, deserved an honour guard. By the 1990s, when I went again, there *was* the real thing, returned at last from Kentucky and exhibited with other royal regalia in a room of its own at the museum. I was more moved by it than by any appearance of living royalty. It was, after all, nearly a thousand years old! It had seen fifty-three monarchs come and go! There were no other visitors about when I went to see it on a wintry morning. The great doors of the crown room opened with a vast and echoing creak, and there in the dim-lit chamber, guarded by a solitary elderly janitor dozing on a chair in the corner – there ablaze with light stood the holy crown. Nothing could seem much holier: its gems and pearls all gleaming there, its enamelled ancient saints from old Byzantium, its ancient Greek and Latin lettering, the precious stones hanging on gold chains from its rim, and, most touching of all, the golden cross mounted cockily or even tipsily skew-whiff on the top of it. I could easily imagine men dying for it.

## 15  *Two royal ladies*

Kings and queens, though, generally thought the continuance of dynasties more important than the preservation of crowns, and in the heyday of the monarchies royal scions galore were available for the marriage market. In Germany alone, until the unification of the country in the nineteenth century, there were some 350 petty princedoms, each with its own administration, its own toy army, its own royal schloss in a park, its own high-born sons and daughters only awaiting suitable matches. Bismarck called the house of Saxe-Coburg, an especially fertile source, 'the stud-farm of Europe'. The interchange of princesses, in particular, defies enumeration, and played an incalculable part in the long intricate process of calculation and compensation by which the royal families of Europe enmeshed the continent.

Some of these ladies were by no means mere ciphers, but played powerful parts in the affairs of State and society. One such was the formidable Princess May of Teck (Victoria Mary Augusta Louise Olga Pauline Claudine Agnes), daughter of the Duke of Teck, a princedom which by then consisted of nothing much but a ruined castle on a hill. She was also a granddaughter of the Duke of Württemberg, and although she was born and brought up in England she never lost her severe Teutonic dignity. She was engaged first to Edward VII of England's disreputable eldest son, the Duke of Clarence, but when he suddenly died in 1892 she married his brother instead, and finally became an unnerving Queen Mary to the hardly more cuddly King George V. I remember her well, and vicariously disliked her always. Majestic in her long dove-grey coat and toque, clasping her umbrella, she was once deferentially ushered (probably at her own demand) into the incorrigibly misogynist library of one of the oldest and stuffiest of London clubs, where never a woman had dared set foot unless she was going to clean the carpet or empty the ashtrays. Stately the Queen of England entered, attended as I imagine it by an obsequious club secretary, and an elderly member looked up from his newspaper. He saw the First Lady of Europe, descended from kings herself, married to the King of England, pausing at the doorway to raise her lorgnette and inspect the furnishings. 'Ha,' was all the old member said, returning to his paper. '*The thin end of the wedge.*'

At the other end of Europe I once went in search of Marie Alexandra Victoria, who made the most of being Queen of Romania in the first half of this century. She was the daughter of the then Duke of Edinburgh, and thus a granddaughter of Queen Victoria. She was also a great-granddaughter of Tsar Alexander II, while her children married into the royal families of Greece and Yugoslavia, and her husband, King Ferdinand, was a Hohenzollern from Germany. However she strongly resisted the usual royal homogenization, and remained her own Englishwoman from first to last, besides taking the trouble to learn the Romanian language. At Sinaia, in the Transylvanian mountains, the Romanian royal family possessed a fantastic fairy-tale castle, Peleş Castle, a mock-Renaissance flourish of pinnacles, terraces, ornamental staircases, gables, crests, clocks and bits of half-timbering. Queen Marie preferred not to live in it (so, years later, did President Ceauşescu, who thought he would catch dry rot from it). Instead she moved into a gentler house nearby, the Pelisor Castle, and here against all the cultural and historical odds she imposed her own taste. I much enjoyed it when I followed her there half a century after her death. Retreating defeated from the forbidden extravagances of Peleş (see page 152), I found myself wonderfully soothed in Pelisor by an elegant synthesis of art nouveau, Byzantium and Celtic design, gracefully complemented by Romanian motifs. Marie designed it all herself. She allowed Ferdinand a few Teutonic blasts in his study, but elsewhere all is cool restraint, white walls, lovely wood, golden stuccoes from the Bosporus.

Away on the Black Sea, in an area that now forms part of Bulgaria, she built herself another characteristic retreat. It stands beside the sea at Balchik, with gardens up the hills behind. Marie called it 'The Quiet Nest', and although we are told that in her day guardsmen stood throughout the twenty-four hours motionless at its gates (she was not a queen for nothing), its intentions are unpretentious, all rustic red tiles and slabbed steps and small waterfalls, miscellaneous follies, and a chapel in a yard. Balchik was largely Muslim in those days, and Marie was always keen to reconcile Romania's Muslims with its Christians, so she went out of her way to absorb Islam into the Quiet Nest aesthetic. The little palace is crowned by a minaret. Among the gardens are many old Muslim gravestones. And it was Marie's pleasure to entertain Muslim ladies from the town in her private smoking-room, where they shared the consolations of Turkish coffee, gossip and opium – all of which the daughter of the Duke of Edinburgh was apparently rather fond of.

Queen Marie it was whose persuasive gifts brought Romania into the First World War on the side of France and England, and she went heroically to war herself as a Red Cross nurse. She published several books. She was said to be fabulously beautiful. She was a fine horsewoman. She died in 1938, and, while her body was buried in the garden at The Quiet Nest, where it remains, her heart was placed under the altar of the chapel: when during the Second World War that part of the coast passed from Romania to Bulgaria, the queenly organ was taken away to Bucharest, and Marie Alexandra Victoria is honoured among Romanians to this day.

## 16 'Comment', 1926, by Dorothy Parker

> Oh, life is a glorious cycle of song,
> A medley of extemporanea;
> And love is a thing that can never go wrong;
> And I am Marie of Roumania.

## 17 If . . .

A good place to think about royal connections is the pleasant German town of Celle, near Hanover. Its decorous streets and beautifully preserved half-timbered houses all seem to look with affectionate respect towards the schloss that stands in a moated park on its edge. In this house was born King George I of England, whose great-great-great-granddaughter was Queen Victoria, whose great-great-great-great-great-great-great-granddaughter would be Queen Elizabeth II. The Hanoverian link ensured that from then onwards the British royal family would be essentially Germanic, sometimes speaking in a thick German accent, and never looking in the least like a family of English gentry. Queen Victoria used to say that if she were *not who she were* she would go and live in Coburg, where her paternal forebears came from: until the First World War her dynasty was still called the House of

Saxe-Coburg-Gotha, only changing its name to Windsor to distance it from
the enemy.

I am told that now and again Prince Charles, as I write the heir to the
British throne, has paid a visit to Celle – I suppose to contemplate the
fact that from here his great-great-great-great-great-great-great-great-
grandfather George Ludwig, Elector of Hanover and Duke of Celle, set off
for London to become King of England too. If history had gone in other
ways Charles might now just be Duke of Celle himself, living in that agreeable
white castle at the head of the town, and one day in the 1990s, when he was
even more than usually embroiled in marital difficulties and London's tabloid
tittle-tattle, I amused myself by imagining that he was. How content he
would be, I thought, as the beloved and respected sovereign of that little
State, Karl Philip the Good of Celle! No ravishing English aristocrats to mess
him about, no tabloids to mock, no paparazzi to haunt him, only his dear
Duchess Kamilla to stroll arm in arm with him through the gabled streets of
his capital, like a prince and princess in a fairy tale, to visit the dukely
stud-farm or the State Institute of Beekeeping (talking to the bees being, as
is well known, one of His Highness's little foibles). Celle really is a kind of
story-book capital for this amiable duke. The schloss itself, four-square and
multi-turreted, stands moated in a park through which the ever-loyal citizenry
is encouraged to wander, and outside its gates the whole town seems to bear
itself with a proper deference, awaiting the palace wishes. It is like a very
large estate village somewhere, looking no further than the manorial lodges
for its allegiance and its welfare. The Duke's mild Germanic eye misses little,
I am assured, and he can only be pleased by what he sees on his promenades
– it is all a dukely dream!

But quick, look, over there by the garden café – there they are Themselves,
and coming this way too! See how the waitresses wave and simper! See how
Their Highnesses pause to watch the ducks! The children stare, sucking their
thumbs. The elderly ladies curtsey. '*Guten tag*, Your Highness, a lovely day
in Celle!' Karl the Good smiles sadly at us. 'Ah so. I do not – er – speak very
much English, but it is, how do you say, er, terribly nice to see you here –
is it not so, *meine Liebchen*?' '*Terribly* nice,' says the Duchess. 'We've been
down to see the bees.'

Fancies, only fancies – the stuff of what might have been!

## 18  *In Ruritania*

To sense the dynastic system at its most allegorical, though, the only place to go is Cetinje, former capital of the mountain republic of Montenegro, which, with Serbia, is all that is left in the late 1990s of the old Yugoslavia. I drove there in the 1970s up the precipitously corkscrew road that used to be called the Ladder of Cattaro, away from the flowered Adriatic coast to the harsh high plateau of the Lovćen massif – waterless, apparently soil-less, and stubbled only with arid patches of scrub. Crouched in a declivity of this wilderness is Cetinje, which was for a decade or two around the turn of the twentieth century the undisputed capital of Ruritania. When the Turks swept this way in the fifteenth century, spreading the word of Islam all across the Balkans, the Montenegrins maintained their Christian independence, led by a line of fighting prince-bishops, and in 1910 a descendant of those heroic clergymen declared himself a king – King Nicholas I of Montenegro. It was the very heyday of the monarchical networks, when emperors, kings and princes lorded it all over Europe, and Nicholas enthusiastically joined their company. Sixty years later his royal palace in Cetinje still seemed to me a very encapsulation of royalty, a cabinet of kingship. Observe the dinner service presented by Napoleon III. Note the portrait of the future King George V of England. What staggering profusions of medals and orders, stacked with their gaudy ribbons in big glass cases, surmounted by the lions, the elephants, the peacocks, the bears and the chimeras of international chivalry! What elaborations of chinoiserie, rococo or Second Empire, presented to His Majesty by this fellow potentate or that to celebrate one formal occasion or another!

Nicholas fathered three princes and nine princesses, and their several marriages linked this remote Balkan villa astonishingly with the royal castles and palaces of Europe. One daughter married the King of Italy, one the King of Serbia, two became the pair of grand duchesses who introduced Rasputin to the Russian court, one became a German princess, and one gave birth to the future King Alexander of Yugoslavia. In Cetinje I toured the embassies of the Powers which had been accredited to His Montenegrin Majesty, together with the court chapel, the opera house and the offices of State with which Nicholas equipped his village capital. Imagine the life that hummed around these anomalous structures in the days before the First World War, while the wind off the plateau whistled all around – the presentations at the palace, the soirée invitations delivered by sashed messengers, the confiding and betraying of courtly secrets, the encounters of diplomatic and ministerial wives on Sunday promenades! King Nicholas adored it all, and made sure that no monarchical nicety was neglected: on badges and buttons, cutlery and cannon, the double-headed eagle of Montenegro, elevated to the status of a royal cipher, gave notice of his admission to the company of the Habsburgs.

## 19  *Long lines of soldiers*

Most of these royal aristocrats traced their ancestry back to the Germanic heartlands of Europe, and the German patriciate is still hard to escape, if only in memory. The *Almanach de Gotha* is, after all, a German institution, founded in 1863 when the unification of Germany must have made the future of the German nobility uncertain. Off the highway south of Riga I came by chance upon an old German estate which had its origins, I imagine, in the days of the Teutonic Knights. Those alarming warriors, members of a Christian fighting order, had entered the pagan Baltic countries in the thirteenth century, and their descendants had established themselves as a German governing class which survived the rule of the tsars and was extinguished only when the three republics gained their independence after the First World War – remaining after that, too, in the part of East Prussia which is now the Russian enclave of Kaliningrad. The estate I stumbled upon had long been requisitioned and communalized, of course, but it was peopled by ghosts for me. The big plain manor-house stood in the heart of it, surrounded by tall trees, and there were rambling outbuildings all around, with tumbled cottages which were once the serfs' quarters, I supposed, and a pretty lake with ducks on it. I imagined the Grafs and baronesses of long ago, the von Thises and von Thats who amounted to local society, big, confident, haughty people, sitting over the candle-lit dinner-table of the big house exchanging local scandal, speculating *sotto voce* about the future of the tsardom and execrating the laziness of the local peasants, whose language they seldom understood and whose race they despised. I felt I knew them well, if only from the pages of *Keisri Hull* ('*The Czar's Madman*'), a 1987 masterpiece by the Estonian novelist Jaan Kross which is their communal memorial.

Two other books, in particular, have also opened my eyes to the power and resilience – and often the charm – of the aristocratic network which for so long constituted a kind of supranational autonomy across much of Europe. There were powerful aristocracies, of course, in every European country, but the patricians seem to have been at their most collusive or club-like in central and eastern Europe, in Germany, Austria, Poland, Hungary and the Baltic countries – little kings and queens on their own estates, although it was said of them that as they were often hard up their crowns were fur hats, their sceptres were sticks and their orbs potatoes. Since in those countries they have mostly been swept out of existence, or at least out of recognition, I have met them only through literature. Who can ever forget Patrick Leigh Fermor's odyssey across patrician Europe, in his memoirs of a journey in the 1930s from England to the Black Sea? He mingled with every rank of citizen, as a footloose and adventurous youth, but he regularly stayed in the castles and country houses of aristocrats, and has given us an imperishable picture of life among the toffs of Mitteleuropa before catastrophe fell upon them. Here he learns the game of bike-polo on a stately lawn. Here he listens to nightingales while his host plays fugues on the next-door piano. This count has eccentric notions about the fattening of ducks, this one smokes a hubble-bubble after dinner. Baron Rheinhard von Liphart-Ratshoff points out on the map country houses Leigh Fermor might visit on his onward journey – 'My old friend Botho Coreth at Hochschatten. The Trautmannsdorffs at Pottenbrunn!' Grófnö Lászlo of Lobos gives him a pistol plated with mother-of-pearl to see him safely on his way. Baron 'Pips' Schey introduces him to the works of Proust. From family to family Fermor wandered across Europe, kindly welcomed everywhere (for he was a prepossessing young English gentleman), passed from one castle to another in a generic ambience of comfort, cultivation, selective hospitality and originality. 'We are like potatoes,' one Hungarian nobleman said to him of his family connections: 'the best part is underground.'

A decade later we meet just the same people, in very different circumstances, in the diaries that the adorable Marie Vassiltchikov ('Missie') kept during the years of the Second World War in Berlin. She herself was the daughter of a Russian prince, and throughout the war she maintained her friendships with the aristocratic clans of Germany, some of them pure German, some Russian, some Polish, some Hungarian, Lithuanian, Czech, Austrian or even Swedish. The patrician network was, it seems, scarcely affected by the advent of the Nazis: in 1939 the Hohenzollern family were still the greatest landowners in Germany, with palaces, villas, hunting-lodges and vineyards from Kiel to East Prussia. When Missie went into the country out of the war-blasted, half-starved capital, familiar country houses were always ready to welcome her, and fatten her up with good country food off the estate. Convivial princes, baronesses and counts were always to hand – Prince August-Wilhelm ('Auwi') Hohenzollern of Prussia, Count Axel ('Wolly') von Saldern-Ahlimb-Ringenwalde, Baron Anton ('Tony') Saurma von de Jeltsch, Count Johannes ('Hansi') von Oppersdorff, Princess Helene ('Lella') zu Mecklenburg. Dashing young aristocrats lived dashingly as ever through the squalors of Nazidom and the miseries of war – the night-fighter pilot Prince Heinrich zu Sayn-Wittgenstein, for instance, who sometimes flew into action with a raincoat over his dinner-jacket, or the brave, doomed company of young noblemen who were concerned in the bomb plot against Hitler in 1944.

They were mostly gone by my time, their stylish half-private world shattered by war, ideology, revenge, prejudice or justified grievance. Sometimes I have seen their houses, like that old Baltic manor, but their lives I have only glimpsed through the eye of imagination, or of literature. 'All of us are descended,' said Kross's Baron von Trock to his fellow-nobles of Estonia, 'from a long line of soldiers.' So they were, the old aristocrats of Mitteleuropa. They had won their precedence by the sword, and by the sword they mostly lost it.

## 20  Arts of government

The dynasties of Europe were often extremely shrewd, shifting their positions, their styles and even their convictions to suit the times. Often they allied themselves with the forces of religion. For several centuries the Habsburgs sustained the myth of divine right, with great success. The Medici princes of Florence were sometimes Popes too. The kings and queens of England were officially Defenders of the Protestant faith, and their coronations were profoundly religious ceremonies, invoking the alliance of God himself to help them in their duties, rather as the doges of Venice used to be married ceremonially to the Adriatic Sea.

Sometimes monarchies even associated themselves with that universal Power, the power of art. The Russian artists of St Petersburg, before the Soviet Revolution, seriously thought of taking over the Government and creating 'an artistic dictatorship'. European artists never aspired so high, but they did often join the ruling hierarchy. We read of mighty kings humbling themselves in the presence of artists. The Grand Duke of Tuscany offers his own chair to Michelangelo. Francis I of France attends Leonardo da Vinci's deathbed. King Christian IX of Denmark summons his carriage to pay a call on Hans Christian Andersen. Queen Victoria of England bases her white-palled funeral upon Tennyson's. 'I was born too soon,' declares Frederick the Great of Prussia, himself an accomplished flautist, 'but *I have seen Voltaire.*' And at the city of Weimar one may still enjoy the fruits of a practical political association between Art and Government, because there the enlightened young Duke Carl August took into his administrative employ no less an artist than Johann Wolfgang von Goethe. This was a great success. Goethe became a sort of wazir to the star-struck duke, and did everything from designing public buildings to inspecting the dukely mines, besides attracting to the city other poets, artists and musicians of every kind (when he went away to Italy His Grace paid his stipend anyway). For generations Weimar was a dream of Germany, neither Frenchified nor Prussian, neither nationalistic nor imperialist. Madame de Staël reported that it was not so much a small city as one large, liberal and wonderfully enlightened palace.

I feel Goethe's organizing presence still when I wander the streets of Weimar, as we wandered them together on pages 228–9. He wanted Weimar's visitors to see the little city and its parks as 'a series of aesthetic pictures'. Certainly I know of no city so instinct with the idea of beauty as a political conception, as part of the established order – and not the beauty of pomp and majesty, either, but an amiable, entertaining, chamber-music kind of beauty. The ideology did not last. The young duke might be enlightened, but his people were mostly terribly Philistine, and the dukedom of artists lost some of its delight when Carl August was no longer there to set the tone, or Goethe to supervise the aesthetics. Still, where else in Europe can one find a ruler buried not among his princely peers but between a pair of poets? For if you visit Carl August's simple mausoleum, on its little hillock above his city, you will find that Goethe lies on one side of him, Schiller on the other. Most European sovereigns would rather be buried among racehorses.

## 21 *Two castles*

Among all Europe's petty princelings (none of them, of course, in the least petty to themselves), some of the grandest have been the Wittelsbachs of Bavaria, whose names have echoed through European history since the Middle Ages, and who were sovereigns of their own independent State until

1918. Nowadays the most famous of them is Ludwig II, the so-called Mad King, who died mysteriously in 1886 after having built the original Disneyland, his immensely towered and turreted castle of Neuschwanstein on the edge of the mountains south-west of his capital, Munich. This structure, conceived by stage designers rather than architects, was greatly liked by Ludwig's friend Richard Wagner, and is now one of the supreme tourist destinations of all Europe. It generally raises a sneer among more sophisticated travellers, and really does look rather ridiculous in photographs; but looking at it from the meadows in the flat land below gives a very different impression. From there you can see it as upon an opera stage. Half a mile away, seldom pictured in the postcards, there is another of Ludwig's castles – Hohenschwangau – which is a far more sombre and warlike building, based upon a twelfth-century fortress, with a squat ochre-coloured keep like a genuine citadel. These two great buildings, the one so camp, the other so macho, eye each other in a bemused way across an intervening valley. Behind them the mountains rise marvellously into the Bavarian blue. Sweet green fields lie in front, speckled with white houses; hang-gliders soar; an occasional helicopter whirrs around the towers of Neuschwanstein; the combination of majesty and frivolity, pretension and domesticity, seems to me irresistibly engaging. Lying flat on my back in the flowered stubble there, in the middle of a meadow on a summer morning, I once called Wales on my mobile telephone, and sent a breath of High German romance into the grey stones of home.

## 22  *A smell of wild garlic*

The Bavarian dynasty still has its political supporters, for many Bavarians still feel themselves Bavarians first, Germans second, and show it even in the clothes they wear – lederhosen and feathered hats for the proletariat, beautiful green caps for the smart set. In 1996 the respected Prince Albrecht, who had distinguished himself in his youth by refusing to join the Nazi Party, died at the age of ninety-one and was buried in the family plot at the monastery of Andechs, where I met the disagreeable monk on page 45. I visited his grave a few days after the funeral, when morose Bavarian gardeners were clearing away the wreaths. No memorial plaque had yet been raised, but all around the green cemetery garden, with its crucifix in the middle, were the names of recent members of the dynasty, princes and princesses, all given (although

Germany has been a republic since 1918) the old honorific of 'Royal High-ness'. While the gardeners brushed up the leaves and took the wreaths away, I rooted idly through the funeral ribbons and sashes which lay in a pile on the grass – a pile of silken reds, yellows and blues. What a mess of royalty was there! Crowns and coronets and embossed princessly initials lay in a crumpled, discarded heap – the detritus, I thought, of a long discredited idea, in a monastic garden where only Royal Highnesses could be buried, and surly gardeners would soon be throwing the whole lot into the dirty back of a truck. There was a smell of wild garlic about, I see from my notebook.

## 23 *Still trying*

In 1900 there were only two republics, France and Switzerland, in the whole of Europe, and it has been only within my own fifty years that the last royal dynasties of Europe have begun to lose their lustre and their significance. For long after the Second World War the Austrian Republic still banned all Habsburgs from setting foot on Austrian soil; only in the 1960s was the gentle pan-European Archduke Otto allowed to visit Vienna. 'Ah well, what the hell,' one seems to hear history saying then. King Farouk of Egypt once prophesied that by the end of the twentieth century only five royal courts would be extant – the courts of Clubs, Spades, Hearts, Diamonds and England: by the 1990s even the English were having their doubts.

Several other royal houses of Europe kept trying – in 1996 nine hereditary monarchies were still in office. As we have seen, the King and Queen of the Belgians, though they had lately given up court balls, were still living regally enough, and so were the reigning princes of Monaco and Liechtenstein. Others compromised with history. King Juan Carlos of Spain was thought to be a prime champion of democracy in that old despotism. The old palace of the Swedish king and queen, in Stockholm, now flew far fewer flags, and looked much less regnant, than the Grand Hotel across the harbour. When I first went to Sweden I saw His Majesty's destroyer *Gävle* (1,040 tons), of the Royal Swedish Navy, parked bang outside the palace front steps: but by the 1990s King Carl Gustav XVI and his Queen were seldom there, the *Gävle* had finished up as a floating generator at a nuclear power station, and no public authority might call itself 'royal', not even the Navy. The Dutch royal family seemed to have established the same equilibrium with democracy, a harmless arrangement which pleased the tourists and appeared to satisfy the indigenes. The toy soldiers I sneered at in Denmark, in their peaked bearskins and cross-straps, still foolishly marched up and down at the royal headquarters in Copenhagen: but when the Royal Danish Ballet ended its command performances the company bowed first to the general public and only secondly to the royal box. The Norwegian monarchy was celebrated with an affectionate dignity that edged endearingly towards humour. The royal palace stood, properly pillared, surrounded by parkland on a hill almost in the middle of Oslo. Sentries in feathered hats and striped trousers stood guard outside the house, now and then marching up and down a bit, or ceremoniously stamping their feet, and at lunch-time every day they shifted duty with a ritual of bands and sword salutes. This was hardly the changing of the guard at Buckingham Palace – when the parade was over a tuba-player was quite likely to be left smoking a cigarette on a bench outside the guardroom, his legs stretched comfortably out and his cap on the back of his head. In London he would soon be bawled out by a sergeant-major: in Oslo he helped to give the little ceremony an easy assurance that I found at once moving and entertaining – just what a modern monarchy needs.

## 24  A perfectly good job

As for ex-King Michael of Romania, or Crown Prince Alexander of Serbia, or ex-King Simeon II of Bulgaria, or ex-King Constantine of Greece, all of whom are sometimes tipped for a return to their abolished thrones, for myself I would not put my money on them: but then I am a Welsh republican, and sympathize with Prince Charles Castroit de Renzi, who says he is unlikely to claim the throne of Albania to which he might apparently be entitled, having a perfectly good job already as an electricity clerk in Stoke-on-Trent.

## 25  The third spasm

I have a particular aversion, not entirely inherited, to the greatest advocate of European unity by family network, the author of my third European spasm – the little bugger Napoleon, as he was defined by his contemporary Marshal Pierre François Charles Augereau. It always astonishes me that in Paris Napoleon Bonaparte is still honoured as a national hero, his tomb in the Invalides still a place of pilgrimage, his memory presented as all but holy.

A century and a half after his death, I have been unable to get away from him. Wherever I go he has been, with his arrogant poses, his bullying armies, his preposterous pretensions and his false claims to liberalism. I detest him. I despise him for sacrificing the lives of hundreds of thousands of men, from almost every country in Europe, for the sake of his personal ambition. I loathe him for his impudence in removing from Venice the golden horses of St Mark and erecting them in self-glorification on a triumphal arch in Paris. It infuriates me to find yet another sycophantic plaque commemorating his visit to a city, or just the house he spent a night in somewhere. Where did Napoleon *not* spend a night? He is as ubiquitous a lodger as George Washington in the United States, and generally much less welcome.

For a few years Napoleon did more or less achieve a unity of Europe. It is true that he in effect himself put an end to the old Holy Roman Empire, but he created a holy empire of his own. He saw himself as the direct descendant of Charlemagne, whatever the Habsburgs said, and adopted many of the mystical suggestions of the old Empire. Was there ever a more sickening scene than the one depicted in Jacques Louis David's painting of Napoleon's coronation in Notre-Dame, still attracting its worshipping hundreds at the Louvre? Grouped around the high altar of the cathedral are his cronies and toadies, most of them atheists or at least violent anticlericists, ridiculously dressed up in the ruffs, feathered hats and pantaloons decreed for them. The simpering Josephine kneels to be crowned herself by her husband, and the members of Napoleon's Corsican family look on in complacency from their box behind. Napoleon himself stands centre-stage, of course, the very image of upstart arrogance in his ribbons, sashes and robes, with a wreath of golden laurel leaves on his head: meekly behind him sits Pope Pius VII, insolently summoned all the way from Rome despite his age and ill-health, holding his hand up in a febrile gesture of blessing. Almost everything about the picture is false, in one way or another. A priest had married the demure Josephine to Napoleon only the night before, in order to legitimize her own coronation. Napoleon had already crowned himself, having snatched the crown from the high altar before the Pope could reach it. Napoleon's family was not in fact present at the ceremony, and David was obliged by imperial order to paint in the Pope's benedictory hand, long after the event. Napoleon himself, far from being chosen or anointed by divine unction, was hardly more than a sort of sexy Hitler, and almost every clause of his coronation oath he was presently to perjure.

## 26 *The empire of vulgarity*

It was all the essence of vulgarity, and Napoleon's restoration of the monarchy, his absurd scattering of trumpery kingdoms, princedoms and dukedoms across Europe, is the best argument for republicanism I know. His vision of a Europe united by his own dynastic arrangements came to nothing, the revolutionary and nationalist nineteenth century being the wrong time for it. Nevertheless his empire lasted a decade, and has left its stamp upon Europe ever since. Napoleon and his brothers and sisters ruled in France, Italy, Holland, Spain and Germany, and, having rid himself of Josephine, he married a Habsburg princess who gave him the King of Rome as an heir. His fighting marshals, mostly the sons of the petite bourgeoisie, became sovereigns too: Soult the Duke of Dalmatia, Murat King of Naples, Bernadotte King of Sweden (from whom those pleasant contemporary monarchs in Sweden are descended). He must sometimes have been confused himself as to the number and even the location of his puppet kingdoms. When he summoned a conclave of his ancillary sovereigns, in 1809, there sat in his salon the rulers of Saxony, Württemberg, Naples, Holland, Spain and Westphalia, with Napoleon and Josephine presiding over them all as undisputed Emperor and Empress of the new Holy Roman Empire. The Imperial Guard included units from Italy, Germany, Lithuania, Poland and The Netherlands.

## 27 *Napoleon's island*

In the end, of course, Napoleon overreached himself. His empire collapsed into its constituent parts, and he was banished almost as far from the continent as it was possible to be banished. For ten months, though, before his final abasement at Waterloo, he was exiled to the comfortable Mediterranean island of Elba, which became his sole sovereign principality. There even a bigot like me finds his memory more endearing than repulsive. His Empire of Europe reduced in scale to an island eighteen miles long, he behaved himself rather well, and proved an able and sensible ruler of his little fief. For me he is more alive in Elba than anywhere else – far more vividly than in Corsica, his birthplace, or in Paris, the stage of his grandiloquent climax. He set out, as always, to engrave his own personality upon the place, and the island remains palpably Napoleonic to this day.

His modest summer palace there is his best memorial of all, to my mind. It is not a very grand house, but even so it is said that he could not afford to buy it until his sister Pauline came to his rescue by selling some of her jewels. In it he spent the hot island days with a couple of generals, a small domestic staff, Pauline and his mother, and the Napoleonic reminders which are scattered all over the property have lost their pomp and hauteur – the eagles, the crests, and above all the bees, sculpted, plastered, drawn and modelled, which also appear on the flag Napoleon himself designed for his principality. The flag still flies in Elba, and there are many other reminders of his presence, too. There is a spring called Napoleon's Fountain, whose excellent water is collected by islanders with flasks, and commercially bottled with bees on its label. There is a sweet and lonely hermitage, lost among woods, where Napoleon spent two happy days with his mistress Marie Walewska. There is a death-mask of Napoleon in the Church of the Misericordia. There is a thronelike rock, traditionally called Napoleon's Chair, where the ex-Emperor is said to have spent lonely meditative hours looking out to sea, longing for France, dreaming of greater days . . .

But there, I see that like everyone else I am succumbing to the romance of Bonaparte. Napoleon was a monster, but he was undeniably fascinating. Despite myself I still pause to read those plaques, wherever in Europe I glimpse his name upon them, and here I stand beside Napoleon's Chair, looking across the blue Tyrrhenian, with a perceptible frisson of sympathy. How pathetically romantic a fate, to be reduced from the command of Europe to the squiredom of this small island! How touching the bees! How noble the death-mask! How loyal his brave generals were! How poignant that brief meeting with his love at the hermitage! Just for a moment I am seduced, as millions have been seduced before me. I have to pull myself together, to remember that when Napoleon was gazing so wistfully towards the horizon he was probably plotting his escape from Elba and a return to violence: which he presently achieved, sacrificing a few score thousand more lives in a resumption of his heartless aspirations, before getting his well-deserved come-uppance at Waterloo, and his final banishment out of Europe altogether. If he had lived in our time they would have put him on trial for war crimes.

## 28  *As to those horses*

As to those horses of St Mark, which the little bugger stole, like many another work of art they are emblematically citizens of Europe themselves, so often have they been the objects of international envy and theft. They were made by some ancient genius of Greece or Rome, were stolen by the Venetians when they plundered Constantinople in 1204, were trundled away to France in immense horse-drawn wagons when Napoleon seized Venice in 1797, became Austrian subjects when Venice fell under Habsburg rule in 1814, and Italian subjects when Venice became part of Italy in 1866. In the two world wars they were taken down from their balcony on the Basilica San Marco and carted away for safety's sake. Now they have been replaced up there by lifeless replicas, and are stabled immune from pollution in dark rooms behind the belvedere from which, for a thousand years, they proudly surveyed the Piazza to the wonder of all who saw them. I was in Venice when they were removed, apparently for ever, and it seemed another of the seminal moments of my life, like that train journey under the English Channel: the moment when Venice, the city that had so long bewitched me, reconciled itself to its future as a civic museum.

I wept a little to recognize this moment of acceptance, because it reminded me of the last Doge's remark when, as Napoleon's forces approached, he handed his ceremonial hat to his valet – 'Take it away,' he said, 'I shan't be needing it any more.' Besides, the golden horses of St Mark had always brought out the emotional in me. They had stood there for so long, so nobly, so gently, with the dull-gold ripple of their magnificent bodies, their hoofs raised so majestically, their lovely heads turned one towards the other with such magnanimous tenderness. I had known them all my adult life, and the thought of them immured in those cavernous chambers out of the sunshine, off the stage at last, struck me as infinitely poignant – more poignant, actually, than their removal by Napoleon to be exhibited as the ultimate trophies of war on his triumphal arch on the other side of the Alps. In a book I wrote about Venice in 1960 I claimed to have heard these glorious creatures stamp their hoofs at midnight, and call to each other in a kind of whinny. One of my less friendly critics called the work 'impossibly fey and self-indulgent', but I was not the first to have such fancies.

## 29 *From* An Itinerary, *1617, by Fynes Moryson*

And above this gallery, and over the great doore of the Church, be foure horses of brass, guilded over, very notable for antiquity and beauty; and they are so set, as if at the very first step they would leape into the market place.

## 30 *The Second Reich*

I was in Berlin one day when I saw a strange spectacle at the east end of Unter den Linden. During the Communist period the East German Government had built itself a vast House of the People on the site of the Königliche Schloss of the German emperors, the headquarters of the Second Reich, which the Russians had destroyed at the end of the Second World War more for ideological than for strategic or aesthetic reasons. Now it was time for the House of the People to be eliminated in its turn, and as a sort of socio-aesthetic-historical experiment the whole building had been covered with painted canvas sheets showing what things would look like if it were decided to rebuild on its site, just as it had been, the old royal palace. Most of the bystanders that day seemed to think it a bad idea – 'It makes my flesh creep,' one man told me – and in the end it was abandoned. I was rather sorry. I knew the look of the old palace very well, from old photographs – a lumpish vainglorious thing, four-square beside the Spree, attended by the usual statues, stables, ceremonial entrances and watergates, and I would like to have seen it hugely standing there again.

I felt myself that the memory of that old empire was so faded and ancient as to be innocuous. The Second Reich was my fourth spasm, the next attempt after Napoleon's to make a whole of Europe – if only, to begin with at least, German Europe. The German States, kingdoms, duchies, princedoms, theoretically retained their separate identities until the twentieth century – German soldiers were sworn in by a dozen different oaths – but in the 1860s they were welded into a national cohesion by the power of Prussia, led by its Iron Chancellor Bismarck. The King of Prussia became the Emperor of Germany, the Kaiser: and it was under the two Hohenzollern kaisers, Wilhelm I and Wilhelm II, descended from a Grand Master of the Teutonic Knights, that Germany became the strongest Power in Europe, humiliating the French, overawing the Austrians, extending its power into Poland and the Baltic countries, challenging the British even on their own element, the sea. 'Germanization,' declared Bismarck in 1869, looking around him at the Europe of his day, 'is making satisfactory progress . . . by which we do not mean the dissemination of the German language, but that of German morality and culture.'

I need hardly say that the Hohenzollerns were allied by marriage and descent to most of the royal families of Europe – Queen Victoria was Wilhelm II's grandmother – but in retrospect their style of sovereignty seems to have been particular to themselves, more flowery and plumed, more resolutely imperial perhaps, a little more defensive or self-conscious than any other. It seemed long beyond resurrection to me. I thought a rebuilt schloss would be about as wicked as the Albert Hall, and I wouldn't have cared if they had also rebuilt the equestrian statue of Kaiser Wilhelm I which used to stand above the Spree opposite the palace gates. I knew this figure well, too, from photographs of its unveiling in 1897, an almost orgiastic parade of plumedness, greatcoatism and thighbootery. It was an absurd piece of nineteenth-century braggadocio, all horses and flags and snarling lions, and, far from raising horrid spectres of aggression in the mind of passers-by, would surely remind us for ever how preposterous self-glory can be.

## 31  *Kaiserstadt*

For me there was no need to rebuild the schloss, anyway, to revive the Wilhelmine feeling in Berlin. One day in the early 1990s I took my Baedeker's *North Germany*, edition of 1913, and went for a contemplative walk through the history of the capital. The Iron Curtain had only lately collapsed, the Berlin Wall was being demolished. The capital was recovering its proper shape again, and the longer I wandered the more it seemed to me that both the Communist and the Nazi experiences were hardly more than terrible aberrations, and that the city's presiding era remained the time of the Prussian monarchy. At least in historical suggestion, with that old Baedeker in my hand, this was Kaiserstadt still. 'The glory of the Parisians robs Berlin of its sleep,' Wilhelm II had observed, as he consciously set out to make his capital 'a world city'. Dear God, it was pompous! Of course a century ago pomposity was the general European style, but no capital flaunted itself like Wilhelmine Berlin, and on skyline and façade there still preened the emblematic champions of its self-regard – armoured and muscular, with swords, trumpets and cannons, attended by chimeras sometimes, astride lions, taming wild horses, brandishing flags or exhibiting trophies. Here was Frederick the Great flanked by cavalry generals, here Marshal Gneisenau stood next to Blücher in the shade of the Operncafé trees. The museums of Royal Berlin stood learned as ever on their island in the Spree. Even the Communists' bulbous television tower looked, to somebody in my mood, acceptably Hohenzollern, and imperial ghosts were everywhere. The vestige of a colonnade, a cracked plinth, or simply a name on my Baedeker map – Wilhelmstrasse, Lustgarten, Kaiser-Wilhelm-Brücke – conveyed me magically to the Berlin of my fourth spasm. In my mind's eye I wondered still at the fashionable brilliance of Pariser-platz beside the Brandenburg Gate, with the Adlon Hotel at the corner where *everyone* stayed, and the gleaming lines of carriages around the ornamental gardens. I had coffee at the same spot, on the corner of Friedrichstrasse and Unter den Linden, where once Johann Krantzler held sway over his world-celebrated café. I all but heard the mounting of the Prussian Guard (clanking of weaponry, screeching of commands) outside the New Guardhouse. I looked up towards the vanished window of the Königliche Schloss where, long before, old Wilhelm I used each day to take the salute, bolt upright at his window, while the band played and the watching crowd cheered. They seemed to me picturesque shades, long disarmed, and the monarchs themselves almost mythologically comical. I had to remind myself that it was the kaisers, their chancellors and their generals whose bombastic ambitions for their Fatherland had helped to embroil Europe in one of the most dreadful of all its wars. 'The Fatherland,' said Mussolini, 'is a spook . . . like God, and like God it is vindictive, cruel and tyrannical.'

## 32 *The fifth spasm*

And presently along came Hitler, creator of the Third Reich and the fifth spasm, which he called his New Order. He was infinitely worse than the kaisers and the Habsburgs, a good deal worse than Napoleon or any of the Holy Roman Emperors. Yet he succeeded in making a unity of all Europe more nearly than any of them. At the height of his power the entire continent was under German control, with the exception of Britain, Ireland, Spain, Portugal, Sweden, Switzerland and Liechtenstein – and if it had been expedient he could probably have acquired most of them too. Never had Europe so coalesced. For anyone of my generation it is impossible to travel around

Europe without thinking of that evil Reich, which was designed to last a thousand years, like Charlemagne's Reich before it, but which fortunately for us all lasted only twelve. It was not altogether a unity imposed, either. In almost every country the New Order had its enthusiastic supporters. There were opportunist politicians, like Quisling in Norway. There were frightened and befuddled patriots trying to do their best for their countries, like Pétain in France. There were passionate anti-Communists. There were racist fanatics. Many thousands of men of many nationalities willingly fought in the German armies, not least in that huge praetorian guard the SS. It was an Austrian general who, as the Germans withdrew from northern Norway, saw to it that every last little fishing-hamlet was burnt to the ground. They were French SS men who, in the last desperate days of the war, defended the Reichstag in Berlin against the Red Army. Spanish volunteers fought alongside the Wehrmacht in Russia. Russians and Ukrainians defected to it. Hungarians, Italians, Romanians, Croats, Danes, Norwegians, Swedes all fought for Hitler's cause. The forces that finally demolished the Third Reich, and suppressed my fifth spasm, were forces from all over the world – every continent, every colour, every faith and language: but the army that fought on Hitler's side was a truly European army. The SS division of French volunteers was called the Charlemagne Division.

## 33 *Memorials*

Yet it came and went like a bad dream – twelve short and terrible years, from Hitler's accession to power until the end of him: no longer than it takes for a baby to grow into a boy. If the Third Reich had lasted longer it would certainly have built for itself some monstrous monuments. Berlin, as Germania, the capital of the New Europe, was to be transformed with ceremonial highways, vast buildings of Government, a gigantic triumphal arch through which the city traffic would pass as though in obeisance, and a Hall of the People capped with a dome higher than the Eiffel Tower and designed to hold standing audiences of 150,000 people. In Vienna the Ringstrasse was to be extended by two avenues running in parallel to the Danube; between them a neoclassic plaza, a Nazi forum, was to replace most of the city's Second District (conveniently occupied chiefly by Jews): in the event nothing was built, and the only architectural legacy of the Nazis in Vienna was a ring of concrete anti-aircraft towers which proved indestructible. Granite blocks were imported from Sweden to build a mighty victory monument in Warsaw; some of them ended up as a memorial to the heroes of the Ghetto Rising against the Nazis in 1943. Linz, near Hitler's birthplace at Braunau in Austria, was to have been metamorphosed into a mighty exhibition of Germanic culture, and we may assume that in all the subject capitals there would have been erected overbearing physical monuments to the might of the Reich. As it happily is, there is remarkably little to see of Hitler's empire. Within Germany the Germans got rid of most Nazi relics in shame: in the rest of Europe there was not much time to build anything except military works. Talk about Ozymandias! Kaiser Bill left far more behind him than Adolf Hitler.

In occupied Europe, however, one tremendous and proper memorial to Nazi values may still be seen: the Atlantic Wall on the coast of France, built by hundreds of thousands of slave labourers to defend United Europe from invasion. To this day the gigantic bunkers and gun-towers of the Atlantic Wall look authentically monstrous and handsome. They are the most impressive architectural mementoes of the Nazi era – some designed, as it happens, by Albert Speer, who designed Hitler's new Berlin too (the plans for Linz were Hitler's own). They are a true cenotaph to the Thousand Year Reich, and all its illusions attend them. One or two strongholds have been made into museums, some are shattered wrecks, but many still stand just as they were built, among the windswept sandy turf of the Atlantic coast.

Sometimes I wander through one, when I have time to kill before catching a Channel ferry, and as I pass through its massive concrete portals, rather like the gateway of the other world in an Egyptian tomb, all sorts of uncomfortable images pass through my mind: jackbooted generals on tours of inspection – prisoners bowed deep below the weight of concrete blocks – collaborationist mistresses perhaps, brought here after dinner for the pornographic thrill of it in ribbed Volkswagen staff cars. The Atlantic Wall is like Nazidom in concrete, horrible and compelling, and like Nazidom itself it abjectly failed.

## 34  *The burden*

I used to suppose that the world would soon be forgetting and forgiving such images of Nazi Germany, but I have come to doubt it. In our time the cinema has made history more vivid than ever, and many future generations will find their attitudes towards the Germans affected by the images of film.

The slaves of the Atlantic Wall will still be alive to my great-grandchildren; the Gestapo will be sinister as ever; death trains will still be rumbling through the late-night movies: it is another of the burdens that the Germans, a people of equivocal destiny, are condemned willy-nilly to bear.

And it could be said, too, that the most unforgettable of all the Nazi monuments is the central monument of our time. Everyone knows, from film and literature, the look of Auschwitz-Birkenau, and the high arched tower through which the trains passed to their last terminal: but I did not grasp the awful power of the place until I climbed that tower myself, and looked down as the Nazis looked over the immense desolation of their camp. It is enormous. As far as the eye can see stand the remains of the barrack huts, and all around is the terror of barbed wire and watch-tower. There was no need for me to visit the museum, so full of famous horrors. All alone up there above Birkenau I realized that I was looking at the worst place in the world – the worst place there had ever been, where every hint of kindness was banished. This was where mankind had reached the bottom: perhaps things could only get better.

## 35  Haunted

Hitler haunts us all still, and nowhere does his presence linger more disturbingly than at his birthplace, Braunau am Inn, near the German border of Austria. This is an adorable little town, compact, very old, with a fine wide market street, friendly cafés, and a picturesque city gate. Hitler never forgot his origins here. He was proud to have reunited Austria within Greater Germany, and hoped to be honoured always by that great cultural complex along the road at Linz, which would doubtless have been named for him. At Braunau his memory is treated with studied matter-of-factness. 'Just down the road,' said a man in the bookshop, when I asked where the birthplace was – 'beyond the arch, on the left-hand side.' 'The yellow house over there,' said the policeman – 'the one with the big stone outside.' The stone turned out to be a memorial to some of the millions who were victims of the Nazis, but I detected no embarrassment or shame when I asked citizens about the Führer connection. They seemed to think it more a curiosity than anything else. I could not help imagining, though, how Hitler would be remembered in Braunau if he had won the Second World War. What plaques and memorials would mark the birthplace today! What a plethora of memoirs and sycophantic biographies would fill the shelves of that bookshop! Statuettes and medallions would be on offer in the souvenir shops, and a tall statue of the Leader would dominate the lovely market street, hand outstretched in perpetual salute, kept forever garlanded by sweet old ladies.

## 36 'At your feet . . .'

Unfair, perhaps. These are generational responses, the last echoes of suspicion in a mind tempered by a wartime youth. Remember that German TV crew I travelled with, back on pages 230–31? When we were filming in Venice I saw the producer being rowed along the Grand Canal with his young assistant. The producer sat in the *sedile nobile*, facing the prow, and looked positively majestic, with his coat slung over his shoulders in the impresarian manner, and his eyeglass on a cord around his neck. Opposite him, with his back to the prow, his assistant sat in a posture of profound respect.

The gondola disappeared behind a house, and when I next caught sight of it, further up the canal, the two men had changed places. Now the assistant sat in the grander seat, looking suave and self-possessed. The producer was altogether deflated by the exchange, his coat huddled around him now, his eyeglass askew, his attitude almost cringing. 'At your feet or at your throat' – God forgive me, I remembered the Churchillian saying.

## 37 The sixth spasm

My last spasm of unity is different in kind from all the others, and must bring my book to an end just as it concludes Europe's twentieth century. The *Zeitgeist* of the time, a millenarian stress perhaps, is an exhaustion with almost every kind of violence, racism, sexism and nationalism: the often floundering efforts of the late-twentieth-century Europeans to unite are instinctive impulses towards a friendlier, quieter life for everyone. I was not terribly impressed, all the same, when for the first time in my life I visited the headquarters of this movement, successor to Hitler's Berlin, Kaiserstadt, Napoleon's Paris, the Habsburgs' Vienna, all the way back to the Aachen of Charlemagne. The centre of the European Union turned out to be an unlovely conglomeration of buildings in a charmless quarter of Brussels. The most pessimistic Euro-sceptic need hardly fear, I thought, that this colourless congerie could ever replace in our diverse affections the Palace of West-minster, the Élysée Palace or the Reichstag by the Spree. Only a few flags flew listlessly that day in the capital of Europe, coveys of bureaucrats scurried morosely by, and when I reached the Palais Berlaymont, the famous home of the European Commission, designed to be the crown of a continent, I found it all deserted. It was having the asbestos ripped out of it. The sunken garden all around was littered with rubbish, and because of the drizzle I could hardly see the memorial to Robert Schuman, the Father of the New Europe, among the unkempt dripping trees. It was going to cost countless billion francs, a passer-by told me, to do the place up. 'The price of history,' I said sententiously. 'Yes, and who's going to pay it?' said he.

The Europe of the *fin de siècle* has at least achieved this: for the first time in the history of the continent all its States share, at least in theory, a single ideology – capitalist democracy, which has overcome theocracy, monarchy, Fascism and Communism alike to give every capital in Europe a more or less freely elected Government. This means that my sixth spasm, though much the most promising – the most benevolent too – is easily the dullest. Officially it proceeds slowly and fitfully, by vote, debate, conference and referendum. All the other attempts to make a unity of Europe have been, one might say, *aesthetic* attempts: high-flown, richly coloured, inflamed with hate, violence, faith, the love of glory or illusion. Even Hitler's manic dreams had to them a ghastly symmetry, and nobody could deny Napoleon a painterly breadth of vision – as if he saw the whole continent, all its armies in the snow, all its marshals and kinglets, through the eyes of a David or a Delacroix. As for the parade of the dynasts, those hyphenated princesses and plume-helmeted archdukes, processing this way and that across Europe in an endless succession of marriages, conspiracies and family conflicts, at least in retrospect they contributed something to the gaiety of nations. Churchill called magnifi-cently for a United States of Europe, based upon 'the resolve of millions to do right rather than wrong', and there was nobility too to Schuman's original conception of a twentieth-century united Europe. It might have been pre-sented at the start as a matter of coal and steel, but it was really a dream of reconciliation between those two great enemies of the Rhine, France and Germany, which would develop over the years into a far wider comity – and so it did develop, too, if only in nomenclature: first into the European Economic Community and then into the lofty abstraction of the European Union, so inadequately represented for me on that drizzly day in Brussels.

But all the man said was, Who pays?

## 38 From 'We are the Music-Makers', 1874, by Arthur O'Shaughnessy

They had no vision amazing
Of the goodly house they are raising;
They had no divine foreshowing
Of the land to which they are going . . .

But we, with our dreaming and singing,
Ceaseless and sorrowless we!
The glory about us clinging
Of the glorious futures we see . . .

## 39 Towards the great republic

Of course we would all rather have our affairs run by economists than by geneticists, religious zealots or even genealogists. Even so, for a temperament like mine the European twentieth century, which had developed in such fire and tragedy, had promised such hope and vision, seemed to be ending bathetically. Like most Europeans I had gone through mixed feelings about my sixth spasm. 'Are you for or against united Europe?' a Canadian had asked me in London not long after the war, when it was first dimly realized that something called the European Coal and Steel Community might well develop into the latest Holy Roman Empire. 'Would it make Britain more or less interesting?' I asked him. 'Decidedly less.' 'Then I'm against.' But almost half a century had passed since then, and I had long been seized by the grand romance of the idea, the prospect of all our peoples united in comradeship at last. I had matured from Britishness to a passionate Euro-Welshness. I was thrilled to feel, as I wandered around Europe, that the old antipathies really were fading. I still remember with delight the very first time when, as I drove my car off a ferry at Cherbourg, the French customs officer did not even bother to look at my passport – half a century ago one needed a visa just to make a day trip to Boulogne! I flaunted a European car sticker on my car, beside the national emblem of Wales, because I had come to think that the best chance for all the peoples of Europe, for the Powers as for the impotent minorities, lay in the creation of a single confederal community, a Europe of all the regions, 'a kind of great republic', as Voltaire called it two centuries ago.

But the States stubbornly hung on. The Powers remained incorrigible. If here and there the minority nations seemed to be achieving some autonomies at last, for the most part the old sovereignties were paramount still. The cruel war in Yugoslavia, yet another European civil war, had been a sad disillusionment. In the former Communist countries organized crime had become almost a Power in itself. Party rivalries degraded and impeded everything. Above all, the dismal science had taken over. 'Poor Rome,' as the Emperor Augustus said about his stodgy successor Tiberius, 'to be chewed between those slow jaws!' Dull materialism had proved the most powerful ideology of them all, *embourgeoisement* was the general trend, and the finance ministers in their chancelleries, the bankers in their banks, the economists in their lecture halls, the corporational executives in their suites spoke for Europe more insistently than any poets, idealists, music-makers or fond romantics.

Never mind, my sixth spasm was happening anyway, with or without benefit of Government. Euro-sceptics resisted in vain. It was no grand revolutionary splurge, no splash of colour, but slowly those regions really were becoming less alien to one another, learning each other's tongues, watching each other's TV programmes, surfing the same net. The growing power of women everywhere was breaking down the rigidities of machismo. Young people all over Europe were discarding false loyalties and national taboos. It was an irresistible organic process, beyond politics, beyond economics, beyond States or Powers, developing inescapably all across our nations, and only waiting for Voltaire's republic to catch up.

# AN EPILOGUE

*

## 1  *Back on the Audace Jetty*

So you find me, half a century on, back on the Molo Audace in Trieste. *What's become of Waring?* I still live in Wales, and always shall, but hardly a year has passed since the end of the Second World War when I have not returned to spend a few days here at the cusp of Europe, where the races meet, where I can look one way towards Rome and Paris and London, the other towards Belgrade and Bucharest and Athens. Trieste has not greatly changed during my half-century's acquaintance with the city. The traffic of tourism has swept through it, generally without stopping; fearful wars have flamed nearby; it spent many years in political flux and economic limbo. But in character, in temperament and even in structure it remains much the same place as it was when I sat on my bollard here, all those years ago, to write my essay about nostalgia.

It has never quite refound itself. There is something wistful to the place that touches me still, as it touched me when I first travelled here across the ravaged continent of my youth. This is another reason I like to come back to Trieste, and why I see it still as my personal epitome of Europeanness: for at the end of the twentieth century, as the nations of the old continent so fitfully grope their way towards comity, there is something wistful to the spectacle of Europe too. I am young no longer, and, just as I am yearning for the fulfilment of my small country, so I am impatient for the unity of my great continent, an end to its silly differences, and the creation of a fraternity in which all its peoples, great and small, will render unto Caesar the things that should belong to Caesar, but cherish for themselves those matters of faith and language, ways of living, ways of loving, that properly belong to God. I know now that I shall not see it in my own lifetime, and that even my grandchildren will probably grow up amidst the same bickering prides of States and Powers that have so long disfigured this continent – Goethe's 'superfluous memories and futile frays'. The nostalgia that I felt here fifty years ago was, I realize now, nostalgia not for a lost Europe, but for a Europe that never was, and has yet to be.

## 2  Viva Europa!

But we can still hope and try, and be grateful that we are where we are, in
this ever-marvellous and fateful corner of the world. 'Better fifty years of
Europe,' Lord Tennyson thought, 'than a cycle of Cathay'! One evening
years ago a friend and I went aboard a sailing-vessel from Split, down the
Dalmatian coast, that was lying in the bay of Trieste. There are no such ships
now. It was one of the very last generation of European working sailing-ships,
blunt-prowed, broad of beam, with red sails and big painted eyes at its bows,
to bring it luck. We took with us a few bottles of cheap sparkling wine, not
being able to afford anything better, and there in the wide harbour, as the
ship gently rocked, we shared them with its captain: while he, lying back
against a coiled rope, opening his heart to the assembling stars, sang sad
Puccini arias into the evening. I agree with Tennyson. '*Viva Europa!*', as I
cried to so little effect that day at Epidauros.

# INDEX

373